21世纪英语专业系列教材·新世纪翻译系列教程

英汉翻译:方法与试笔
AN ENGLISH-CHINESE TRANSLATION COURSEBOOK
（第三版）

主编　祝吉芳

编者　张光明　顾　翔
　　　陈红梅　罗天妮

图书在版编目(CIP)数据

英汉翻译：方法与试笔/祝吉芳主编．—3版．—北京：北京大学出版社，2015.8
(21世纪英语专业系列教材·新世纪翻译系列教程)
ISBN 978-7-301-26118-7

Ⅰ.①英… Ⅱ.①祝… Ⅲ.①英语—翻译—高等学校—教材 Ⅳ.①H315.9

中国版本图书馆CIP数据核字(2015)第175334号

书　　名	英汉翻译：方法与试笔（第三版）
著作责任者	祝吉芳　主编
责 任 编 辑	郝妮娜　宣　瑄
标 准 书 号	ISBN 978-7-301-26118-7
出 版 发 行	北京大学出版社
地　　址	北京市海淀区成府路205号　100871
网　　址	http://www.pup.cn　新浪微博：@北京大学出版社
电 子 信 箱	bdhnn2011@126.com
电　　话	邮购部 62752015　发行部 62750672　编辑部 62759634
印 刷 者	北京虎彩文化传播有限公司
经 销 者	新华书店
	730毫米×980毫米　16开本　24.25印张　480千字
	2004年8月第1版　2009年7月第2版
	2015年8月第3版　2023年5月第5次印刷
定　　价	69.00元

未经许可，不得以任何方式复制或抄袭本书之部分或全部内容。
版权所有，侵权必究
举报电话：010-62752024　电子信箱：fd@pup.pku.edu.cn
图书如有印装质量问题，请与出版部联系，电话：010-62756370

本教材获得以下项目资助

中央高校基本科研业务费专项资金(项目编号:2014B10814)
河海大学"十二五"本科校级规划立项
河海大学 2015 年校级重点立项教材建设项目
特此致谢!

前　言

"译"无信不立。诚实守信的翻译主要体现在准确、忠实地再现原文上。然而,许多翻译初学者由于翻译不得要领,翻译实践中往往做不到准确和忠实。因此,我们集各人所长编写了本教程。

本教程专供高等院校英语专业高年级学生翻译课课前预习、课堂讲练、课后实践之用。为此,本书一方面力求内容丰富多彩、精炼易懂,通过自学便可基本掌握所需翻译理论、方法及技巧,为课堂讲练腾出时间;另一方面,为提高学生的翻译能力,本书在每章之后专门设计了课堂讲练材料及课外扩展练习材料,材料内容有趣,体裁、题材多样,难点、容量张弛有度,与每章内容相关性大。同时本书还提供译文参考,旨在抛砖引玉,鼓励多样化译法及译文,提倡通过对比,汰劣存优,为读者的翻译实践活动提供参照。

另外,考虑到有志于从事翻译工作的在校生和往届生的需要,我们力争使本书的设计和编写与"全国翻译专业资格考试"考试委员会规定的考试大纲接轨,增加了类似翻译教材上少有的语篇翻译内容,以加强语篇翻译的学习力度。同时,本书尽力使所涉及的理论和实践方法具有普遍意义,既适用于英译汉,也基本上适用于汉译英,帮助考生迅速熟悉翻译途径更有效、更快捷地完成本科阶段翻译课程及"全国翻译专业资格考试"指定用书的学习。

本书译例大部分选自国外最新出版的书报、杂志,参考时应持批判的态度。参加本书编写的教师分工如下:第一章和第二章由祝吉芳撰写;第三章由河海大学顾翔教授编写;第四章第五节由祝吉芳编写,另外九节均由国际关系学院英语专业博士生导师张光明教授编写;第五章第一节由张光明教授编写,第二、三、四节由祝吉芳编写,后四节均由中国药科大学陈红梅教授编写;第六章由东南大学罗天妮教授编写;第七章由祝吉芳编写;资深教授柏成鹏老师为第七章提供了宝贵的参考意见。
　　愿本书能给您的翻译学习和翻译实践带来便利。

祝吉芳
2015年4月于
南京河海大学外国语学院

目　录

第一章　翻译标准及译员素质的培养 ………………………………… (1)
　　第一节　翻译的标准——忠实、通顺 …………………………… (1)
　　第二节　翻译标准与读者关照 …………………………………… (6)
　　第三节　译员素质的培养 ………………………………………… (7)

第二章　翻译的基本方法 ……………………………………………… (10)
　　第一节　翻译的基本步骤 ………………………………………… (10)
　　第二节　音译、零翻译、直译和意译 …………………………… (13)
　　第三节　异化法和归化法 ………………………………………… (18)

第三章　英汉语言的对比 ……………………………………………… (27)
　　第一节　词汇现象的对比 ………………………………………… (27)
　　第二节　句法现象的对比 ………………………………………… (38)
　　第三节　英汉思维的差异 ………………………………………… (46)

第四章　词语的翻译 …………………………………………………… (52)
　　第一节　词语的翻译 ……………………………………………… (52)
　　第二节　英语习语的翻译 ………………………………………… (62)
　　第三节　英语俚语的翻译 ………………………………………… (72)
　　第四节　英语比喻的翻译 ………………………………………… (86)
　　第五节　英语变异现象的翻译 …………………………………… (94)
　　第六节　英语矛盾修饰法的翻译 ………………………………… (98)
　　第七节　英语双关语的翻译 ……………………………………… (108)
　　第八节　英语拟声修辞格的翻译 ………………………………… (116)
　　第九节　富有英语文化特色的词语翻译 ………………………… (123)
　　第十节　可译性与不可译性的补救 ……………………………… (129)

第五章　句子的翻译（一） ······ (134)
　　第一节　词义的确定、引申和褒贬 ······ (134)
　　第二节　转译法 ······ (149)
　　第三节　增益法 ······ (161)
　　第四节　减词法 ······ (172)
　　第五节　重复法 ······ (181)
　　第六节　反面着笔法 ······ (190)
　　第七节　合译法 ······ (201)
　　第八节　分译法 ······ (207)

第六章　句子的翻译（二） ······ (214)
　　第一节　被动语态的几种译法 ······ (214)
　　第二节　名词从句的翻译 ······ (219)
　　第三节　定语从句的翻译 ······ (224)
　　第四节　状语从句的翻译 ······ (231)
　　第五节　标点符号的灵活处理 ······ (237)
　　第六节　长句的翻译（一） ······ (245)
　　第七节　长句的翻译（二） ······ (252)

第七章　语篇的翻译 ······ (263)
　　第一节　语篇的理解和翻译 ······ (263)
　　第二节　描写文、记叙文和小说的翻译 ······ (279)
　　第三节　论说文的翻译 ······ (288)
　　第四节　说明文的翻译 ······ (293)
　　第五节　新闻报道的翻译 ······ (296)
　　第六节　演讲语篇的翻译 ······ (303)
　　第七节　科技语篇的翻译 ······ (311)

参考译文 ······ (319)

第一章　翻译标准及译员素质的培养

所谓翻译,是把一种语言文字的意义用另一种语言文字表达出来的语言转换过程或结果。就题材而言,翻译可分为文学翻译(literary translation),如诗歌、戏剧等的翻译,以及实用翻译(pragmatic translation),如科技、商务或其他资料翻译。根据工作方式,翻译可分为口译(interpretation)、笔译(translation)、全自动机器翻译(machine-aided translation)。口译又可分为连续翻译(consecutive interpretation)和同声传译(simultaneous interpretation)。根据处理方式,翻译还有全译、摘译、编译、译述、缩译、综述、述评、改译、阐译、译写、参译等之分。

第一节　翻译的标准——忠实、通顺

翻译是按照原文的形、神、义、情、谋篇布局进行再创造的劳动。这种劳动虽然复杂多变,包罗万象,但仍有章可依,有标准可循。翻译标准是衡量译文优劣的尺度,是指导翻译活动的明灯。无论翻译理论出自何门何派,均无例外首先会涉及翻译的标准问题。言及翻译标准,晚清时期启蒙思想家严复的"信、达、雅"必盈于心。时光荏苒,一个世纪过去了,我国译界对这三字标准始终难以割弃,只是囿于汉语的现有发展,"雅"字标准似有局限性。有鉴于此,经过长期不懈的实践,针对翻译初学者,很多理论家主张把翻译标准概括为"忠实、通顺"(faithfulness; smoothness)。

一、忠实

古今中外,无论做人、处世,抑或翻译,均强调以信为本,即"忠实"。"忠实"具有双重含义,既要求翻译忠实原作内容,不得篡改、歪曲、缺失或随意增删原作内容,还要竭诚维持原作形式,其中包括原作的文化元素、体裁、风格。风格包括民族风格、时代风格、语体风格及原作者的个人风格。如果原作西方气息浓郁,洋气十足,译文就不得充满中国文化色彩,土腔土调,而需尽量保持原汁原味；如果原作采取通俗的口语体，译文就不得译为文绉绉的书面体，而须尽力保持原文特色；如果原作简练明晰、朴素无华、通俗流畅，译文行文就不得隐晦、艰涩。不过，任何事情都不是绝对的，不能排除特例的存在，例如曾经有译者在处理原作的民族主义思想内容及意识形态上的内容时，就进行了淡化处理或适当改变，灵活传译出原文并达到了较好的翻译效果。

但是无论如何，"忠实"作为基本的翻译规则，译者须首先予以遵守，不得在翻译中犯"失信"的错误。现举例加以说明：

> When electing Presidents of the United States, Americans haven't been partial to one type of man. Commanders in Chief of all kinds—tall and short, handsome and homely, well-educated and barely schooled, scoundrel and saint—were sent to Washington to serve.
>
> 美国人选举总统时，并不偏好某一类人。三军总司令无论是高是矮，仪表堂堂还是相貌平平，有文化还是没文化，无赖还是圣人，都会被派往华盛顿任职。

该句的原意是"美国人在选举总统时，并不对某一类人情有独钟。无论是高是矮，仪表堂堂还是相貌平平，有文化还是没文化，无赖还是圣人，都会入主白宫担任美国最高行政长官和三军总司令"。但译者并没仔细体会原文意思，而是抓住"were sent to Washington to serve"进行逐字翻译，不仅有违常理，还歪曲了原意，因而背离了"忠实"原则。所以，许多有经验的译员认为，领会原文真正含义，不因原文内容或结构形式而作茧自缚，是初学者很难做到但又必须学会面对的。

> More than twenty-five-million soldiers and civilians had died during the six years of fighting.
>
> 在为期六年的战争中，两千五百多万士兵和平民命丧黄泉。

该译文虽然简洁、顺畅，但过于汉化。看了译文，稍有民俗常识的人就会发出疑问："黄泉"这一中国道教术语，怎么跑到美国人嘴里去了？为避免此类"错位"导致的文化上的不忠实，还是应该以原语文化为依托，将其译作"丧命"或"不幸遇难"等为宜。可见，初学者要做到忠实，不仅需要照顾汉语读者阅读习惯，更须考虑原语文化。再举例：

> Do you want to be a dragon lady or a woman behind your man?

你想做一个龙女,还是做个男人背后的小女人?

文化味道过浓的表达在翻译时宜谨慎使用。如"龙女""龙子"出自西方人之口,易引起汉语读者不必要的联想,从而背离忠实原则。这儿不妨译作:"做个女强人还是做个男人背后的女人?"

Deliberate September—in its own time and tempo—begins to sum up another summer.

缓慢的九月——以自己的时间和步子——开始总结又一个夏季的经验。

为解决好忠实问题,初学者应力争使译文的语体与原作一致,需将原作的修辞手段传译给读者。原作是一篇用词考究的抒情文,译语文字也需传达同样的美感。此句不妨译作:"从容的九月,踩着悠悠的节拍,迈着闲适的步伐,去收获夏日的累累硕果。"

Both "herb" and "herbalist" are misnomers. Materials used in the aromatic but often bitter brews are not limited to the vegetable kingdom. Minerals and animal substances are also ingredients.

"草药"及"草药郎中"皆以讹传讹而成。这芳香四溢、苦涩难咽、救死扶伤的汤汤水水并非仅限于植物王国,矿物与动物也夹杂其间。

原文为一篇科普短文,用语简明扼要,因而译者遣词造句不得因喜欢文言词语,而使译文文白混杂语义不明;不得因乐于堆砌辞藻,而因词害意,歪曲原意;更不得不顾原文语言特点,过于修饰文字。在此不妨译为:"英语里所谓的'草药'及'草药郎中',都是误称。那些略带香味但多半苦涩的汤药,其实用料并不限于植物王国,矿物与动物也常是药中的成分。"

二、通顺

所谓"通顺",是指译文语言流畅易懂,不与译语语法规范及语言习惯有过大偏差。一般而言,译文语言须明白晓畅、文理通顺、结构合理、逻辑关系清晰,无死译、硬译、乱译、语言晦涩难懂的现象。但是,遇到作者为刻画人物或渲染气氛等目的故意采用非规范化语言的情况时,译者不宜片面追求合理性,应力图加以效仿。如:

Often, when we found ourselves up against a seemingly insuperable difficulty, he would stand up, put his pipe on the table, and say in his quaint English, "I will a little tink".

很多次,当我们遇到看似无法攻克的难题时,他(爱因斯坦)就总是站起身来,把烟斗往桌上一放,用带口音的英语道:"让我来晌(想)一晌(想)。"

另外,译文追求通顺时不能一味强调"地道",过于"地道"的译文难免流于平板陈腐,可能有损异国情调,背离读者对文字的期待。如:

Although you insist loving on your own is also called love, one palm can not make noises.

虽然你一直强辩说,单相思也是一种爱情,但单用一只手掌是拍不出声音的。

"loving on your own"虽然实质上是指"单相思",但若译作"单恋",文字可能会更新鲜抢眼,更能满足读者对文字的期待。

不过,避免译语平板陈腐,追求生动新颖的文字,不能以牺牲文字通顺为代价。如:

The great French leader Napoleon was shorter than everybody around him, so you'd have to call him a little shrimp. But for a shrimp, he certainly made the rest of Europe tremble.

法国伟大的领导人拿破仑比他周围的人都矮,所以你可以说他像只小虾。但是作为一只小虾,他却让欧洲其他地方发抖。

后一句的译文明显带有硬译的痕迹,使人不知所云。在此,应考虑挣脱原文的束缚,不妨译成:"但是作为一只小虾,他却震撼了整个欧洲。"

总之,"通顺"就是选用汉语读者认知能力以及汉语文化可接受限度内的语言,把原意清楚忠实地表达出来,尽可能消除生硬拗口、欧化过度、过分"本土化"、过于"地道"等弊端。

三、忠实与通顺的关系

忠实与通顺既对立又统一。忠实的译文须是通顺的,而译文的通顺则须以忠实原文为根本基础与前提。不过,鉴于英汉两种语言差异巨大,翻译原则的遵循以灵活为宜,毕竟过分注重忠实,难免有碍通顺,一味要求通顺,形式上又难以忠实。倘若忠实但不通顺,则忠实的意义尽失;倘若通顺但不忠实,则背离了翻译基本原则及标准。所以,译者的任务是在对立中寻求统一,适当处理好两者关系。忠实是第一位的,翻译时不可望文生义,生搬硬套;通顺虽是第二位的,但翻译实践决不可只重忠实,不顾通顺,二者须统筹兼顾,不得任意偏废。

在翻译标准的掌握上,初学者易走两个极端:一是过分拘泥于原文的字面意义,依葫芦画瓢,译文生硬拗口,与原文貌合神离;二是滥用成语,生搬硬套,译文陈腐俗滥,走腔变调,异国情调尽失。试比较:

> I didn't say it was your fault; I said I was blaming you.
> A:我没说是你的错,我说我怪你。(过于"忠实",其结果适得其反。)
> B:我可没怨你!我是在谴责你!(看似与原文有些出入,但并不影响原文意义,且符合汉语习惯,有可取性。)

"And what am I going to do when I want to talk to you?" But God had an answer for that question too. "Your angel will place your hands together and will teach you how to pray."

> A:"如果我想与你说话怎么办?"上帝胸有成竹地回答:"你的天使会将你的双手合拢,教你如何祈祷。"(符合汉语表达习惯,可读性较强,但形式上与原文有差距。)
> B:"如果我想与你说话怎么办?"上帝仍是有问必答:"你的天使会将你的双手合拢,教你如何祈祷。"(虽与原文有出入,但基本忠实原文,有可取性。)

上述两种现象我们应予以足够重视,以更好地处理忠实与通顺的关系,拿出最佳译文。

四、翻译标准的原则性、灵活性及译文的多样性

翻译标准要求译者在任何情况下都须"忠实、通顺"地再现原文,这就是翻译标准的原则性。

然而,实际翻译中,不同体裁、不同题材、不同读者对象、不同翻译目的和不同的工作方法,对翻译要求不一,这便需要译者在忠实原文的前提下,相应地采取灵活机动的态度,而非将翻译标准视作一成不变的教条生搬硬套,这就是翻译标准的灵活性。

原则性是恒定的,而灵活性是变化的,其目的旨在提高忠实程度。翻译需要灵活性,但灵活是有条件和限度的,须以可读性、读者层次及读者群体

为依据,由此必然产生翻译的多样性。

在翻译中注意译文的多样性十分重要。用丰富多彩、贴切精当的语言形式,把反复出现而又意思不变的句子、词组、成语、词语译得生动活泼,为同一句子、词组、成语、词语拿出多种译法,就是所谓翻译中的多样性。多样化译法可出自一人之笔,也可出于多人之手,有助于开拓译者的思路,增加译文的选择余地,如 fat 可译作:胖、富态、肥实、滚圆、胖乎乎、肥墩墩、肉坨坨、心宽体胖、丰满、丰盈、丰腴、珠圆玉润、肉感、臃肿、大腹便便、脑满肠肥,等等。译文选择范围愈宽,最佳译文产出的可能性愈大,这样读者就能欣赏到既忠实于原作,又行文流畅、生动活泼、可读性强的文字。不过,译文的生动活泼与可读性是相对的,在很大程度上受读者的社会背景和地域影响,如在一个读者群中通俗易懂的译文,放在另一群体中可能显得不伦不类,不知所云。

所以,译者在任何时候都须将原则性和灵活性有机结合起来,把原则性放在第一位,但又须有适当的灵活性,同时注意译文的多样性。

第二节 翻译标准与读者关照

求"信",难免艰涩;求顺,又恐失"信";求原汁原味,又怕翻译腔太足;意欲本土化,又恐损失异国情调;想紧跟作者,又担心失去读者;打算关照读者,又怕背离作者……正确处理忠实与通顺的关系,较好地处理翻译标准与读者关照(readers' consideration)的关系,使译作"不折不扣"地再现原作原有风貌——很难!

首先,翻译行为并非发生在真空之中,注定会打上译者生活时代及译语文化的烙印。所以,在介绍异域文化时,译者就不能无所忌惮,而要考虑译语文化的主导意识,考虑出版商的意愿要求,考虑译文读者的情趣和接受力,适当地对原文做出战略性叛逆。如在处理艰涩难懂的原文时,译者须考虑读者理解程度及市场接受能力,做出一定的明晰化处理。

其次,翻译作为一种有目的的行为,自然受目的的制约。自有翻译活动以来,翻译这项交流和宣传工具,不是被统治者用以维护统治,就是文人学者用来表达自身意识形态。众所周知,晚清文人在大量译介西方作品的过程中就曾经背"信"弃"忠"。他们遵循小说的"怨世、诋世、醒世"功能,顺应当时的社会现实与文化现实,通过夹译夹作、改译改作等具体方法,从事翻译活动。其中最具代表性的莫过于名译家林纾。尽管狄更斯的小说 *The Old Curiosity Shop* 并没宣传孝道的思想,但鉴于"孝"为当时的主流行为内容,且在中国文化中根深蒂固,所以为争取读者,林纾顺势而行,选择了改译原作译名的这一权宜之计,于是便有了译本《孝女耐儿传》,结果收到了较好的市场反映。

另外,翻译对译者有着多方面的要求,既要求译者保留原文的风味,又要求译者照顾译语读者的语言及思想文化接受程度。以《安妮日记》(*Ann Frank's Diary*)的德译本为例。由于原作多处夹杂侮辱仇视德国人的语言,译者在将其翻译成德文的过程中,酌情对原文进行了淡化、改动、删除或解释等变通处理,由此避免了可能引起的麻烦或不快。这样做虽有"不忠"之嫌,但事实证明不无可取之处——既有利于寻求销路,也考虑到了德国读者的情感接受能力。又如在婚姻伦理方面,中国人含蓄自律,崇尚伦理道德;西方人则有自己的准则,作品难免露骨的描写,所以,朱生豪在翻译莎士比亚作品时做了一定的淡化处理或删改,因此朱译莎士比亚被公认为"洁本"。

第三节 译员素质的培养

从某种意义上说,翻译比写作困难,写作时至少可以就自己的能力扬长避短,自由发挥,翻译则需忠实原文,不得偷工减料,也不得添油加醋。学习英语,翻译最需要真功夫。那么,翻译对译员究竟有什么业务素质上的要求呢?

首先,英语基础要扎实,特别是阅读理解能力和文字鉴赏能力要强,才可能对原作有尽握其妙的工夫。实践证明,少量的英语语言知识,少许支离破碎的语法概念,不多的文化习俗方面的知识,依赖词典进行字字对应的文字转换,定然做不好翻译。

第二,要有熟练驾驭、自如运用汉语的本领。为此,须大量阅读汉语原著,进行经常性的汉语写作训练。汉语水平的高低,是决定译文质量优劣的第二大要素。

第三,要树立正确的是非判断标准。在实际翻译中,常需译者根据自己对事物的衡量标准以及语境因素将一个词译成不同的对应词。以 good 为例,最基本的汉语对应词是"好",但跟不同的词搭配起来又可用不同的汉语表达,翻译时必然涉及译者个人对"好"的界定。如:

a good Christian 可译：虔诚的基督徒；热心助人的基督徒

a good mother 可译：慈祥的妈妈；一心为孩子着想的母亲；勤劳朴实的妈妈；合格的妈妈

a good child 可译：孝顺的孩子；有出息的孩子；学习优秀的孩子；尊老爱幼的孩子

a good wife 可译：贤良的妻子；忠实的妻子；贤惠的妻子；能干的妻子

a good husband 可译：忠实的丈夫；尽责的丈夫；能干的丈夫；会赚钱的丈夫

a good president 可译：勤政爱民的总统；日理万机的总统；政绩卓越的总统；万民拥戴的总统

可见，翻译涉及的不仅仅是语言能力问题，也涉及译者为人处世的标准问题。

第四，应熟悉英汉两种语言在语音、词汇、句法、修辞、使用习惯等方面的种种差异，使译文既规范通顺，又"洋气"适度。

第五，译者知识须是宽口径的。翻译是传播文化知识的媒介，译者的知识结构越广博越好。除专门知识和相关知识外，译员要全面了解世界各国历史、地理、政治、经济、军事、外交、科学技术、风俗习惯、宗教信仰、民族心理、文化传统等方面的百科知识，同时还须通晓本国的百科知识。唯有如此，才可能在翻译中做到明察秋毫，得心应手，准确无误。一言以蔽之，即便做不了专家，做一个通古博今、上知天文、下晓地理的多面手也是必要的。

第六，翻译策略须合理。译者须自觉地探讨翻译原理，建立自己的翻译策略。如果英语基础较好、汉语表达较弱而性格又较为拘谨，可偏重字对字的直译或尽量紧靠原文作者的异化方法；如果汉语基础好、生性较为自由，可偏重意译；作为初学者，应力避"走偏锋"，宜选择适中的翻译策略，不断实践，不断摸索，掌握翻译的规律、方法和技巧。

第七，了解语言信息中所包含的文化内涵，了解本民族的文化，以便敏锐地体察两种文化的异同，做一个真正意义上的文化使者。翻译只是一种文化交流工具，无法做到"语言传真"，但可力争"文化传真"。有时，一句话，从语言对等的角度考虑，可以得出一个译法，而从文化传真的角度翻译，可能得出另一译法，甚至可能是技高一筹的译法。

第八，须培养认真负责、谦虚谨慎的学风。翻译是项复杂仔细的工程，需要付出艰苦的劳动,还要倾注大量的热情,更要耐得住清贫,守得住寂寞,通过虚心汲取前辈的翻译经验和技巧不断提高翻译水平。

最后,好的译员在遇到难题时,知道到哪里寻找答案,知道如何运用工具书、翻译软件和因特网。每个翻译初学者都需准备纸货或电子词典,养成勤查词典的习惯。查词典时,要以分析、推测为前提,要警惕词的多义性;要有一丝不苟孜孜以求的精神,养成考据求证的习惯;翻译时,要脑勤、手勤、口勤,不乱猜胡译,一定要把翻译建立在有根有据的基础之上。

学好翻译具有重要的现实意义和深远的历史意义,翻译初学者一定要有意识地健全和培养自己的翻译素质,走好翻译的第一步。

附　课堂讲练材料

Advertising

Advertising has become a very specialized activity in modern times. In the business world of today, supply is usually greater than demand. There is great competition between different manufacturers of the same kind of product to persuade customers to buy their own particular brand. They always have to remind the consumer of the name and the qualities of their product. They do this by advertising.

The manufacturer advertises in the newspapers and on posters. He sometimes pays for songs about his product in commercial radio programmes. He employs attractive salesgirls to distribute samples of it. He organizes competitions, with prizes for the winners. He often advertises on the screens of local cinemas. Most important of all, in countries that have television he has advertisements put into programmes that will accept them. Manufacturers often spend large sums of money on advertisements. We buy a particular product because we think that it is the best. We usually think so because of the advertisements that say so. Some people never pause to ask themselves if the advertisements are telling the truth.

(Jack Franklin)

第二章 翻译的基本方法

成功的翻译有赖于一定的具体途径,即所谓的翻译方法。不同的翻译方法产生风格迥异的译文,直接影响译文质量的优劣程度。有关翻译的基本方法,建议初学者熟练掌握,大胆运用。

第一节 翻译的基本步骤

合理的翻译过程是正确理解原文,创造性运用另一种语言,准确无误地再现原文的过程。翻译初学者须遵循这一固有程序,认真完成理解、表达、校核三步骤,实现成功翻译。

一、理解

翻译的关键前提在于理解(comprehension)。对土生土长的中国人而言,理解英语的难度与用汉语表达的难度不可同日而语。英汉两种语言不仅在词法、句法上,更在逻辑、思维、文化、风俗等方面存在巨大差异,要透彻理解原文的每一词、每一短语、每一句、每一段乃至全文的精神谈何容易!英语词汇浩如烟海,一词多义现象俯拾皆是,习语俗语千差万别,文章谋篇布局各藏"机关",历史、地理、风土人情、生活习俗包罗万象,一个生长在汉语环境中运用汉语进行思维的人很难通晓。因此,理解"不到位"的现象时有发生,其结果往往是误译、错译。如:

Anna was thin and black, a very umbrella of a woman.
安娜是个又瘦又黑的女人,上身粗大,下身细长,简直像一把雨伞。

这个句子翻译难度并不大,但译文却自相矛盾,显得十分诡异。究其原因,是译者对伞的理解与原文作者对伞的理解不一致造成的。在中国,人们只在下雨或大夏天才撑着伞(很多时候是花伞)出门,所以伞对中国人而言是胖大的;而英国人由于其气候的特殊性平时出门常拿把黑颜色的伞以备不时之需,所以伞对他们而言是细长黑瘦之物。因此,这里可考虑将原文译成；安娜是个又瘦又黑的女人，活像一把细长的雨伞。

不过，理解作为翻译活动的第一步，无论困难多大，都得勇敢地迈出去。稳打稳扎的理解一般始于原文的语言现象（如词汇意义、句法结构、修辞手法、惯用法等）对比研究，其次是将语言的文化背景、逻辑关系和具体语境融会贯通。为此，对原文宜至少阅读三遍：第一遍"浅尝"，其间对疑难词句按层次做圈点，并把握全文大意；第二遍"细嚼"，其间须逐词逐句逐段地答疑解惑，既要咬文嚼字，避免随心所欲，又要细心揣摩，避免望文生义，生搬硬套，以便译文恰如其分，清楚明朗；第三遍"通吃"，以将全文精神融会于心，这既要求读通全文，又要求落实词义、句义、段义。

在通读三遍的同时，可对原文进行语言分析。首先宜借助词典，通过词义辨析和语法分析，捕捉原文确切意义；第二可考虑从细致入微的语境分析入手，抓住语言片段的确切意义；第三可运用逻辑分析方法，将语言分析和逻辑分析有机结合起来，力求语言明了，逻辑清晰，理解正确；第四可在原文之外做文章，掌握原文的背景知识以及各种相关的专门知识。若原文写的是某个人，就尽可能详细地了解该人的生平事迹；若原文提到某一作品，就至少了解一点该作品；若原文为标书，那就学习一点招标投标常识……总之，理解过程中要做到"逢山开路，遇水架桥"，否则在表达阶段就会举步维艰。

二、表达

表达（expression）是翻译过程中的第二步。

作为成功实现由原语至译语信息转换的关键，表达须把已经了然于心的原作内容，用汉语恰如其分地表述清楚。表达的好坏，是否能做到忠实、通顺，取决于四方面的因素：一是译者对原作理解的深度；二是译者汉语的修养程度；三是译者对两种文化、历史、风土人情等要素的正确把握；四是译者真正抛弃原文束缚，遣词造句尽量贴近原文，同时按汉语的规律和习惯从容翻译。如将 The winds of November were like summer breezes to him, and his face glowed with the pleasant cold. His cheeks were flushed and his eyes glistened; his vitality was intense, shining out upon others with almost a material warmth. 译成"十一月的寒风，对他就像夏天吹拂的凉风一样。舒适的冷空气使他容光焕发，两颊通红，两眼闪光。他生气勃勃，叫别人感到是一团炙热的火。"英语 a material warmth 字面意思是"物质的温暖"，这里具体表达成"一团炙热的火"，言明意明，让人一看就懂。试比较：

Evening news is where they begin with "Good evening", and then proceed to tell you why it isn't.

晚间新闻总是以"晚上好"开头,再告诉你为什么好不了。

此外,忠实、通顺的翻译原则还要求译者摆正克己意识与创造意识之间的关系。有人曾形象地将译者比作"披枷戴锁的重刑囚犯",无权享受完全的创作自由,只有忠实原文的可能,因而只能尽量压抑自我的创造冲动,将创造欲融于原文,与原文作者合为一体,竭力使译文内容、风格、表现手段与原文无二。译者仅有的自由,局限于语言层面,如对原语所有、译语所无的语言点或现象,译者可在准确达意不露"翻译腔"的情况下,发挥创造能力,创造出新颖生动的译文语言。问题的关键是如何把握好分寸,这便要求初学者在实践中认真摸索,最终走出一条适合自己的翻译之道。

表达是理解的结果,但理解正确并不意味着表达必然准确到位。在表达上不仅需要掌握下面将介绍的两对翻译基本方法概念,还要求在以后章节将要提到的许多具体翻译技巧上面下足工夫。

三、校核

校核(revision)是翻译的最后一期工程,是确保译文质量的最关键一环。

对翻译初学者而言,"锦上添花"简单,"瘦身减肥"易行,而"剜疮削骨"式的校核则有些勉为其难,难就难在对自己的"劳动成果"割舍不下,下手做不到精、准、劲、狠。但是,为了求得读者认可,最好严守翻译过程最后的这个关口。

谁都难免疏漏,谁都难以一挥而就、一字不易,这与细心程度、功力深厚没有直接联系,倒是与校核功课是否做足不无关联。校核的主要目的旨在:检查译文是否存在遗漏、失误或不妥;检查译文是否精确(accurate)、自然(natural)、简练(economical);检查理解与表达是否需进一步深化;对译文语言做进一步推敲落实。一般情况下,须校核三遍:第一遍着重校核内容,同时进一步揣摩原文,彻底吃透原文精神。第二遍阅读译文时不妨将原文放在一边,边看边改,这样可以免受原文表达形式的束缚和影响。这样修改后,再对照原文看一遍,看是否与原意有出入。第三遍摆脱原文,铲除一切生硬拗口的表达,对译文进行修订、润色、雕琢。

常言道"好文章是改出来的",译文亦如此。从某种程度而言,成功的翻译就是反复修改反复校核的结果。

第二节 音译、零翻译、直译和意译

谈到翻译方法,人们会提到音译、零翻译,更会提及直译和意译这一对翻译界的传统术语。

一、音译

所谓音译(transliteration),是一种译音代义的方法。音译又称转写,即用一种文字符号(如汉字)来表示另一文字系统的文字符号(如英语)的过程或结果。《现代汉语词典》将音译界定为译音,即把一种语言的语词用另一种语言中跟它发音相同或近似的语音表示出来的翻译方法。这里所讨论的是英译汉中广义的音译法,包括纯音译法、音意兼译法、音译加类法、半音译半意译法。

纯音译法亦称直接音译法,即根据英语的读音选择读音相同或相近的汉字组合在一起,这些词组在汉语中常常没有任何意义,如 Motorola 摩托罗拉(手机)。纯音译法常用来翻译专有名词,如 Eugene Nida(尤金·奈达),Houston(休士顿)等;还用来翻译表示民族特有事物的名词,如 toast(吐司),ballet(芭蕾)等;也用来翻译无对应词的词语,如 hacker(黑客),cholera(霍乱),clone(克隆)等。

音意兼译法,又名谐音双关法,即在翻译时选取能激起联想的谐音词汇或词组。汉字有很多同音异义字,因此在翻译时可自由选择发音响亮、意境优美或意境深远、贴近人物个性身份性格的字来表现。音意兼译法还用来翻译人名,如考虑到人的职业身份将美国著名艳星 Monroe 译作"梦露",却将美国第五任总统 Monroe 译作"门罗";将著名小说人物 Jane Eyer 译成"简·爱",而非"珍妮·艾尔",因为简是个孤女,译成珍妮似有不妥。英美文学作品中有些名字是由具有一定意义的词构成的,这些词的含义反映出人物的个性特征。译这些人物的名称时,如果只靠纯音译法,译出来的名字有时听起来不伦不类。译此类人物名字,无疑音意兼译是一种较为理想的办法,既弥补了纯音译过程中丢失双关语所表达的双重意义的不足,又使得通过意译而得的译名仍能保留原文的音趣。如杨必先生在译 William Thackeray 的代表作 *Vanity Fair* 时,将 Rebecca Sharp 译成"夏泼",便是一不可多得的佳译。英语中,sharp 一词意为"精明的、有洞察力的",但又暗含"狡猾、诡诈"之意;而译文将"泼"赋予这样一位泼辣、精明,有时甚至于不择手段的名利场中的女性人物,是再恰当不过的;同时,"夏泼"与 Sharp 在读音上颇为接近。而当作为一种电器商标时,Sharp 却译作"夏普","普"字很好地表达出"推广、普及"的内涵。

音译加类法,指音译后或前附加解释性注释,如 hippy(嬉皮士),ballet(芭蕾舞),cartoon(卡通片),New York(纽约市),AIDS(艾滋病),Mecca(麦加圣地),pizza(比萨饼),Benz(奔驰车),sauna(桑拿浴),Hamburger(汉堡包),El Nino(厄尔尼诺现象)等。

半音译半意译,指的是在翻译时对一些复合词采取一半音译一半意译的方式,二者合为一个新词,如 miniskirt(迷你裙),water ballet(水上芭蕾),Big Ben(大本钟)等。

二、零翻译

近年来汉语中出现了大量的字母词,即由西文字母或西文字母加汉字构成的词语,例如 DNA,NBA,DVD,WTO,GDP,B 超,U 盘,维 C,IP 卡等。与此同时,英语中也出现了 shi fu 等汉语拼音。这些都是零翻译的结果。

与缩写词一样,零翻译也具有经济、简洁、入耳、鲜明、实用的特点。试想一遇到类似 MP3 的字母词,就用其中文全称"一种常用的数字音频压缩格式",岂不既冗长低效又拘谨刻板?

三、直译

所谓直译(literal translation),是把一种语言所传达的内容和形式变换为另一种语言和形式的过程或结果。在翻译过程中,直译要求基本保持原语的表达形式及内容,不得更改,同时要求语言流畅易懂。直译强调"形似",主张尽力将原文内容按原文的形式逐一翻译出来。原文的形式一般包括词序、语序、段序、表达方式、修辞方式、语体风格、地方色彩、个体风格、民族特色等。例如:

1. He went to bed tired and he woke up tired.
   他上床累,起床也累。

2. Living without an aim is like sailing without a compass.
   生活没有目标,犹如航海没有罗盘。

3. Women love cats. Men say they love cats, but when women aren't looking, men kick cats.

女人喜欢猫,男人说他们也喜欢,但当女人看不到时,男人踢猫。

4. The relentless pursuit of perfection.
   不懈追求完美。
5. God gives every bird its food, but He doesn't throw it into its nest.
   上帝给了鸟儿食物,但他没有将食物扔到它的巢里。

很多时候,直译的成功使用,主要是由于在汉语中能找到与英语完全等值或基本等值的词或句子表达。如:

talk show	脱口秀	cat walk	猫步
exit speech	退选演说	social dancing	交谊舞
gene therapy	基因疗法	vanity fair	名利场
financial crisis	金融危机	dark horse	黑马
chain reaction	连锁反应	life or death choice	生死抉择

直译方法的成功使用,不仅能忠实地再现原文,还能满足作者对新鲜生动文字的期待,更能丰富本民族语言词汇系统。倘若没有直译方法恰如其分的运用,很难想象我们现在早已司空见惯的词汇中会有"象牙塔""洗礼""牛市""赤字"等词。

初学者需注意的是,不可将直译与"死译""硬译"、生搬硬套、逐字照译相混淆,不分青红皂白地对号入座,这样不仅达不到直译效果,还可能制造一些常识性的笑话,如 lucky dog(幸运儿)误译为"幸运狗",adaptor(多向插头)误译成"适应器",bicycle people (骑自行车的人)误译为"自行车人",cat people (养猫的人或爱猫的人)误译为"猫人",black sheep(害群之马)误译为"黑羊"。

四、意译

英汉两种语言中的词汇、语法结构、表达方式及谋篇布局都有其特殊性,翻译过程中译语与原语形式上往往会因此产生矛盾冲突,需要译员借助意译予以化解。

所谓意译(free translation)是指将一种语言所表达的意义用另一种语言做释义性解释,在转换过程中不必过分拘泥于原文形式。例如 follow one's nose 不能照字面直译为"跟着鼻子走",而应意译为"跟着感觉走";

day student 不能直译成"白天的学生",而宜意译为"走读生",in the dark 不能按字面理解为"在黑暗中",应译作"一无所知",battery eliminator 译为"电池消除器"让人如堕云雾,若译成"稳压电源"就能达到文从字顺的效果。意译强调"神似",主张依照原文的意义,灵活机动地把原文意义创造性地表达出来。又如:

1. Shopping is not a sport, and no, we are never going to think of it that way.
   逛街购物不是做运动,永远都不是。我们(男人)绝不会将二者等而视之。

2. We must accept finite disappointment, but we must never lose infinite hope.
   我们必须接受失望,因为失望是有限的,但千万不可失去希望,因为希望是无穷的。

3. A man can fail many times, but he isn't a failure until he begins to blame somebody else.
   一个人可以失败很多次,但只要他没有开始责怪旁人,就还不是一个失败者。

4. He had never felt so lonely in his life, abandoned, defenseless.
   有生以来,他从未像此刻感到这样孤独,仿佛被人遗弃,只身无援。

5. A successful man is one who makes more money than his wife can spend. A successful woman is one who can find such a man.
   成功的男人是能挣比他太太花的更多的钱;成功的女人是能找得到这么个给他钱花的男人。

意译还包括许多翻译技巧,如转译、分译、合译、增词、减词、重复等等,灵活掌握意译这一基本翻译方法,有助于成功地再现原文风姿。不过,作为初学者,应把意译与"乱译"的概念区分开来,应认识到意译绝不是任意嫁接、随意剪枝,歪曲原意,更不是胡译、乱译、过分意译,如:

1. It's not the fall that kills you, it's the sudden stop at the end.
   跳楼时,"啊——"的时候还没死,"啪!"那才是死了。(译文过分意译,偏离原作思想。)

2. A clear conscience is usually the sign of a bad memory.

   无愧于心哈？记性不好吧？（过度表达，与原文差异较大，显得有些随意。）

3. To appease their thirst its readers drank deeper than before, until they were seized with a kind of delirium.

   为了解渴，读者比以前越饮越深，直到陷入了昏迷状态。（译文死抠原文形式，死抠字典释义，翻译腔严重，让人难以明白其意思。可改译为：读者为了满足自己的阅读渴望，越读越想读，直到进入如痴如醉的状态。）

五、直译与意译

直译重意义和表达形式，意译则着重意义。在不违背汉语语言规范尽量用原文形式表达原文思想内容的前提下，直译有助于保留洋腔洋调，有助于引进新鲜生动的词语、句法结构和表达方式，从而丰富汉语，完善汉语，发展汉语。为此，能直译时宜尽力直译。但是，英汉两种语言差异较大，翻译时往往需改变原文的表达法，即采用意译，因为意译便于调和原文与译文形式上的矛盾，使译文通顺流畅，符合汉语语法规范和表达习惯。

直译和意译不是绝对概念，二者界限并非泾渭分明，而是互补互助，殊途同归。翻译实践中，应本着最能忠实、通顺地表达原文含意的原则，灵活选用或交替使用这两种方法，该部分直译便不全部直译，该选择部分意译就不全部意译。任何译者在翻译中都会有意无意地兼用两种方法，整体倾向上并无侧重。如：

The Italians are wise before the deed, the Germans in the deed, the French after the deed.

意大利人事前聪明，德国人事中聪明，法国人事后聪明。

译文既紧扣原文做了直译，又摆脱了原文进行了意译，达到了较好的翻译效果。另外，大量实践表明，即便是同一话语，有时也是既可直译又可意译的，如：

Smashing a mirror is no way to make an ugly person beautiful, nor is it a way to make social problems evaporate.

直译：砸镜子不能使五八怪变漂亮，也不能使社会问题烟消云散。

意译：砸镜子并不能解决实际问题。

直译和意译的取舍去留，主要取决于三个因素：翻译目的、读者层次和语篇类型。若以再现原文的表达形式为目的，就须采用严格的字对字的直译，如合同、条约、法典、政府公文等，一般性学术理论、科技文章及著述可基本直译，而新闻报道和分析、报刊特写等一般要求直译但须考虑可读性。如果以文化层次较低的读者为对象，就须采用简单易解的意译为主，如幼儿童话等；如果翻译古典诗歌、抒情散文、剧本、小说等要求以获得最佳可读性与艺术性为目的的题材，也须以意译为主，甚至为获得更理想的效果，不妨采取改写的办法。

第三节 异化法和归化法

近年来，在阐述翻译方法时，许多学者常抛开直译和意译，转而采纳另一种提法——异化法（foreignizing method）和归化法（domesticating method）。

异化和归化与直译和意译是两对不能等同的概念，从历史角度而言，前者是后者概念的延伸和继承。直译和意译主要集中于语言层面，重点关心的是如何在语言层面处理形式和意义的关系；异化和归化则突破语言的范畴，立足于文化大语境下，将视野扩展到语言、文化、思维、美学等更广阔的领域。

一、异化法

所谓异化法，是接受原文与译文的语言、文化等差异，忠实传达原文内容，把读者带入异国情景。该方法要求译者向原文作者靠拢，力争采取相应于原语的表达方式，即鲁迅先生提及过的"异国情调"和"洋气"。现在，异化法正为越来越多的译者视为主要翻译方法。的确，从长期的翻译实践来看，异化法的使用往往能够更加准确、充分、原汁原味地传达出原文的意义。如：

It gives me very great pleasure to see Chinese children shooting up like beansprouts, full of vitality and energy.

看到华裔儿童像豆芽一样冒出来，充满生机和活力，我十分高兴。

原文用"像豆芽一样冒出来"形容英国华人社区华裔下一代越来越多这

一事实,很传神,很新颖,用异化译法不落俗套。

　　While it may seem to be painting the lily, I should like to add somewhat to Mr. Alistair Cooke's excellent article.

　　我想给阿利斯太尔·库克先生的杰作稍加几笔,尽管这也许是为百合花上色,费力不讨好。

在西方人眼里,百合花是高贵、贞洁、美丽的象征,故为百合花上色自然是做徒劳无益之事。对此译文,读者一看即明白,同时还可能产生一种阅读欣喜,因为用"为百合花上色"表示吃力不讨好,给人印象实在太深刻了。

　　It was as if a band of Italian days had come from the south, like a flock of glorious passenger birds, and lighted to rest them on the cliffs of Albion.

　　仿佛有一群意大利天气,像欢乐的过路鸟从南方飞来,栖息在阿尔比恩的悬崖上。

在《简·爱》中,祝庆英先生保留了很多原文的表达方式和句子结构。孤立地看,这种译文翻译腔十足,晦涩生硬不自然,但事实是他的译本不但没遭到唾弃,反而达到了很高的发行量,让许多中国作者都喜欢上简·爱这么一个长相平平但聪明独立的女性形象。

许多人看过美国著名影星梅利尔·斯特里普主演的影片《穿普拉达的女王》,但很少有人知道这部电影还有另一个译名——《时尚女魔头》。为什么?因为"普拉达"是世界时尚界顶级名牌,1913年由意大利人Mario Prada创立。用异化法翻译"The Devil Wears Prada"没有超出汉语读者的接受能力,反而有助于增强影片的号召力,强化读者对世界企业文化的认知。

　　This organization is today collapsing on its clay feet. Its organs have been cut out, dissected and reshaped so that they may perform the way the puppet masters want.

　　今天,这个泥足支撑的组织正在瓦解。它的器官被阉割、肢解、整形,它像木偶一样受人摆布。

这是马来西亚总理马哈蒂尔2004年年初在第58届联合国大会上狠批联合国是强国的傀儡时说的一番话。用异化译法既没破坏其原汁原味,还将原文生动形象的暗喻忠实传神地表达了出来。

由上可见,采取异化译法,既可充分传达原作的"异国风味",还可引进一些原语的表达方式,丰富汉语的语言词汇。正是由于翻译工作者们在翻译中力求异化,汉语里不仅有"炮火的考验",还有了同义词(baptism of fire)"炮火的洗礼";不仅有"政治本钱",还有了同义词(political capital)"政治资本";不仅有"换汤不换药",还有了同义词(new wine in old bottles)"旧瓶装新酒";不仅有"杀手锏",还有了同义词(trump card)"王牌";不仅有黑名单(black list),还有了白名单,更有了"君子协定""丘比特之箭""双刃剑""武装到牙齿""欧佩克""亚佩克""回到谈判桌来""卖点""斯芬克斯之谜"……此外,读者对语言不是不存期待的,总是盼望新颖生动,腻烦陈词滥调,不甘平淡无味,而异化译法力求保留原文的笔调和情趣,有可能满足读者这种对新鲜、刺激文字的期待。

  总的说来,译文要忠实传达原文原貌,语言要不落俗套,就不能不选择异化译法。初学者可把异化视为翻译的主要方法,但采取异化的译法,有几个方面的问题要加以注意。

  首先,主张翻译以异化为主要方法,并非意味着异化是万能的,可以毫无顾忌地"从一而终",那样就会走上极端。实际上,异化法的运用有一定限度,这种限度具体体现于译语语言文化的限度及译语读者接受能力的限度,即译者在运用异化法时,既不能超越译语语言文化的规范限度,也不能超过读者的认知能力。如将"Every time I see my grandfather, he gives me a big bear hug."译成"每次见到爷爷,他都要给我一个大大的熊式拥抱。"那么译文就陷入了字字对译的死胡同,读后让人不知所云。其实,"a big bear hug"意为"抱得很紧"。若译成"紧紧地拥抱我",便一目了然。可见,异化法的使用要考虑读者的认知能力。

  其次,过分的异化,就是不顾读者的接受力,不顾目标语的语言习惯,一味追求眼下原文的形式对应,结果会导致译文晦涩难懂。这种译法,严格说来,不能算作异化翻译,而只能视为"伪异化"。如将"Do you see any green in my eye?"译作"你从我的眼睛里看到了绿色吗?"该译文给人的感觉岂止别扭,简直令人费解,因为损害了原文的表达效果,还违背了汉语语言习惯。此处,可考虑译作"你以为我是好欺骗的吗?"

  诚然,引进西方语言的某些表达方式有助于丰富我们自己的语言,但毫无节制、不加筛选地兼收并蓄则会损害汉语的纯洁性,降低译文可读性,其结果无疑会影响译作的流传。因此,翻译中应避免使用过分"欧化"的表达及晦涩难懂的句子。

二、归化法

与异化法相反,归化译法要求译者向译语读者靠拢,采取读者关照的态度,使原文符合译语的文化价值观,把原文作者带入译语文化之中。为避免在异化的使用上走极端,弄巧成拙,初学者宜将归化作为辅助手段。归化的译法旨在译文通顺易懂,能为译语读者所接受。如:

1. How many winter days have I seen him, standing blue-nosed in the snow and east wind.
   许多冬日,我总是看见他鼻子冻得发紫,站在飞雪和寒风里。
2. She is the most beautiful and perfect ladyboy in Thailand.
   她是泰国最完美的变性女孩。
3. To me, the past is black and white, but the future is always color.
   对我而言,过去平淡无奇;而未来,却是绚烂缤纷。
4. It looks like that it's a shotgun marriage for those two.
   看上去这两个人好像是奉子成婚。
5. You'd think he has ants in his pants.
   你会觉得他坐立不安。

语贵适度,写作如此,翻译也概莫能外。如果异化译法行不通,译者就应摆脱原文语言形式,尽量从原文词法、句法结构、谋篇布局的条条框框中跳出来,设法寻找汉语在同样场合的习惯表达,用通顺易懂的汉语译出原文内容的精神。如 a bread and butter letter 若译作"面包黄油信",会给人一种不得要领的感觉,而译者经过融会贯通,按照汉语的表达习惯,将其译成"表扬信",可谓文从字顺。对原文中此类形象语言,有两种情况可采取归化译法:一是原文的语言虽然形象,甚至很新鲜,但无法照实传译。如 a mare's nest 若译作"母马的巢"就可能造成理解困难,因为知道母马从不筑巢的人并不多,因而最好译为"子虚乌有的事情";二是原文的语言已不再新鲜,用不着照实传译。如 a political "Dear John"可归化成"政治上的绝交信",就流畅自然得多了。

谈到译文的归化,自然要提到汉语成语的运用。汉语成语具有结构工整、语言简练、含义深刻等优点,翻译中若能恰如其分地加以运用,确实会增强译文的表现力,给译文增添光彩。如:

Good To The Last Drop
滴滴香浓，意犹未尽！

　　这是著名的麦氏咖啡(Maxwell House Coffee)的一个成功广告口号，据说源自美国第 26 任总统西奥多·罗斯福(Theodore Roosevelt)对它的评价。用四字成语加以翻译，加深了中国消费者的印象，无疑增大了该产品的附加值。这样运用归化译法，使广告文字简洁易记，还给人以美好的想象。

　　诚然，求归化可解决异化译法解决不了的翻译问题，可使译文达到连贯易懂、语句通顺、表达地道的境界，但实践中若不注意适度，就会出现"归化过头""添油加醋"或"偷工减料""偷梁换柱"的现象。事实上，翻译实践中通常"一不小心"就可能触犯"归化过头"的大忌，有关问题归纳起来主要集中表现在以下两个方面：

　　一方面，归化时，译者往往不顾原文的语言形式，不顾原文的民族文化特征，一味追求译文的通顺和优美，读起来颇像原文作者在用译语写作一样。这是归化过头的一种表现。如：

　　　　One dollar and eighty-seven cents. That was all. And sixty cents of it was in pennies. Pennies saved one and two at a time by bulldozing the grocer and the vegetable man and the butcher until one's cheeks burned with the silent imputation of parsimony that such close dealing implied. Three times Della counted it. One dollar and eighty-seven cents. And the next day would be Christmas.

　　　　一块八毛七分钱。全在这儿了。其中六毛钱还是铜子儿凑起来的。这些铜子儿是每次一个、两个向杂货铺、菜贩和肉店老板那儿死乞白赖地硬扣下来的；人家虽然没有明说，自己总觉得这种掂斤播两的交易未免太吝啬，当时脸都臊红了。德拉数了三遍，数来数去还是一块八毛七分，而第二天就是圣诞节了。

　　译文中"凑""硬扣""臊红"等忠实传神，反映出译者翻译过程中高度的灵活性和创造性。但是，"一块八毛七分钱"和"铜子儿"似乎过于归化，带有明显的中国文化痕迹，尤其后者是典型的中文表达，会让译文读者误以为原文作者本人的说话风格就是如此。若用异化法照实传译，在使读者享受精彩译作的同时能体味到原汁原味的异域文化，译文可能更受欢迎。固然，归化不失为一种解决异化难题的好方法，但过度使用，有时会损害原文意义。又如：

They wandered here and there with their absurd long staves in their hands like a lot of faithless pilgrims bewitched inside a rotten fence.

他们手里都拿着一根可笑的哭丧棒,从这里溜到那里,像一群失去信心的香客,让鬼魅给迷在这一圈乱树丛中了。

由于"哭丧棒"和"香客"都是典型的中国文化概念,可能使读者产生"文化错位",不仅不利于读者对异域文化兴趣的提高,还有"偷梁换柱"之嫌,不妨老实地译作"长棍子"和"朝圣者"。

有些译者为了迎合读者的口味而让译文归化,有时甚至不惜曲解原作,如把 When Greek meets Greek, then comes the tug of war. 译作"张飞杀岳飞,杀得满天飞"(其实可考虑译为"两雄相遇,其斗必烈"),把 Solomon(所罗门,古以色列国国王大卫之子,以智慧著称)译成"诸葛亮",把 Spring, the sweet spring, is the year's pleasant king. 译为"春,甘美之春,一年之中的尧舜"。中外翻译史上这种归化过头的译文不少。

另一方面,滥用汉语成语也是归化过头的一个常见表现。汉语成语大多具有浓郁的中华民族文化特征,翻译中不顾实际情况滥搬滥用,有可能破坏原作异国情调,给译语读者制造一种虚假感觉,结果只会造出一种与原语文化不相协调的汉文化,无形中给读者一种文化误导。这种以"本土文化"替代"洋文化"的弊端,可从下例看出端倪:

"A second take!" he quipped before kissing Alicia when they remarried last June. "Just like a movie."

去年6月,在复婚仪式上,拉什亲吻阿丽西亚之前妙语连珠,他说:"我们是梅开二度,就像演电影一样。"

乍一看,这个译文通顺地道,特别是"梅开二度"尤显顺畅。但从异化的角度来看,这一译法存在一个不容忽视的问题——"梅开二度"是个有深刻文化印记、中国文化意味浓厚的成语。但是该成语由拉什使用似乎有些滑稽,从而造成"文化失真"。在很多情况下,译者只有循着作者的思维、表达方式,采取谨慎的异化译法,才能充分反映原文的文化特征,充分表达原文真实意义,否则不恰当的归化译法,特别是汉语成语的不谨慎运用,可能使译文失去原文文化特征,给读者造成"文化错觉"。又如:

I'm full of scholarship; I'm full of genius; I'm full of

information; I'm full of novel views on every subject.

我学富五车,才高八斗,茹古含今,对一切问题都有最独到的见解。

该译文虽然鲜明地表现了译者的"神化"之功,充分展示了译者娴熟地道的汉语表达技能,但"学富五车"和"才高八斗"作为汉味浓厚的成语,具有文化的独特性。若用于英译汉中,极易让读者产生不知身在何方之感,形成"文化失真"。

在英译汉时,许多译者认为有五类汉语成语宜慎用:一是反映中华民族特殊习俗的,如九霄云外、义结金兰、生辰八字、负荆请罪、卧薪尝胆等;二是带有汉字特征的,如一字长蛇阵、有眼不识金镶玉、目不识丁等;三是含有中国地名的,如江东父老、逐鹿中原、乐不思蜀、庐山真面、逼上梁山等;四是含有中国人名的,如女娲补天、东施效颦、廉颇老矣等;五是涉及中国古老传说或故事的,如三顾茅庐、嫦娥奔月、盲人摸象、暗度陈仓、指鹿为马等。也就是说,译文在力求易懂的同时,还应注意保持原作文化风姿,不能将中国文化拼接到异域文化作品中去,否则会剥夺中国读者欣赏异国风情品尝异域独特风味的机会。因此,译者在使用汉语成语进行翻译时,宜采取谨慎态度。

三、异化、归化并用互补

翻译是一个充满无奈的过程。归化过度,可能被人叱为"挂羊头卖狗肉";异化过头,可能降低译文的可读性,有"脱离读者"之嫌;力求"文化传真",又恐制造"文化错觉";减少"文化失真",又难免"偷梁换柱",引起读者不必要的联想;用汉语解释原文的方法如实翻译,又怕满足不了读者对新鲜文字的期待。

诚然,翻译的根本任务是忠实地再现原作的文化、思想和风格,而原作的文化、思想和风格都带有浓厚的异国情调,因此翻译时不采用异化方法是不可能的,异化也就成了矛盾的主要方面,因而是第一位的。与此同时,既然要求译文像原作一样通顺,译者在语言表达中就不得不进行必要的归化。作为解决语言障碍的折中手段,归化法也就成为矛盾的次要方面,是第二位的。虽然异化和归化有主次之分,却不存在劣良之别,它们各具优势,各有缺陷,顾此失彼、厚此薄彼的做法都不能圆满地完成翻译任务。因此在可能的情况下,初学者应尽量争取异化,在难以异化的情况下则需退而求其次——进行必要的归化。即该异化时异化,该归化时归化。所以,很多译者,无论是偏爱异化还是重视归化,往往都两者并用,如此这般的结果很明显;许多译文都成了两种方法交错运用的产物。具体操作过程如下:

首先,可能的情况下,尽量实行异化译法。一般而言,形神皆备的译文,通常是异化译法的结果。因此,初学者在酝酿表达的过程中,应先从异化译法试起。如果异化译法能够晓畅达意,则坚持异化译法。如"You toil and work and earn bread, and I'll eat it."译成:"你们辛勤劳动换来面包,我坐享其成。"其中"面包"就是一个很好的处理,若归化为读者熟悉的"米饭",则有悖于西方的饮食文化特征,弄巧成拙,剥夺了读者了解异域文化的权力。

第二,如果异化译法不能完全达意,或者不能完全晓畅,则可考虑汉语的行文习惯,做一定的归化处理。如"... it was wrong in her situation. I wanted her to stay at home and rest this morning but she would come with us; she longed so much to see you all."译成:"她身子不方便,我要她上午待在家里好好歇着,可她偏要跟我们一道来。她多么渴望见见你们一家子啊!"如此翻译,兼有异化和归化的因素,既贴近作者委婉的表达方式,又符合汉语的语言习惯。

第三,若异化译法彻底行不通,译者不必勉为其难,可采取归化译法,舍其表层形式,传达其深层含义。如将"The good seaman is known in bad weather."译成:"惊涛骇浪,方显英雄本色。"

第四,译者在语言转换的过程中,常会遇到由于语言文化差异、思维差异等因素造成的种种障碍,有些障碍甚至无法逾越,如果一味坚持异化译法,势必导致译文的晦涩难懂。在这种情况下,译者只能退而采取归化译法,将自己的译笔纳入汉语语言文化规范的轨道。如"Well, she's certainly no spring chicken."译成"她当然不再是小丫头了",效果就较好。不过,如果一味坚持归化译法,势必导致译文"文化失真"。如哈代的小说《苔丝》中,苔丝的弟弟对苔丝说:Our great relation will help'ee to marry a gentleman.有译家采取归化的表达方式译作"咱们那个财主本家,要给你攀一门好亲,叫你嫁一个体面人",没有忠实地再现原文,后有译者改译为"俺们那个了不起的亲戚将帮你嫁一个高贵的绅士",效果则好多了。

翻译初学者应树立一个明确观念:归化主要表现在纯语言层面上,在文化层面上则应力求最大限度的异化。这就是所说的适度原则,分寸原则。异化时不妨碍译文的通顺易懂,归化时不改变原作的风味,特别不能"偷梁换柱"导致"文化失真"。

总之,译文的语言既不可能是纯粹的异化语言,也不可能是纯粹的归化语言，只能是原语和译语的混合物。其中，异化的成分该占多少，归化的比例又当如何，不可能形成一个统一标准，初学者当合理把握一个字，那就是"度"。

附　课堂讲练材料

Youth

　　Youth is not a time of life; it is a state of mind; it is not a matter of rosy cheeks, red lips and supple knees; it is a matter of the will, a quality of the imagination, a vigor of the emotions; it is the freshness of the deep springs of life.

　　Youth means a temperamental predominance of courage over timidity of the appetite, for adventure over the love of ease. This often exists in a man of 60 more than a boy of 20. Nobody grows old merely by a number of years. We grow old by deserting our ideals.

　　Years may wrinkle the skin, but to give up enthusiasm wrinkles the soul. Worry, fear, self-distrust bows the heart and turns the spirit back to dust.

　　Whether 60 or 16, there is in every human being's heart the lure of wonder, the unfailing childlike appetite of what's next and the joy of the game of living. In the center of your heart and my heart there is a wireless station: so long as it receives messages of beauty, hope, cheer, courage and power from men and from the infinite, so long are you young.

　　When the aerials are down, and your spirit is covered with snows of cynicism and the ice of pessimism, then you are grown old, even at 20, but as long as your aerials are up, to catch waves of optimism, there is hope you may die young at 80.

(Samuel Ullman)

第三章　英汉语言的对比

英汉翻译的所有理论、方法和技巧都建立在英汉两种语言的对比之上,对于初学者而言,研究两种语言之间的异同,尤其是差异,有助于探索出翻译特点,培养译文质量优劣的甄别能力,重视翻译难点,揣摩译文的多样性,扩大译文选择空间,从而走出一条适合自己的翻译之路。

翻译实践表明,英汉两种语言的差异主要体现在词汇、句法及思维三个方面。

第一节　词汇现象的对比

一般情况下,英汉词汇比较主要从词义、词序及词的搭配三方面展开。

一、词义

通过比较,不难发现以下现象有助于译者做出精当的词义选择。

(一) 完全等值

英汉翻译过程中,人们时常发现某些英语表达与汉语表达在语法意义、语用意义(包括表征意义、表达意义、联想意义、祈使意义、社会意义)以及文化意义上完全相同,形成一一对应的关系。完全等值是翻译中时常碰到的一种现象。这种现象常见于专业术语、专用名词及日常生活用语。如:

  filial son　　　　　　　　孝子
  acceptance speech　　　　获奖感言
  earthquake hazard hunt　　地震隐患排查
  family earthquake drill　　家庭防震演习

(二) 部分等值

英文词语有时与汉语中的某些词存在部分等值,可根据语境、搭配、句子间的逻辑关系来加以甄别,以明晰其言内之意及言外之意。如:

ambition	雄心；野心
man	男人；仆人；兵；侠；丈夫；男子汉
flatter	恭维；讨好

(三) 英语所有、汉语所无

翻译时译者会遇到英语所有、汉语所无的词语,特别是新词、杜撰词及反映最新科技、最新理念、英美社会特殊习俗、风气或事物的词。译者可根据语境或句间逻辑关系及文化等因素或力求异化,或进行归化处理。如:

pandemonium
　　地狱;魔鬼居住的地方(有人将其归化为"阎王殿",殊不知"阎王殿"是个反映中国独特文化的词语,不仅在文化上不能与原词等值,还易使中国读者产生"文化错觉",还是根据其字面意义翻译为好。)

Troika
　　欧盟三套车(这是欧洲理事会现任轮值主席国、前任轮值主席国、继任轮值主席国联合组成的一套外交机制,采取异化译法既符合设想者及读者所积累的认知经验,又生动形象地说明了欧盟外交机制的复杂性。)

(四) 一词多义

英语语言最重要的特征之一便是一词多义,因而在众多英语意义中选择既忠实原文又符合汉语表达习惯的译词显得尤为困难。遇到一词多义现象时,初学者不妨首先根据词语搭配进行词义的筛选。请比较形容词 sloppy 及其汉语对应词的选择。

sloppy weather	潮湿的天气
a **sloppy** racetrack	湿漉漉的跑道
to use **sloppy** English	操不地道的英语
a **sloppy** young man	穿着邋遢的年轻人
sloppy trousers	肥大的裤子
sloppy sentiment	脆弱的感情
a **sloppy** pudding	烂糟糟的布丁

其次,可参考语境。请比较一下动词 touch 及其汉语翻译:

to **touch** sb. on the shoulder
轻轻碰某人的肩膀

to **touch** one's lips to the child's forehead
轻轻地吻小孩的前额
to **touch** glasses
碰杯
to **touch** the high point in one's career
达到某人的事业顶峰
to be **touched** to the quick
触及痛楚
hair **touched** with grey
有点花白的头发
to **touch** sb. to the heart
触动某人的心弦

再次,可看某词汇是否为引申义。如下面的广告词:

Give your hair a touch of **spring**.
译文一:给你的头发增添一缕春色。
译文二:给你的头发春天的格调。
译文三:给你的头发增添弹性。

与原文内涵相比,以上三种译文的信息都有所缺损。所以,从某种意义上讲,翻译是一种时常与缺憾为伴的活动。现比较一下汉语译词从字面义的选取到引申义的确立:

tiger   老虎——残暴
king   国王——主宰
entree   进入——入场券——敲门砖

最后,可根据词汇的褒、贬或中性程度来进行词义的选择。试比较 aggressive 及其汉译:

an **aggressive** salesman   一个积极肯干的推销员
Hitler's **aggressive** policy   希特勒的侵略政策

对于英语词汇一词多义的现象,无论怎样处理,都要本着"忠实、通顺"的翻译原则,尽可能正确地传递原文的多重意义,以争取原文和译文最大程度的等值。

二、词的搭配

英语和汉语在词的搭配方面存在差异。以形容词 light 为例，light music 即"轻音乐"，light loss 即"较小的损失"，light car 即"轻型汽车"，light heart 即"不专一的心"，light step 即"轻快的脚步"，light manners 即"轻浮的举止"，light voice 即"轻声"。可见，英语词汇的搭配能力很强，需要用不同的汉语词汇来翻译同一个词。因此，译者有必要在平时的翻译练习中对词语搭配所反映出的英汉语之间的异同进行认真研究，仔细推敲，揣摩翻译的精妙之处及正确处理方法。试比较下列例子：

financial policy
货币政策

financial crisis.
金融危机

the **Financial** Accounting Standards Board (FASB)
财务会计准则委员会

in **financial** difficulties
处于财政困难之中

The store was a **financial** failure and soon closed.
该店赔本，很快就关闭了。

另外，英语中还存在大量的固定搭配、习惯搭配以及非固定搭配。所谓固定搭配就是人们约定俗成的搭配；习惯搭配就是人们习以为常且经常使用的搭配；非固定搭配就是在人们交流中表达相同含义的多种表达方式，这取决于一个人的创造性表达能力。无论是翻译固定搭配、习惯搭配还是非固定搭配，切忌望文生义，否则就可能成为笑谈。如：

1. It is **out of the question** that you should become the president of the company.

    错：你当这个公司的总裁不成问题。

    可参考：你要当这个公司的总裁是绝对不可能的。

2. They were **anything but** sparing their efforts to finish the construction work.

    错：他们绝不愿努力完成这一建设工作。

    可参考：他们为完成这项建筑工程而不遗余力。

3. There is no way to **black out** the news.
   错:无从发布消息。
   可参考:无从封锁消息。

4. They are trying to **get round** the income taxes.
   错:他们为绕开收入税而绞尽脑汁。
   可参考:他们为逃避收入税而绞尽脑汁。

英语中固定搭配、习惯搭配或短语种类繁多,其中动词性短语或搭配、名词性短语或搭配、形容词性短语或搭配、副词性短语或搭配尤为重要。

(一) 动词性短语及搭配

A. 动词+小品词。请比较:

1. We must **bring** the chairman **around to** our point of view.
   我们必须**劝说**会议主席**转而支持**我们的观点。
2. The Asian countries along the coast of the Pacific all **came out against** the US new military base in Japan.
   太平洋沿岸亚洲各国都**宣布反对**美国在日本新建军事基地。
3. Though they are running out of food and drink, the men are cheerful and confident that they will **get out** soon.
   他们几乎水尽粮绝,但情绪很好,自信很快就能**走出困境**。

B. 动词+名词。请比较:

fake moves	花拳绣腿
face the music	勇于承担后果
jump the queue	插队
miss the boat	错失良机
make the grade	取得成功

C. 动词+介词短语。请比较:

beat about the bush	旁敲侧击;拐弯抹角地谈话
play for one's own hand	为自己的利益而去做

(二) 名词性短语及搭配

A. 形容词/分词短语+名词。请比较:

fond dreams	黄粱美梦

narrow escape	九死一生
the adoptive family	收养子女的家庭
a beaten path	现成的路；惯例
bushy hair	浓密的头发

B. 名词＋介词＋名词。请比较：

a wolf in sheep's clothing	披着羊皮的狼
a blessing in disguise	塞翁失马；因祸得福
a fly in the ointment	美中不足之处；使人扫兴的事
a bed of flowers	安乐窝
a man of family	名门子弟
kiss of death	死神之吻；乍看有益但会导致毁灭的行为

C. 名词/专有名词＋'s＋名词。请比较：

cat's paw	被利用的人
King's English	纯正英语
Achilles' heel	唯一致命的弱点
Penelope's web	永远完不成的工作

D. 名词＋and＋名词。请比较：

resourcefulness and tenacity	智慧勇气
rank and file	普通的士兵们
flesh and blood	亲骨肉；亲属
part and parcel	重要或必要的组成部分
the pros and cons	赞成者和反对者；正反理由
end and aim	目的
happiness and sorrows	喜悦与惆怅
aid and abet	伙同作案；同谋
man and wife	夫妻

E. 名词＋名词。请比较：

divorce lawyer	办理离婚案件的律师
brain trust	智囊团

riot police	防暴警察
people skills	做人技巧
stage fright	怯场

(三) 形容词性短语及搭配

A. 形容词＋and＋形容词。请比较：

high and mighty	趾高气扬；神气活现
pure and simple	完完全全的；十足的
honest and true	诚实的
weak and feeble	虚弱的
null and void	无效的；不再有约束力的

B. 介词＋名词。请比较：

in the dark	蒙在鼓里的
beyond description	无法形容的
on fire	起火；非常激动的
on guard	在岗的；警惕的
behind the time	不合时宜的

C. 形容词＋介词＋名词。请比较：

wide of the mark	毫不相关的
slow off the mark	起跑慢的；行动迟缓的
up in the air	悬而未决的

D. as＋形容词＋as＋名词。请比较：

as bald as an egg	光秃秃的
as black as a raven/coal/night	漆黑
as blind as a beetle	视力非常坏的；两眼一抹黑的
as bold as brass	厚颜无耻的
as bright as a new penny	光泽鉴人的；非常整洁的
as proud as a peacock	非常高傲
as cheerful as a lark	兴高采烈的；非常快乐的
as clear as day	一清二楚的
as quiet as a mouse	非常安静；不声不响

as busy as bees　　　　　　　忙忙碌碌

(四) 副词性短语

A. 名词＋名词。请比较：

heart and soul　　　　　　　全心全意地
bag and baggage　　　　　　完全地；彻底地

B. 副词＋副词。请比较：

really and truly　　　　　　　完全地
thick and fast　　　　　　　　密集地

C. 介词＋名词。请比较：

in a breeze　　　　　　　　　轻松地
with flying colors　　　　　　出色地；成功地
behind the scenes　　　　　　在幕后
at a gallop　　　　　　　　　用最快速度；飞快地；急速地

三、词序

英汉句子中的主语、谓语动词、宾语或表语的词序基本一致，只是定语和状语的秩序同中有异，时有变化，所以在此主要针对定语及状语的不同进行英汉语词序对比。

(一) 单词作定语

英语与汉语一样，在用单词作定语时，通常把它置于被修饰词的前面；不同的是，英语有时还将定语后置。某些以-able,-ible 结尾的形容词，与every, all, only 或形容词的最高级连用作定语修饰名词时，可以放在名词前，也可以放在名词后，意义相同。试比较：

all the means possible　　　　一切可能的方法
all the possible means　　　　一切可能的方法

值得注意的是，英语中的某些单词修饰名词时，前置词和后置词意义迥然不同。试比较：

the present students　　　　　现在的学生
the students present　　　　　出席的学生；到场的学生

a responsible man	一个负责任的人
a man responsible (for sth.)	对某事负责的人
a concerned look in one's eyes	(对某事)眼中关切的神情
people concerned	(与某事)相关的人
interested people	(对某事)感兴趣的人
people interested	(与某事)有利害关系的人
an involved sentence	复杂的句子
people involved	与某事有牵连的人

另外,英语名词多作定语,但这种情况在汉语中十分少见,因而翻译过程中宜注意根据上下文的逻辑含义,做一定的技术处理。试比较:

1. A high-tech **transportation supervision and coordination** center will play a major role in easing traffic. Other systems for **traffic** monitoring, guiding and **accident** reporting will also contribute to better **transportation** conditions. Concentrating on **traffic** organization and direction, a scientific **transit management** system will be built up based on an integrated **traffic information** management and guaranteed by **traffic police** management.

   高科技的**管理协调**中心将会在缓解交通压力方面发挥重要作用。其他**交通**监控监测系统、交通指挥系统以及交通事故报警系统届时都会有助于改善**交通**状况,从而形成以**交通**组织指挥为龙头、综合**交通信息**管理为基础、交通警务管理为保障的科学**交通管理**体系。

2. In his own life, Barack Obama has lived the American dream, as a **community organizer**, in the **state senate**, as a **United States senator**. He has dedicated himself to ensuring the dream is realized. And in this campaign, he has inspired so many to become involved in the democratic process and invested in our common future.

   身为社区组织者、州议员和**联邦参议员**,贝拉克·奥巴马自己的生活就是美国梦的写照。为确保这个梦想的实现,他全力付出。在这次竞选中,他鼓舞那么多人参与民主进程,致力于我们共同的未来。

初学者应仔细研究相关译文,特别要注意译者对定语的翻译处理技巧和措辞。

(二) 短语作定语

英语中修饰名词的短语一般都放在被修饰词的后面,汉语一般则放在被修饰词的前面。

短语作定语可分为分词短语作定语、动词不定式作定语、介词短语作定语这三种情况。

A. 分词短语作定语

1. Consult the references **given at the end of the chapter**.
   请参阅本章末尾的参考文献。

2. There is the challenge, **more clearly defined than ever before**, to scientists to apply the results of science and technology for the benefit of mankind.
   科学家们面临的挑战比以往任何时候都要明确——如何用科技成果造福人类。

B. 动词不定式作定语

1. There are children **for her to look after** and **a big house to take care of**.
   她要照看孩子,还要打理一所很大的房子。

2. We have no place **to go and have fun**.
   我们无地方可玩。

C. 介词短语作定语

1. Women **at 30** are more likely to put relationships above career.
   30岁的女人重爱情轻事业。

2. It's not necessary to provide yet another analysis **of the disintegration of the family** or the breakdown **of the social fabric** or the price **of democracy** to explain what had happened to our society.
   要解释我们的社会问题,没必要再从家庭解体、社会结构瘫痪以及民主代价这些方面进行分析。

(三) 单词作状语

英语与汉语一样,在单词作状语时,常放在被修饰词或状语的前面。不同的是,英语单词作状语修饰动词时,一般放在动词之后,而汉语则一般置于动词之前。另外,英语表示程度的状语在修饰状语时既可前置又可后置,而汉语一般全部前置。试比较以下句子:

1. **Fortunately** for imperfect men, however, not all women go for the Gyllenhaal ideal.
   对不够完美的男性而言**所幸**的是,并非所有女性都喜欢吉伦黑尔这种类型的。(前置)

2. Height is **apparently** more important than looks to women looking for Mr Right, a survey claims.
   一项调查发现,与长相相比,女性在寻找意中人时**显然**更看重对方的身高。(后置)

(四) 短语作状语

英语短语状语可置于动词前后,汉语则视情况而定;英语的地点短语状语多在时间状语之前,汉语时间状语则在地点状语之前;英语时间短语状语和地点短语状语一般由从小到大的秩序排列,而汉语恰恰相反。试比较以下句子:

1. **On May 12, 2008**, an earthquake of 8 magnitude struck Sichuan. Everyone in China was shocked, and quickly became heartbroken as reported deaths climbed from 10,000 to 32,000 to more than 62,000 people. The death toll is still rising, and the number of injured and missing is many times more.
   2008年5月12日,四川发生里氏8级大地震。每一个中国人都非常震惊,继而感到心碎。据报道,遇难同胞人数从1万很快上升到3.2万,随后达到6.2万以上。目前,这个数字仍在增加,受伤和失踪的人数则数倍于此。(前置)

2. The ship ploughed her way **through the huge waves**.
   船**在惊涛骇浪中**破浪前进。(后置)

第二节　句法现象的对比

句法现象主要体现在句子结构、句序、句子内容的表现手段三个方面。

一、句子结构

英汉两种语言在句子结构方面虽有共同之处，但差别也很大，主要表现在被动句、倒装句、简单句、复合句等句子结构的使用上。

（一）被动句

英汉两种语言都使用被动句，但在形式及使用频率、使用范围等方面存在差异。一般情况下，英语被动句一目了然，而汉语被动句却因使用"被""为……所""受""由""加以""予以""得到""是……的"等被动词而不易识别。

从使用频率看，日常会话及文学著作中的英语被动句式要远高于汉语，科技英语文体则更高，所以一些语言学家将被动句式的大量使用归纳为科技英语的两大特征之一。

从使用范围看，使用主动句式还是被动句式只是从两个不同角度出发叙述同一事件，并不涉及说话人或当事人对整个事件的评价，因此英语中不管好事或坏事还是其他任何事都可用被动句式。而汉语则不同，"被"字句原先主要说明主语受难或遭遇到某些损害或不愉快的事情，不过随着时代的变化，汉语被动句式的适用范围扩大了，现代汉语中被动句也可以表示令人愉悦的事情了。但在口语中，被动句式基本上仍表示不幸或不愉快，如"我喜欢的礼物都被别人抢走了。"

（二）倒装结构

倒装结构在汉语中很少存在，但在英语中却是一种常见结构，且形式多样，种类繁多。

第一类：将 here, there, now, then, out, up 等副词或副词短语放在句首，且谓语动词多为 be, come, go, exist, live, follow 等不及物动词时，句子完全倒装。试比较下列句子：

1. Here is the very passport that you have lost.
   这就是你丢失的那本护照。
2. There stands a great temple on the top of that mountain.
   山顶上矗立着一座宏伟的寺庙。
3. Up went the rocket into the space in an instant.

顷刻间,火箭"嗖"的一声飞向太空。

4. Then came the day we had been looking forward to.
我们盼望的这一天终于到来了!

第二类:(not) only 修饰状语放在句首时的倒装。如:

1. Only in this way can you succeed.
只有这样,才能成功。

2. Only when one is ill does he realize the value of health.
人只在生病时,才意识到健康的价值。

3. Only by reading extensively can you widen your horizons.
只有通过广泛阅读,才能拓宽视野。

4. Not only was Jack London a well-known novelist, but (he was) also a poet.
杰克·伦敦不仅是一个著名的小说家,还是一位诗人。

第三类:表示否定意义的副词或副词短语位于句首时的倒装结构,如 little, seldom, hardly, scarcely, never, nowhere, in no case, under no conditions, under no circumstances, not in the least, not at all, in no way, by no means, on no account 等。试比较:

1. Never in my life have I heard of such a strange thing!
我这辈子从没听说这么离奇的事情!

2. Under no circumstances should we yield to difficulty.
我们在任何情况下都不应向困难屈服。

3. In no case will China be the first to use nuclear weapons.
中国决不第一个使用核武器!

4. On no account are visitors allowed to feed the animals.
游客不得给动物喂食。

第四类:在 so ... that 结构中,so 放在句首时的倒装句。试比较:

1. So fast did he walk that none of us was his equal.
他走路非常快,谁都不是他的对手。

2. So absurd did he look that everyone stared at him.
他看起来滑稽可笑,人人都盯着他瞧。

第五类:虚拟条件句如果省略 if,也用倒装。试比较:

1. Had you worked harder, you would have succeeded.
   再努一把力,你就会成功。

2. Were it not for you, I would fail.
   如果没有你的帮助,我肯定会失败。

第六类:在 Hardly ... when 和 No sooner ... than 以及 Not until 等句型中,否定词或否定词组放在句首时所用的倒装结构。试比较:

1. Hardly had I arrived when I had a new problem to cope with.
   我刚到就碰到一个新问题要处理。

2. Scarcely had we started lunch when the doorbell rang.
   我们刚开始吃午饭,门铃就响了。

3. No sooner was she back at home than she realized her mistake.
   她一回家,就意识到自己犯了个错误。

第七类:为保持句子结构的平衡或强调句子中的表语部分,经常把表语放在句首时所用的倒装结构。试比较:

1. Gone are the days when China had to depend on foreign oil.
   中国依赖洋油的时代一去不复返了!

2. Faint grew the sound of the bell.
   铃声越来越弱。

3. At the head was Dr. Bethune on horse-back, followed by a donkey loaded with medical supplies.
   走在前面的是白求恩大夫,他骑着马,后面跟着一头驴,驴身上驮满了药品。

第八类:惊叹句常用倒装。试比较:

1. What a cute dog it is!
   多可爱的狗!

2. Isn't cold!
   真冷!

3. Am I fed up.
   烦!

第九类:地点状语放在句首时,主谓的结构要倒装。试比较:

1. On the bed lay a very beautiful woman.
   床上躺着一位美妇人。
2. On the floor were piles of old books and newspaper.
   地板上堆放着旧书和报纸。
3. On a hill in front of our school stood a great shopping mall.
   我们学校前面的小山上有一家大卖场。

第十类:倒装结构用于表示祝愿的句型中。试比较:

1. May you live a long and happy life!
   祝您幸福长寿!
2. Long live the People's Republic of China!
   中华人民共和国万岁!

第十一类:其他倒装结构。试比较:

1. Such was the force of explosion that all the windows were broken.
   爆炸的威力十分了得,所有窗户都震破了。
2. Young as she is, she has seen much of the world.
   她年纪轻轻,可见过不少世面。
3. Starved and tired enough he was.
   他饿得要命,累得要死。

第十二类:正常的语法性倒装。试比较:

1. Are you a teacher or a student?
   你是教师还是学生?
2. Why did you do it without your parents' permission?
   你做这件事为什么不经父母许可?

(三) 简单句及复杂句

众所周知,英语的句子与汉语的句子一样,也有简单句和复杂句之分。英语简单句主要结构有以下五种,试比较:

1. China is a great nation.
   中国是个伟大的国家。(注:这是典型的SVP"主语+动词+表语"句型结构)

2. A new problem arose.

   新问题出现了。（注：这是典型的 SV "主语＋动词"的句型结构）

3. Every coin has two sides.

   凡事都有两面。（注：这是典型的 SVO "主语＋谓语＋宾语"的句型结构）

4. The teacher gave that student a passing score.

   老师给那位学生一个及格分数。（注：这是 SVOiOd "主语＋动词＋间接宾语＋直接宾语"的句型结构）

5. The parents consider their child a genius.

   家长都认为自己的孩子是天才。（注：这是典型的 SVOCo "主语＋动词＋宾语＋宾语补足语"的句型结构）

从以上五个简单句来看，英语及其汉译几乎是等值的关系，但复杂句的情况则相反，常常需要在理解的基础上用忠实易懂的汉语去对原文进行解释性翻译。试比较以下英语长句及其汉译：

1. And when our own tears have dried and the hangovers have subsided, we will all emerge as winners from the greatest tournament on earth.

   泪水已干、醉梦方醒之时，我们将以胜利者的姿态走出这世上最伟大的赛事。

2. I was seized with sadness as I thought of how the ancient city had been spared during the Second World War and now might be destroyed by an impending riot.

   想到这座古老的城市在第二次世界大战时得以幸免而现在可能要遭到即将来临的暴乱的毁灭，我不禁悲从中来。

3. Michelle Obama's understated chic has injected a welcome dash of class into the run-up to today's G20 as world leaders descend on London amid rowdy protests in the City of London financial district.

   米歇尔·奥巴马低调雅致的着装为今天即将开幕的 G20 峰会增添了些许新鲜气息。当出席峰会的各国首脑齐聚伦敦时，迎接他们的是伦敦金融城举行的闹哄哄的抗议活动。

4. And he believes that when you have worked hard, and done well, and walked through the dooway of oppoutunity, you do not slam it shut behind you, no, you reach back, and you give others the chances that helped you succeed.

他相信,当你努力奋斗,出人头地,并通过那扇机会之门后,你不会自私地随手关掉它,而会转身回去伸出援手,给普通人那些曾帮助你成功的机会!

二、句序

英汉复合句中的主句和从句之间在时间顺序、逻辑顺序等方面不尽相同,因此先后顺序也有所不同。

(一) 英汉复合句中的时间顺序

在英语复合句中,表示时间的从句可放在主句之前,也可放在主句之后,而汉语则视表达习惯而定。试比较下面的例句,并注意英汉在时间表达上的差异:

1. **As it is nearing the Christmas season**, such programs have multiplied.

   圣诞将至,此类项目多了起来。

2. **As soon as Tortoise heard of the great feast in the sky** his throat began to itch at the very thought.

   乌龟一听说天上的盛宴,不禁垂涎三尺。

3. I want to ponder my chances of success **before I take action**.

   行动之前,我得考虑成功的几率有多大。

(二) 英汉复合句中的逻辑顺序

在表示因果关系的复合句中,表示原因的从句可放在主句的前面,也可放在主句之后;而汉语一般为前"因"后"果"顺序。试比较:

1. The beauty of a woman must be seen in her eyes, because that is the doorway to her heart—the place where love resides.

   因为眼睛是心灵的窗户和爱居住的地方,所以一个女人美不美得看她的眼睛。

2. Obie didn't bother to answer. You couldn't ever win an argument with Archie. He was too quick with the words.

Especially when he fell into one of his phony hip moods. Saying man and cat, like he was a swinger, cool, instead of a senior in a lousy little high school like Trinity.

奥比实在懒得答,跟阿奇争辩,你永远也别想赢。他太伶牙俐齿了,尤其是当他学起嬉皮士调侃的时候,经常满嘴的"大哥""小弟",像个潮人,很酷,一点也不像三一高中这个小破学校的学生。

3. She married Robert because she thought she loved him.
   她以为自己很爱罗伯特,所以才嫁给了他。

4. Jim, your father is very uncomfortable with you for your getting into trouble again.
   吉姆,你又惹麻烦了,爸爸对你很生气。

在表示条件(假设)与结果关系的复合句中,条件(假设)从句的位置可以在表示结果的主句之前,也可以在主句之后;而汉语中多数情况则是条件(假设)在前,结果在后。试比较:

1. Suppose you have a million dollars, what will you do with it?
   假设你有一百万美元,你会用它做什么?

2. If he woke while he was being buried, they would think he was a demon and beat him to death.
   如果他在被活埋时醒来,村民们会把他当成魔鬼活活打死。

3. If you ask a question you don't want an answer to, expect an answer you do not want to hear.
   如果你们问我们一个不想知道答案的问题,那么请做好心理准备去听你们不想听到的答案吧。

在表示目的与行动关系的复合句中,多数情况是行动在前,目的在后。汉语大多数情况下,也是行动在前,目的在后,但有时为了强调目的,也把目的放在行动之前。试比较:

   To prove their point they scaled up a chicken to the size of Tyrannosaurus rex and found the giant chicken probably would not have been able to stand.
   为了证明自己的观点,他们按比例把一只鸡放大到霸王龙大小,结果发现这只巨鸡无法站立。

在表示结果与理由关系的复合句中,多数情况是理由在前,结果在后;而汉语一般亦如此。试比较:

1. Las Vegas spent the 1990s trying to attract families by transforming itself into a kid-friendly entertainment paradise.
   为吸引以家庭为单位的游客,拉斯维加斯用20世纪的最后10年努力把这座城市建设成一个孩子们的娱乐天堂。
2. The considerable credit that is due to him is not for having invented a method which others had pioneered.
   他之所以大受赞扬,并不是因为他在前人开创的战术方面有什么新的建树。

(三) 英汉语复合句中其他表达顺序之间的关系

关系一:转折

Although he seems hearty and outgoing in public, Mr. Cook is a withdrawn, introverted man.
虽然库克先生在公开场合显得亲切而随和,实际上却是一个性格孤僻内向的人。

关系二:同位

The key is resolution, **which helps children feel secure that their families will stay intact.**
关键是要解决问题,要让孩子在完整的家庭中有安全感。

关系三:假设

What if **you wrote all day and all night and never slept for a hundred years**?
如果100年不睡觉,不分昼夜地写,会怎么样?

关系四:让步

1. Making a practice of checking in with the insurance company in advance, **no matter what care you are receiving**, could avoid a lot of heartache later on.

不管投什么险种,事先到保险公司咨询可省却日后许多麻烦。

2. **In spite of what I'd done**, I believed he would listen to mine.
无论我做错了什么,相信他还是愿意听我祈祷的。

关系五:总结

In short, the scientific revolution, as we call it, was largely the improvement and invention and use of a series of instruments.

简而言之,所谓的科学革命,主要是指一系列工具的改进、发明和使用。

关系六:选择

When he retired from the CIA after 24 years, **rather than seeking a job among Hollywood makeup artists**, Barren decided to help people, "giving them back their identity."

24年后从中央情报局退休时,巴伦没有去好莱坞当化妆师,而是选择帮助毁容者"重塑自我。"

第三节 英汉思维的差异

人类与动物最大的不同是能够思维,不过由于历史、文化、生活环境、地域等方面的不同,人类的思维方式有所不同,形成了各民族特有的思维定式。这种思维定式的存在为研究对比各种思维模式提供了便利。近年来,翻译工作者们越来越清楚地认识到思维对翻译过程的影响,一致认为对比两种语言在思维方式上的差异可以更忠实更准确地传达原文的内涵,实现成功翻译。

一、英美人与中国人思维的差异

(一) 英美人偏好抽象思维,中国人偏好形象思维

在地域文化传统以及长期的历史积淀等因素影响下,英美人一般重视用抽象概念表达具体的事物,长于抽象思维的运用,长于分析事物;中国人恰恰相反,往往运用形象的方法表达抽象的概念,重综合,重归纳,重暗示,重含蓄,不太强调纯粹意义上的抽象思维。这种思维形式的不同在语言上表现为:

1. 英语语言常常使用大量的含义概括、指称笼统的抽象名词来表达复

杂的理性概念。如：**Science is a method** that ignores **religion**, race, nationality, **economics**, **morality**, and **ethics**. 这里的 science, method, religion, economics, morality 以及 ethics 全是抽象名词,因此给中国读者以一种"虚""泛""暗""曲""隐"的感觉。而中国人则习惯使用具体形象的词语来表达虚的概念,这种表达给人一种"实""明""直""形""象"的感觉,如"画饼充饥"中的"饼"与"饥","指鹿为马"中的"鹿"与"马","指桑骂槐"中"桑"与"槐","窈窕淑女,君子好逑"中的"淑女"与"君子"等。

2. 英语中被动语态的大量存在,也是英语语言偏重抽象思维形式的一个集中体现。

(二) 英美人偏重直线思维,中国人偏重曲线思维

美国学者卡普兰(Kaplan)在对英语和东方语言(包括汉语)学习者写的英语文章进行对比分析之后发现文章的谋篇布局方式能反映人的思维模式。通过进一步研究,他得出结论认为：英语篇章的组织和发展是"直线型"(linear),即直截了当地陈述主题,进行论述,习惯把要点首先表达出来,然后再把各种修饰语或其他次要内容一一补进。这种情况在英语中具体表现为句式结构多主句,从句相互交错,主句中有从句,从句中可能还有主句,从句套从句,盘根错节,异常复杂。然而,中国人则习惯于从侧面阐述外围的环境,最后点出话语的信息中心,所以汉语表达方式常呈"螺旋形"(circular/spiral),即不直接切入主题,而是在主题外围"兜圈子"或"旁敲侧击",最后进入主题。这可能与中国人为人谦虚、追求含蓄这一民族特性相关。正是由于中西思维的巨大差异,在翻译过程中,许多初学者往往不知所措,误译、错译的情况时有发生。试比较：

> It spread its wings anew and soared upward, at first carefully and tentatively, soon with greater boldness and assurance, until at last with a wild scream of joy it swung itself high up in the air and made a great circle.

> 它重新张开双翅向上飞越。起初,它谨慎地尝试着飞翔,但很快胆子就大了,飞得更稳了。最后,它发出一声欣喜的尖叫,直冲云霄,展翅盘旋。

其实,这句主要结构非常简单,就是：It spread its wings anew and soared upward. 其他成分都是修饰成分,如果不仔细分析,有可能译错。

(三) 英美多用复杂句，汉语崇尚简约

正如张光明教授在其《名译赏析导论》中所指出的那样，"英语句式最大特点之一是句式冗长，结构复杂，层层叠叠，绵延不断。"与此相比，汉语偏重使用短句、简单句。了解这一差别有助于译者处理好句式转换这一翻译环节。试比较：

  Translation is first a science, which entails the knowledge and verification of the facts and the language that describe them—here, what is wrong, mistakes of truth, can be identified.

  首先，翻译是一门科学，它需要知识，需要求证，需要懂得描述的语言。翻译时，错误的内容，错误的事实，可能得以甄别。

(四) 英语严格区分主、客体，汉语主、客体相互交错，相互交融

英语语言中的思维注重客观事物对人的作用和影响，因而他们对主体和客体有着严格的区分，而汉语语言中的思维往往以"人"为中心，认为只有人才能做出有意识的动作，或具有有意识的行为，因此汉语语言一般对思维的主体和客体不加区分，具体表现为：汉语常以有生命的名词作主语，句子的语态呈隐含式；而英文则多用无生命名词作主语，主动与被动两个范畴泾渭分明。试比较：

  Whether these stories are cartoons, jokes told by a slap-stick comedian, or a cross-talking team, they appeal to people everywhere as funny stories because they have a note of reality to them, and the unexpected punch line is quite funny.

  漫画故事、喜剧笑话和群口相声作为人们喜闻乐见的幽默形式，因其贴近现实生活，加上出其不意的搞笑方式，广受各地人民喜爱。

(五) 英语偏重形合，汉语偏重意合

英语语言偏重形式逻辑，但不排斥辩证思维；相比之下，汉语语言思维更偏重辩证思维，不太重视形式逻辑。这种思维差异在语言上表现为英语重"形"合，汉语重"意"合，即英语注重运用各种有形的联结手段达到语法形式与逻辑形式两方面的完整，概念指代分明，句子组织严密，层次一环套一环，句法功能呈外显特性；而汉语语言表现形式受意念引导，看上去概念、判断、推理都不严密，句子松散，句法功能呈隐含形式。试比较：

  He, amply provided with liberal accomplishments, and bound, if he kept the straight road, to attain all distinctions, was goaded by a spirit of haste, which impelled him to outpace first his equals, then his superiors, and finally his own ambitions: an infirmity fatal to many, even of the good, who, disdaining the sure and slow, force a premature success, though destruction may accompany the prize.

他是个很有才华的人,如果走正道,将来一定能成功。只可惜他心浮气躁,急于从同层次的人中脱颖而出,继而超过比他地位高的人,结果野心迅速膨胀。包括某些优秀人士在内的很多人身上也都有这种致命弱点,他们不屑于稳步升迁,一味追求早日成就功名,甚至不惜身败名裂。

(六)英语重静态,汉语重动态

英汉两种语言另外一个明显的区别是,英语偏重静态的描写,而汉语偏重动态的描写。从语言形式上看,英语一般多用名词、动名词,较少使用谓语动词或其他表示运动意义的词;在词汇方面,英语常用动词的同源名词、同源形容词、副词及其介词(英语被一些语言学家称之为"介词"语言)。而汉语表达则多用动词,如使用大量的"兼动式或连动式",这样可以使所描写的人或事跃然纸上,显得生动活泼,让读者产生身临其境的感觉。试比较:

The whole armada, equipped at once for **sailing** or propulsion by the oars, was a **striking** and **formidable** spectacle.

整个船队既可**扬帆航行**,也可划桨前进,其规模蔚为壮观,令人生畏。

二、思维差异对翻译的影响

英汉两种语言在思维方面存在上述诸多差异,为英译汉实践造成许多困难,具体表现为:

(一)思维习惯不同,造成词义理解困难,可能影响译文的准确性

由于英语注重抽象思维,因而抽象表达法在英语里使用得相当普遍,尤其在社会科学论著、官方文章、报刊评论、法律文书和商业信件等文体中。而汉语缺乏英语中抽象表达的手段,其词义表达形式没有形态变化。因此,英语语言中的大量抽象名词往往难以找到相对应的汉语表达方式,这就给翻译带来一定难度。试比较:

So we drove along between **the green of the park and the stony**

lifeless elegance of hotels and apartment buildings...

车子朝前行驶着，路两旁一边是**青翠的公园**，一边是**死板乏味的豪华旅馆和公寓大楼**……

这里的 green, elegance 都是抽象名词，在翻译时要特别注意其汉语对应译语。

(二) 思维风格不同，句子重心各异，可能影响译文的连贯性

试比较下面的句子：

1. Much attention in international economic and political affairs **understandably** focuses on the welfare gap between the developed and developing countries.

   人们在国际经济和政治事务中对发达国家与发展中国家之间的贫富差距给予了极大关注，这是可以理解的。

2. Of the seven deadly sins, **I'm convinced** that greed is the worst.

   现在我深信，"贪"真是万恶之首。

(三) 思维中心不同，可能造成误译、错译

We went away as **wise** as we came.

错译：我们离开的时候跟我们进来的时候一样明智。

参考译文：我们走时跟来时一样——一窍不通。

(四) 思维侧重点不同，造成表达形式各异，甚至有时可能出现"欧化"汉语，进而影响译文的自然、流畅和忠实

Few nations are willing to give up much of their sovereignty and accede to direction in their economic affairs from the outside unless they see offsetting gains or they have no other choice.

"欧化"的译文：很少有国家愿意放弃他们的主权，忍受外国对其经济事务进行干预，除非能得到相应的好处，或者是由于别无选择。

参考译文：要不是因为有甜头可享，或者被逼无奈，没有国家愿意放弃主权，忍受别国对自己的经济事务指手画脚。

总之，在英译汉的过程中，我们首先要正确理解英语原文，然后以符合汉语思维和表达习惯的方式把原文作者的思想内涵准确无误地表达出来，避免由于思维差异出现不忠实现象以及理解和表达方面的失误。

附　课堂讲练材料

What I Lived for

Three passions, simple but overwhelmingly strong, have governed my life: the longing for love, the search for knowledge, and unbearable pity for the suffering of the mankind. These passions, like great winds, have blown me hither and thither, in a wayward course, over a deep ocean of anguish, reaching to the very verge of despair.

I have sought love, first, because it brings ecstasy—ecstasy so great that I would often have sacrificed all the rest of life for a few hours of this joy. I have sought it, next, because it relieves loneliness—that terrible loneliness in which one shivering consciousness looks over the rim of the world into the cold unfathomable lifeless abyss. I have sought it, finally, because in the union of love I have seen, in a mystic miniature, the prefiguring vision of the heaven that saints and poets have imagined. This is what I sought, and though it might seem too good for human life, this is what—at least—I have found.

With equal passion I have sought knowledge. I have wished to understand the hearts of men. I have wished to know why the stars shine. And I have tried to apprehend the Pythagorean power by which number holds sway above the flux. A little of this, but not much, I have achieved.

Love and knowledge, so far as they were possible, led upward toward the heavens. But always pity brought me back to earth. Echoes of cries of pain reverberate in my heart, Children in famine, victims tortured by oppressors; helpless old people a hated burden to their sons, and the whole world of loneliness, poverty, and pain make a mockery of what human life should be. I long to alleviate the evil, but I cannot, and I too suffer.

This has been my life. I have found it worth living, and would gladly live it again if the chance were offered me.

(Bertrand Russell)

第四章 词语的翻译

第一节 词语的翻译

从事英汉翻译工作,难免会跟数字(numeral)打交道。由于英汉两种语言在表达数字以及倍数增减方面存在一定的差别,翻译时应十分小心,稍有不慎,就可能出现错误。本节介绍几种基本方法,希望对读者有所裨益。

一、表示"不多不少""恰恰正好"的翻译策略

表示"不多不少""恰恰正好",英语一般使用 clear, cool, exactly, flat, just, sharp, whole 等。如:

1. Professor Johnson finished the experiment in twenty-four hours **flat**.
   约翰逊教授完成这一实验**正好**用了 24 小时。
2. The physician treated **cool** 30 patients that day.
   这位内科医生那天**正好**看了 30 个病人。
3. The plane takes off at 8 o'clock **sharp**.
   这架飞机 8 点**整**起飞。
4. The machine worked for ten **whole** days.
   这台机器**整整**运转了 10 天时间。
5. The wire measures **exact** twenty meters.
   这条导线**刚好**920 米长。

二、表示"大约""不确定"的翻译策略

英语一般常使用 about, some, around, round, nearly, towards, somewhere about, estimated, approximately, in/ of/ on the border of, close to 等词修饰数字,表示"不确定""大约""上下""将近""几乎"等。如:

1. The volume of the sun is **about** / **some**/ **around**/ **round** 1,300,000

times that of the earth.

太阳的体积**约**为地球的 130 万倍。

2. It is **nearly/ toward(s)** 4 o'clock.

现在已是**将近**4 点了。

3. The price of this new machine is **in the neighborhood of / on the border of** a thousand dollars.

这台新机器的价格**约**1,000 美元。

4. It has been reported that noise figure is **in the border of** 4 to 5 db at 2 GHz.

据报道,在 2,000 兆赫时,噪音系数**约**为 4 — 5 分贝。

5. According to the weatherman, the temperature will be up 5℃ **or so**.

据天气预报,气温将升高 5℃**左右**。

三、表示"高于""多于"的翻译方法

英语常用 more than, odd, over, above, long, past, or more, upwards of, higher than, exceed, in excess of 等词修饰数字,表示"超过""以上""有余""高于""多于"等。如:

1. Pig iron is an alloy of iron and carbon with the carbon content **more than** two percent.

生铁是铁碳合金,其中碳含量**超过**2%。

2. Only when a rocket attains a speed of 18,000 **odd** miles per hour, can it put a man-made satellite into orbit.

只有当火箭速度达到每小时 18,000 **多**英里时,才能把人造卫星送入轨道。

3. **Over/ Above/ More than/ Not less than** 100 chemical elements are known to man; of these about 80 are metals.

人类已知的化学元素有 100 种**以上**,其中约 80 种是金属。

4. **Upwards of** seven thousand medical workers and twenty thousand PLA men have left for the earthquake district.

有 7,000 **多**名医务人员和 20,000 **多**名解放军前往震区。

5. The patients are children of three years old **and upwards**.

这些病人是三岁及三岁以上的儿童。

四、表示"少于""差一些""不到"等的翻译方法

英语常用 less，less than，below，no more than，under，short of，off，to，within，as few as 等词修饰数字，表示"少于""不到""以下"等。如：

1. It took one month **less than** three years for them to develop the new material.
   他们花了三年差一个月时间研制这种新材料。

2. Helium in the air is **a little under** 1%.
   空气中氦的含量略低于1%。

3. The efficiency of the best of these engines is **under/ below/ less than/ no more than** 40%.
   这些发动机中效率最好的也不到40%。

五、形容数目、数量多时的翻译方法

英语中常用 full，solid，at least，all of，no less than，as...as 等词来修饰数字，强调数目之大、数量之多。如：

1. They covered **full** twenty reference sources on fluidics in a single day.
   仅用了一天时间，他们就看完了足足20种有关射流的资料。

2. The motor ran 450 **solid** days on end.
   马达连续运转了足足450天。

3. The experiment will take three months，**at least**.
   实验至少需要三个月时间。

4. The temperature at the sun's center is **as high as** 10,000,000℃.
   太阳中心的温度高达摄氏1,000万度。

5. There were **no less than** 62,000 dead and injured in the 5·12 earthquake.
   在5·12地震中，死伤者达62,000多人。

六、形容数目小、数量少时的翻译技巧

英语中常用 only，merely，barely，scarcely，but，at most，no more

than, scant 等词修饰数字,强调数目小、数量少。如:

1. There is **at most only** room for one person.
   至多只有可容纳一个人的空间。
2. That solar-energy car weighs **only**/ **merely**/ **barely**/ **scarcely**/ **but**/ 500kg.
   那辆太阳能汽车重量仅有500公斤。
3. Inspection time for the installation was **no more than** 2 hours.
   检验安装工作仅用了两个小时。

七、表示两者或多者范围数量的翻译

英语中常用 from...to, between...and(to)来修饰数字,表示范围,它们通常可译为"从……到……""在……之间"等。例如:

1. The energy of the fuel wasted by the reciprocating steam engine is **between 80 and / to 85** percent.
   往复式蒸汽机浪费的燃料能量为**80%**到**85%**。
2. The ladle refining time takes on average **between 3 and 4** hours depending on the treatment required.
   桶内精炼时间平均为3至4小时,这要视所需要的处理量而定。

八、需要换算数词的翻译

由于英语数字的表达与汉语数字的表达方式不同,汉译时需要换算。数字的换算看起来似乎很简单,但翻译时往往会因为不小心而犯错误,可谓失之毫厘、谬之千里。例如:

  ten thousand(10个千→一万)
  one hundred thousand(100个千→十万)
  ten million(10个百万→一千万)
  one hundred million(100个百万→亿)
  one billion(十亿)(美语)
  ten billion(10个十亿→百亿)
  one hundred billion(100个十亿→千亿)
  one trillion(万亿)

九、英语中表示倍数的翻译

英语中表示倍数的翻译,有两点应引起注意:一是英汉倍数的表达法;二是英汉两种语言的单位表达法。

(一) 用系动词或行为动词和包含有数词 n 的词语相搭配

具体表达方式有如下几种,分别译作"是……的 n 倍""n 倍于"或"比……大(n-1 倍)":

be n times ＋形容词(或副词)＋ as...

1. This substance reacts **three times as fast as** the other.
   该物质的反应速度是那种物质反应速度的 3 倍。(或:该物质的反应速度比那种物质的反应速度快 2 倍。)

be n times ＋比较级＋than

2. This line is **two times longer than** that one.
   这条线的长度是那条线长度的 2 倍。(或:这条线比那条线长 1 倍。)

be＋比较级＋than＋名词＋by n times

3. Mercury weighs more than water **by about 14 times**.
   水银的重量约为水的 14 倍。(或:水银比水重 13 倍。)

be＋比较级＋by a factor of n

4. The error probability of binary AM is **greater than binary FM by a factor of at least 6**.
   二进制调幅的误差概率比二进制调频至少大 5 倍。(或:二进制调幅的误差概率至少是二进制调频的 6 倍。)

(二) 在系动词或行为动词后接"as ＋ 形容词或副词 ＋ again as"或接"again as ＋ 形容词或副词 ＋ as"

这些搭配通常可译作"是……的两倍""比……多一倍"。另外需注意,如果 again 前再加 half,则表示"比……大(长、宽……)半倍"。例如:

1. This wire is **as long again as** that one.
   这根金属线的长度是那根的 2 倍。(或:这根金属线比那根金属线长 1 倍。)

as many /much again(as)(比……)可译作"多一倍":

2. Professor Li has books **as many again as** I do.
   李教授的书比我的书多一倍。

3. This wire is **half again** as long as that one.
   这根金属线的长度是那根金属线的1倍半。(或:这根金属线比那根金属线长半倍。)

4. Brown has **half as many books again as** Peter does.
   布朗的书比彼得的书多1/2。

(三) 用带有"增大"意思的动词(increase, rise, grow, go up 等)和下列包含有数词 n(表示数字、百分数或倍数)的词语相配合

具体表达方式有:"动词＋n times""动词＋by＋n times""动词＋to＋n times""动词＋n-fold""动词＋by a factor of＋n"等,可译作"增加到n倍""增加了(n-1)倍"。例如:

1. The sales of industrial electronic products have **multiplied** six times.
   工业电子产品销售额增加了5倍。

2. The strength of the attraction **increases** by four times if the distance between the original charges is behalved.
   如果原电荷的距离缩短一半,则引力就增大到原来的4倍。(或:如果原电荷的距离缩短一半,则引力比原来大3倍。)

3. By 2014 the production of primary copper has **increased** fivefold.
   到2014年,原铜产量增长了4倍。

4. The drain voltage has been **increased** by a factor of 4.
   漏电压增加了3倍。

(四) 用带有"增大"意思的动词(increase, rise, grow, go up 等)连接"(by)n＋单位(或 n％)",表示净增量,数词 n 可照译。

例如:

1. The output **went up 45,000 tons**.
   产量增加了45,000吨。

2. The production has **increased by 45％**.
   生产已增加了45％。

3. Automation will help us to **raise** the output of production by thirty percent.

   自动化能帮助我们提高产量30％。

4. Industrial output **rose by** 0.9 percent in June.

   6月份产量增长了0.9％。

(五) 用表示倍数的动词表示量的增加

其中，double 表示"是……的2倍""增加1倍"或"翻一番"；treble 表示"是……的3倍""增加两倍"或"增加到3倍"；quadruple 表示"是……的4倍""增加3倍"或"翻两番"；quintuple 表示"是……的5倍""增加至5倍"或"增加了4倍"；sextuple 表示"使成为6倍"；septuple "使成为7倍"；octuple 表示"使成为8倍"。例如：

1. The new airport will **double** the capacity of the existing one.

   新机场是现有机场容量的2倍。

2. The population has nearly **trebled** in forty years.

   人口在40年中增加了近2倍。

3. The company **quadrupled** output to around 20 million tons.

   该公司把产量增至2,000万吨左右，是原来的4倍。

4. The output has been **quintupled** since 2013.

   2013年以来，产量已增长了4倍。

(六) 英语中用"an increase of n"或"a n increase of"表示净增的数量，n 可照译

例如：

1. There is **an increase of** 4.5 million tons of steel as compared with last year.

   钢产量比去年增加了450万吨。

2. There is a 25％ **increase of** steel as compared with last year.

   钢产量比去年增加了25％。

十、英语中表示减少(倍)数的翻译

(一) 用表示"减少"的动词(decrease, reduce, fall, lower 等)连接" by n 或 n ％"，表示净减量；用系动词连接"n less(than)"表示净减量，所减数字均

可照译

例如：

1. 180 **decreased** by 90 is 90.
   180 减去 90 等于 90。
2. The cost **decreased** by 40%.
   成本下降了 40%。
3. This new process used 35% **less** fuel.
   这种新工艺少用了 35% 的燃料。

（二） 用表示"减少"的动词（decrease, reduce, fall, lower 等）连接"by n times""n times""n times as ＋形容词或副词＋ as""by a factor of n"等均可译作"减少了 n 分之(n－1)"或"减少到 n 分之 1"

因为英汉语言在使用分数方面的差异（如汉语的分母中极少使用小数点），如果英语减少的倍数中有小数点时，则应换算成分数。例如：

1. The enterprise management expenditure this year has **decreased by three times** as against that of 2014.
   该企业今年的管理开支比 2014 年降低了 2/3。
2. The pre-heating time for the new type thermal meter is **shortened 5 times**.
   这种新型热电式仪表的预热时间缩短了 4/5。
3. The error probability of the equipment was reduced by **2.5 times** through technical innovation.
   通过技术革新该设备误差概率降低 3/5。

根据表达习惯英语中的 2.5 times，汉语一般不说"二点五分之一"，这时应换算成整数分母，即"降低到五分之二"或"降低了五分之三"。

附一　课堂讲练材料

1. The output was reduced to 25%.
2. By the year 2018 the world's annual oil output is expected to fall to 50%.
3. The error probability of this equipment was reduced by 2.5 times.

4. This year, the production of this kind of machine in our plant is estimated to increase to 3 times compared with 1980.

5. Johnson finished the 200-meter dash in 22 seconds flat.

6. Doctor Smith treated cool 30 patients that day.

7. The explosion is complete in a few thousandths of a second.

8. Hundreds of tall buildings have sprung up in the metropolitan city of Nanjing this year.

9. Tens of millions of yuan have gone into the building of this auditorium with modern electronic facilities.

10. The renovated model of lathe turns twenty percent faster than the previous one.

11. There is an about 100% increase of steel in this steel works in 2013 as compared with 2012.

12. The principal advantage over the old model of refrigerator is a four-fold reduction of both noise and weight.

13. As the high voltage was abruptly trebled all the valves in the precision instrument burnt at once.

14. In the older type of coaxial system amplifiers are requiring every eight miles. In the newer type coaxial system, the signals transmitted are much higher in frequency and amplifiers are required every four miles.

15. The Royalty rates indicated in Attachment of Contract shall be applicable for five years following the date of receipt of the technology, after which, they will be reduced by one percent per annum.

16. In addition to the payments under the preceding paragraph, the employer will make commission payments to the employee based on 2.50% of gross sales. This commission will be paid monthly on the last day of the following month.

附二　课外扩展训练材料

Impressions of Zhu Rongji

When our family was invited to spend the first day of Chinese New Year with Xiamen officials and business leaders, my sons were excited until they heard there would be speeches. "No way!" they protested. So Susan stayed home with the boys. She regretted it later, for the guest speaker was no other than Zhu Rongji!

Like many Americans, I have little patience for politicians and speeches, but Mr. Zhu came across not as a politician but as a grandfatherly figure, or even a friend, simply sharing his concerns and hopes for China. And he had the audience laughing almost from beginning to end.

Mr. Zhu tackled serious subjects, like the reform of State-owned enterprises and the burgeoning bureaucracy, China's commitment to her Asian neighbors and determination not to devalue her currency, the need to clean up the environment or root out corruption. All the while, people sat on the edge of their seats, alternately nodding in approval or holding their sides with laughter, while this spry statesman and grandfather kept a dignified poise and poker face that reminded me a lot of America's beloved talk show host Johnny Carson.

He also shared his likes and dislikes. Everyone chuckled when he rolled his eyes and said he hated TV commercials for VCDs— too many of them. And then he confided to us that his favorite programs were talk shows, and that he wished more people would share their frank opinions. That wasn't too surprising, for Mr. Zhu certainly does not beat around the bush about anything.

I suspect that ever since Zhu Rongji's birth into a poor family in Hunan, he has been a man of vision. He has always concerned himself with working towards the future rather than worshiping the past or entrenching himself in the present. He doesn't fear confrontation and doesn't mince words. His directness has annoyed some who seek to preserve the comfortable status quo, but has earned him the admiration of those who want not politicians and promises but leadership and results.

And that was the final impression Mr. Zhu gave me—that he was not a politician but a leader with vision. Politicians must cajole and manipulate and change their platform to fit the occasion or audience, but leaders with visions never lack a following.

China is fortunate to have had many great leaders, each seemingly custom-made for the occasion! It took Chairman Mao to end a century of foreign oppression and unite the Chinese behind the revolution. It took Deng Xiaoping, the architect of the socialist market economy, to lead the nation in her transition to maturity. And today, after Premier Li Peng's decade of stability and solid growth, China now enters what may be the most rewarding and most difficult phase, for as the old Chinese saying goes, "To start an enterprise is difficult, to maintain it after completion is not easy."

We Xiamen people (us adopted foreigners included) were proud to have Zhu Rongji start off our new year with his visit, and we are thankful to know that with Zhu Rongji at the helm, China's greatest days are yet ahead.

(William N. Brown)

第二节 英语习语的翻译

习语(idiom)是语言发展中长期积淀的精华,是人类长期使用的、形式简洁而含义精辟的定型词组或短句。英语词汇量极为丰富,习语纷繁多姿,渗透着浓郁的西方文化气息。

此处把 idiom 统称为习语只是为了讲述的方便,实际上习语涵盖面较宽,至少包括了如下意思:(1) set phrases;(2) proverbs;(3) sayings;(4) epigrams;(5) slang expressions;(6) colloquialisms;(7) quotations 等。

翻译英语习语方法较多,而且译者也可能喜欢选用自己偏爱的方法。本文主要提出如下几种常用方法,供读者参考。

一、习语对等翻译法

部分英语习语和汉语习语有相近或相似之处，若能照直翻译，汉语读者可较好理解其寓意。采取这样的翻译方法，不仅能够使读者见到其原有意义，还可以欣赏原语所表达的形象与文字风格。例如：

1. They insist on **an eye for an eye, a tooth for a tooth**.
   他们坚持要**以眼还眼，以牙还牙**。

英语成语 an eye for an eye, a tooth for a tooth 与汉语的成语"以眼还眼，以牙还牙"正好等值，形式与意思都很接近。

2. He **shut his eyes to** our joint petition.
   他对我们的联合请愿**充耳不闻**。

shut one's eyes to something 说的是对某事装作看不见，可借用汉语中成语"充耳不闻"译之。

3. Everybody knows that John **lost his shirt** when that business he had invested in failed.
   大家都知道，约翰的财产在他投资的企业倒闭后**损失得精光**。

lose one's shirt 主要喻指损失惨重，此处采用比较形象的比喻，"连衣服都输掉了"，用"精光"这一形象译法，与原文形象相去不远。

4. We're not talking about **the castle in the air**—the donkey's carrot. No, I mean something we've all shared.
   我们并不是在谈论什么**空中楼阁**——那些挂在驴鼻子前面的胡萝卜一样的东西。我指的是一些大家都有份的事情。

build the castle in the air 是说在"沙堆上建楼房"，喻指根基不牢，此处译者将英语习语直接转换成汉语同类成语，容易为读者所接受。

5. He **set his teeth** and felt discontented when he watched the rich drive the poor into a tight corner.
   他一看到富人将穷人逼入绝境，就气得**咬牙切齿**表示要打抱不平。

set one's teeth 指对某事愤愤不平，在汉语成语"咬牙切齿"之前加两字

"气得",把原文话题范围和形象如实反映出来。

  6. Those who like to **make a scene** will never get advantage.
   那些喜欢**无理取闹**的人永远讨不到便宜。

make a scene 是指喜欢闹事,此句译文用"无理取闹"四字译之,可以说算是点出了核心内容。

  7. To **requite like for like** is a common practice.
   一报还一报是人们通常的做法。

requite/ return like for like 含义为"一报还一报",英语的习语用汉语的谚语译之。

  8. Since you are **raising a Cain**, how can we hope to get peaceful days?
   你在那儿**兴风作浪**,我们怎么可能期望会有安宁日子过?

raise a Cain/ hell/ the devil 有"作怪或兴风作浪"的含义,可用汉语的习语进行对等翻译。

二、形象意义兼顾法

  由于使用汉语和英语的两个民族文化差异较大,各自的某些习语含义或比喻意义虽然基本相同,但表达方法差异很大。对这样的习语要采取形象意义兼顾法,即:可以直译的部分尽量保持原文形象,不能直译的可用解释或其他方法进行适当弥补。如:

  1. You need much more prudence when you are going to **take up a quarrel**.
   若人家争吵时你去**袒护**其中一方,那可要多加小心哟。

人家争吵,你去 take up a quarrel(拉一方打一方),即偏袒某一方,肯定不是明智之举。

  2. They **put their heads together** and decided on a gift.
   他们经过**碰头商量**,最后决定选购一件礼物。

put their heads together 是指大家把"头"放在一起想主意,此处用"碰头商量"译之应该算是成功的。

3. He **put on high airs** with his learning.
   他**装腔作势**,以饱学之士自矜。

汉语中有个成语"趾高气扬",形容某种"得意忘形"的人,put on high airs(装腔作势)与此有异曲同工之妙。

4. George was enjoying himself to **the top of his bend**.
   乔治快乐到了**极点**。

the top of his bend 指狂欢到了顶点,top 即指高点,此处译为"快乐到了极点"。

5. It was **in the cards** for the son to succeed his father as head of the business.
   子承父业,他后来**顺理成章**地接替父亲成了该企业的老板。

to be in the cards 喻指很可能会发生,或者意料之中的事,此处根据句子的深层含义,译为"顺理成章"应该算是适度的。

6. His life savings **went down the drain** in a bad investment.
   因为一项错误的投资,他的一生积蓄全部**化为乌有**。

go down the drain 直译为"顺下水道流走了",喻指损失殆尽,用"化为乌有"成语代之,较为成功。

7. He's now **keeping body and soul together** and he must die sometime or other.
   他现在只是**苟延残喘**,一定不久于人世了。

三、意译改造法

英汉语有些习语意义大致相等,二者的差别主要在于形象和风格,翻译时,只要略加化解改造,就可以再现原文意义,同时又不违背原文习语的结构与习惯。例如:

1. I am here **like a fish out of water**.
   因为环境生疏,我在这里感到**不自在**。

出水的鱼躺在干地上肯定很不舒服,当然也肯定不会感到自在了。

2. For months after her husband's death, Joan simply **ate her**

heart out.

琼自从丈夫死后,好几个月都**悲痛欲绝**。

eat one's heart out 主要指极度悲伤,译为"悲痛欲绝"基本传达了含义。

3. She has a bad habit of **buying a pig in the poke.**
   她有**见物就买**的坏习惯。

成语 buy a pig in the poke 是说有些人到商店以后,见啥都觉得好,有见啥都想买的购物癖。

4. Worship carries her **off her feet.**
   宗教使她**痴迷癫狂**。

carry one off one's feet 喻指狂热得飘飘欲仙,失去了理智。

5. He **got the sack**, because he could not deal with a great rush of business.
   他**被解雇**了,因为他不能处理突发事件。

习惯用法 get the sack 是指被上司或老板解雇。

6. He **keeps his memory green** in doing things.
   他头脑清楚,做事绝不糊涂。

keep one's memory green 是指某人头脑很清楚,做事不糊涂。

7. According to the new theory of medicine, **to live on air** is the most effective method of treatment.
   按照医学新理论,**绝食**是最有效的治疗方法。

live on air 直译过来是说"依靠空气生活",汉语中有句"不吃饭,喝西北风"的俗话,意思与本句原文较接近。

8. He's not honest to you;he's **turning you round his finger.**
   他不是在真诚待你,只是**玩弄你于股掌之间**。

turn/ twist a person around one's finger 若直译是"把某人玩弄于手指间",似可勉强译为"玩弄某人于股掌之间"。不过请注意:本句英语主要含义是"笼络"某人,但没有诚意;而"玩弄某人于股掌之间"则可能带有一定政治色彩。

9. One who mastered the secrets generally **makes no figure**.

真正的高手一般**深藏不露**。

make no figure 主要指不愿出风头,不露锋芒,不露头角。

四、优势互补翻译法

这种方法主要是前面几种方法无法起到有效作用后采取的一种发挥汉语优势的方法,译者应尽其之所能,把原文含义确切生动地表达出来,可用汉语中的对偶、对仗甚至对联等形式,只要效果堪与原文媲美就算成功的译文。例如:

1. Don't waste your time. We have already decided to **nail the colors to the mast**.

不要浪费时间了。我们已经决定**坚持到底,决不投降**。

nail the colors to the mast 含有"立场坚定""决不投降""誓死不屈"的意思,用上面四字结构译之,铿锵有力,朗朗上口。

2. She **bowed me to the earth**.

她使我**羞愧难当,无地自容**。

bow a person to the earth 直译为"头碰地赔礼",有"使人羞愧得无地自容"的含义,译文用四字结构,显得很有力量。

3. He carried on a business, but **brought his pigs to the wrong market**.

他接手一笔生意,可是几乎**血本无归**。

bring one's pigs to the wrong market 的含义是"老本都蚀掉了",译文四字结构"血本无归"恰到好处。

4. A man of a stiff neck hardly **makes a market**.

冥顽不化的人很难**赢得人心**。

make a market 有"博取人心"的意思,译文使用了四字结构,显得干脆利索。

5. He did it **as well be hanged for a sheep as a lamb**, and finally committed a crime.

他一不做二不休,终于误蹈法网。

英语习语 as well be hanged for a sheep as a lamb 喻指"一不做二不休"。

6. Wherever he works, he always **wins his chief's ears.**
   他无论到哪工作,总能得到上司的**宠顾**。

英语习语 have/ win one's ears 表示"受某人宠顾""得到某人关爱"或"引起某人注意"等。

7. Don't poke your nose into other people's business; then you can well **keep your nose clean.**
   如果你能少管闲事,就完全可以**明哲保身**。

keep one's nose clean 与汉语习语"明哲保身"意思相近,有异曲同工之妙。

8. You don't have to explain it anymore. I see you just **fit the cap on me.**
   你无须再解释什么,我知道你在**指桑骂槐**。

英语习语 fit the cap on 意思与汉语成语"指桑骂槐"相差无几,故而用之。

9. Don't **meet trouble halfway**, otherwise, you keep on worrying about things like this, you will get a nervous breakdown.
   不要杞人忧天,否则你总是担心这担心那的,会精神崩溃的。

meet trouble halfway 说的就是无事瞎担心,有点儿庸人自扰的味道。

附一 课堂讲练材料

1. live in a small way(俭朴过日子):Though he is very rich, he lives in a small way.
2. miss by a mile(差之甚远):John tried to guess on the test, but his answers missed by a mile.
3. pull up one's socks(提心吊胆):Don't pull up your socks for him; let him do as he pleases with it.

4. coin money(快速致富):Ever since he went into that business he has been coining money.
5. take a leaf out of one's book(模仿某人):Boys very much like to take a leaf out of others' book.
6. on the carpet(在考虑中):Your proposal is just on the carpet.
7. hum and haw(支吾其词):Common people are used to hum and haw when they do evil.
8. take one's words with a grain of salt(怀疑某人所讲的话):I take his words with a grain of salt because he has ever told me a lie.
9. pour water on the hands of somebody(侍奉某人):He always blows his top, but she still pours water on his hands.
10. be meat and drink to do something(做某事是非常快乐的事):It is meat and drink to chat with a sweetheart till midnight.
11. fly off the handle(发怒;激动):He is an odd fish;when we are joking, he flies off the handle.
12. heap coals of fire on one's head(以德报怨使其惭愧):John stole the bishop's silver, but the bishop heaped coals of fire on his head by giving the silver to him.
13. talk like a Dutch uncle(谆谆教诲):A teacher talks to his pupils like a Dutch uncle.
14. hold water(正确;合理):This is a theory that can hold water.
15. break a fly upon the wheel(小题大做):It's not necessary to break a fly upon the wheel.
16. sow dragon's teeth(种下祸根):By insisting on a fiercer religious persecution than ever, the government sowed dragon's teeth, destined to spring up plots and violence.
17. turn the tables(改变局势):He has a power to turn the tables, but he always takes a back seat.
18. get the key of the street(无家可归):The beggar gets the key of the street.
19. cook one's goose(毁人名誉):His aim of circulating a false rumor is to cook your goose.
20. throw a wet blanket(扫人兴致):It's not polite to throw a wet blanket.

21. leave no stone unturned(千方百计):He left no stone unturned to get an official job, but it's of no use.
22. bring down the house(博得全场喝彩;使欢声雷动):As soon as he has finished his speech, he brings down the house.
23. know/learn the ropes(熟知内幕):In doing anything, one who knows the ropes gets much chance of success.
24. wise up to(恍然大悟):He never wised up to the fact that the joke was on him.
25. pass by on the other side(不予同情):He has been over head and ears in debt, but you have passed by on the other side.
26. marry with the left hand(尊卑通婚):Though you love your maid very much, your parents must object to your marrying with the left hand.
27. give a stone for bread(假装给予援助):He's a hypocrite, and he gives you a stone for bread.
28. run circles/rings around(轻易地就比某人做得更好):Frank ran circles around the other boys on the basketball team.
29. run in a groove(墨守成规):A man cannot live a broad life if he runs only in one groove.
30. lie in/on the bed one has made(自食其果):I can use no stronger condemnation but that she must lie in the bed she has made.
31. punch line(故事、笑话等的精彩之处):This poem has its punch line at the very finish.
32. face the music(接受事实):Come on now, buck up, face the music!
33. make an omelet without breaking eggs(不劳而获):He most dislikes a man who makes an omelet without breaking eggs.
34. in the melting mood(因感动而流泪):Having read the story, he was in the melting mood.
35. go on the air(广播):The president went on the air, making a speech to his people.
36. have other fish to fry(另有他事待做):He said he could not go to the opera this evening, for he had other fish to fry.
37. give the air(一刀两断):If you do so, I will give you the air.
38. fall/land on one's feet(幸运;运道好):Some people always seem to fall

on their feet.

39. work like the devil(拼命工作):He works like the devil in order to keep his family.

40. talk through one's own hat(信口雌黄):If you talk through your own hat, you will be regretful of it.

41. lay it on thick(夸张):There are people who say that all you have to do in advertising is to lay it on thick.

42. jump through a hoop(遵照他人的话做):Bob would jump through a hoop for Mary.

43. go on a tear(纵情):Every once in a while he goes off on a tear and drinks for three days without stopping.

44. like water off a duck's back(毫无影响或效果):Your golden words for him are nothing but like water off a duck's back.

45. goo-goo eyes(含情脉脉地注视):They sat there making goo-goo eyes at each other.

46. have a crow to pluck with sb.(与之理论;吹毛求疵):I have a crow to pluck with the butler. I want to know why he sent the messenger off with an uncivil word yesterday.

47. wear the trousers/or pants(为一家之主):Mr. Wilson is henpecked by his wife; she wears the trousers in that family.

48. skeleton in the cupboard /closet / house(家丑):The skeleton in our family closet was Uncle Willie. No one mentioned him because he drank too much.

49. a cup too low(意气消沉):You're a cup too low. A glass of claret will make you feel more cheerful.

50. let the cat out of the bag(泄露秘密):She let the cat out of the bag and the surprise was gone.

51. put on the dog(摆威风):He works in the bank, but from the way his wife puts on the dog, you would think he owned the bank.

附二　课外扩展训练材料

Body Language

All of us communicate with one another nonverbally, as well as with words. Most of the time we're not aware that we're doing it. We gesture with eyebrows or a hand, meet someone else' eyes and look away, shift positions in a chair. These actions we assume are random and incidental. But researchers have discovered in recent years that there is a system to them almost as consistent and comprehensible as language.

Every culture has its own body language, and children absorb its nuances along with spoken language. A Frenchman talks and moves in French. The way an Englishman crosses his legs is nothing like the way a male American does it. In talking, Americans are apt to end a statement with a droop of the head or hand, a lowering of the eyelids. They wind up a question with lift of the hand, a tilt of the chin or a widening of the eyes. With a future-tense verb they often gesture with a forward movement.

(English Language Learning)

第三节　英语俚语的翻译

英语俚语(slang)数量很大,其中大多数都与西方英语或非英语国家的地域文化有着密切的关系。翻译英语俚语时,一般都要借助有关词典,才能较准确理解俚语的基本意思,并根据词语的上下文准确判断出某具体词条的确切含义。具体翻译方法,除了可参考成语的翻译方法外,还可从以下几个方面进行翻译。

一、以俚译俚

俚语与其他文雅文字不同,本来就是泼辣的"乡姑",你怎么能让她装成"林妹妹"呢?这里主要应考虑原文风格的需要,既要有"阳春白雪",又要有"下里巴人"。俚语本来就是土的东西翻译时就应还它一个"土"。请看译例:

1. Peter can't understand anything. He's such **an airbrain**.
   彼特什么都不懂,真是个**呆瓜**。

airbrain 或 airhead 俚指呆子,故用之。

2. This restaurant went **belly up** after being open for only three months.
   这家餐厅才开张 3 个月就**关门倒闭**了。

belly up 俚指"垮台了""完蛋了"(源于"死鱼肚子朝上漂在水里")。

3. Mary thinks she owns the world. She's a real **bitch**.
   玛丽认为整个世界都是她的,真是**臭美**得不得了。

bitch 俚指喜欢臭美的女人。不过,千万不要同骂人的 bitch 混为一谈。

4. Hey, **dude**! What's up?
   嘿,**老兄**!什么事啊?

dude 俚指家伙或穿戴讲究的公子哥儿,此处译为老兄,也可译为老伙计。

5. You're a **hit**! The audience loved your performance.
   你真是个**大热门**!观众喜欢你的表演。

hit 俚指"热门",这个词近年来用得很"热"。

6. That is a really **far out** hairdo. Where did you get it done?
   很棒的发型。你在哪里做的?

7. This theory is too **far out** for me.
   这个理论对我来说简直太**玄妙**了。

far out 这个用法在不同场合可有不同含义,即一指"很棒",二指"怪怪的",故有上述两个句子。

8. Jane likes to live a life in the **fast lane**. Wherever there's a party, she is sure to be there.
   简喜欢过**刺激兴奋的生活**。哪儿有聚会,她就会去哪儿。

life in the fast lane 俚指刺激、兴奋的生活(直译为快车道,开快车对于某些人肯定无比刺激)。

9. Jenny told Greg to go **fly a kite** after he told her he had to break their date.

格雷格告诉珍妮必须取消他们的约会后，珍妮让他**滚蛋**。

go fly a kite 直译为放风筝，风筝断了线就要永远再见，转义为"滚蛋"。

10. John **grossed little Sue out** when he waved a snake in front of her face.

约翰在小苏面前摇晃着一条蛇，使她恶心得直想吐。

gross someone out 英俚，指让人觉得恶心、无法忍受。

11. I'm going to **hit the hay**. it's been a long day and I'm exhausted.

我要去**睡觉**了，从早忙到晚我都要累趴了。

hit the hay / sack 英俚，指瞌睡、睡觉。

12. He thinks he's **hot stuff**, but everybody else thinks he's a jerk.

他自以为**了不得**，但其他人认为他是个傻瓜。

hot stuff 英俚，指大人物。

13. I have to **go to the john**. Wait for me in the car.

我要上**一号**（或直接说厕所）。在车里等我。

john 英俚，指厕所。

14. Grace is always correcting other people. She thinks she's just a **know-it-all**.

格雷斯总是在纠正别人，她觉得自己简直是个**万事通**。

know-it-all 英俚，指啥都行的万事通。

15. That handsome young man is a real **lady-killer**.

那个年轻英俊的小伙真是个**小帅哥**。

lady-killer 英俚，指帅哥、英俊小伙，也可直译成"师奶杀手"。

16. All Jeff's hard work is paying off. He's a **leg up** on the rest of his competitors.

杰夫的努力是有回报的。他在与竞争对手的较量中**占了上风**。

leg，a leg up 英俚，指占上风。

17. This flat is a **real lemon**. I've bought it for only a year and already had it repaired four times.
    这套公寓房真**差劲**。我才买了一年就找人修了四次。

lemon 英俚，指烂货、质量差的东西。

18. Next time I see Rick，I'm going to **let him have it**.
    下次我看到里克**要叫他好看**。

let someone have it 英俚，指要让某人好看，要摆平某人。

19. Thanks for the good news. You've **made my day**.
    谢谢你的好消息，你让我**觉得很"爽"**。

make my day 英俚，指让我觉得很"爽"。

20. Kathy is such a **motor-mouth**. I can never get a word in.
    凯西真是个**话匣子**，她说话时我一句也插不进去。

motor-mouth (= chatterbox)俚语，意指话匣子。

21. Don't **mouth off** at me, young man! Where are your manners?
    年轻人，别**顶嘴**！你懂不懂礼貌？

mouth off 英俚，指顶嘴。

22. She dare not do anything to me, because I **have her number**.
    她不敢对我怎么样，因为我**对她的底细了解得一清二楚**。

have someone's number 英俚，指清楚某人的底细；看穿某人的把戏。

23. Tom thinks Mary is a **hot number**.
    汤姆认为玛丽真是个**尤物**。

number/ hot number 英俚，指新鲜、迷人的人或事物。

24. He seems **out in left field**. Nobody ever understands what he is talking about.

他似在**发神经**,没有人知道他在说些什么。

out in left field 英俚,指疯了。

  25. This food is **out of this world**. I'll have to get your recipe.
    这食物**好吃极了**!把配方告诉我。

out of this world 英俚,指太棒了,好极了。

  26. That team was not very good. We **beat the pants off** them. The final score was 21:3.
    那个球队真差,我们最终以 21:3 的比分把他们**打得落花流水**。

beat the pants off 英俚,指打得落花流水。

二、以俗语译俚语

  我们在上面讲述了以俚译俚并列举了大量例子。实际上除了用俚语译俚语之外,还可以使用较通俗的表达形式来翻译英语的俚语,通俗表达形式包括习惯表达法、人们喜闻乐见的日常用语、俗语等。如:

  1. This furniture cost me **an arm and a leg**, but it was worth it.
    这家具花了我**一大笔钱**,不过值得。

an arm and a leg 英俚,指昂贵的价格。

  2. Ever since Howard borrowed 5,000 dollars from Mike and never paid him back, there has been **bad blood** between them.
    自从霍华德向迈克借了 5,000 美元不还后,他们之间就有了**隔阂**。

bad blood 英俚,指不和、敌意。

  3. Follow the school rules and you won't get **chewed out**.
    遵守校规你就不会**被刮胡子**了。

chew someone out 英俚,指责骂某人、谴责某人。

  4. It will be a **cold day in hell** before I agree to marry that jerk Harold.

要我同意嫁给哈罗德那个笨蛋除非**太阳从西边出来**。

cold/ a cold day in hell　英俚,指不可能的事。

5. They **hit it off** instantly and have been good friends ever since.
   他们一见面就很**投缘**,从此成了好朋友。

hit it off　英俚,指投缘、一见如故。

6. That blonde didn't work hard, but she always tried to cheat on her test by sneaking in **crib cards**.
   那个金发女孩学习不努力,考试时总是想**夹带小条作弊**。

crib card / sheet　英俚,指用小条作弊。

7. The garment exhibition is **dead ahead** about 2 miles from here.
   服装展设在**正前方**两英里处。

dead ahead　英俚,指正前方。

8. Dick is a real **freeloader**. He's been staying with Steve and eating all his food.
   迪克真是一个**爱占便宜的**人,他一直住在史蒂夫家里白吃白喝。

freeloader　英俚,指利用别人的慷慨、占便宜的人。

9. **Gag me with a spoon**! Please don't tell me such disgusting stories anymore.
   我快吐了!请别再讲这么恶心的故事了。

gag sb. with a spoon　英俚,指快吐了。

10. It's not good to concentrate all your efforts on just writing. You should **get your feet wet** and try painting or dancing.
    一天到晚写作对你不好,你应该**涉猎**一下绘画或舞蹈。

get one's feet wet　英俚,指参与、开始做某事。

11. Don't **get in his hair**. He doesn't like to be bothered when he's working.
    别去烦他。他不喜欢工作时被人打扰。

get in someone's hair 英俚，指烦某人，惹某人。

  12. Joan had never skied before, but she decided to **give it a shot**.
    琼从没滑过雪，但她决定**试试看**。

give it a shot / whirl 英俚，指试试看。

  13. When Laura asked if she could borrow his bicycle, Bob said, "**Be my guest.**"
    劳拉问鲍勃能否借用一下他的自行车，鲍勃说："**随时都可以**。"

guest/ be my guest 英俚，指请便。

  14. We intend to **have a ball** at the amusement park today.
    我们打算今天到游乐场**玩个痛快**。

have a ball 英俚，指寻开心、痛快地玩。

  15. The contract will be ready to sign as soon as we **iron out a few of the kinks**.
    我们把一些小问题**解决**之后就可以签合同了。

iron out the kinks 英俚，指解决小问题。

  16. Nobody makes me as mad as David does. He really knows how to **push my buttons**.
    没有人像大卫那样惹我生气。他真知道怎么**惹我发火**。

push someone's button 英俚，指惹火某人、激怒某人。

  17. **I put my ass on the line for you**. I know you'll do the same for me someday.
    我现在**为你两肋插刀**。我知道将来有朝一日你也会为我这么做。

put one's ass on the line 英俚，指两肋插刀。

  18. I can't make it to dinner with you tonight because I already made other plans. Can I have a **rain check** though?
    我今晚有事不能和你一块去吃饭。**改天**再吃好不好？

rain check 英俚，指改天再做。

19. Today is Jane's birthday. Don't **rain on her parade.**
    今天是珍妮的生日,别**扫她的兴**。

rain on someone's parade 英俚,指扫某人的兴。

20. After her mother's death, she started **hitting the sauce again.**
    妈妈死后,她又开始**喝得昏天黑地**了。

(the) sauce 英俚,指酒。

21. **Shake a leg!** We're already ten minutes late.
    快点儿! 我们已迟到10分钟啦。

shake a leg 英俚,指赶快。

22. Her **sob story** really moved me. it's so sad.
    她**悲伤的故事**真的打动了我。真令人难过!

sob story 英俚,指悲伤的事情。

23. Genny is such **a stick in the mud.** She never wants to try anything new.
    杰妮**很保守**,从不想尝试新鲜事物。

stick in the mud 英俚,指保守的人。

24. Don't buy things from that store. It **sucks.**
    别去那个店里买东西,那个店很**差劲**。

suck 英俚,指差劲。

25. I'm so tired. I think I'll just **turn in** and see you in the morning.
    我真累。我想我要去**睡觉**了,明天见。

turn in 英俚,指上床睡觉。

26. To figure out what the problem is, we're going to have to **zero in on** this area.
    为了查出问题的症结所在,我们必须将**注意力集中**在这一领域。

zero in on 英俚,指集中注意力。

27. Why is it that every time I have a hot date, I **break out with a big zit** on my face?

为什么每次我有重要约会,脸上都会冒出一个很大的青春痘呢?

zit 英俚,指青春痘。

三、用习语译俚语

英语俚语有时也可以根据需要适当运用汉语的常用习语译之,不求雅只求通俗易懂,易记,易用。这种方法在其他方法不十分奏效的情况下偶尔用之,会使句子增色不少。请看译例:

1. Joanna always shows up at work **bright-eyed and bushy-tailed**.
乔安娜上班工作时总是神采奕奕。

bright-eyed and bushy-tailed 英俚,指精神焕发、神采奕奕。

2. **Don't have a cow**! I'll pay for the damages.
别大惊小怪! 我会赔偿损失的。

don't have a cow 英俚,指别大惊小怪。

3. The amount of money Mr. Howell spent on a new Rolls-Royce was just **a drop in the bucket** compared to his annual salary.
豪厄尔先生买一辆新劳斯莱斯的钱和他的年薪相比只不过是九牛一毛。

a drop in the bucket 英俚,指九牛一毛、沧海一粟。

4. After Betty dumped Chuck, Chuck went to the bar to drown his **sorrows over a beer**.
查克被贝蒂甩了后,就到酒吧喝酒消愁。

drown one's sorrows 英俚,指借酒消愁。

5. Johnson didn't put in his full effort and he still won **hands down**.
约翰逊虽未尽全力,却依旧轻松取得了胜利。

hands down 英俚,指易如反掌、轻松。

6. Mike is **in the doghouse** for missing his curfew.
迈克因违反宵禁而被**打入冷宫**。

in the doghouse　英俚,指被打入冷宫。

7. I've never seen Teresa **pop her cork before**. I always thought she was a very laid-back person.
我从没见过特里莎**大发脾气**。我原以为她是个好好小姐哩。

pop one's cork　英俚,指大发脾气。

8. This is a **red-letter day** for Susan; she made her first sale to a very important client.
今天是苏珊的**大好日子**,她和一个非常重要的客户做成了第一笔生意。

red-letter day　英俚,指大好日子。

9. You don't have to **rub it in**. I already feel bad enough as it is.
你不要再**火上加油**了,我已经够难过的了。

rub it in 英俚,指火上加油。

10. What did he say to her? She's **all shook up**.
他刚才跟她说了些什么,让她这么**惊慌失措**的?

(all) shook up 英俚,指惊慌失措。

11. Don't **spill the beans**. It's supposed to be a secret.
千万别**告诉他人**,这可是个秘密哦!

spill the beans　英俚,指泄露秘密。

12. Don't be such a **worry wart**; you have to learn how to relax.
别**杞人忧天**了,你要学会放松自己。

worry wart　英俚,指杞人忧天的人。

四、用四字格形式译俚语

为了更好地发挥汉语的优势,使英俚的翻译方式丰富多彩一些,有时不妨适当运用汉语的四字格,增加一定的色彩。当然,运用四字格翻译俚语绝不应以损失英俚的原有文字风格和意义为代价,而且四字格的运用也要适可而止。

1. You just **bite the bullet** and get it over with.
   咬紧牙关完成这件事吧!

bite the bullet 英俚,指咬紧牙关、忍受痛苦。

2. The detective was careful not to let the drug dealer know he worked for the police. He didn't want to **blow his cover**. The drug dealer thought the detective was a junkie.
   侦探很谨慎地不让毒贩知道他替警方工作,尽力避免**泄漏身份**。毒贩还以为侦探真是个瘾君子哩。

blow one's cover 英俚,指泄露底细。

3. The other boys said that Henry was **rocking the boat** by wanting to let girls join their club.
   其他男孩子说亨利要让女生加入他们男生俱乐部是**自找麻烦**。

rock the boat 英俚,指坏大事、自找麻烦。

4. America is experiencing a **new breed of ambitious and educated**, young businessmen.
   美国出现了一批**雄心勃勃、受过教育的新生代**青年企业家。

breed/ a new breed of 英俚,指新生代。

5. The best way to stop smoking is to quit **cold turkey**.
   戒烟最好的方法就是说戒就戒,**绝不含糊**。

cold turkey 英俚,指立即(戒除坏习惯)、二话不说。

6. He gave me **diddly squat** for all my hard work. See if I ever help him again.
   我这么卖命,而他给我的**报酬微不足道**,看我以后会不会再帮他。

diddly squat 英俚,指微不足道的报酬。

7. He certainly has a **green thumb**. All his plants flourish.
   他真有**园艺天赋**。花草树木经他侍弄都生机勃勃。

green thumb 英俚,指园艺天赋。

8. He takes a **hands-off** approach when it comes to raising his children. He leaves all the decisions up to his wife.
他用**顺其自然**的方式教养孩子,一切事情都交给太太决定。

hands-off   英俚,指顺其自然。

9. She **went whole hog** in planning her New Year's Eve party.
她**竭尽全力**筹办新年晚会。

go whole hog   英俚,指全力以赴。

10. Don't **jump the gun**. We have to be patient for a while.
不要**草率行事**,我们应耐心等一会儿。

jump the gun   英俚,指草率行事。

11. **Keep your shirt on**. He didn't mean to offend you. That's just the way he talks.
冷静克制。他平时就这么说话,并非有意冒犯你。

keep one's shirt on   英俚,指保持冷静。

12. She **knocked her friends out** with the delicious meal she spent all day preparing.
她用一天时间准备的丰盛大餐让朋友们吃得**大呼过瘾**。

knock someone out   英俚,指让某人高兴得忘乎所以。

附一 课堂讲练材料

1. pet peeve(英俚,指最厌恶的事):My biggest pet peeve is the way Mike slurps his soup. It drives me crazy.
2. play games(英俚,指捣鬼):Don't play games with me, Jane. I'm on to your tricks and manipulations.
3. polish off(英俚,指狼吞虎咽地吃光):We were so hungry that we polished off Mom's apple pie in ten minutes.
4. pull a fast one(英俚,指欺骗):He tried to pull a fast one on us, but we

caught on before he got away with it.

5. pull strings(英俚,指利用关系):He pulled some strings and managed to get us front row seats for the concert.

6. punch line(英俚,指好笑的部分):I can't tell the joke; I forgot the punch line.

7. Russian roulette(英俚,指玩命的事,原意为俄罗斯轮盘):Drinking and driving is like playing Russian roulette.

8. screw loose(英俚,指脱线、神经不对头):Bill must have a screw loose somewhere; he's acting really strangely.

9. space out(英俚,指魂不守舍):He didn't hear what you said. He's spaced out.

10. string someone along(英俚,指对某人卖关子):Don't string me along. Tell me exactly where things stand now.

11. suck eggs(英俚,指可恶、烂):How could they cancel the concert? This really sucks eggs!

12. suck up to(= brown-nose) someone(英俚,指拍某人的马屁):Smith gets ahead by sucking up to the boss.

13. third wheel(英俚,指电灯泡、第三者):You two go on ahead. I don't want to be a third wheel.

14. wishy-washy(英俚,指脚踩两只船):Don't be so wishy-washy. You have to take a stand one way or the other.

15. miss the boat(英俚,指错失良机):We really missed the boat this time! That deal would have made us millions.

16. pig out(英俚,指狼吞虎咽):We pigged out on potato chips and cookies until our bellies ached.

17. zone out(英俚,指避开):Living in New York City, you learn how to zone out the noises around you.

18. twist someone's arm(英俚,指勉强某人、好说歹说地劝某人做某事):I wasn't going to come, but he twisted my arm.

19. use one's head(英俚,指动脑筋):If you'd use your head once in a while, you wouldn't get into such messes.

20. walk out on(英俚,指丢开不管):You can't walk out on me; I really need your help.

21. yuck /yucky(英俚,指难吃):This meal tastes yuck! Who burned it?
22. bad-mouth(指说话不好听、臭嘴、说某人的坏话):Paul was always bad-mouthing his superiors until his boss threatened to fire him.
23. brown-nose somebody(俚指拍某人的马屁,此处可以俚译俚):Harold is always brown-nosing the boss.
24. couch potato(俚指一天到晚盯着电视看个不停,意为电视迷):Mary is definitely a couch potato. She snacks in front of the TV all day.
25. joy ride(俗话指兜风):We went for a joy ride in Peter's new corvette.
26. make waves(俗指引起轩然大波):If my wife finds out about this, she's really going to make waves.
27. big goose egg(英俚,指成绩微小、一点点):My score in the incredibly difficult exam appears to have been a great big goose egg.
28. big fish(英俚,大人物):That man looks likes a big fish.
29. small potato(英俚,小人物):I'm just a small potato, and my words carry no weight.
30. Forget it(英俚,算了、别提了):Forget it, she never intended to go.
31. doc(英俚,原为 doctor 的口语简化形式,相当于老兄):Hey, doc, where is the exit?
32. basket cast(英俚,指绝望无助、意志消沉的人):When Sam's wife left him, he was a basket case for weeks.
33. A:Does he know that he's already at his wits end?
    B:I think he's realized that. But he's still whistling in the dark by putting up an act.
    A:He might be driven up a wall. You should handle your relation with him with kid gloves.
    B:But when I noticed that he was left in the cold, I couldn't help wanting to help him to get out of the situation.

附二 课外扩展训练材料

Reasons to Study Culture

Culture hides much more than it reveals, and strangely enough what it hides, it hides most effectively from its own participants. Years of study have convinced me that the real job is not to understand foreign culture but to understand our own. I am also convinced that all that one ever gets from studying foreign culture is a token understanding. The ultimate reason for such study is to learn more about how one's own system works. The best reason for exposing oneself to foreign ways is to generate a sense of vitality and awareness—an interest in life which can come only when one lives through the shock of contrast and difference.

The best reason for the layperson to spend time studying culture is that he/she can learn something useful and enlightening about himself/herself. This can be an interesting process, at times harrowing but ultimately rewarding. One of the most effective ways to learn about oneself is by taking seriously the cultures of others. It forces you to pay attention to those details of life which differentiate them from you.

(《跨文化交流》)

第四节　英语比喻的翻译

比喻(metaphor)被誉为"诗的语言",是语言的美学功能和信息功能的巧妙结合。所谓"比喻",是指说话者借助"喻体"和"本体",即某种类似性质去说明比较复杂或深奥难懂的道理。从认识论的角度进行观察,自然界的复杂性、人类认识的有限性,以及语言系统自身在表达上的局限性,迫使人们通过比较简单的事理去说明复杂的道理。比喻长盛不衰的魅力主要表现在它的内涵美方面,比喻能运用其能指(形式)与所指(意义)之间多变的联系,调动听众、读者的联想,丰富他们的想象。

一、比喻的主要类型

本节所说的比喻是宽泛的比喻,包括明喻和暗喻。人们有时将英语的比喻粗略分为形似、神似及形神兼备三种类型。

(一) 形似的比喻

"形似"就是本体与喻体在音响、形状与外貌上某一点或某几点有相似之处,这样的比喻可称之为"形似的比喻"。如:

1. And the whining schoolboy, with his satchel and shining morning face, **creeping like snail** unwillingly to school... （明喻）(William Shakespeare)

   背着书包的学童,有一张朝阳般明媚的面容,嘟哝着不愿去上学,像只蜗牛慢慢向前挪动。

这里的相似点,取自学童上学时步履缓慢犹如爬行缓慢的蜗牛,惟妙惟肖地描绘出他厌学的心态和情状。

2. The hallway was **zebra-striped** with darkness and moonlight. (Kurt Vonnegut, Jr.)（隐喻）

   大厅里有的地方黑黑的,有的地方透进了月光,整个大厅就像黑白相间的斑马线。

作者抓住黑暗与月光交替的景象与斑马身上花纹的相似来设喻,十分形象生动。

3. In the morning the dust hung like fog, and **the sun was red as ripe new blood.** （明喻）(John Steinbeck)

   早上尘埃迷漫,犹如漫天浓雾,朝阳则鲜红似血。

这里朝阳之鲜红与血之鲜红是个相似点,尘埃弥漫与浓雾弥漫相差无几又是个相似点。这两个比喻生动地再现了当时人们面临的漫天尘埃、炎热和干涸的情状。

(二) 神似的比喻

神似就是指喻体与本体在形式、外观及表面毫无相似之处,而在精神或实质内容的某一点可能极其相像,如 as happy as a cow, as cunning as a dead pig 等。这些比喻中,喻体与本体几乎毫无外在相似点,却有其内在的相似点,而这一点恰好是本体最根本的、本质的特点。

1. **Men are April** when they woo, **December** when they wed, **maids are May** when they maids, but **the sky changes** when they are wives. (William Shakespeare)

   男人求爱时如和煦的 **4月**,婚后却像寒冬腊月;闺中少女则**宛若温暖的 5月**,而为人妇后却像易变的天气阴晴莫测。

2. The thought **was fire** in him. (J. London)

这种想法如同他心中的**满腔烈火**。

激愤的情绪与烈火存在着内在的相似点,热烈高涨,大火无法立即平息,情绪也不能一下子平静下来。

(三) 形神兼备的比喻

在许多情况下,一个比喻可以同时兼有形似和神似的特点,所以人们称之为"形神兼备"的比喻。如:

> My heart is like **a singing bird**
> Whose nest is in a water'd shoot;
> My heart is like **an apple-tree**
> Whose boughs are bent with thick-set fruits...
> 我的心像一只歌唱的小鸟
> 鸟窝在一支浇了水的嫩枝上;
> 我的心像一棵苹果树
> 压弯的枝条上果实累累。

诗人的心(heart)与歌唱的小鸟(singing bird)具有两个类似点:一是本体与喻体心情都很愉快,这是内在的相似,即神似;二是心脏的跳动与小鸟欢快的蹦跳之间有外在的相似。鸟儿歌声婉转清脆,像要唱出人们心中的歌;苹果树果实累累,是心中承载不下的快乐和满足。简单的比喻,丰富的联想,使人共鸣于作者的情感中,感受到一种"激情之美"。

二、比喻的翻译

依据翻译美学的基本原则,对比喻性修辞格的翻译,可采用的方法很多,实际上每位译者因审美观的不同做法也肯定会有所不同,译者对此不应强求一致。为此,我们仅介绍几种最基本的方法。

(一) 保留喻体,等值再现

任何一种语言都有某种"异化可容性",以此调动读者的主观能动性,所以在读者可以接受的基础上同时又不会产生误解的情况下,尽可能保留原作的比喻形象,让读者体验不同民族情调的差异美。例如:

1. Look at the woebegone walk of him. Eaten a bad egg. **Poached eyes of ghost.**

   A:瞧,他走路的这副愁眉苦脸的样子。吃了个坏鸡蛋。水煎荷包活见鬼。

B：然而，瞧瞧他走路时那副狼狈相，仿佛是个在事业上一败涂地的人。一对**荷包蛋般的幽灵的眼睛**。

2. Passion was to **go to sleep** in the presence of Mrs. General and **blood was to change to milk and water**.

在詹勒罗夫人跟前，一个人的激情会变得**麻木不仁**，热血也会变成**掺了水的牛奶**。

牛奶虽有滋味，但掺了水后是何等性质，汉语读者同样可以理解并领悟到它的讽刺意味。

3. He is **as strong as a horse** / bull / lion / ox.

他**强壮如牛**（一般不说：强壮如马、公牛、狮子）。

4. Her heavy earbobs with their long gold fringe hung down from loops of tidily netted hair swinging close to her brown eyes, **eyes that had the still glean of a forest pool in winter when** brown leaves shine up through quiet water.

两个沉甸甸的耳坠，上面吊着长长的金流苏，垂在用发网整整齐齐兜着的鬓角边，贴近那双棕色眼睛，晃晃悠悠，眼睛幽幽闪亮，**犹如冬天森林里两泓池水**，平静的水面上黄叶泛光。

作者用"水"作喻体，描绘女子的双眸，可谓神态毕肖。

（二）更换喻体，突出喻义

当差异的存在不利于理解，而汉语里恰有相对应或类似的比喻时，译者可用符合中国人习惯，且能引起读者同样联想、同样情感的比喻予以部分或全部更换。从审美角度看，客体形式的改变，正是为了产生相同的审美效果，再现译入语的接受美学功能。例如：

1. That guy Morrow was about as sensitive **as a goddam toilet seat**.

要说敏感，莫罗那小子**像个榆木疙瘩**（不宜译为：……和讨厌的马桶坐垫差不多）。

2. Also, he had money in his pocket, and, as in the old days when a payday, he **made the money fly**.

还有,当口袋里有点钱的时候,像过去发薪的日子一样,他**挥金如土**。

这个"挥"字与原文的 fly(飞)有异曲同工之妙,形象地说明了用钱的挥霍,富有动感,全面再现了原比喻的韵味。

3. His mother is **as happy as a cow.**
   他母亲高兴得**像只云雀**。(不宜直译为:高兴得像头母牛。)

4. Mr. Smith may serve as a good secretary, for he is **as close as an oyster.**
   史密斯先生可以当个好秘书,因为他**守口如瓶**。

瓶口小和蚌嘴紧,喻体异但含义似,形象也较鲜明。

(三) 放弃比喻形式,保持动态对等

如果原文比喻形式因语言差异原因不能保留,也找不到合适的比喻取而代之,只有放弃使用比喻形式。这样做,原语语言形式上的美学价值肯定会有所损失,原有的感染力也会削弱,退而求其次的办法是设法发挥汉语的优势,借助其他手段来弥补损失的美学价值,以获得审美效果上的动态对等。例如:

1. The ship **plows** the sea.
   船在海上**乘风破浪**地前进。

plow 比喻的是船像犁铧翻土似的翻起浪花在海上前进,描写它沉稳有力。现在用"乘风破浪"代替,四字成语简洁有力,是没有形象的形象描写,读者同样可以感受到一种动态的画面,有一定气势。

2. His **intellectual productivity** has decreased in recent years.
   他的**学术成果**近几年少了。

用 productivity 形容成果,说明原来的数量大,而后来数量却日渐减少。

3. WIt's very plain that the old man and I will remain **at daggers drawn to the end of our lives**, and that I have nothing to expect from him.
   很明显,我与老头子至死都**势不两立**,我也不会从他身上得到任何东西。

此句译文利用了很有力度的成语,虽不是剑拔弩张,但其含义已清楚地表明,形不似而神似,求得了动态的对等。

4. ... the wind is **as cold as charity**, we are much more comfortable here, are we not?

外面**冷风飕飕**,我们这儿要舒服多了,是不是?

用汉语的叠字"飕飕"再现了原文比喻的生动性。

5. Whenever he was challenged, he habitually tried to **beat his brain** for an idea to fight back.

他一遇到挑战,就习惯性地**冥思苦想**,想办法回击。

用汉语成语"冥思苦想"再现 beat one's brain。

6. Mr. Brown is a very **white** man. He was looking rather green the other day. He has been feeling blue lately. When I saw him he was in a brown study. I hope he'll soon be in the pink again.

布朗先生是个非常**忠实可靠**的人。那天,他脸上颇有病容。近来他闷闷不乐。我见到他时,他在沉思之中。希望他早日恢复健康。

附一 课堂讲练材料

1. We need to take the rough edge off that idea, hone it down, and smooth it out.
2. He was like a cock that thought the sun had risen to hear him crow.
3. That idea just won't sell.
4. It's important how you package your ideas.
5. It's a rough idea; it needs to be refined.
6. Advice and correction roll off him like water off a duck's back.
7. Even with the most educated and the most liberate, the King's English slips and slides in conversation.
8. He won't buy that.
9. There is always a market for good ideas.
10. That's a worthless idea.

11. Mary and her mother are as like as two peas (in a pod).
12. I guessed when he asked for an interview that Smith had an axe to grind.
13. We're really turning (cranking, grinding) out new ideas.
14. We've generated a lot of ideas this week.
15. He pronounces new ideas at an astonishing rate.
16. Every family is said to have at least one skeleton in the cupboard.
17. Don't monkey with my hi-fi radio, please.
18. Those naughty boys thumbed their noses at each other.
19. He doesn't have an idea of his own. He just parrots what other people say.
20. That young lady just has bats in the belfry.
21. He leaves his company, like a rat deserting the sinking ship.
22. Paris is a morgue without you; before I knew you, it was Paris, and I thought it heavens; but now it is a vast desert of desolation and loneliness. It is like the face of a clock, bereft of its hands.
23. All that I had to show, as a man of letters, were these few tales and essays, which had blossomed out like flowers in the calm summer of my heart and mind.
24. Some books are to be tasted, others to be swallowed and some few to be chewed and digested.
25. Ill-gotten wealth is like a palace built on the sand.
26. On his wise shoulders through the checker work of leaves the sun flung spangles, dancing coins.

附二　课外扩展训练材料

Seeking Popularity

A poet published a collection of his newly-written poems. He, of course, was proud of his success. But to his disappointment, few people would buy his book. He was troubled. The poet told a friend of his about it. "The problem is," said his friend, "that nobody has ever heard of you.

You should become popular and win acclaim, then your book will sell well." "I see," said the poet. "But what can I do?"

"You bookworm! Why not put an advertisement in the newspaper?" said his friend with a smile on his face.

"But I can't put an advertisement saying I'm a bright poet and my book is worth reading."

"No, but don't worry, I can help you with it."

What his friend said brought him some relief. And after that he looked in the newspaper every day, paying special attention to the columns of advertisements. But to his disappointment, he had never found any advertisements of his poems. And as time went by, he almost forgot all about the matter.

One morning, the poet was having breakfast. The doorbell rang. He got up and answered it. When he opened the door, he saw a big man with a big dog standing in front of him.

"I've come for the reward!" the big man said in a bad-tempered voice.

"What reward is it?" said the poet, "perhaps you mistake me for someone else."

"Nonsense!" said the man. "Two pounds you offered to pay for the dog!"

"But I don't want any dogs," said the poet.

"Aha! You don't want the dog!" in an impatient voice the big man said. "You let me come here all the way for nothing!" He was ready for a fight.

"I'm too weak, and that fellow is so strong," the poet thought. "I can't be his match," so he had no choice but to buy the dog for two pounds.

Having fed some meat to the dog and locked it in the kitchen, the poet went back to his work. It was not long before the doorbell rang again. He looked out through the window and found at least six men with six dogs in front of his door. "What's the matter?" he said to himself.

And all of a sudden, he thought of the advertisement. He picked up a pile of newspaper and began to look through them one by one. And suddenly one of the Found and Lost advertisements caught his eyes. It read:

"Mr. Cock offers 2 pounds reward for the return of his faithful dog that first awakened the ideas of writing his new book of poems."

(D. H. Barber)

第五节　英语变异现象的翻译

一、语音变异的翻译

语音变异现象(distortion)常见于日常交际中,更常见于幽默语言之中。幽默之所以能成为一种雅俗共赏的语言形式,语音变异恰如其分的使用,功不可没。美国著名的老牌杂志《读者文摘》(*Reader's Digest*)多年来就一直设有"All in a Day's Work""HUMOR IN UNIFORM""Laughter, The Best Medicine""Life in These United States"等栏目,专门登载幽默笑话,其中有相当一部分笑话借用了语音变异这一功能。

为清楚语音变异这个概念,在此不妨借用《读者文摘》上的一个小幽默:

My friend and I were celebrating our 40th birthday the same year. As a gag gift, I gave her a CD by the band **UB40**.

For my birthday, she retaliated with a CD as well. The group **U2**.

该故事的基本意思是:我和我朋友同一年过40岁生日。为插科打诨,我送给她一盘由UB40乐队演唱的CD。她回敬给我的生日礼物也是CD,由U2乐队演唱。UB40的英语发音同英语"你40岁生日"发音一致,而U2的英语发音又与英语"你也一样"发音一致,如此机缘巧合,其中的小智慧不能不让人会心一笑。

问题是,作为译者应该如何克服英汉两种语音的差异,将同样的语音变异机巧地传达给译文读者?

(一) 译文适时加注,避免缺损

由于英汉语言差异较大,为达到翻译效果,需要译者尽力弥补译文语言效果方面的失真与缺损,以使译文达到与原文大体相同的效果。对此,译文加注不失为一个较好的解决办法。适时加注,如夹注、中注、脚注或尾注,有益于避免译语信息缺损,消除信息失真现象。如:

At the school where my mother worked, the two first-grade teachers were named **Miss Paine and Mrs. Hacking.**

One morning the mother of a student called in the middle of a flu epidemic to excuse her daughter from school.

"**Is she in Paine or Hacking**?" the school secretary asked.

"**She feels fine**," said the confused mom. "We have company and I'm just keeping her home."

原文巧妙地利用了姓氏 Paine(潘恩)与 pain(疼痛)及姓氏 Hacking(哈金)与 hack(不住干咳)发音相同但意思迥异的特点,利用不熟悉该学生的校秘书之嘴发问:"Is she in Paine or Hacking?"使不了解学校教师情况的学生家长联想不到秘书是在问女儿"在潘恩小姐班上,还是在哈金夫人班上?"误以为秘书在问女儿哪儿"疼还是在干咳",所以回应道:"她感觉好着呢!"一个问东,一个答西,打岔似的摩擦爆出幽默的火花。为迎合中文读者的阅读习惯和欣赏口味,很好地传达出原文的幽默效果及言外之意,译者可先尝试将姓氏 Paine 意译成"疼"的同音字"滕",Hacking 译作"咳"的近似音字"柯",因为"滕"和"柯"是中国的两个姓氏。如此处理,既可照顾中国读者的姓氏认知能力,又可化不可译的语音变异为可译,还能为笑料的出彩做好铺路架桥工作。在此试译如下:

我妈妈学校有两个一年级教师,一个姓**滕**,一个姓**柯**。
流感高峰期的某天上午,一学生家长打电话到学校为女儿请假。
"她老师叫什么?姓**滕**还是**柯**?"校秘书问。
学生家长不解地答道:"她好着呢,**不叫心疼,也不咳**。这会儿正和我在一起。我想要她今天不上去学。"

如此翻译,有关原文姓氏 Paine 与疼痛 pain 及姓氏 Hacking 与咳嗽 hack 的处理不仅意韵合拍,而且风趣可乐。另外,适时增加"不叫心疼,也不咳。"这样的夹注做说明,可以弥补不同表达方式造成的译文不足及信息缺失问题。

(二) 用归化手段,再现原文神韵
受语言差异的干扰,译者常常不能运用完全相同的语言手段再现原文语音变异所传递的信息,此时,宜选择与原文不同的表现手法传递其言外功能,在一定的限度内创造性地运用归化手段,再现原文内容。如:

Willette B. Long

When my wife and I showed up at a very popular restaurant, it was crowded. My wife went up to the hostess and asked, "Will it be long?"

The hostess, ignoring her, kept writing in her book. My wife again asked, "How much of a wait?"

The woman looked up. "About ten minutes."

A short time later we heard an announcement over the loudspeaker: "Willette B. Long, your table is ready."

这一故事落笔很淡,不动声色,实则暗藏机关,特别是最后一句不可小视,它是本故事的精髓,所以译者不能莽撞挥笔而就。特别值得注意的是,原文中的 Willette B. Long 是一语音变异,为本段子"包袱",奇巧新颖,可算神来之笔,若译作:"威利特·B. 龙先生",便会造成译文的失真,从而歪曲了原文的妙趣。为再现 Willette B. Long 与 Will it be long 的语音、语义、语境关联,达到译文作者与原文作者的反应对等,可将 Will it be long 译成"等多久"以使其同后面的变异 Willette B. Long 相呼应,为将其汉译为中国人名"邓夺玖"埋下理据,巧妙传达出幽默语言中语句变异、语音变异所造成的语义变异、语境变异,减少或避免译语信息缺失,再现原文的幽默神韵。

上面的翻译处理看似过于归化,实则是一个妥协的结果。虽然忠实原文是翻译的基本要求,但语音变异毕竟不同于一般的语言行为,它具有独特的审美功能,所以要避免翻译时译语的缺失或失真,并非只是要求传达语言表层的含义,更重要的还在于是否传达了作者所要传达的精妙内容及意趣。

二、反常规词语的翻译

反常规词语是运用反常规构词方法形成的一种临时语(nonce word),最常见的是使用连字符进行任意合成,语法上属于复合词。翻译时宜在充分再现原文意思的基础上,根据汉语表达习惯进行翻译。如:

1. I saw an **I-told-you-so** air on his face.
   我看见他脸上流露出一种"我早跟你说过"的神情。

2. My grandfather displayed a **never-to-be-too-old-to-learn** spirit.
   祖父表现出"活到老,学到老"的精神。

3. It's a **you-can-see-through** bag.

这是一个**透明**的包。

4. As **anxiety-maker**, examinations are second to none.

要说**让人焦虑**,最使人焦虑的莫过于考试。

5. A spirited discussion springs up between a young girl who insists that women have outgrown the **jump-on-the-chair-at-the-sight-of-a-mouse** era and a colonel who says that they haven't.

这时一位年轻的女士同一位上校展开了热烈的辩论。她坚持认为女性已有很大进步,不再像过去那样一见到老鼠就吓得跳起来。

附一 课堂讲练材料

Oh, No!

Sean Lennon, his famous mom, Yoko Ono, and a group of friends arrived at a busy New York restaurant. Lennon's girlfriend went to the host and requested a table for seven.

"There'll be a 45-minute wait," he said. "Do you want to leave a name?"

"Ono," the young woman said.

"So you don't want to wait?" asked the host.

"Ono," the woman repeated.

Thoroughly confused now, he asked, "Do you want a table or not?"

The woman finally pointed to Yoko Ono. Within minutes everyone was seated.

(Readers' Digest)

The Words

The dictionary is abundant in sunny words, healthy words and happy words. Words to utter the good. There is plenty of good to be uttered, certainly. There has been a lot of cause for rejoicing in the lives of you and me. It is not suggested that we should never utter a syllable about the dark side of events. Of course not. But in building an attitude that has a healthiness and constructiveness about it, what kinds of words should we advise ourselves to use? It is simply a psychological fact that we can do immense good to ourselves, and can avoid a great deal of self-poisoning, just taking a bit of care about what words we use. Out of words, in a very real sense, we build a picture of life that becomes our reality. By words we create the "powers", dark or smiling, that companion and can rule us.

附二　课外扩展训练材料

Immune

Not long ago a well-known member of Parliament met a newsboy doing his daily round of delivery. The lad was of such diminutive size, and the load of newspapers he was carrying so great, that the honourable gentleman was moved to pity.

"Son," he asked, "don't all those papers make you tired?"

"No, sir," cheerfully replied the bit of humanity, "I can't read."

(Readers' Digest)

第六节　英语矛盾修饰法的翻译

意义上互相排斥、互不协调的两个词语放在一起,即矛盾修辞。矛盾修饰语乍读起来感觉突兀,细嚼之后又觉得入情入理。

英语矛盾修饰法(oxymoron)细分起来有多种形式,对此,李定坤先生做过很好的归纳。

一、矛盾修饰法的基本结构

(一) 形容词修饰语＋名词

"形容词修饰语＋名词"这种用一个含义与中心词相反的形容词来修饰一个名词的结构,是英语矛盾修饰法中最为普通的结构,大多数英语矛盾修饰法都是以这种形式出现的。请看例句:

1. His **cruel kindness** is simply beyond words.

他那**害人不浅的仁慈**(不宜译为"残忍的仁慈")简直难以用言语表达。

kindness 表示的是善良、仁慈等好的品质,可是用 cruel(残忍的)进行修饰,意思突然之间有了根本性的转变。

2. We don't understand why some young people are never bored with their **laborious idleness**.
   我们不明白为什么有些年轻人对那种**令人腻烦的闲散**反而乐此不疲。

laborious(辛苦的)表示不惜花气力去做某事,idleness(闲散、不愿做事)表示不愿花气力做事情,两种意思可说是大相径庭。从整个句子看,确实有那么一些人,正事不愿做,歪事却很舍得花力气。

3. She agreed to this, with a touch of **sorrowful gladness** that they would go back to the rectory and be arranged on the accustomed walls once more...
   她认为这一番评价恰如其分,想到这些书将回到教区区长的住宅里,放回到原来的壁架上,她不禁有点**悲喜交集**……

故事说的是一位教区区长的女儿破产后,不得不拍卖家产,连先父的藏书也难逃厄运,所以感到非常难过。但书被人买走后将会放到其父生前藏书的地方,因此由悲转喜。

4. It (New York) has the **poorest millionaires**, the **littlest great men**, the **haughtiest beggars**, the **plainest beauties**, the **lowest skyscrapers**, the **dolefulest pleasures** of any town I ever saw.
   这座城市(指纽约)里有的是**心灵最空虚的百万富翁**,**人格最渺小的伟人**,**最目空一切的乞丐**,**最使人瞧不上眼的美女**,**最卑鄙龌龊的摩天大楼**和**最令人悲伤的娱乐**,比我所见到过的任何城市都有过之而无不及。

欧·亨利在这一句话里一连用了六个矛盾修饰语,在翻译的时候,译者在准确理解并再现词语基本含义的前提下,又根据句子的上下文和译文读者的语言表达习惯进行了程度不同的引申,比如把 poorest(基本义为最贫穷的)引申为"心灵最空虚的",把 littlest(本义为最短小的)引申为"人格最渺小的",把 haughtiest(本义为最傲慢的)译为"最目空一切的",把 plainest(本义为最普通的、最丑的)引申为"最使人瞧不上眼的",把 lowest(本义为最低矮的)引申为"最卑鄙龌龊的",把 dolefulest(本义为最令人悲哀的)引申为"最令人悲伤的"等。

  5. Writing is **busy idleness**.
   写作是**忙碌的清闲**。(类似于忙中偷闲。)

  写作本来是很辛苦、很占时间的,但作者却从哲人的高度,说它是忙中的清闲。可见对任何事情,角度不同,看法也不会完全一样。又如把 You are talking delightful nonsense. 译成"你信口胡诌,倒也蛮有情趣。"

  (二)副词修饰语＋形容词(或分词)
  "副词修饰语＋形容词(或分词)"这种结构的矛盾修饰语也较多,翻译起来一般不会非常困难,译时应根据句情和汉语的习惯表达适当进行一定的归化处理。例如:

  1. That young man was **strenuously idle**.
   那个青年人**闲得非常难受**。

  一般人可能喜欢悠闲,但也有人愿意做事,悠闲反而使他觉得无聊。

  2. They told their friends that they enjoy that kind of **painful pleasure**.
   他们对朋友说喜欢那种**痛苦的喜悦**。

  pleasure(本意为愉快、快乐等)本是乐事,可是偏偏加了个 painful(痛苦的)来修饰。尽管如此,说话者还是甘心情愿接受的。

  3. She looked tall and **splendidly alone**.
   她个子高高的,**好像鹤立鸡群,显得格外俊俏靓丽**。

  splendid(本意是壮丽的、极姣美的)修饰 alone(孤独的、独一无二的)似乎不太合乎情理,因为后者往往给人一种不太好的联想。译者对此做了恰当的调适,译文较好地传达了原文的内涵意义。

  4. It was a big squarish frame house that has once been white, decorated with cupolas, and spires and scrolled balconies in the **heavily lightsome** style of the seventies, set on what had once been our most select street.

那是一幢曾漆成白色的近似方形的大木屋,坐落在当年一条最考究的街道上,还装点着(19世纪)70年代风味的圆顶、尖塔和涡形的花纹阳台,具有**庄严而轻快**的气氛。

5. She was **agreeably grieved** by the news.
   那消息使她感到**悲喜交集**。

心焦如焚地等待某一可能会不吉祥的消息,最终等到了结果,而且出乎意料,一般都可能会"悲喜交集"。

(三)名词或名词词组+作修饰语的介词短语

"名词或名词词组+作修饰语的介词短语"这种结构也是较为常用的,但较前两种要复杂困难一些,望读者多加体会。请欣赏例句:

1. Alas, that love, whose view is muffled still,
   Should, without eyes, see pathways to his will!
   Where shall we dine? O me! What fray was here?
   Yet tell me not, for I have heard it all.
   Here's much to do with hate, but more with love.
   Why, then, O **brawling** love! O **loving hate**!
   O any thing, of nothing first create!
   O **heavy lightness**! **Serious vanity**!
   Misshapen chaos of well-seeming forms!
   Feather of lead, bright smoke, cold fire, sick health!
   Still-waking sleep, that is not what it is!
   This love feel I, that feel no love in this.

   (Shakespeare:*Romeo and Juliet*)

   唉!想不到爱神蒙着眼睛,
   却会一直闯进人们的心灵!
   我们在什么地方吃饭?
   哎哟!又是谁在这儿打过架了?
   可是不必告诉我,我早就知道了。
   这些都是怨恨造成的后果,
   可是爱情的力量比它要大过许多哦。
   啊,吵吵闹闹的相爱,亲亲热热的怨恨!
   啊,无中生有的一切!

啊,沉重的轻浮,严肃的狂妄,
整齐的混乱,铅铸的羽毛,
光明的烟雾,寒冷的火焰,憔悴的健康,
永远觉醒的睡眠,否定的存在!
我感觉到的爱情正是这么一种东西,
可是我并不喜爱这一种爱情。

作者在这段话里,运用了大量的矛盾修饰法,如"亲亲热热的怨恨""沉重的轻浮""严肃的狂妄""寒冷的火焰""憔悴的健康""觉醒的睡眠",等等。其中 Misshapen chaos of well-seeming forms 和 Feather of lead 便是由"名词词组+作修饰语的介词短语"构成的。

2. ...
   Dove-feather'd raven! Wolvish-ravening lamb!
   Despised substance of divinest show!
   Just opposite to what thou justly seem'st
   A damned saint, an honourable villain!
   ......
   披着白鸽羽毛的乌鸦!
   豺狼一样残忍的羔羊!
   圣洁的外表包裹着丑恶的实质!
   你的内心刚巧和你的形状相反,
   一个万恶的圣人,
   一个庄严的奸徒!

本文所选六句全都用了矛盾修饰法,而带有着重点的两行诗句,是从 Dove-feather'd raven! Wolvish-ravening lamb! Despised substance of divinest show 译过来的,它们也是由名词词组+"作修饰语的介词短语"这种结构构成的。

二、矛盾修饰法的理解方法

理解是翻译的前提,李定坤提出五种理解方法,如运用对立统一的观点、根据背景情况、故事情节、人物身份地位、言谈举止等方面去理解。本节主要选用最常用的三条,供读者参考。

第四章 词语的翻译

(一) 从认知心理角度去理解矛盾修饰法

人类的认知心理有差异也有共性,共性大于差异,承认这一点,译者就有可能设身处地地进行换位思考,经过认真思考后,答案便可能较容易找到。例如:

> Then had I not been thus exiled from light,
> As in the land of darkness, yet in light
> To live a life half dead, a **living death**,
> And buried; but, O yet more miserable!
> (John Milton: *Samson Agonistes*)

> 那样,我就不会这样流放于光明之外,
> 身在光天化日之中,宛在黑暗世界,
> 过半死不活的生活,一个**活死人**,
> 被埋葬了,但比埋葬更为悲惨。

本诗说的是斗士参孙被妻子出卖,落入敌手,受尽折磨,在煎熬中过着半死不活的日子。肉体虽活着,但精神上所受的折磨却比死了还难受,这正是 living death 要表达的主人公的心境。

(二) 从分析上下文入手,找出答案

分析上下文是做任何翻译都必不可少的一步,翻译矛盾修辞法也不例外。深入分析句中的关键词,许多困难便可迎刃而解。例如:

1. '**A tedious brief scene** of young Pyramus,
   And his love Thisbe; very **tragical mirth**. '
   Merry and tragical! Tedious and brief!
   That is **hot ice** and wondrous **strange snow**.
   (Shakespeare: *A Midsummer-Night's Dream*)

   "关于年轻的皮拉摩斯及其爱人提斯柏的**冗长的短戏**,非常**悲哀的趣剧**。"悲哀的趣剧!冗长的短戏!那简直是说灼热的冰,发烧的雪。

戏既然"很短"(brief)怎么又会"冗长"(tedious),既然是"趣剧"(mirth)怎么又变得令人悲伤(tragical)?若细读下段剧中人的旁白,答案就会赫然显现。

2. A play there is, my lord, some ten words long,
   Which is as brief as I have known a play;
   But by ten words, my lord, it is too long;
   Which makes it tedious; for in all the play
   There is not one word apt, one player fitted.
   And tragical, my noble lord, it is;
   For Pyramus therein doth kill himself.
   Which, when I saw rehearsed, I must confess,
   Made mine eyes water; but more merry tears
   The passion of loud laughter never shed.
   (Shakespeare: *A Midsummer-Night's Dream*)

   殿下,一出一共只有十来个字那么长的戏,当然是再短也没有了;然而即使只有十来个字也会嫌太长,叫人看了厌倦;因为在全剧之中,没有一个字是用得恰当的,没有一个演员是支配得恰如其分的。那出戏的确很悲哀,殿下,因为皮拉摩斯在戏里要把自己杀死。可是看他们预演那一场的时候,我得承认确曾使我的眼中充满了眼泪;但那些眼泪都是在纵声大笑的时候忍俊不禁而流下来的,再没有人流过比那更开心的眼泪了。

(三) 根据常识、阅历、生活经验等去理解

生活经验丰富的可以凭借经验理解原文,阅历不甚丰富的可以通过间接经验去仔细体会、琢磨,只要思路对头,一样可以弥补经历的不足。例如:

1. The mother is undergoing the **joyful pain**, and the **painful joy of childbirth.**
   这位母亲正经受着分娩时那种欢乐的痛苦,痛苦的欢乐。

   成年人一般大都能体会"伟大的母亲"这句话的深厚含义,它不仅指母亲博大的胸怀、无私的爱,包含了母亲不仅孕育了子女的血肉之躯,还有分娩时令人难以忍受的阵痛。阵痛虽然难以忍受,但作为母亲,自己能为人类增加一条可爱的生命,那种欢乐是压倒一切痛苦的。上面这句话讲的就是这个道理。

2. He was **restlessly tired**, even as he lay in bed.
   他累了,然而一点也不安宁,即使躺在床上也不安宁。

三、矛盾修饰法的翻译

(一) 等值翻译法

矛盾修饰法的等值翻译法就是把原文的形式和结构不作多少改变移植到汉语中来。请看例句：

1. "What had happened," he said, "was a **normal aberration.**"
   他说："所发生的事不过是一次**正常的越轨**。"

aberration 原意为反常、不正常，可是该词前面的修饰词又说是"正常的"(normal)，这会引起读者的特别注意。细心分析之后，读者可能会从中得出答案：有些发生的事看似荒唐，却有其内在的原因。

2. There was an **audible stillness**, in which the common voice sounded strange.
   这是一片**听得见的寂静**，连普通的声音听起来也显得异样。

寂静本来是无法听到的，可是此处却说能听到，这就是特定情况下的特殊意境。

3. The (Vietnamese) withdrawal sparks mixed feelings among Kampucheans, who are historic enemies of the Vietnamese but for nine years have viewed Hanoi's army as a **necessary evil**.
   越南从柬埔寨撤军令柬埔寨人一下子产生出一种矛盾的心情。历史上柬埔寨是越南的夙敌，但这九年来，柬埔寨人把越军的进驻视为一个"**必要的恶行**"。

既然是恶行，就要制止或革除，为什么还说是必要的(necessary)呢？这里隐含着一个矛盾的心理：当时的形势可能确实需要一支部队稳定社会治安，但与此同时，当地居民又不喜欢外国军队留在那里。

(二) 对称拆译法

对称拆译法就是在充分理解原文的基础上，适当调动汉语文字的优势，将矛盾各方的概念、内涵充分表达出来。这种方法可使用汉语的某些套路，如"既……又……""又……又……""……但……""……却……"等。如：

1. He sat there and watched them, so **changelessly changing**, so

bright and dark, so grave and gay.

他坐在那儿注视着,觉得眼前的景象,既始终如一,又变化多端,既光彩夺目,又朦胧黑暗,既庄严肃穆,又轻松愉快。

如果把原文中几对粗体字照直翻译过来,如"不变化的变化""明亮的黑暗""严肃的轻快"等,读者可能会感到一头雾水。拆开后,把压缩的信息稍做调适,可帮助读者更深刻地理解原文。下面几句大都属于这种情况。

2. Parting is such **sweet sorrow.**

(Shakespeare: *Romeo and Juliet*)

别离是如此的**既甜蜜又令人心酸**。

3. It will enable them to do so by finding out more about the many different kinds of usage that are all covered by the **deceptively simple** word "English".

这本教程可令他们达到上述目的,因为他们可以找出更多的用法,而所有这些用法全都包括在"英语"这个**简单却又令人难以捉摸**的词里了。

4. Though he was a great genius, yet he was an out-and-out **cheerful pessimist.**

他是个了不起的天才,但也是个地地道道的**纵情于酒乐的厌世者**。

前面一个修饰词说的是愉快的,而后面的中心词却说是不愉快、厌恶一切,两词合在一起,正好描绘出一种人生态度,即:纵情于酒乐却悲观厌世。俗话说"一酒解百愁",果真有那么灵验吗?

(三) 融会贯通法

融会贯通法主要是指把两个互相矛盾或排斥的概念融会贯通在一起,以比照的方式翻译过来。例如:

1. Hereditarily disposed to myopia, he recognizes only the persons and habitats of his own species among which he passes **an existence of competitive tranquility.**

(John Galsworthy: *Forsyte Saga*)

他有点遗传性近视,因此只认得自己的同类及同类的巢穴,且只在同类中间过一种小打小闹的安生日子。

2. Some of the people of the chateau and some of those of the posting-house, and all the taxing authorities, were armed more or less, and were crowded on the other side of the little street in a purposeless way, that way **highly fraught with nothing**.

酒堡的人和驿站的人,加上全体税务人员,都已或多或少地武装停当,漫无目的地聚集在小街的另一边,真好像是**无事自扰**似的。

3. We are **terribly pleased** to hear the good news.

听到这一好消息我们真是**欣喜若狂**。

terribly 派生自 terrible(糟糕的),基本意义为"极坏地、糟糕地";口语中释义为"极大地"。该词与 pleased 合在一起,有一种先忧后喜的意味。

附一 课堂讲练材料

1. And, in keeping with its relentless democracy, the new Bartlett's greatly increases the space devoted to the works of anon.
2. As a Forsyte myself, I have no business to talk. But I'm a kind of thorough bred mongrel.
3. He had a friendly contempt for the huge, stupid loggerheads, yellow in their armour-plating, strange in their love-making, and happily eating the Portuguese men-of-war with their eyes shut.
4. For once, Jim Hall was right. He was innocent of the crime for which he was sentenced. Jim Hall believed that the judge knew all about it and was hand in glove with the Police. It was, when the doom of fifty years of living death was uttered by Judge Scott that Jim Hall, hating all things in the society that misused him, rose up and raged in the court-room until dragged down by half a dozen of his blue-coated enemies.
5. He knew he could bear hunger; for that power of endurance had been called forth when he was a little child, and had seen his mother hide her daily morsel to share it among her children, and when he, being the eldest, had told the noble lie, that "he was not hungry, could not eat a

bit more", in order to imitate his mother's bravery, and still the sharp wail of the younger infants.

6. "How you shot the goat and frightened the tiger to death," said Miss Mebbin, with her disagreeably pleasant laugh.

7. I don't mean to imply that we are suddenly threatened in the United Nations with harmony.

附二 课外扩展训练材料

All's Well That Ends Well

It was fine and warm one afternoon, and Will decided to go for a bicycle ride in the country. He was enjoying the sunshine and the peaceful roads, and when he came to a steep hill he let his bicycle run down it much too fast. But there was a sharp bend at the bottom of the hill. When he was nearly there, a dog rushed out of a farmyard, barking and jumping up at him.

Will put his brakes on. He managed not to hit the dog, but he was going too fast to get round the bend safely. The bicycle ran across the road and hit the bank at the other side. Fortunately, no vehicle was passing, so there was no danger of a collision. As Will was picking himself up, the farmer came out. When he saw that there was no damage, he brought Will back to the farmhouse and gave him a glass of fresh milk.

Will was soon ready to go on with his ride. "All's well that ends well," he said to the farmer when they wished each other goodbye.

第七节 英语双关语的翻译

英语修辞格双关(pun)又称 paronomasia(文字游戏)，这是由其自身特点决定的。双关的特点是：用一个词或一句话表达两层或多层意义，这种假借可使语言生动活泼，甚或借题发挥，旁敲侧击，收到由此及彼的幽默效果。

《柯林斯英语词典》为 pun 下的定义是：the use of words or phrases to exploit ambiguities and innuendoes in their meaning, usually for humorous effect. (通过对词或词组的运用,造成语义歧义或暗指,通常以此获得幽默效果。)

一、英语双关的分类

在英语文学作品中,双关运用得相当广泛。英语双关通常为谐音双关(homophone)和词义双关(homograph)两种格式。谐音双关是利用词义不同、词音相同(或基本相同)构成的。词义双关是利用一词多义的特点构成的。对此我们将分别简述如下:

(一) 谐音双关

谐音双关(homophonic pun)主要指依靠意义不同但是音同、音似、音近等特点构成的双关。谐音双关若运用得当,可以给读者意外的幽默和美的享受。例如:

1. First they **get on**, they **get honour**, then they **get honest**.

(Humphrey Rolleston)

他们得努力工作,立下**功劳**,最后得到公认。

这句原文听起来层次感非常强,把 on 作为原级,依次为:原级(on)→比较级(on+er)→最高级(on+est),韵味十足,效果奇佳。

2. **Not on thy sole but on thy soul**, harsh Jew,
   Thou makest(=make)thy knife keen.
   O world! **Thou wast**(= you are) **the forest to this hart**,
   And this, indeed, O world! **The heart of thee**.

(Shakespeare)

无情的犹太人,他们磨刀不用**鞋底蹭**,
却用自己的**灵魂**。
世人呀!这听起来使人感到鲜血淋淋,却恰似世人的心。
是啊,这正是你那颗歹毒的心。

原文中使用了同音异义词 sole(鞋底)和 soul(灵魂),hart(公鹿)和 heart(心脏)。这两对同音异义词主要是通过对比,刻画一个人丑恶的灵魂。译者把 Thou wast(= you are) the forest to this hart 这句译为"这听起来使人感到鲜血淋淋,却恰似世人的心",而未译成"听起来像是雄性红鹿的家园"。因为那样译,没有什么实际意义。原作者只是借助谐音表明一种看法,而不是要介绍雄性红鹿。

(二) 一词多义带来的双关

一词多义的双关,即我们所说的语义双关(homographic puns),主要是利用一词多义的特点构成的双关,要透彻理解其中的双关含义,译者首先要对该语言比较熟悉,语感较强,否则一下子难以明白其中双关意义的奥妙。例如:

The clerk (entering): Are you **engaged**?

Augustus: What business is that of yours? However, if you will take the trouble to read the society's papers for this week, you will see that I am **engaged** to the Honourable Lucy Popham, youngest daughter of ...

The clerk: That isn't what I mean. Can you **see** a female?

Augustus: Of course I can **see** a female as easily as a male. Do you suppose I'm blind?

The clerk: You don't seem to follow me, somehow. There's a female downstairs: What you might call a lady. She wants to know can you **see** her if I let her up.

秘书(上楼进办公室后)问:你正忙着呢?(to be engaged 有两个意思:一、正忙于做某事,二、已经订婚。听者因为一直想着某件好事,所以自然就将上边那句理解为:你订婚了吗,回答也就顺其思路下来了。)

奥古斯都斯:这与你有何关系?不过,你要是不嫌麻烦,读一下本周报纸上有关上流社会新闻,就会知道我和尊贵的露西·波帕姆订了婚。她在其姊妹中年龄最小,是……

秘书:我不是问这个。你现在能见(看见)一个女子吗?(see 含双义:接见或看见。秘书用前一个意思,而奥却理解成了后一种意思。)

奥古斯都斯:当然能看见,我看见女子如同看见男人一样轻而易举。你以为我是个瞎子吗?

秘书:看起来你没明白我的意思。楼下有一位女子,你可以称她为女士的一位女子。她想知道,如带她上楼来,你能否接见她。

上面这个答非所问的对话,皆由 engaged 和 see 两词引起:engaged:(1)忙着;(2)订婚。see:(1)接见;(2)看见。秘书所用的是第一个意思,而老板却听成了第二个意思,所以答非所问。在阅读欣赏双关所带来的幽默乐趣时,读者也会领略到作者是如何讽刺老板满脑子都在想如何巴结名门望族那一副可笑嘴脸的。

二、双关的翻译

英语双关的翻译要比一般的翻译困难,有些文化特异性强的双关甚至根本就无法翻译,只能用解释或其他方法说明大概意思。尽管如此,有些双关语还是可以翻译的。归纳起来,人们主要运用如下方法翻译英语的双关修辞格。

(一) 直译法

所谓直译法,是指尽量按原文的表现形式,照译过来,形式相似但意思能否相似,有时确实很难保证,就算翻译大家有时也很难做到形神皆似。

1. Let's see how the wind blows, then decide whether we should **swim against or with the stream**.

   咱们先看看风向如何,然后再决定是逆流而上还是随波逐流。

译文是照原文直译过来的,译者没有作文字的改变。从字面上看,两种文字都是说的游泳,但在深层意义上又都不是只谈游泳,而是谈做事的策略应审时度势。

2. A: Come on, boy. Can you cut off a man's head?
   B: If the man is a bachelor, sir, I can. If he is a married man, that is, he is his wife's head, I can't. I never **cut off a woman's head**.
   A:过来,小子。你会砍人头吗?
   B:老爷,他要是单身汉,我会砍。可万一他已娶妻,那他就是他老婆的头,让我去砍女人的头,我可下不了手。

译者按照原文直译,读者对"女人的头"这句中的"头"有了新的理解。

3. Behold, it is threatening to shower. We are **in the same boat, let's provide against the rainy days**.

   看,风云如此险恶。我们风雨同舟,宜早作未雨绸缪之计。

英语双关语 in the same boat(在同一条船上),表面上看似乎讲的是坐船,实际上深层含义指"同舟共济"。provide against the rainy days 字面上指"事先做好防雨准备",实际则指"做好预防各种事变的准备"。原文含义深长,译文形神皆似,非常成功。

(二) 意译法

双关语非常突出地体现出民族文化的特性,在另一种文化中找出完全对等的双关语确实有一定困难,要找到完全形神皆似的双关对应语更加困难。遇到这种情况,只有部分或大部分舍弃原文双关语的修辞妙趣,取其基本意义。

A:His words are as plain as **ABC**.
B:But I am **DEF**.
A:他的话说得明明白白。
B:可惜我耳不聪目不明。

原文的双关风趣主要体现在两个方面:一是在英语字母 ABC,二是在由字母组成的谐音 DEF(音 def,立刻使人想到 deaf 耳聋)。前者意指"简单明了,容易听明白。"后者三个字母用得很巧妙,你说得简单,我也让你听得明白:我耳聋。弦外之音是:你说得再清楚我也听不进去,即不买你的账。原文有趣,译文也很传神。

(三) 翻译阐释法

有些英语双关可以说是根本无法两全其美地再现其风貌神韵,对这些双关语,一般只能译出其主要方面,或者说译出其中一层含义,另一层含义可用阐释方法进行补充。

1. My doctor says one million people are over-weight. Those, of course, are **round figures**.

   译文一:我的医生说有 100 万人超重了。当然啦,这 100 万可是个**整数**哟。

   译文二:我的医生说有 100 万人超重了。当然啦,那些人可都是**圆圆墩墩**的。

这句话里有两层意思,一层意思说超重的人很多,特别强调这个数字,round figures 可不是个小数字,整整 100 万哪。第二个意思是指那些胖人的体形。他们可都是实实在在的胖子,又胖又圆,胖人也有可爱的时候嘛。

2. What does that lawyer do after he dies?
   Lie still.

   译文一:那个律师死后能干什么?——**静静地躺着**。

译文二:那个律师死后还能干什么? ——**躺着说鬼话**。

译文一没有体现出原文中律师说谎的幽默效果,译者没有从读者期望心理角度考虑译文,结果不仅没有制造幽默效果,可能还使读者感到莫名其妙。译文二避免了前一译文的问题,着力从读者角度考虑译文,最大限度地再现了原文的幽默和讽刺效果,不失为一则佳译。

3. Two ghosts walked into a bar and asked the bartender.
" Do you serve **spirits**"?
译文一:两个幽灵走进酒吧,问酒保:"你们卖不卖**烈性酒**?"
译文二:两个幽灵走进酒吧,问酒保:"你们为**幽灵服务**吗?"

此处的 spirits 至少有两个意思:一是指通常喝的烈性酒,二是平时不太使用的"幽灵"。到底应如何译,还要看句子的上下文。再比如:

4. A:Tomorrow, I am scheduled to cut the largest diamond in the world.
B:Oh, really?
译文一:A:我准备明天去切割世界上最大的一颗**钻石**。
B:啊,真的?
译文二:A:我准备明天去世界上最大的一块**棒球场**割草。
B:啊,真的?

diamond 一词在这个句子中两个意思都有可能存在。如果说话人不是经营钻石这个行当的,很可能只是指除草。

5. An ambassador is an honest man who lies abroad for the good of his country.
译文一:大使是为其本国利益在国外**说谎**的诚实人。
译文二:大使是为其本国利益在国外**居住**的诚实人。

lies 可表示撒谎或居住。该句的译文,两种都对,任君视情况选择,选择的依据主要看说话者的用意。

6. A:"My business is **looking up**", said the astronomer.
B:"Mine is **going up** in smoke," complained the cigar-maker.
C:"Mine is **all write**," chuckled the author.
D:"Mine is just **sew, sew**," remarked the tailor.

E: "Mine is **growing**," the farmer boasted.

F: "Ours is pretty **light**," snapped the electric light man.

G: "Mine is **picking up**," smiled the cheerful rag picker.

H: "Mine is **looking better**," opined the optician.

上面几个人的对话中,每句话都含有两层含义,这主要取决于读者从何角度进行理解。译文如下:

A:天文学家说:"我的工作是**向上看**。"(或"我的生意正在**好转**。")

B:雪茄制造商嘟哝着说:"我的工作是**烟雾升空**。"(或"我的企业将**化为灰烬**。")

C:作家抿嘴笑着说:"我的工作全都是**写啊写的**。"(或"我的**生意相当不错**。")(all write 与 all right 属谐音双关)。

D:裁缝说:"我的工作只是**缝缝补补**。"(或"我的生意马马虎虎。")(sew,sew 与 so so 属谐音双关修辞格。)

E:农庄主夸口说:"我的工作是**栽栽种种**。"(或"我的**生意蒸蒸日上**。")(grow 有栽种和成长、上升等含义。)

F:电灯工人说:"我们的工作是给人们**带来光明**,"(或:"我们的工作**相当轻松**。")(light 有光明和轻松等含义。)

G:快乐的破烂王说:"我的工作是**拾拾拣拣**。"(或"我的生意在**加速发展**。")(pick up 有拾捡东西和某工程或企业蒸蒸日上、不断发展等义。)

H:眼镜商说:"我的工作是**改善视力**。"(或"我的生意**越做越好**。")(look better 既可以表示比原来看得更清楚,视力好转,也可以表示某情况越来越好。)

(四) 代替法

有些英语双关很有意义,有一些则完全是为了增加说话的趣味性,尤其是那些谐音双关。翻译此类双关,译者可根据汉语的语言特点和读者的欣赏趣味,另拟出一种谐音双关来。例如:

在 *The Sound of Music*(《音乐之声》)这部电影中,有这么一段插曲和歌词:

Doe... a dear, a female deer. Ray... a drop of golden sun. Me... a name I can call myself. Far... a long long way to run.

Sew... a needle pulling thread. La... a note to follow sew. Tea... a drink with jam and bread. That will bring us back to doe.

译文一:Doe 是鹿,是一头母鹿,Ray 是金色阳光,Me 是我,是我自己,Far 是奔向远方,Sew 是引针穿线,La 跟在 Sew 后面走,Tea 喝茶加点心。那就重又回到 Doe。

译文二:朵,美丽的花朵。来呀,大家都快来!密,你们来猜秘密。发,猜中我把奖发。索,大家用心思索。拉,快点猜莫拖拉。体,怎样练好身体,做茁壮成长的花朵。

从上面所给的原文和译文看,文字除了让人记住几个乐符之外,没有更深的含义。押韵是本段的主要特征,目的是增加趣味性,上口易记。译者只要提供朗朗上口的有情趣的文字就可以了,没有必要准确译出原文每个字符的意义。从这个角度看,译文二似乎略胜一筹。

附一 课堂讲练材料

1. A customs officer: Have you got anything to declare?
   Man: Well... Yes. I would like to declare that I love my wife.
2. Son: How much am I worth, Mom?
   Mom: You're worth a million dollars to me, Son.
   Son: Well, could you lend me five of them?
3. Patient: Doctor, I snore so loudly I keep myself awake. What can I do?
   Doctor: Sleep in another room.

附二 课外扩展训练材料

Enigma of the Panther

As she stands in the jungle she is calm, independent, self-possessed, radiating animal magnetism that cloaks her like an aura. She commands attention without manipulation or artifice. In the moonlight her glossy coat is jet beneath her skin like sparks from flint, only hinting at the unleashed power, the electrifying speed within. She is savage without cruelty, noble without pride, bewitching but never flirtatious.

Suddenly she is aroused by some unseen force, connecting with it through her focus, her intensity, the fire of her soul smouldering through emerald agate eyes. What does she see in the shadows? Is it a mate whose brilliance matches hers, whose domination will liberate her tender spirit? Or prey to fall powerless at her feet, felled by one deft stroke of her piercing talons? She has an intuitive understanding of when to strike, and awaits the perfect moment.

As she stalks, liquid motion flows through her body like molten lava. Undulating movement ripples from her breastbone, through her solar plexus, her haunches, her sinewy legs. Her movement has power without strain, energy without effort. Her strong paws pad silently in hypnotic rhythm as they caress the ground, her arched spine curves like a hunter's bow poised to release. She coils like a snake about to strike, then spring into the air with a burst of lightening fury.

What fate awaits her? Is she the huntress or the temptress?

(L. B. Collet)

第八节 英语拟声修辞格的翻译

在英、汉词汇中,拟声词(onomatopoeia)数量虽占比例不大,但若用得恰如其分,能给文章增添"声情并茂"的效果,而且拟声也是一项较有用的修辞手段。拟声词的翻译,一般不会有太大困难,但却有严格的要求,选词得当与否,能体现出译者语言水平的高低。概括起来,拟声词的翻译主要有:对等译、转类译、匹配译、拟声词非拟声译、非拟声词拟声翻译和创造新的拟声词。

一、对等译

英汉两种语言中若有对应的语音形式的模仿事物或动作的声音的拟声词,翻译时较好处理。比如:

1. **Thump**! A table was overturned!
   "哗啦"一声,桌子推翻了!
2. "Boom...Boom...boom-boom..." the thunderous sound rolled in from the other side of the mountain.

"轰——轰——轰轰",巨大的爆炸声从山后那边滚滚而来。

3. A mosquito **hums and hums**,
   Two flies **drone and drone**.
   一个蚊子**嘤嘤嘤**,
   两个苍蝇**嗡嗡嗡**。

4. The car **chugged** with difficulty up the winding road.
   小汽车**呼哧呼哧**,艰难开上盘旋曲折的山路。

5. The leaves **rustled** in the breeze.
   树叶在微风中沙沙作响。

二、转类译

由于英汉两种语言的拟声词在句法功能上有所不同,在翻译这些拟声词时,译者虽保留其拟声的本质和意义,但却不得不改变其词性以求更加符合译文的表达习惯。此外,英语拟声词大多作名词、动词或动词派生词使用,而汉语中的拟声词则大多具有形容词或副词的作用。因此,在进行英汉拟声词的翻译时,要注意进行形容词和副词转类,在进行汉英拟声词的翻译时,要注意进行名词和动词转类。请看以下例子:

1. The cart **rumbled** past.
   大车**轱辘辘**(地)开了过去。(动词→副词)

2. "What's that?" he suddenly exclaimed, hearing a **rustle**; and they both looked up.
   他听见一种**沙沙**的声音,就突然叫道,"什么声音"?接着俩人同时抬头望去。(名词→形容词)

3. The center door **creaks** half-open.
   正中的门"**呀**"地开了一半。(动词→副词)

4. A north wind is **whistling**.
   北风**呼呼**地吹着。(动词→副词)

三、匹配译

英汉两种语言中,有的同一个拟声词可兼指几种不同事物的声音。在英汉翻译时,译者需考虑译文中拟声词的习惯搭配并根据新组合重新搭配。例如英语拟声词 rumble 可同时兼指雷声、车辆声、肚饿声等,在译成相应的词语时，要酌情调整。如：

1. Thunder **roared and rumbled** in the black night sky.
   黑暗的夜空中雷声**轰鸣**。
2. The racing train **rumbled** on.
   飞驰的火车**隆隆**前行。
3. The young man's stomach **rumbled** with hunger.
   年轻人饥肠**辘辘**（肚子饿得**咕咕噜噜**地响）。
4. The old woman **rumbled** to herself as she went out.
   老妇人**嘟嘟哝哝**地走了出去。

英语中模拟动物声音的词十分丰富。几乎每种动物都有专门的拟声词来描绘其独特的声音，甚至有些动物的雌雄老幼都有相应的词表示其不同的叫声。比如：

An ape gibbers. 无尾猿吱吱叫（猿啼，猿啸）。
A buffalo boos. 水牛哞哞叫。
An ass/ donkey/ brays hee-haws. 驴咴咴叫。
A bear growls. 熊咆哮。
A bee hums/ buzzes/ drones. 蜜蜂嗡嗡嗡。
A beetle drones. 甲虫鸣叫。
A bull bellows/ lows. 公牛（大声）哞哞（吼）叫。
A camel grunts. 骆驼发出呼噜声。
A cat miaows/ miaus/ mews/ purrs. 猫咪咪叫。
A cow lows/ moos. 母牛（尖声）哞哞叫。
A calve blats/beats. 小牛（细声）哞哞叫。
A bird twitters/ chirps/ chirrups. 小鸟喊喳地叫。
A bittern booms. 鹭鸶鸣。
A chick cheeps/ pips/ peeps. 小鸡唧唧叫。
A cicada chirps/ chirrups. 蝉鸣（知了叫）。
A cock crows. 公鸡喔喔啼。
A crane whoops. 鹤唳。
A cricket chirps/ chirrups. 蟋蟀唧唧叫。
A crow caws/ croaks. 乌鸦呱呱叫。
A dear bleats. 鹿叫。

A dog barks/ yaps/ yelps/ bays/ snarls/ growls/ howls. 狗汪汪叫(或狂吠等)。

A dove coos. 鸽子咕咕叫。

A duck quacks. 鸭子呱呱叫。

An eagle screams. 鹰尖声鸣叫。

An elephant trumpets. 大象(低声)吼叫。

A fly hums/ buzzes/ drones. 苍蝇嗡嗡叫(或发出嘤嘤声)。

A fox croaks. 狐狸叫。

A frog croaks. 青蛙呱呱叫。

A goat bleats. 山羊咩咩叫。

A goose cackles/ gaggles. 鹅咯咯(或嘎嘎)叫。

A hen cackles/ chucks/ chuckles/ clucks. 母鸡咯咯叫。

A horse neighs/ whinnies/ nickers. 马叫(或嘶、鸣、萧萧)。

A hound bays. 猎狗汪汪叫(或连续狂吠)。

A lamb bleats/ baas. 小羊咩咩叫。

A lark warbles. 云雀啭鸣。

A lion roars. 狮子吼叫。

A magpie chatters. 喜鹊喳喳(啾啾)叫。

A monkey screeches/ chatters/ gibbers/ jabbers. 猴子唧唧叫(猿啼、猿啸)。

A mosquito hums/ buzzes/ drones. 蚊子哼哼(嗡嗡、嘤嘤)叫。

A mouse squeaks/ peeps. 老鼠吱吱(唧唧、啾啾)叫。

A nightingale jugs/ jug-jugs. 夜莺歌唱(鸣)。

An owl hoots/ screeches/ whoops. 猫头鹰鸣叫(尖叫)。

A parrot squawks. 鹦鹉咯咯呱呱叫。

A pig grunts/ squeals. 猪咕噜咕噜(哼哼)叫。

A pigeon coos. 鸽子咕咕叫。

A puppy yelps. 小狗猎吠。

A rat squeaks/ peeps. 老鼠吱吱(唧唧、啾啾)叫。

A raven croaks. 渡鸦呱呱叫。

A sheep bleats/ baas. 绵羊咩咩叫。

A snake hisses. 蛇声咝咝(发出咝咝声)。

A sparrow twitters/ chirps/ chirrups. 麻雀吱吱喳喳叫。

A thrush whittles. 鸫啭鸣。
A tiger growls. 虎咆哮（或吼叫）。
A turkey gobbles. 火鸡咯咯叫。
A whale blows. 鲸鱼（扑扑）叫。
A wild-goose honks. 雁（鸣）叫。
A wolf howls/ growls. 狼（嚎、嗥）叫。

四、拟声词非拟声译

因为拟声词具有较强的文化特异性，各种非生物的声音在英语中有专词传达，而在汉语中却只是笼统地以"……声"或"……响"来表达，基本没有拟声色彩。这类英语拟声词在译成汉语时一般都失去了拟声效果。碰到这种情况，译者应该依据上下文采取不同的翻译策略，能将拟声词译成相应的拟声词，当然最理想，如果勉强为之，倒不如干脆译成非拟声词。如：

1. We heard the machines **whir**.
   我们听到了机器的**轰鸣声**。
2. The train whistle **tooted**.
   火车汽笛声响了。

英语里有些动物的专有拟声词，在汉语里找不到专指的拟声词，所以在译成汉语时，能将拟声词译成相应的拟声词，当然最好，如果无法做到，也可采取非拟声译法。如：

1. The frogs in the fields outside the town were **croaking** cheerfully.
   青蛙在郊外的田野里（咕呱咕呱）起劲地叫着。（括号里的拟声词如果能补上，拟声效果可能会更好些，如果没有加上，句子也算对。）
2. The cock in the coop **crowed** it first round.
   鸡笼里的雄鸡已（喔喔）叫头遍了。（此句中的拟声词 crowed 译或不译都可，视文章风格而定。）
3. The train **puffed** towards Beijing from Shanghai.
   火车（噗噗地）从上海开往北京。（此句中的拟声词 puffed 还是不译为好）

五、非拟声词拟声译

拟声词具有使所描写的事物栩栩如生的效果。为了突出这一效果,译者可根据内容需要,设法把非拟声词译成拟声词,以增强原有的声色效果。英译汉过程中,许多名词或动词常需添加拟声的形容词或副词,以使译文更加生动活泼。这种添加的形容词或副词常以叠音的形式出现。如:

1. He had lost his way when riding in the mountains, and after a day without food he began to **grow** hungry.
   他在山里骑马时迷了路,由于整整一天没吃东西,现在感到饥肠**辘辘**。
2. Edward **fell asleep** almost immediately when he lay down.
   爱德华几乎一躺下就**呼呼**睡着了。
3. We don't know why the kids are **crying loudly** over there.
   我们不明白为什么孩子们在那边**哇哇**大哭。

六、创造新的拟声词

英语拟声词再生能力很强,词汇也较丰富。汉语的单音拟声词,尤其是叠音拟声词也较丰富。如果某种拟声词在汉语中无法找到相应的表达法,译者可以根据字音音译拟声词。

1. She drew one match out. **R-ratch**! Now it sputtered and burned.
   她抽出一根火柴,**哧**!**啪**! 一下子就点燃了!
2. We are charmed with the pretty **prattle** of children.
   孩子们动听的**咿呀**学语声真让人陶醉。

附一 课堂讲练材料

1. Ancient girders creak and groan, ropes tighten and then a trickle of oil oozes down a stone runnel into a used petrol can. Quickly the trickle becomes a flood of glistening linseed oil as the beam sinks earthwards, taut and protesting. Its creaks blend with the squeaking and rumbling of the grinding-wheels and the occasional grunts and sighs of the camels.

2. There is no retreat, but in submission and slavery! Our chains are forged! Their clanking may be heard on the plains of Boston!

3. There was a large, low-ceiled room, with clacking, rattling machines at which men in white shirt sleeves and blue gingham aprons were working. She followed him diffidently through the clattering automatons, keeping her eyes straight before her, and flushing slightly.

4. The seizure of the station with a fit of trembling, gradually deepening to a complaint of the heart, announced the train. Fire and steam, and smoke, and red light; a hiss, a crash, a bell, and a shriek; Louisa put into one carriage, Mrs. Sparsit put into another; the little station a desert speck in the thunderstorm.

5. Discovering voice, the child tries tentatively to use it the very first day, usually it begins to shriek as though in pain. After a month it begins to coo and gurgle, and later it hums gently to itself. Presently teeth appear, and voice-making becomes possible.

6. Zenith, with its saloons, was fifteen miles from Mohalis and the University Winnemac; half an hour by the huge, roaring steel interurban trolleys, and to Zenith the medical students went for their forays.

7. With a wild rattle and clatter the carriage dashed through streets and swept round corners, with women screaming before it, and men clutching each other and clutching children out of its way.

8. I decline to accept the end of man. It is easy to say that man is immortal simply because he will endure; that when the last ding-dang of doom has clanged and faded from the last worthless rock there will still be one more sound; that of his puny inexhaustible voice, still talking. I refuse to accept this. I believe that man will not merely endure: he will prevail.

9. The seasons came and went and they revolved around Joshus. He was the center of Jenifer's world. She watched him grow and develop day by day and it was a never-ending wonder as he began to walk and talk and reason. His words changed constantly and he was in turn, wild and aggressive and shy and loving.

10. Gradually, the curative powers of conversation made us all feel better, until a booming clap of thunder shook the windows only inches from the phone Pat and I were using.

附二　课外扩展训练材料

Time Urgency

Many people today want to do so many things within so little time. This sense of time might be called time urgency. It is a syndrome of behavior in which the person continually tries to accomplish more than can be humanly accomplished. Until very recently, time urgency was thought to be a characteristic of Americans, particularly American males in the generation born in the period from the Great Depression through to the end of World War II.

It should be obvious that this sense of time urgency is no longer a cultural characteristic of just this one generation of American males. It is a characteristic of the Asian "salaryman", and is spreading through the world rapidly as one aspect of the internationalization of business.

One of the most important effects of this sense of time is that in communication it will almost always produce a negative evaluation of the slower participants by the faster participants. Those who share in this concept of time urgency will come to see anyone who moves more slowly than they do as conservative, as uncooperative, as resistant to change, and as opposing progress. Behind the concept of time urgency is the idea that what lies ahead in the future is always better than what lies behind in the past; it is based solidly on the belief in progress.

(《跨文化交际英语课程》)

第九节　富有英语文化特色的词语翻译

东西方文化渊源和背景有很大差异,中国拥有五千多年的灿烂文化,儒、释、道思想贯穿其中,诗、词、曲、剧、名人典故尤为突出;西方文化渊源于古希腊、古罗马文化,《圣经》对西方文化的影响也是无处不在,这些都给翻译带来了一定难度。对此,译者要十分留意,设法捕捉其中的含义,努力提供上乘的译文。本节主要从语言使用差异、文化差异等方面做一简要介绍。

一、语言差异

语言差异表现在许多方面,从对人的称谓,到较为复杂的书面语言等都有可能给译者带来困难。平时写信时的抬头如 Dear Sir /Dear Madam,无须译成"亲爱的先生"或"亲爱的女士",实际上这是语言表达的差异,只是一种称呼,无亲热之意。再比如:

1. It **served him right to give him the gate**.
   译文一:应该把他领到门口。
   译文二:他被开除是罪有应得。

本句有几个难点,比如 serve 一词就有起码两个意思,一为"服务",一为"对待"。serve one right 是个成语,意思是"活该如此、罪有应得"。give one the gate 不是领着某人送到门口,而是"对某人下逐客令"或"开除某人"。由此判断,译文二较为准确。

2. He knows what it is to have **a boy idle**.
   译文一:他知道有个**懒惰的孩子**会是个什么样子。
   译文二:他知道让孩子**游荡**是很不好的。

have a boy idle 与 have an idle boy 意思不同,前者是指"让孩子闲逛、游荡",后者则指"有个懒惰的孩子",idle 置前或置后,差别很大,所起语法作用也不同,置前作定语,置后作补语。这种语言差异,稍不留心,就可能引起误译。

3. They were not **framed** for such pressures and oppressions.
   他们的心理承受不了这么大的压力,肉体也忍受不了这么多的迫害。

动词 frame 有"制订,设计"等意思。原文与译文之间在思维方式上有一定的差异,为了使译文读者能较好理解并接受汉语的表达方式,需要对动词及与其联系最密切的宾语做一定的化解工作。

4. **I would never** have believed in the simple **bliss of being**, day

after day, at sea.

我**以前绝不可能**相信这种日复一日的海上生活竟会如此令人陶醉。

这个看似简单的句子里隐含着一个虚拟语气成分,即 I have come to believe in the bliss of being at sea at last。此处有两点需注意:(1)汉语没有助动词 would 等形式,而此处正是因为有了它,才表达出虚拟成分;(2)never 在此处不是表示否定,而是表示肯定,这与汉语有所不同。

5. They have become **dead political rivals** in the provisional government they helped create.

   他们在自己协助创立的临时政府中反目成仇,成了**势不两立**的政治敌手。

译者在理解原文深层含义的基础上,考虑到两种语言的表达差异,照顾到译文读者的语言习惯,增加了"反目成仇",使语义更加突出明了。

6. **Mighty is the man** who conquers himself.

   最坚强的人就是那些战胜自己的人。

用倒装句来表示强调,也是英汉两种语言的差异之一。英语一般把强调的部分置于句首,汉语则用加词法强调突出部分。翻译这类句子时,应先译出强调部分。

二、宗教、哲学、文化差异

教会、家庭、学校被西方人称为社会的三大支柱,宗教及相关知识是英语文化中一个重要部分,译者对此要有明确的认识。请看例句:

1. However, as the boat, bristling with twenty passengers, was rowed to shore, he felt the joy of creation and domination—even though Mr. Hospice was ostensibly in charge—for certainly no other than Leonard Lumlye had led out these **bleating Israelites** from their Egypt—had set the strong machinery of these rowing Lascar's arms in motion.

这段描述选自英国女作家斯特拉·本森的幽默短篇小说《恰恰相反》。故事中的主人公伦纳德·伦姆莱自命不凡,无论对错,总要表现自己与众不同。一次乘船航行途中,因船需卸货,航行至滩边停泊,伦姆莱自告奋勇,领着船上的英国乘客上岸观光游览。既然讲的是英国乘客,为何又冒出 Israelites(以色列人)? 不仅如此,还在该词前冠以 bleating(咩咩叫的……),而且还谈到了 from their Egypt(出埃及)!

原来,作者在此借用了《圣经·旧约》Moses(先知摩西)带领以色列人逃出埃及这个典故。在语言的发展中 Moses 一词渐渐"升级"为"伟大领袖"。作者用此典故旨在揶揄故事主人公伦纳德·伦姆莱的自恃和愚妄。在他看来,他比谁都伟大英明,别人只不过是一群咩咩待领的羔羊。对这一文化背景和典故充分了解之后,译文便可应运而出:

> 然而,在拥拥挤挤坐满 20 位乘客的小船摇向岸边时,他因自己富有创造性的想法,并能支配他人而沾沾自喜(尽管名义上的领队是霍西皮斯先生):除了他伦纳德·伦姆莱之外,肯定没有第二个人能带领这群**叽叽喳喳的以色列人**走出埃及,没有第二个人能让这些印度水手,用其强壮得如同机器般的手臂摇船前进。

同理,God, Jesus, Christ 在下句 2 中就不一定要译成"上帝""耶稣"或"基督"。

2. "My God, you think he did this?"
   "I don't know. Yes."
   "Why? Wait, you just said, to silence her. **Jesus**, Jonelle, I don't know. I'll help you uncover every stone."
   "我的天哪,你认为这是他干的?"
   "我不知道。是的。"
   "什么? 等等,你刚才说是为了灭口。**啊呀天哪**,琼莉,这我可不知道。我来帮你查个水落石出。"

3. He is not invincible. He has his own **Achilles' heel**.
   他并非坚不可摧。他身上也有像"**阿喀琉斯的脚踵**"那种致命的弱点。

4. Ben frowned, clearly disturbed. "I don't know," he answered finally. "Just...some kind of freaking **Frankenstein** or **Dracula** or something. **Honest to God**, I don't know."
   本双眉紧锁,显得心神不定。"我不知道。"他最后答道。"就是……**弗兰肯斯泰因式的怪物**或者**德古拉式的吸血鬼**或者别的什么。**对天发誓**,我也说不清楚。"

在此,Frankenstein 和 Dracula 分别为英国作家玛丽·雪莱(Mary Shelley)和布兰·斯多噶(Bram Stoker)小说中的两个怪物。

三、风俗习惯差异

语言学家马林诺夫斯基(Malinowski)说过,语言基本上植根于该语言的民族文化、社会生活和习惯之中。翻译时,应该时刻记住这一点。例如:

1. The boy had just eaten his dinners and been called to **the bar.**
   译文一:这个男孩刚刚吃过晚饭,就**被叫到酒吧间**去了。
   译文二:这个年轻人刚刚**取得律师资格**,就当上了**律师**。

在我们弄明白上句是美式英语还是英式英语之前,不好轻易下结论说哪个译文对或错。换言之,若是英式英语,那译文一就是误译,译文二就是正确的,因为在英国律师界有个长期沿袭的做法,大学法律专业学生每学期必须到律师公会参加若干次的聚餐(dinners),然后才有资格当律师。本句中的 dinners 就是指律师公会所举行的聚餐会。

2. Excuse me, Sir, could you show me your **green card**?
   译文一:打扰一下,先生,能否给我看看您的**绿卡**?
   译文二:打扰一下,先生,能否给我看看您的**境外驾驶保险卡**?

green card 在美国可译为"绿卡",指对外籍人士发放的准许其长期居住并可以在美国找工作的许可证;在英国,则指为防止驾驶汽车的人在国外遭遇意外而提供的保险卡,通常译为"境外驾驶保险卡"。根据这些差异,我们可以判断上述哪个译文更符合原义。

3. John can be relied on. He **eats no fish and plays the game.**

我们知道,英国是个岛国,四面环水,盛产鱼虾。俗话说靠山吃山,靠水吃水,鱼自古以来就是英国人的主食。相传在罗马人入侵英国时,人们在星期五普遍吃鱼,只有极少数人不吃,以示对英皇的效忠。从此,eat no fish 深含忠诚、值得信赖之意。了解到英国人的风俗习惯后,上句英语可译为:约翰**忠诚正直,值得信赖**。

附一 课堂讲练材料

1. I'm from Missouri.
2. Three men on horses have already ridden out of a wall in the background, and all but the last flank of the fourth horse has emerged. He is a pale steed, representing Death. The men are the Four Horsemen of the Apocalypse.
3. This report will be laid aside in the safe, but he knew Pandora's box cannot always be kept shut.
4. You think you can defeat one who warred with God? You think you can defeat one who struck down great Michael to the Earth? Do you?
5. Tell me of that great strength that was taken from you at Golgotha!
6. Look, Barn, it frankly doesn't take a rocket scientist to figure out She's had really good karma when it comes to finding a story. Suspicion is natural.
7. Mrs. Robert "Oastie" Charles, grande dame of Washington's Old Guard, warmly grasped Jonelle's hand in the receiving line, and said, "Lovely to see you, and thank God you're the last."
8. "That's Larry Woldt."
   "Who is he?"
   "One of the paparazzi in New York. He's got the biggest collection of JFK Junior photos in the world."
9. He wasn't quite asleep, but he seemed to dream. He had forgotten something. He was in some school. His college. Apparently, going into an examination, he had tried to summon the entire course into his mind, and something was missing. He could see a room, filled with row upon row of desks, and he had forgotten something. He couldn't remember what it was. Wein's formula, Raleigh's and Jeans', Planck's, Stefan's law, Boltzmann's constant... Radiant excitance, Wm, for a given wavelength, lambda, equals the first constant times the reciprocal of lambda to the fifth times. Names, formulas, equations—all rushed through his mind. He was trying to remember everything at once, and couldn't; something was lost. His mind raced, around and around, looking for

it. Finally, with a start, he awoke, or became conscious. Staring up into the darkness, he suddenly whispered, like a prayer, or the element of a catechism, "5.6697 times 10 to the minus 8 Wm to the minus 2 K to the minus 4," and then repeated this twice, mindlessly, for a moment not aware of what the expression meant. But then he realized that it was the actual value of Stefan's constant, sigma, which allowed one to find the radiant flux per unit area emitted by a black body for a given temperature.

附二 课外扩展训练材料

The Backpacker

Chinese state media warned Monday that the joyful reception given the new U.S. ambassador in Beijing should not be mistaken for a solution to the two countries' problems. Gary Locke, the first Chinese American to serve as U.S. ambassador to China, created a media sensation when he arrived on Friday carrying his own luggage and traveling from the airport in a modest car.

But the official Xinhua news agency, which labeled him "the backpacker," noted a number of problems that Locke will have to deal with, including strains over trade, military relations and the U.S. debt. It said Locke's mission will be "much heavier than the bag he carried on the way to China." *The Global Times newspaper* also noted Locke's modest arrival and described him as "possibly the most recognizable American ambassador to China in history." But it said his Chinese origins will not mean a softer stance when it comes to defending U.S. interests.

第十节 可译性与不可译性的补救

一、可译性与不可译性的问题

关于可译性(translatability)与不可译性(intranslatability)的讨论早已

有之。威廉·洪堡特说过：任何译者毫无疑问是在试图完成不能完成的任务。还有人说：翻译者即叛逆者。话虽说得有点绝对，但也从侧面说明了翻译之难。不可否认，不同民族、不同语言中的异质特性，有些是无法翻译的，或者说是无法等效翻译的。翻译过程中出现的"损耗"或"失彩"是不可避免的。如英语中的双关语、用双关语组成的谜语、汉语中带双关的歇后语、英汉语少量的回文、汉语中标点符号的文字游戏、拆字游戏等，无论怎么译，它们的意思都无法充分译出。这就是所谓的不可译性，或者说可译度很小。

不过，可译性与不可译性是相对的，没有什么是绝对不可译的，加点注解能让人看懂也可算是具有可译性，所以有人认为用可译度这一说法比较科学。

在翻译过程中，文化和语言差异较大的内容可采用"直译加注释""解释性翻译""变换角度译"等方法进行补救。

二、处理文化差异过程中的补救方法

(一) 直译加注释翻译法

直译加注释翻译法就是在直译的基础上，译者根据需要，增加一些必要的背景介绍，以帮助读者更准确地理解原文，并顺带了解一些异国表达法。请看例句：

1. The **May-day dance**, for instance, was to be discerned on the afternoon under notice, in the disguise of the club revel, or "club-walking", as it was there called.
比如那天下午证明，**五朔节舞**的旧风俗是以联欢会（或者以本地人所说的游行舞会）的形式出现。

五朔节舞是英国一项民俗活动。每年1月5日，人们奏乐吹号，撒树枝，采野花，装饰门窗，在草地上竖起五朔节柱，围柱跳舞，并选出五朔节皇后。此风古时极为盛行，现在只在一些偏远的乡村才可见到。

2. He came safe from **the East Indies**, and was drowned in **the Thames.**
译文一：他从**东印度**安然归来，却在泰晤士河里淹死。
译文二：他**涉过无数惊涛骇浪**，却在小小阴沟里翻了船。

东印度即现在的南亚次大陆及东南亚等地。17世纪英国开始在该地区扩张,18世纪建立殖民地。当时来往于该地区和英国之间须绕经非洲好望角,海程万里,水险浪大。泰晤士河为英格兰内河,流经伦敦,长仅336公里。上句喻指人们能安全闯过大风大浪,却跨不过一条小河沟。

(二) 解释性翻译法

解释性翻译主要指若用直译或其他方式,读者有可能不明白其中含义,甚至产生一些不好的联想。遇到这种句子,还是采取解释性翻译法为好。比如:

1. He is as pleased as **a dog with two tails**.
   他高兴得**手舞足蹈**。

尽管在西方狗被当作人类忠实的朋友,主人对狗有时比对家人还要亲,人与狗的关系胜过人与人的关系,但上句还是不宜直译。如果直译成:"他像狗长着两条尾巴一样高兴。"恐怕不太能为读者所接受。又如:

2. How she wished she could send that man to **the Furies**—for the punishment she thought he deserved.
   她多么想把那个男人交给**复仇女神**去狠狠惩罚一下,让他罪有应得。

Furies(常译为福里埃)是古希腊、罗马神话中复仇三女神,此外喻指慓悍、厉害的女子。

(三) 变换角度翻译法

变换角度翻译法主要指运用汉语成语、谚语、俗话、对联、对偶句等读者喜欢的精炼语言,翻译或化解原文中浓重的文化异质。比如:

1. Misfortunes **seldom come singly**.
   译文一:祸不单行,福无双至。
   译文二:屋漏更遭连阴雨,船破又遇顶头风。

此句英语是一句谚语,译者也尽量用言简意赅的谚语或对仗语句译之,保持原文的风貌。再比如:

2. In the **end** things will **mend**. (When things are at the worst, they will mend.)
   车到山前必有路,船到桥下自然直。

原语有两个押韵的字,读起来朗朗上口,译文也应如此。所以用汉语中人们喜闻乐见的对称句译英语中浓缩的民谚,不失为一种较好的方式。也可以直、意译结合:事到最后总有救。

除了上面介绍的方法外,还可能有其他一些可行的方法,希望译者不断总结、整理,为翻译研究做出应有的贡献。

附一　请欣赏下列英语句子及其汉译

1. A:What is given to you, it belongs to you, but others use it more often than you? (什么东西给了你之后就属于你,可是别人使用它的次数倒比你多?)
   B:Your name. (名字。)

2. A:The man who made it did not want it; the man who bought it did not use it; the man who used it did not know it. What is it? (造它的人不要它,买它的人不用它,用它的人不知道它。这是什么?)
   B:Coffin. (棺材。)

3. A:The more you get from it, the bigger it becomes. What is it? (你从它那儿拿走的越多,它反而变得越大。请问它是什么?)
   B:Hole. (洞。)

4. A:What is the strongest day of the week? (一星期里哪天最强?)
   B:Sunday, because all the others are weekdays. (星期天。因为其他几天都弱。weak 与 week 均发同一个音,译文无法传达原文的幽默和谐趣。)

5. A:Which is the longest sentence? (什么监禁最长?)
   B:Life imprisonment. (终身。)

6. A:What has teeth but can't eat? (什么有齿不吃东西?)
   B:Comb. (梳子。)

7. A:Barking dogs seldom bite. What dog never bites? (会叫的狗不大咬人,那么什么狗从不咬人呢?)
   B:A hot dog. (热狗。)

8. A: What will you break even if you just mention it? （提一下就打破的是什么？）
   B: Silence. （沉默。）
9. She sells seashells on the seashore. （她在海滩上卖海贝。但这种原本只是用来区分 /s/ 和 /ʃ/ 的句子，其功能无法译出。）

附二　课外扩展训练材料

Damler Quality Line Pork

Damler and supplier guarantee each pork has its own ID card to record its origin, race, age, breeder, breeding period and breeding process.

Scientifically formulated food, non-polluted breeding environment and strict control medication to guarantee better taste and full safety.

To become a Quality Line "partner", the staff of the farm commits to respect animal's well-being and strictly follow the relevant rules of breeding, slaughtering and delivering.

To ensure the taste and quality of the pork meat, all the genetic model come from certified breeders and will grow up in farms appointed by Damler.

To guarantee the quality and the freshness of the pork meat, from slaughtering to Damler counter, we maintain the temperature within 0－4 degree centigrade all the time.

(Ad for Damler Pork)

第五章 句子的翻译(一)

第一节 词义的确定、引申和褒贬

一、词义的确定

英汉两种语言都有一词多类、一词多义的现象。一词多类就是指有的词可能属于好几种词类(性),每个词性的意义都可能会有某些程度的不同,要求译者细心判别。一词多义就是说同一个词在同一个词类中很可能有好几个不同的含义,同样也需要译者认真辨别,从中细心挑选。我们拟从两个方面讨论这一问题。

(一)根据词类(part of speech)确定词义

选择某个词的词义时,首先根据句法结构判明这个词在原句中应属于哪种词类,然后进一步确定词义。例如:

1. An electron is an extremely small corpuscle with negative charge which **rounds** about the nucleus of an atom.
   电子是绕着原子核转动带有负电荷的极其微小的粒子。(动词)

2. The earth goes **round** the sun.
   地球环绕太阳运行。(介词)

3. **Round** surface reflector is a key unit for the solar energy device.
   弯曲面反射器是太阳能装置的关键元件。(形容词)

4. The tree measures forty inches **round**.
   这棵树树围有40英寸。(副词)

5. This is the whole **round** of knowledge.
   这就是全部的知识范围。(名词)

又如 base 一词及其翻译:

1. Plastics was at first **based** on coal and wood.

最初，塑料是从煤和木材中提取的。（动词）

2. The government **based** its conclusions on some intelligence agency false reports and fabricated stories.

   政府根据情报部门提供的虚假报告和无稽之言做出了结论。（动词）

3. As we all know, a **base** reacts with an acid to form a salt.

   众所周知，碱与酸起反应变成盐。（名词）

4. Iron and brass are **base** metals.

   铁和黄铜为非贵重金属。（形容词）

5. It is **base** to cheat in any kind of examination.

   无论在什么样的考试中作弊都是可耻行为。（形容词）

（二）根据上下文（context）确定词义

英语中的同一词类常有多种意思，用于不同场合其含义可能大不相同，因此译者在确定某一词所属词类的基础上，应根据上下文，即根据专业特点和具体语境来确定其确切含义。例如：

1. The electronic microscope possesses very high resolving **power** compared with the optical microscope.

   与光学显微镜相比，电子显微镜具有极高的分辨率。

2. **Power** can be transmitted from the Yangtze Gorges Power Station over a long distance to the metropolitan city of Shanghai.

   电力可以从长江三峡水电站输送到很远的大上海。

3. The fourth **power** of three is eighty-one.

   3 的 4 次方是 81。

4. Though the enemy used modern ships turned by steam **power** while we guerillas used sailing boats driven by wind **power**, we succeeded in defeating the Japanese aggressors in our Weishan Lake area.

   尽管敌人使用的是由蒸汽驱动的汽艇，我们游击队只有靠风力行驶的帆船，我们还是在微山湖区打败了日本侵略者。

5. The Seventh Fleet in American navy is a mighty **power**.

   美国海军第七舰队是一支强大的武装力量。

6. She has strong **powers** of concentration when she studies or works.

   她在学习或做事时有极强的专注力。

7. It's been proved again and again in history that some **powers** always tried to dominate and bully other small and weak countries.

   历史无数次反复证明：某些大国总想控制和欺侮弱小国家。

上面几个句子中，句1是物理学上常使用的术语，如放大率、分辨率等；句2是电力上的术语，译为"电厂""电站"等；句3是数学上使用的术语，如"幂""乘方"等；句4即是我们常说的"动力"；句5中的power则应译为"武装力量"，即指一支部队；句6指某人的能力、天赋；句7是一个政治术语，指国家或大国，如superpower（超级大国）。由此可见，同一个词，尽管都是名词，但意义却有很大的不同，翻译时要认真分析上下文和句义，然后拿出恰当、准确的译文。

二、词义的引申

词义的引申(extension)，主要是指把原文词句所包含的意思在译文中显现出来。虽然原文的意思与译文中引申的意思基本一致，但两者也会多少发生一些变化，主要体现在三个方面：(1)译文中的说法和形式不一样，原文隐含，译文显现；(2)原文蕴含的意义在译文中得到进一步的挖掘，因此深度和广度都有可能超过原文；(3)为了使译文更加符合汉语表达习惯，使读者更容易接受译文的行文措辞，需做必要的"归化"处理。

词义引申不仅仅体现在文学作品中，在科技、政治、军事、经济、医学等文体中都有程度不同的体现。词义引申主要有名词引申、动词引申、形容词引申等，此外还有词组引申和句义引申。

（一）名词引申

我们在翻译过程中，经常发现词典释义不尽如人意。译者在参阅词典时，不能也不应完全照搬词典提供的释义或表达法，需要进行一定的变通。例如：

1. Feel the new **space**.

   感受新**境界**。

此为三星电子的广告词。space 的释义是：太空、空间、场所、地位、间隔、距离、空白、时间、空幻状态、篇幅等。若照此直译不进行引申,就不太符合人们对产品的美好预期,宣传效果难免打折扣,因此有必要进行引申。

2. Another factor in the development of dermatology has been the growth of societies, regional and national, at which much **cross-fertilization** of minds took place.
   皮肤病学获得进展的另一个原因就是地区性和全国性皮肤病学会的成立。在这些学会中,人们得以**彼此自由地交流想法**。

cross-fertilization 根据词典释义,有"异花受精"等意思,可是思想怎么会"异花受精"呢？因此,考虑到上下文词句的关联,将其译为"交流想法"。

3. This little, frail old man... sought comfort in the **past**. He was bewildered by the present, and afraid of the future.
   这位矮小瘦弱的老人,从**已经逝去的岁月**中寻求慰藉,对今天感到迷惘,对未来充满恐惧。

past, present 和 future 本义是"过去""现在"和"将来"。但是,此句的 past 前面有介词 in,"在过去寻求慰藉"显得词语搭配不够和谐,引申为"从已经逝去的岁月中寻求慰藉",读起来就显得顺畅多了。

4. A personnel **deficit** has existed for years.
   人手**不够**的现象已经存在好几年了。

deficit 一般作财政上的"赤字""亏损""逆差"解释,现代英语中,往往又从这些释义中引申出"不足"或"短缺"之意。说"人员亏损(逆差、赤字)"在汉语里是讲不通的。又如:

5. The EU's Common Agricultural policy is a **dinosaur** which is adding £13.50 a week to the food bill of the average British family.
   欧盟的共同农业政策早已**不合时宜**,因为该政策使英国家庭平均每周在食品开销上多支出 13.50 英镑。

dinosaur 的词典释义是"恐龙",指一种史前早已绝迹的庞大动物。在现代英语里,dinosaur 又常被引申为"要被废弃的落后的庞然大物",如 the country's industrial dinosaur 指"该国庞大而陈旧的工业体系"。落后而要被废弃的东西当然也是过时的或不合时宜的,故此处作这样的引申。

6. The huge increase in oil prices in the 1970s cast a **cloud** over the development plans of many developing nations.
20世纪70年代石油价格猛涨,曾对许多发展中国家的经济发展计划投下一抹**阴影**。

cloud 在现代英语里可表示"使人产生未曾想象到的伤心或不愉快"。故本句作此引申。

7. She felt that this moment of interview for her first job was a tremendous **inch** in her whole existence.
她觉得第一次的求职面试在她整个人生中占有重要的**地位**。

如果把 inch 直译为"英寸",译文不通。译者将其引申为"地位",十分准确地表达了原文的意思。

8. He who seizes the right moment, is **the right man**.
谁把握机遇,谁就**心想事成**。

the right man 引申为"心想事成",较符合原义。

(二) **动词引申**

动词在英汉两种语言中使用频率都很高,且十分灵活。动词用得好,会为译文增色添彩。要想提供上乘的译文,译者经常需要做一些意义上的引申和变通。例如:

1. A threatened king in chess must be **protected**.
下棋时国王受到威胁必须**保驾**。

protected 有"保护"等释义,上句译成"……保护"也未尝不可,但与国王连在一起用时,用"保驾"似乎要雅一些。这里的引申主要根据上下文词句的关联影响。

2. Hanoi **romanced** its Asian neighbors for six years before winning its membership in ASEAN.
河内对其邻国进行了六年的**亲善努力**后才成为东盟的一员。

romance 作动词用于个人之间时,可指"向……求爱"或"追求某人"。可是用于国家与国家之间,却不能说彼此间求爱或求婚,因此 romance 在句中需要引申,意思即为"以亲近的方式来改善国家间的关系"。

3. But the run-up to the meeting has been **coloured** by acrimony over financing the new plan, and sharp differences between developed countries and developing countries.

会前准备**弥漫着一种不协调的气氛**:在为这项新计划提供资金的问题上,与会者唇枪舌剑,争得面红耳赤;不仅如此,在许多问题上发达国家与发展中国家立场观点尖锐对立。

colour 作为动词用是"给……上颜色""给……改变颜色"。在现代英语里,它又可被引申为"影响(思想、情绪、氛围等)"等一类意思,上面句子中 colour 的汉译"弥漫着一种不协调的气氛"即是基于这样的引申而产生的译文。

4. Scandal **clouded** the popular president's reputation.
   丑闻**玷污**了深得民心的总统的声誉。

cloud 作动词用时,有"含混不清""不易看懂或理解""变得难以判别""玷污诽谤""玷污"之义。

5. **Take** TOSHIBA, **take** the world.
   拥有东芝,**拥有**世界

(三) 形容词引申

形容词或复合形容词虽然比较好译,但有时也需要做一定的引申或必要的调整,使表达更容易为读者所理解和接受。否则照词典释义译,译文可能显得生硬别扭。例如:

1. Influenza is an acute **self-limited** infection and is characterized by constitutional symptoms, although the infection is restricted to the respiratory tract.
   流感是一种**定期自愈**的急性传染病,虽然传染只限于呼吸道,但其症状却是全身性的。

self 表示"自身的""靠自身的或为自身的",与 limited 组成一个合成词,意思是"受自身限制的""自限的"。如果不做引申,总感到哪里说得不地道,译文稍加引申,读起来就使人感到很有点味道。

2. That is a **no-win** dilemma.
   这可是一个**两头都不讨好**的难题。

no-win 原意是"无法取胜的",如 a no-win war 是"一场打不赢的战争"。但这里与 dilemma 搭配,就是指"不可能同时满足双方要求的困境"。因此把 no-win 变换为"两头都不能讨好的",把 dilemma 变换为"难题",既照顾到上下文,也比较符合汉语的表达习惯。

  3. Hi, **Handsome**. My name is Rose. I'm eighty years old.
    嗨,帅哥!我叫罗丝。我80岁了。

(四)词组引申

原文含义比较抽象、概括、含蓄的词或词组,翻译时需要根据语境和译入语使用习惯加以引申,使表达明朗清楚,让读者明白其中的含义。不过,这些都必须建立在不曲解原义和原文风格的基础之上。例如:

  1. I'll place some wood in the hole, ma'am. Then when a sudden storm comes up, you can **stay warm**.
    我会放一些木材在这个洞里,夫人。这样暴风雪突然来临时,你就可以**取暖**。

如果把 stay warm 按字面意义译为"保持暖和",译文就会前言不搭后语,将其引申为"取暖",就将这两句的内在逻辑关系清楚地表达了出来。

  2. **Rearm your spirits** before it is too late.
    赶快**振作精神**。

英语原文是 rearm...spirits,但汉语译文中不宜出现"重新武装……精神",改为"重振精神"才符合汉语的表达习惯。

  3. When the Sheridans were little they were forbidden to set foot there because of the revolting language and of **what** they might catch.
    谢里登家的人小时候都不准到那儿去,**生怕学到一些下流话,或沾染上什么毛病**。

这句译文除增加了"生怕学到""沾染上"等词外,还将 what 具体引申为"什么毛病",这样处理才能使意思表达得清楚明白。

  4. Westal looked up to see Belfreda **crooking a finger** from the half-darkness of the hall.
    "You back? What is it?" asked Vestal crossly.

薇思德一抬头,看见白菲瑞达在半明半暗的门厅里**弯弯手指招她过去**。

"你回来啦?什么事?"薇思德没好气地问。

crook 一词,原来是"弯曲"的意思,crook a finger 是"弯弯手指"。但在这个特定的上下文中,"弯弯手指"只是其表面含义,"招她过去"才是这个动作所象征的真正隐含意义。译文不把这一点说明,读者就不太容易理解。

5. For many families, especially in Tokyo, **two incomes** are a necessity.

    对许多家庭,尤其是东京的家庭而言,**夫妻俩都去上班赚钱**是迫不得已的事。

two incomes 表面词义为"两份工资",意指"夫妻双双都工作而获得的两份工资",汉译时需将这个特殊意义引申出来,否则读者不一定能理解全句的完整意思。

6. The British suburban garden, that **most revered of national institutions**, is increasingly facing destruction by land-hungry developers.

    英国城郊花园是**最受推崇的国粹**,现在却不断遭到贪吃的土地开发商的破坏。

7. Malaysia, which posted its highest growth rate in a decade, is the region's new **star performer**, with Indonesia close on its heels.

    十年中,马来西亚的发展速度是最快的。它是该地区新出现的**最出色的经济发展国**,紧随其后的是印度尼西亚。

star 这个词在现代英语里可以说是很时髦的,现在用来特指因演出成功而名扬四方的演员或歌星。star performer 当然也可指"扮演最重要角色的演员"或"领衔主演者"。为了更易为读者所理解和接受,需要将 star performer 引申译为"最出色的经济发展国"。

8. At The Mandarin Singapore, flagship hotel of Singapore Mandarin International, we have long practiced service that is **in the tradition of emperors**.

    新加坡文华大酒店乃新加坡国际文华酒店集团的佼佼者。在此,我们长期实行的一整套服务项目都**体现出华贵的皇家风范**。

句末一个词组 in the tradition of emperors 可解释成"按历朝皇帝的传统"。但若该饭店说自己长期按历朝皇帝的传统提供服务,可能给人以陈旧过时的感觉,故译者稍加引申,译成"体现出华贵的皇家风范",立即给人以富丽堂皇、气派非凡的印象。

(五) 习惯表达法引申

习惯表达法浸透一种浓厚的文化底蕴和积淀,其内涵意义非常丰富,译者须仔细揣摩,并根据需要适当加以引申,才能确切传达原文的要旨。

1. The President contemplates retiring with **a hand on the helm**.
主席打算退位,不过**依然参事听政**。

helm 作"船舵"解,说某人 at the helm 或 take over the helm,就表示这个人"居于掌权或领导地位"。主席打算退位,"但仍要有一只手放在舵上",意即他仍要在国务决策中起支配作用,可引申为"依然参事听政"。

2. China joined the growing list of Asian nations **turning their backs on American aircraft-makers.**
亚洲越来越多的国家**不再订购美国制造的飞机**,中国也加入了这个行列。

turn one's back on something or someone 表示对某种事物或某个人的"背弃""抛弃""轻视"或"拒绝"。根据语境,可将其引申成"不再订购(美国制造的飞机)"。

3. All these ideas are **low-hanging fruit** and something most organizations could quite easily have a go at.
这些想法都是**比较容易实现**的,而且大部分组织都能轻松上手。

果树上总有一些树枝是动物和人类不用费劲就能够到的,挂在这些树枝上的果实或许没有高在枝头的那些果实诱人或成熟,但它们数量多且更易摘取。从这一事实便可以引出这个广泛使用的表达 low-hanging fruit,通常指仅用最少的精力就能轻易实现的目标。

4. Resettlement countries, suffering **"compassion fatigue"** years

after the end of the Vietnam War and faced with their own domestic socio-economic pressures, have also indicated a lower resettlement rate in future.

越南战争已经结束多年,难民接受国**对难民再也同情不起来了**。这些国家因各自面临的社会和经济压力,都表示今后要减少接受难民安置数量。

compassion fatigue 较难处理。有一工程技术术语 metal fatigue,通译成"金属疲劳",指的是金属因张力过度而损裂。但"同情疲劳"的说法在汉语里却不宜,因而需要做上述的引申。

5. Rich and poor, black and white, young and old, Virginians by the thousands lined up last week at courthouses and police stations seeking permits for carrying concealed weapons. **The common denominator** was fear of crime.

上星期成千上万的弗吉尼亚人,不分贫富、肤色和年龄,在法院或警察局门口排起长队,申请可随身携带武器的许可证。**他们这样做出于一个共同的原因**:对犯罪事件不断上升感到恐惧。

句中的 The common denominator 原是数学上的一个术语(即公分母),在此可引申成为"共同点"或"共同行为(态度)"等一类意义。

6. Many senior officers believe that expanding the roles of women to infantry units and other direct-combat jobs **would disrupt the cohesion of fighting forces** and could compromise readiness of the US military.

许多高级军官认为,把女性在军队后勤二线所担当的职责扩展到步兵单位及其他直接作战的岗位,**会使作战部队乱了阴阳**,有可能削弱美军的临战能力。

句中 disrupt the cohesion of fighting forces 若按一般的翻译处理,可能会产生这样的汉语表述:"破坏作战部队的聚合力"。这样的译文当然表面上也勉强过得去,但毕竟没有完整传达出其要义,因此需要做出上句那样的引申。

7. Food was food, hunger was hunger, and his half-empty belly and the perfume of roast meat established a rapport that it would

take the Devil to cut in two.

食物归食物，饥饿还是饥饿；他那只填饱了一半的肚皮和那烤肉的香味之间建立的亲善关系，只有**魔鬼才能割断**。

如果把 cut in two 按字面意义译为"分割成两半"，不仅文理欠通（关系不可能具体割成几段），用词也不简练。为提供较理想的译文，译者用"魔鬼才能割断"进行了整体的考虑和引申。

（六）句义的引申

某些句子也不能按字面意义来翻译，须结合语境和汉语表达习惯加以引申。例如：

1. Look, we're not tennis people. We wouldn't **feel right** there. I wouldn't **feel right** there.

   听我说，我们不是网球圈里的人。那儿不是我们去的地方，也不是我去的地方。

   后两句若直译为"我们在那儿会感到不好，我在那儿会感到不好"，意思模糊，令人费解。译者根据上下文，把句子意义做了引申，确切地表达了原文的含义。

2. That doesn't worry me as much as that **sullen look**, as though she's going to get out a razor.

   我觉得最可怕的还是她那副**凶狠的模样**，就好像马上要掏出一把剃刀把你宰了似的。

   如果译者不把 sullen look 在句义上引申和后边的"宰"就连不起来，就不能忠实地体现原文的内容和神韵。

3. The leader publicly insinuated that he possessed **compromising information** about Mr Obama that was liable to harm his bid for the White House.

   这位领导人公开表示，他掌握着有关奥巴马先生的**负面材料**。这些材料一旦公开，会危及奥巴马为入主白宫而参加的竞选活动。

   compromise 意思为"妥协"和"损害"，也可表示"放弃""改变""修正""修改"等，但在此处 compromising information 似可解释为"对某人不利的情报、情况",引申为负面材料。

三、词义的褒贬

英汉两种语言的词义都有褒贬之分(complementary or derogative terms)。当原文中有些词本身就表示褒或贬意义时,就应该把相应褒贬意义恰如其分地表达出来;当有些词语孤立地看似乎是中性意义时,汉译时也要视上下文准确、忠实地把它们的褒义或贬义表达出来。

(一) 传达原文本身含有的褒贬意义

英语句子中有些词本身含有褒贬意义,汉译时要用相应的词语表达出来。如:

1. Your country is a consistent and resolute **champion** of all the peoples who struggle against terrorism.
   贵国坚定不移地始终**站在**反恐**前列**。
2. It is the **champion** of apartheid.
   它是导致种族隔离的**罪魁祸首**。
3. Mary always gets what she wants by playing **office politics**.
   玛丽总靠耍**手腕**来达到其目的。
4. The arrogant policeman is very **humble** towards his superiors.
   那个傲慢无礼的警察对上司**奴颜婢膝**。
5. Mr. Carter has **engineere**d a radical change in the management of his chain stores, which survived a bankrupt.
   卡特先生对连锁店的管理**精心**进行了一番彻底改革,使之起死回生。

(二) 视上下文传达褒贬意义

一般而言,英语中的褒义词或贬义词远比汉语少,因此英译汉时,词的褒贬大多靠上下文决定,这就要求初学者做出正确判断。这类可褒可贬的词有:

results(褒:成果;贬:苦果)
plot(褒:故事;贬:阴谋)
trick(褒:窍门;贬:诡计)
clever(褒:聪明;贬:狡猾)
story(褒:新闻;贬:谎话)

future（褒：前途；贬：下场）

As luck would have it.（褒：很走运；贬：真倒霉）

在任何一种语言中，词语都可能带有一定的感情色彩，或褒或贬或中性，译文的褒贬必须以原文的立场为基础，而不能以译者的个人感情为标准。请比较下面的句子：

1. Sex and sin **make a comeback** in Las Vegas.
   色情和罪恶在拉斯维加斯**卷土重来**。

2. This man came with a good recommendation from his last job, but it turns out he's just **a turkey** who simply can't do anything right!
   这个人来的时候，他以前的工作单位还给他写了很好的推荐信。可是，他原来是个**笨蛋**，什么都干不好。

3. Should the couples split up or **stay together** for the sake of the kids?
   这样的夫妻应该离异，还是为了孩子**凑合过下去**？

4. The **unexamined** life is not worth living.
   浑浑噩噩的日子不值得过。

5. My dear girls, I am **ambitious** for you, but not to have you make a dash in the world—marry rich men merely because they are rich, or have splendid houses, which are not homes because love is wanting
   亲爱的姑娘们，我对你们**期望很高**，可并不是叫你们在世上出人头地——要你们去嫁给富人，仅仅因为他们有钱，有奢华的住房，缺少爱情的话，豪华的住房算不上家。

ambitious 既可表示"雄心壮志的"，也可表示"野心勃勃的"，这里选用褒义词"期望很高"翻译比较妥当。

附一 课堂讲练材料

1. Vladivostok is gradually ending its hermetic existence, receiving increasing numbers of foreign visitors each year. They still come only on

special invitations, but even this trickle of outsiders is enough to tax the city's modest tourist infrastructure.
2. A legion of con men and contraband specialists are taxing Germany's ability to police its newly acquired eastern borders.
3. Farmers migrated in droves to Seoul in search of higher paying jobs and better education for their children. Over the past eight years for example the country's farmers have dropped from 27% to only 18% of the total population. Such hectic growth taxes Seoul and most of the city's urban problems ultimately trace their cause to its population surge.
4. They have their smiles and tears.
5. Some analysts speculate that aircraft acquisitions and a plethora of new routes have severely taxed the airline's financial resources.
6. The situation taxes the ingenuity of the party's reform-minded leaders.
7. The man was lured to a north London house and secretly filmed in a compromising position with the woman.
8. Inspectors would burst into her room at 2 a.m., seeking to catch her in a compromising position.
9. Former US assistant secretary of State for East Asian and Pacific Affairs Richard Holbrooke, in an article for "Foreign Affairs", coinciding with the Pearl Harbour anniversary, argues that: "Japanese are always quick to remind the rest of the world how resource-poor and vulnerable they are."
10. Through luck rather than foresight, I was in Tuman for the year's biggest festival, held on the 15th day of the lunar New Year, to coincide with the first full moon.
11. There is a flurry of hotel construction in metropolitan Manila, unmatched since 1976, when seven new hotels opened to coincide with the annual IMF-World Bank meetings held there.
12. Shenzhen officials are pushing to turn the SEZ into a free trade zone, and are upgrading its port facilities to help cope with the rapid surge in imports and exports it expects.
13. The contract, expected to be signed on the next few months,

represents one of the biggest-ever foreign arms acquisitions by the army, and will help to upgrade its air defense and power-projection capabilities.

14. Shanghai's ambitious plans for an economic renaissance through the development of the Pudong economic zone hang on its ability to raise billions of dollars to upgrade the city's falling transport system.

15. Last year the government (of Malaysia) earmarked substantial funds to upgrade the country's infrastructure.

16. The six-month conflict between Amenia and Azerbajian has sparked mass rallies, strikes and ethnic violence that have kept the Caucasus on the boil since February.

17. Streamlining the work force will make industry more efficient, but it could spark unrest among workers who fear being laid off.

18. The movement has sparked a confrontation between rich industrial nations, which are fresh converts to the environmental cause, and the poorer nations of the Third World, which view outside interference as an assault on their sovereignty.

19. American farm lenders are concerned that last year's agricultural recovery made possible by a shower of federal dollars will be aborted because of the drought.

20. Doctors at a special burns and plastic surgery unit here were trying yesterday to save 10 critically injured victims of the Ramstein air show disaster who were showered with blazing fuel from a crushing aircraft.

21. It was an occasion for journalists to shower questions.

22. Yet when my husband's brother had a boy, she showered him with attention.

23. The birth of the new commonwealth capped a year that turned Yeltsin from a discounted maverick into one of the great figures of modern history.

24. Beginning late November, Bush is likely to visit Japan, South Korea, Australia and Indonesia—capping the trip with a stopover on 7 December in Honolulu for ceremonies marking the 50th anniversary of Japan's attack on Pearl Harbor.

25. At that time nobody were aware of his ambition to break away from the Union.
26. Many famous people are surprisingly humble.
27. The coup-d'etat was engineered by the military backed right-wing faction.
28. I am no Hamlet.
29. The old man said he was an Epicurean for all his life.
30. His income derived from illicit activities—bookmaking, gambling, shylocking, and questionable union activities.

附二　课外扩展训练材料

Lake of Autumn

I remember quite clearly now when the story happened. The autumn leaves were floating in measure down to the ground, recovering the lake, where we used to swim like children, under the sun was there to shine. That time we used to be happy. Well, I thought we were. But the truth was that you had been longing to leave me, not daring to tell me. On that precious night, watching the lake, vaguely conscious, you said: Our story is ending.

The rain was killing the last days of summer; you have been killing my last breath of love since a long time ago. I still don't think I'm gonna make it through another love story. You took it all away from me. And there I stand, I knew I was going to be the one left behind. But still I'm watching the lake, vaguely conscious, and I know my life is ending.

(Crazy English)

第二节　转译法

英语和汉语在词类构成方面有很大的不同。比如,英语有动名词、不定式、关系代词等,汉语则没有这类词。即使两种语言都有的词类,其功能也不尽相同,所以有时要确切地表达原文的内容必须转换词类。转换不是"偷梁换柱"。翻译中,恰如其分地进行转译(conversion)是常用的基本手段。

一、转译成动词

汉语动词灵活多变,其使用频率比英语高,即使一个短句子也可能出现多个动词,例如"请你陪我去走走去看看。"其中"请""陪""去走走""去看看"都是动词。动词多是汉语的一大特点,也是与英语最大的区别之一。英语句法要求每个句子只能有一个谓语动词,因此英语中不少词类,尤其是名词、前置词(也称介词)、形容词、副词在汉译时往往可以转译成动词。

(一) 名词转译成动词

1. Arrogance and complacence turned out to be his **ruin**.
   骄傲自满最终**毁**了他。
2. He says of his **plan** to stand atop a 2-foot-wide pillar standing nearly 10 stories tall in New York City for two days and two nights, with no food, water, sleep, and nothing to sit or lean on.
   他说他**计划**在纽约市一根近10层楼高、2英尺宽的柱子上站立两天两夜,其间不吃、不喝、不睡、不坐也不靠。
3. In some cases, deserts are the **creation** of **destruction** of virgin forest.
   有些沙漠是人为**毁坏**原始森林**造成**的。
4. **Access** to Internet is very simple.
   上因特网很简单。
5. Good **throw** / **catch** / **jump**!
   扔 / **抓** / **跳**得好!

(二) 形容词转译成动词

表示知觉、感情、欲望等心理状态的形容词与系词在一起构成的复合谓语,汉译时均可转译成汉语动词。此类形容词有:

afraid	担心	angry	生气
sure	确信	doubtful	怀疑
familiar	熟悉	ignorant	不知道
grateful	感谢	sorry	遗憾
tired	厌倦	ashamed	惭愧

surprised　　　吃惊　　　　discouraged　　气馁

1. The program was not **popular** with all of the troops.
   部队里并非所有人都**喜欢**这个计划。
2. Are you **satisfied** that he is telling the truth?
   你**确信**他讲的是真话吗?
3. I am **anxious** to learn another foreign language.
   我**渴望**再学一门外语。
4. His parliamentary career was **stormy**.
   他的议员生涯**充满曲折**。

(三) 前置词转译成动词

英语中大量使用的介词,汉译时常常可以译成汉语动词。

1. Dabord said he shot Dele **in** self-defense.
   德伯德辩称他是**出于**自卫才向戴乐开枪。
2. Now ten years later, she has gained her master's degree from Harvard's School of Education and is finally **off** welfare.
   十年后的今天,她获得了哈佛大学教育学院硕士学位,而且终于**摆脱**了救济。
3. After the marriage, Michael adopted Linda's son **by** a former boyfriend.
   婚后,麦克收养了琳达与前男友**所生**的儿子。
4. We are **inside** two marriages.
   我们**在观察**两对夫妻。
5. **After** a 45-minute hike **in** darkness, they finally make their camp. Flashlights and shoes are collected, just in case anyone has thoughts of running away.
   经过45分钟**摸黑**行军,他们终于到达了宿营地。手电和鞋子被收缴了,让他们死了逃跑的心。

许多介词短语常常可以译成汉语动词,如:

　　by means of　　　利用
　　in place of　　　代替
　　in praise of　　　赞扬

in quest of　　　　　寻找
with a high hand　　　用高压手段
for the support of　　 抚养

(四) 副词转译成动词

1. He'll jump **off** the pillar on live TV.

   他将在电视现场转播中纵身**跳下**柱子。

2. Let me **through**.

   让我**过去**。

3. The librarian told me that the book was **out**.

   图书管理员告诉我，那本书**借出去**了。

4. Our machine is **down**.

   我们的机器**坏了**。

5. We are two days **ahead of** schedule.

   我们比原计划**提前**了两天。

6. Pursue your object, be it what it will, **steadily and indefatigably**.

   不管追求什么目标，都应**坚持不懈**。

二、转译成名词

(一) 动词转译成名词

英语中有一些动词的含义难以用汉语动词准确表达，可以考虑转换成汉语名词进行翻译。

1. The ten-year-old girl **behaves** as if she were an adult.

   那个十岁小女孩的**举止**像个成年人。

2. Jane is diabetic and has **survived** breast cancer.

   珍妮有糖尿病，还是乳腺癌的**幸存者**。

3. Edison **patented** over one thousand separate inventions during his life.

   爱迪生一生申请到一千多项发明**专利**。

4. The entire transmitting setup **weighs** less than 3 pounds and runs on rechargeable batteries.

   整个传输装置的**重量**不足3英镑且仅依靠充电电池运行。

5. The murder was **motivated** by deep hatred.
   谋杀**动机**是深仇大恨。

(二) 形容词转译成名词

1. He was found **unconscious** on a Mexican beach, in a coma from an apparent overdose.
   他在墨西哥海岸被人发现时已失去了**知觉**,明显因用药过量而昏迷。
2. Thus a **symbolic** representation of the human world was a cross within a circle.
   于是,中间画着一个十字的圆圈便成了人类世界的**象征**。
3. Glass is more **transparent** than plastic cloth.
   玻璃的**透明性**比塑料布高。
4. The electrical appliances made in China are **competitive** in the world market.
   中国制造的电器产品在国际市场上很有**竞争力**。
5. Tom is **courageous**, **ambitious**, but unintelligent.
   汤姆有**勇气**,有**雄心**,但不怎么聪明。

英语中有一些名词化的形容词,前面加定冠词就可以转换成类名词,表示"……的人或物",译成汉语时转换成名词"人、子、者、员、的"(均为复数名词)等。如:

> Steinbeck defended **the poor** and **the oppressed**.
> 斯坦贝克替**穷人**讲话,为**受压迫者**代言。

又如:

the injured	伤员	the busy	忙碌的人;大忙人
the unemployed	失业者	the needy	有困难的人;穷人
the oppressed	被压迫者	the educated	受过教育的
the uneducated	未受过教育的	the blind	盲人;瞎子
the handicapped	残疾人	the brave	勇士

请注意,当形容词转译成名词时,修饰形容词的英语副词则转译成相应的汉语形容词,如:the better educated 受过良好教育的人。

(三) 副词转译成名词

1. It is **officially** announced that the unemployment rate will get lower next year.
   官方宣称明年失业率会有所降低。

2. He is strong **physically**, but weak **mentally**.
   他体力强，但智力弱。

3. Sodium is very active **chemically**.
   金属钠化学反应很活跃。

4. It is as **morally** hard to turn her away as it is a lost dog.
   从道义上讲，很难将她赶走，就像很难赶走一条丧家犬一样。

三、转译成形容词

(一) 动词转译成形容词

1. Let me see if it **fits**.
   让我瞧瞧它是否合适。

2. The rotten meat **stinks**.
   腐肉很臭。

3. Little islands **stud** the lake.
   湖内小岛星罗棋布。

(二) 名词转译成形容词

英语名词前加冠词或指示代词时，有时可转译成汉语形容词。

1. In all this great **serenity** of ocean it is seldom that we espy as much as another ship.
   在广袤宁静的大海上难得看见其他船只。

2. I can note the **grace** of her gesture.
   我注意到她优雅的手势。

3. It is a **pleasure** to see you.
   见到你真高兴。

4. I am deeply impressed by the **beauty** of the Summer Palace.
   美丽的颐和园给我留下了深刻的印象。

(三) 副词转译成形容词

1. She chirped, blinking her eyes **happily**.
   她叽叽喳喳地说着，两眼闪着**快乐**的光芒。
2. **Hopefully**, the research project can be completed on time.
   按时完成这项研究工作是**有希望的**。
3. It is **commonly** believed that women are the ones who love to spread rumours, and gossip about their friends behind their backs.
   普遍的观点是，女人爱散播谣言，爱在背后议论朋友。
4. Australians held an acrimonious debate in 1999 on whether or not to dump the queen, but **eventually** voted to keep the monarchy.
   1999年澳大利亚人对于是否脱离女王而进行了一场激烈的辩论，**最终的**表决结果是维持君主制。

四、转译成副词

当英语名词转译成汉语动词时，则修饰名词的英语形容词自然转译成相应的汉语副词。

1. With **slight** modification each type can be used for all three systems.
   每种型号只要**稍加**改动就能用于这三种系统。
2. He had a **careful** study of the map before he started off.
   他出发前**仔细地**研究了地图。
3. **Special** care should be taken when handling flammable materials.
   使用易燃材料要**格外**小心。
4. In the morning when you pick them up out of the crib and they're **happy** to see you.
   清晨，把他们从婴儿床里抱出来时，他们会**很开心地**望着你。
5. He has a **persistent** cough.
   他**不停地**在咳嗽。

五、代词的转译

翻译实践中常常要求对原文的代词根据语境、搭配或文体的需要进行省译或转译,即译为其他的代词或名词。如:

1. Man errs as long as **he** strives. 失误是进取的代价。

代词 he 省译后语言简明扼要。

2. Victory won't come to **me** unless I go to it.
胜利是不会向**我们**走来的,**我们**必须自己走向胜利。

此处将 me 转译成复数,针对范围更广,且更具名言特征。

3. **We** often seem to mix our senses in everyday language. We may describe a "sweet" voice, "bitter" cold, or a "warm" color. Most of us do not really mean that **we** can taste a sound or feel a color, however.
人们在日常语言中常将味觉、嗅觉、听觉、视觉和触觉混为一谈,比如用"甜"来描写声音,用"苦"来形容寒冷,用"暖"来表示颜色。**他们**的意思并不是说**他们**真的能品尝到一种声音是甜还是苦,或是能触摸到一种颜色是冷还是暖。

4. You'll find **us** caring, practical, comfortable, not fancy.
一旦入住本店,您会发现**本店**服务体贴周到,经营经验丰富,环境舒适宜人,收费合理。

5. Afterwards, **one** can go out into the charming grounds. One may sun oneself on the turf of the spacious lawns, or stroll by the lily-pond and then enter the little wood that half surrounds it.
而后,你置身于景色迷人的庭园里,可以躺在大草坪上沐浴阳光,也可以在百合花池畔信步漫游,然后走进半绕着池塘的一小片树林。

6. "I can always tell a graduate class from an undergraduate class," observed the instructor in one of **my** graduate engineering courses at California State University in Los Angeles. "When I say 'Good afternoon', the undergraduate

respond 'Good afternoon'. But the graduate students just write it down."

"研究生班和本科生班很容易就能区别开来。"在洛杉矶加利福尼亚州立大学给**我们研究生**上工程学课的老师如是说,"我说'下午好',本科生们回答说'下午好';研究生们则把我说的话记在笔记本上。"

7. If **you** think **you** are fat, **you** probably are. Do not ask **us**.
   如果你们女人觉得自己胖,那么你大概就是胖。不要过来问**我们男人**。

六、指示代词的转译

在翻译指代关系时,译文有时要"张冠李戴"才符合译入语的习惯。除对人及实体的指示功能外,指示代词 that 和 those 还有承上的作用,而 this 和 these 亦有启下的功能,翻译时应引起充分注意。

1. **That**'s right.
   这就对了。

2. **That**'s the end of the program.
   到**此**为止。

3. **That**'s where you are wrong.
   这就是你不对的地方。

4. **Those** are the problems we want to solve.
   这些就是我们想解决的问题。

5. You have to believe in yourself. **That**'s the secret of success.
   人必须自信,**这**是成功的秘诀。

6. My idea is **this**.
   我的想法是**这样的**。

7. For **these** reasons we've decided to cancel the trip.
   我们决定取消此次旅行,理由**如下**。

8. **This** is VOA.
   这里是"美国之音"对您广播。

9. Is this the bus we want? —Yes, That's it.
   这是我们要上的车吗?——**没错**。

英译汉实践中,词性的转换及词语的转换是多种多样的,绝不仅限于以上介绍的几种。同一个词或同一句话,由于处理方法不同,也可能有不同的转译方法。

附一　课堂讲练材料

1. When it comes to recycling, Germans are the world champions.
2. Four years after the launch of the British Government's National Childcare Strategy, there is still only one childcare place for every seven children under eight.
3. To be or not to be married, that was the question.
4. The media exposure of the economical scandals fueled further infighting of the Democratic Party.
5. If one considers the enormous variety of courses offered, it is not hard to see how difficult it is for a student to select the course most suited to his interests and abilities.
6. For example, great efforts are made by the American tobacco industry to sell cigarettes in the Middle East and North Africa where U. S. tobacco exports increased by more than 27 percent.
7. To choose such a line of work is to invite ridicule.
8. And there is also the objection that the city has always been the core from which cultural advancement radiated.
9. More than twenty years ago an American oceanographer, John Isaacs, brought forward the idea of towing icebergs from the Antarctic regions to the drier centers of the world.
10. They are a lot more skeptical when their "pharmacy team" gives them unsolicited advice.
11. And each stunt has an increased amount of danger to keep it interesting.
12. His company's new ball is also more precise and features a "softer" touch.
13. The audience wants all different things.
14. The so called Fevernova model, designed specially for the 2002 World

Cup, is 25 percent more precise and 10 percent faster than Adidas' 1998 match ball, the Tricolor.
15. Hardy also said parents should keep in mind that each of their children has good and bad qualities.
16. Not everyone who is exposed to MMA has an adverse reaction, and some manufacturers say the chemical is no more dangerous than other nail products.
17. Almost every couple fights at some point—about anything from dirty dishes and socks left on the floor to bigger problems of trust and communication.
18. With five cameras and 300 hours of footage, *Primetime* took an unprecedented look into the inner world of two volatile American families.
19. Psychologists have long understood that parental fighting can be toxic to a child's emotional well-being. But new research goes further, suggesting the wounds are both psychic and physical.
20. The skeleton is evidence their common ancestor is "more ancient than we thought".
21. Les and Shannon were high-school sweethearts who were pregnant with their oldest son before their senior prom.
22. She was seeking a single-mom roommate.
23. Once content is available in downloaded and compressed form, it's easier to share—and harder to control.
24. Eight-year-old Tom was born without an ear.
25. As digital entertainment choices grow, industry experts note that consumers will need new ways of finding the glut of diversions.
26. At a busy U.S. airport, those mistakes could mean a thousand passengers a day who would get pulled aside by security, a move that would probably mean lots of missed flights and irate passengers.
27. To prevent their digital programs from being perfectly copied and distributed by pirates, Hollywood studios want digital protection schemes in place.
28. Convinced that he was "a messianic figure of great but secret importance", he frantically scanned *The New York Times* for encoded messages from

aliens, and fiddled with radio dials to pick up signals from space.
29. They worked long hours on meagre food, in cold caves and by dim lamp.

附二　课外扩展训练材料

Animal Athletes

The camel is a slow-moving creature. But what it lacks in speed it gains in stamina. This veritable beast of burden can walk 30 miles a day carrying a load that weighs half a ton.

The kangaroo, with its long, muscular hind legs, is a marvel of fitness. Weighing about 200 pounds, it can thrust its heavy body into the air and clear a fence nine feet high. While airborne, this leaping marsupial uses its thick tail as both a counterbalance and a rudder.

Never underestimate the strength of an insect. The tiny ant can boost burden 50 times its weight. And the brawny bee, when tethered to a small load on wheels, is able to haul up to 300 times its own weight.

The elephant is the monument to muscles. Its trunk alone, which can do everything from bulldozing a tree to delicately picking up a pin, contains amazing 40,000 about 70 times the number of muscles in your body.

One of the world's longest leapers is the flea: it can jump 13 inches—about 350 times its own length. For a person 6 feet tall, this would be like jumping approximately 2,000 feet, or almost seven football fields. No one yet has leaped even as much as 30 feet.

A seemingly inexhaustible jumper is the oriental rat flea: it can jump 600 times an hour for three whole days without stopping.

The fastest muscle movement ever recorded belongs to the mighty midge. This tiny, agile insect can beat its wings 133,000 times a minute, about 100 times faster than a human can blink an eye—which takes all of one twenty-fifth of a second.

By land, air or sea, birds are masters of locomotion. The ostrich outruns any animal on two legs, carrying its 300-pound body at 30 miles an hour. The fight of the Indian swift sometimes exceeds 100 mph. The gentoo penguin, by at least one account, can swim 22 mph. At this speed, the penguin keeps pace with one of the fastest-swimming marine mammals, the dolphin.

(*The World of English*)

第三节 增益法

增益法(amplification)又称增词法(addition)。常听人说"无加减则无数学",套用这句话来概括翻译,即"无加减则无翻译"。翻译中常用的减词法是翻译的减法,而增益法就是翻译的加法。增益法的目的旨在使译文的语法结构、表达方式、修辞、语气以及文化思想和思维方式既保持"洋腔洋调",又符合汉语表达习惯,且更能突显语义。不过,增益并非随意"添油加醋",而是增加原文虽无但有其义的词、词组或句子。

一、根据意义或修辞上的需要

(一) 增补名词

在部分英语名词或动名词前后增补汉语名词是一种常用的翻译处理手段。

1. Even countries with large populations like Britain and the United States are seriously considering imitating the Swedish.
   甚至连人口众多的美国和英国之类的**国家**也在认真考虑仿效瑞典的**这种做法**。

2. In order to improve a certain kind of battery, Edison spent almost ten years and made nearly 50,000 experiments.
   为了改善某种电池的**性能**,爱迪生花费了近十年时间,做了近50,000 次实验。

3. He has difficulty in sleeping, inability to concentrate.
   他不易入睡,也难以集中**注意力**。

4. According to *National Geographic*, archaeologists transformed the town into a dig.
   按国家地理学会提出的**要求**,考古工作者们把整个小城变成了考古挖掘**现场**。

5. Drug companies are paying pharmacies to promote products.
   药材公司出**钱**请药店促销。

增补名词的情况在科技文献翻译中经常遇到,初学者应根据上下文和科技常识,增补恰当的汉语名词。常增补的汉语名词有"方法、技术、现象、效应、作用、局势、状态、化、方案、系统、情绪、部门、工作、结果……"例如:

confusion	混乱局面
saturation	饱和状态
derivation	推导过程
recycling	废物回收利用
measurement	测量方法;测量结果
preparation	准备工作
management	管理部门
redundancy	多余信息
normalization	正常状态
remedies	补救措施
solution	解决方案
modification	修改方案
advantage	有利地位
complacency	自满情绪

(二) 增补动词

根据意义上的需要,可以在名词前后增补动词。如 In the evening after the banquet, the concert and the table tennis exhibition, he worked on the drafting of the final communique. 译成"晚上在**参加**宴会,**出席**音乐会,**观看**乒乓球表演之后,他还得起草最后公报。"此句在名词前增加原文中虽无其词而有其意的动词,形成三个动宾词组。如此处理,意思明确,读起来比较通顺自然,符合汉语习惯。试比较下列句子:

1. He dismissed the meeting without a closing speech.
   他没有致闭幕词就**宣布**结束会议。

2. After the football match, the chairman has got an important meeting.
   观看足球比赛以后,主席要**参加**一个重要会议。

3. Brains or beauty? Women still conflicted.
   要**智慧**还是要**容貌**？女人很矛盾。
4. This was a record increase.
   这是**破**纪录的增长。

无论是文学翻译,还是科技文献翻译,都经常需要增补汉语动词,如"产生,使,加,引起,调整,进行,发生,陷入……"。翻译初学者可根据上下文的具体情况,依靠已掌握的常识性知识,增补恰当的汉语动词。例如：

programming	编写程序
after the concert	出席音乐会之后
No tipping	不收小费
instrumentation	研制仪器；使用仪器

(三) 增补形容词

1. Las Vegas seemed tired, and needed to find a way to set itself apart from the rival gambling establishments that were popping up across the country.
   拉斯维加斯似乎累了倦了,需要找到一条**新**路子,以区别于美国风起云涌咄咄逼人的博彩新秀。
2. They would much rather be citizens than subjects, he said.
   他说,他们宁愿做**有选举权的**市民也不愿做**受人支配的**臣仆。
3. When I watch Ronaldo's moves, our goal seems pretty hopeless.
   看到罗纳尔多**绝妙的**踢球动作时,我感到我们要达到同样的水平,似乎没有希望。
4. Warren Buffett's investment philosophy is impressively simple: Don't lose capital.
   沃伦·巴菲特的投资哲学简单得令人咋舌：切莫蚀掉**老**本。
5. The agency soon moved him from forgery to disguises like mustaches and wigs, which were fairly crude back then in the 1960s.
   很快,中央情报局要他停止造假,改搞化装,如用**假**胡子、**假**发,而20世纪60年代这些东西的制作相当粗糙。

6. Consumption of wines and spirits picked up again before the New Year.
   色酒和白酒的消费量在新年到来之际再一次呈上升趋势。

7. Spend a dime, save your time.
   花点小钱,省您时间。

8. The price of food is soaring.
   食品价格飞涨。

(四) 增补概括性的词

1. The advantages of the meeting room are bright, spacious, fashionable and without echoes.
   这个会议室有**四大优点**:明亮、宽敞、时髦、无回声。

2. The Americans and the Russians have undergone series of secret consultations.
   美俄**双方**已进行了一系列的秘密磋商。

3. The husband and wife agreed to give another try.
   夫妻**俩**同意再试试。

4. American women are more concerned about losing weight than they are about suffering from cancer, heart disease or diabetes, a survey showed.
   一项调查显示,与癌症、心脏病和糖尿病**三大问题**相比,美国女性更关心减肥问题。

(五) 增补解释性的词

由于两种语言与文化以及思维方式的差异,英译汉过程中须做一定的增补,以使原文信息不会在译文中有所缺失或脱节,再现原文。

1. Those were the words that were to make the world blossom for me, "like Aaron's rod, with flowers".
   这些词把一个美好的世界绽放在我面前,**正如圣经上说的一样**:"像亚伦的手杖,开出了美丽的花"。

2. One should love animals. They are so tasty.
   每个人都应该热爱动物,**因为**它们很好吃。

3. The rushing of these school boys was pardonable, but costly.

这些男生的莽撞行为是可以谅解的,但是**为此付出的代价**却是昂贵的。

4. The man who waters his grass after a good rain is carrying coals to Newcastle.
   刚下一场及时雨,那人却又为草坪浇水,真是把煤运到纽卡斯尔,**多此一举**。(纽卡斯尔是英国煤都)

5. "Oh! Tell us about her. Auntie," cried Imogen. "I can just remember her. She's the skeleton in the family cupboard, isn't she?"
   "哦,给我们讲一讲她的事儿吧,好姑姑,"伊莫根嚷嚷道,"我几乎记不得她了,她是咱们家衣橱里的骷髅,**丑得见不得人**,是吧?"

(六)增补承上启下的词

为使译文行文流畅不涩耳,翻译时有必要增补一定的词以实施承上启下的功能。

1. East or west, home is best.
   东好西好,**还是**家最好。

2. Theory is something but practice is everything.
   理论**固然**必要,实践**尤其**重要。

3. Water shortages are a global problem, especially in big cities.
   缺水是一个全球性的问题,大城市**尤为如此**。

4. Survey finds what British women really want in Mr Right. He should be clean-shaven, good-looking and drive a silver Mercedes. And, most important of all, he should be more than 178cm.
   调查发现英国女性心目中的白马王子是什么样子的。他必须刮光胡子,长相要英俊,**最好再**开一辆银色奔驰,最重要的是身高至少要有1米78。

5. When the play was over, the Mayor went up to the stage, shaking hands with the actors and offering his congratulations.
   演出一结束,市长走上舞台,与全体演员一一握手,并祝贺演出成功。

二、根据语法结构方面的需要

(一) 增补以符合汉语语法及汉语表达习惯

在翻译英语不及物动词、动词时态、名词复数、不定冠词以及英语语法允许的省略时,必须依据汉语语法和表达习惯做必要的增补。

1. Old wood best to burn, old wine to drink, old friend to trust, and old authors to read.
   干燥的木头**最**易燃烧,陈年的老酒**最**为好喝,多年的朋友**最**值信任,经典的作品**最**值品读。

2. Say you're afraid of heights, you climb higher and higher, you get exposed and you see nothing awful is going to happen to you. You're afraid the market is going to collapse, you go out and you spend money.
   如果你恐高,**那就**去爬高,你去经历了就会发现其实没什么危险。如果你害怕市场崩溃,**那就**出去花钱吧。

3. Without water, there could be no life on the earth.
   假如地球没有水,就不可能有生命。

4. If I were there!
   我要是在那儿,**就好了**!

5. White lies don't hurt.
   善意的谎言不会伤害**谁**。

6. The nickname stuck to him.
   这个绰号跟随他**多年**。

(二) 增补副词、语气助词或数量词

英汉两种语言的表达差异很大,英译汉中常遇到原语所无但汉语所有的表现手段,特别是汉语的补充副词、语气助词以及数量词。若能准确运用汉语这些常用的表现手段,译文会更加贴近译文读者,并能增加译文语句的表现力。

1. In this mind, I went to diplomatic circles, earnest but only sketchily informed.
   我怀着这种心情进入外交界,满腔热忱,但是知识肤浅**得很**。

2. He said to Essex, "I didn't think you would hold me for political ransom. So nakedly, anyway."

   他**照直**对厄塞克斯说:"想不到你**居然**对我搞政治绑票,至少想不到你会做得如此赤裸裸。"

3. The dense fog melted away.

   浓雾**渐渐**散开了。

4. Take it easy. I'm just kidding.

   不要紧张**嘛**,我不过是开个玩笑**罢了**。

5. The more you learn, the more you know, the more you know, the more you forget. The more you forget, the less you know. So why bother to learn.

   学的越多,知道的越多,知道的越多,忘记的越多,忘记的越多,知道的越少,为什么学**来着**?

6. I'm the daddy and the mama.

   我**既**做爹**又**当妈。

7. Air is a mixture of gases.

   空气是**多种**气体的混合。

8. She finished the race on crutches.

   她拄着**双**拐跑完了比赛全程。

9. The two turbulent streams joined to form a clear, deep pool.

   两**弯**湍急的溪流汇聚在一起,形成了一**汪**清澈的深潭。

10. The taste is great.

    味道好**极**了。

(三) 增补以明确语义

表达习惯的不同要求在英译汉过程中根据上下文做适当的增补。试比较下列句子:

1. As he turned to take the ball, a dam burst against the side of his head and a hand grenade shattered his stomach.

   他正转身接球,**对方球员**"砰"地撞过来拦截,撞在他太阳穴这边,**紧接着**,又给他腹部狠命一拳。

2. When he moved his lips, he tasted the acid of dirt and grass and gravel.

他抿了抿嘴唇，尝到了泥土**夹杂着**青草和沙砾的那种酸味。

3. On the third play, he was hit simultaneously by three of them: one, his knees, another, his stomach, a third, his head—the helmet no protection at all.

   第三节比赛开局伊始，他就同时遭到三个人的围攻。第一个**对准**他的膝盖，第二个**对准**他的腹部，第三个**对准**他的头。他的头盔一点保护作用也没有。

4. Archie turned and smiled at him benevolently, like a goddam king passing out favors.

   阿奇转过脸，友善地对着他微笑，好像一个人神共愤的国王正在施舍小恩小惠，分发礼品。

三、根据文化交流层面的需要

(一) 为专有名词增补附加的文化信息

有些专有名词在原语文化中具有特殊的内涵，翻译时就该对其附加的文化信息进行说明，特别是翻译那些用作比喻的历史人物或地理位置的名称时。如：

1. ... they suggest the grim drawings of Dauminer.

   他们使人联想到**德国著名漫画家兼雕刻家**多米尔辛辣的讽刺画。

2. He flung himself down at little Osborn's feet and loved him. Even before they were acquainted, he had admired Osborn in secret. Now he was his dog, his man Friday.

   他拜倒在小奥斯本面前，死心塌地爱他。他没有认识奥斯本之前，已经暗暗佩服他，如今成了他的狗，他的**忠仆星期五**。

(二) 为典故增补文化信息

一般译语读者对原语典故的文化信息并非十分清楚，所以译者在翻译典故时常常会运用注释，例如：

In this house of his there was writing on every wall. His business-like temperament protested against a mysterious warning that she was not made for him.

在他的这座房子的墙上,到处都写着字,说她天生不是他的人;他的求实气质抗议这种神秘的警告。

由于 writing on every wall 是一典故,需要较多的文字才能解释得清楚,因此不宜把增补的信息放在句中,可以考虑这样放在尾注或脚注:《旧约·但以理书》第五章伯沙撒王受天谴事,预告即将来临的灾难:"当时忽有人的指头显示,在王宫与灯台相对的粉墙上写字……上帝已经数算你国的年月到此完毕。提客勒就是你被称在天平里显出你的亏欠。……当夜,迦勒底王伯沙撒被杀。"

(三) 为用第三语言写的词、词组或句子增补信息

有时原语作者会用另一种语言来书写某些词、词组或句子以达到某种特殊的效果。在翻译中,这种语言被称为第三语言。如果第三语言被直接译到译文中,其特殊的韵味就可能丢失,一部分原语的文化信息在译文中也可能随之丢失。在实际操作中,许多有经验的译员多采取保留第三语言并用注释法加以解释的方法。例如:

"...I believe it was that which made her part with me; and so thank Heaven for French. Vive La France! Vive I'Empereur! Vive Bonaparte!"

原文取自萨克雷的 *Vanity Fair* 第二章,对文中的法语,许多译家主张这样处理:"……我想这就是她让我离开学校的原因。真是感谢上天,法文真有用啊!Vive La France! Vive I'Empereur! Vive Bonaparte!"然后在尾注或脚注增补信息如下:这三句是法语,意为:"法国万岁!皇帝陛下万岁!波拿巴万岁!"

附一 课堂讲练材料

1. The Thompsons also received a letter, complete with a coupon. At the very bottom of the letter was a note, saying the invitation had been "provided by Astra".
2. But He's confident that the chips, which would cost device makers only "tens of dollars", could become pervasive within two or three years.
3. Carol's nails were her pride and joy: long, strong and beautiful.
4. Director George Lucas says he's just telling a tale.

5. "Okay, fight," and you fight and fight until he says "cut".
6. Another sign is the substance's pungent, bitter chemical smell, which can be strong enough to make one's eyes water.
7. We really made a very concerted effort to try and focus on all of the nongambling aspects of Las Vegas.
8. The Visitors Authority launched an intensive advertising campaign aimed at families.
9. Previous information on the Inca culture has come from scatterings of burials, most of only a few individuals, not enough to allow many firm conclusions about Inca ways.
10. Both recognize they may have gotten married too young, and they also struggle with issues of trust, communication, parenting, and the amount of time they spend together.
11. Sullivan figured there were probably more women in the same situation, so she started Co-Abode.com, which developed into a nationwide resource last year.
12. Its climbing ability may have given it an advantage over other mammals in its environment, although That's just speculation.
13. Faster, cheaper and more flicks?
14. One of the bundles included some 300 pounds of raw cotton, the body of an Inca noble and a baby, as well as 70 other items, including food, pottery, animal skins and corn to make a fermented drink known as chicha.
15. The tournament is more than fun and games.
16. The human walk is smooth.
17. I'm going to die anyway, so why drag this hell out? There's nothing good about life.
18. The tapes show other kids passively watching as bullies kick and punch victims.
19. Enter "Will Smith", and the digital hub will sort out from the many devices and "network" it's connected to.
20. Of my students, there are about five Frankensteins.
21. Part of the reason behind the range in comments may be that the

structure of the ball is so new—and perhaps unfamiliar.

22. Can a better ball help even the best play better?
23. So far the ball has gotten mixed reviews from players. Belgium's goalkeeping coach has complained the ball is "too light". Brazilian midfielder Rivaldo was quoted as saying the ball is "too big and too light".
24. Weather anomaly El Nino, blamed for searing droughts and devastating floods worldwide, is awakening from a four-year slumber, but how hard it will hit is unknown.
25. After regaling his listeners with box-office results, Nash joked that he hoped Universal was doing a better job of keeping its books than Enron.
26. One of the triplets is walking, another is crawling, and the third is sitting up. And all three are learning to say "Dada".
27. Blaylock's San Francisco startup, Hairogenics Inc., is offering to preserve the strands until science finds a better cure for baldness.
28. The costs of transportation and energy are the great equalizer.
29. Histories make men wise; poems witty; the mathematics subtle; natural philosophy deep; moral grave; logic and rhetoric able to contend.

附二 课外扩展训练材料

The Land and Its Limits

Once upon a time, the United States seemed to have plenty of land to go around. Plenty of rivers to dam and plenty of rural valleys left over. Plenty of space for parks and for cities. Plenty of forests to cut and grasslands to plow. But that was once upon a time. The days of unused land are over. Now the land has been spoken for, fenced off, carved up into cities and farms and industrial parks.

At the same time, the population keeps growing. People need places to work and places to play. So we need more sites for more industries, more beaches for more sun bathers, and more clean rivers for more fishers. And it isn't just a matter of population growth. Our modern technology has needs that must be met, too. We need more coal for energy, and we need more power plants; cars must have highways and parking lots, and jets must have airports.

Each of these land-uses swallows up precious space. Highways and expressways alone take some 200,000 acres each year. And urban sprawl—the spreading out of cities—is expected to gobble up vast areas of land by the year 2008. But there is only so much land to go around.

第四节　减词法

删减在作品的修改和润色过程中起着重要的作用。试比较：

修改前：兰克想把我从强迫自己写日记的状态中解脱出来，但他并不禁止我写小说。他鼓励我断断续续地记笔记，但没有必要去描写什么。然而当我给他看我对他的描写时，他却很高兴，和亨利以前一样。"毁掉日记！"他们说，"写小说吧！"但当他们看到我对他们的描写时，他们都说："好极了！"

修改后：兰克劝我不要强迫自己写日记，可适当写些小说，必要时做点笔记，但无须描写。不过读了我对他的描写后，他显得十分高兴，一如亨利。"别写日记了，"俩人口径一致，"改写小说吧！"在评价我对他们的描写时，都道："很到位！"

按理，翻译时对原文内容不应该作任何形式的删节或增补。但是，由于英汉两种语言表达方式不同，把原文信息译成译文信息时，常常需要省略一些词，这样做绝不等同于"偷工减料"。在研究原文意义及汉语习惯表达基础上所采用的减词法（pruning 或 omission）并不损害原意，反而使译文更为忠实通顺，意义更加明朗；而"偷工减料"则是不顾原文所进行的"胡译"。对此区别，翻译初学者应有一定的认识，以便在实践中认真而忠实地传达出原文精神。

第五章 句子的翻译(一)

一、从语法角度

(一)省略代词

英语由于语法的需要或为避免重复使用名词而广泛使用代词,特别是人称代词和物主代词,而汉语却较少使用代词,所以英译汉时只要不妨碍意义的表达,代词可以省略。

1. **One** must make painstaking efforts before **one** can succeed in mastering a foreign language.
   要成功掌握一门外语非下苦功不可。

2. Order is order, **we** cannot complain, **we** cannot bargain, **we** cannot question and **we** cannot suggest changes.
   命令就是命令,不得抱怨,不得讨价还价,不得质疑,不得建议修改。

3. Love is photogenic. **It** needs darkness to develop.
   爱情就像照片,需要大量的暗房时间来培养。

4. At Cock's lab in Lima, physical anthropologists from the United States and Canada are examining bones and other remains to try to learn more about these people, their health, what kind of work **they** did and how **they** died.
   在利玛市柯克的实验室里,来自美国和加拿大的人类学者正在对木乃伊的骨骼、遗骸进行研究,以进一步了解他们,包括了解他们的健康状况、工作状况和死因。

5. A person with nerve damage in the spinal cord can grasp objects when **his** or **her** forearm muscles are activated by a device like this one.
   脊髓神经有损伤的人使用这样的装置能激活前臂肌肉,便能抓握东西。

6. Every life has **its** roses and thorns.
   每个人的生活都有苦有甜。

(二)省略冠词

A. 须省略冠词

汉语没有冠词,当英语冠词 a,an,the 放在单数普通名词之前表示该事物的全体时,汉译时冠词不必译出;当 the 在专有名词前时也不必译出。冠词省略后,句子不仅意思不变,反而更加简练明白。

1. Death's approach is accompanied by **a** darkening of the patient's blood.
   死亡临近时,病人的血液颜色会因缺氧而加深。
2. The sun is setting down beyond **the** western hill.
   日落西山。
3. All matter is made up of atoms whether it is **a** solid, **a** liquid or **a** gas.
   任何物质,无论固体、液体或是气体都由原子组成。
4. **A** salmon is born in the river, grows up in the sea, and comes again to the river.
   鲑鱼在河里出生,海里成长,之后又游回河里。
5. **The** Appalachian mountains begin far south in Geogia and continue northwards to Vermont and Canada.
   阿巴拉契亚山脉南起佐治亚州,向北一直延伸至弗蒙特洲和加拿大。
6. **The** fear of being alone is **a** primary reason they are staying together.
   对孤独的恐惧是他们走到一起的最主要原因。

B. 不须省略冠词

当 a, an 第一次提及人、事、物或表示"一"这一具体概念时,应译出;当 the 特指时,也应译出。

1. I take computer lessons twice **a** week.
   我一星期上两次计算机课。
2. There is **the** book you are looking for.
   这就是你在找的那本书。
3. **The** book I bought last week deals with English idioms.
   我上周买的那本书是关于英语习惯用语的。
4. Jane is **an** honest girl and never tells a lie.
   珍妮是一个诚实的孩子,从不说谎。
5. There is not **a** Helen in the class, but we have three Marys.

这个班里没有一个叫海伦的,倒是有三个叫玛丽的。

6. It was **a** different William Carey from the William Carey he had long known.
   这不是他认识很久的**那个**威廉·卡瑞。

7. I lost **a** bat and **a** ball. The bat was found, but **the** ball was gone.
   我丢了一支球拍和一个球。球拍找到了,但**那个**球却没找到。

(三) 省略介词

大量使用介词是英语的特点之一。介词在不同情况下表示不同的意义,汉译时常省译某些表示时间、地点的介词。

1. **With** the weather so stuffy, ten to one it'll rain presently.
   天这样闷,很可能就要下雨了。

2. **On** July 4th, there are celebrations throughout the United States.
   每年7月4日,美国各地都举行各种庆祝活动。

3. She soon fell asleep **with** the light still burning.
   她很快就睡着了,灯还亮着。

4. Watch out **for** the sharp smell.
   小心刺鼻的气味。

注意:表示地点的介词短语在动词之后,有时不能省略。如:

The gunman hid **behind** the door.
持枪歹徒躲在门后。

(四) 省略连词

1. The sun is bright, **and** the sky is clear.
   阳光明媚,晴空万里。

2. It may be a long time **before** an immigrant can fully get used to the customs and habits of the country to which he moves.
   要过很长一段时间,移民才能完全适应所移居国的风俗习惯。

3. **If** winter comes, can spring be far behind?
   冬天来了,春天还会久远吗?

4. The people who get on in this world are the people who get up

and look for circumstances they want, **and** if they cannot find them, make them.

在这个世界上取得成就的人,都努力去寻找自己想要的机会,如果找不到机会,便自己创造机会。

(五) 省略 it

引导词"it"作形式主语、形式宾语时,或在强调句子中作形式主语时,本身没有独立的意义,可省译;在无人称句中或用"it"作主语表示自然现象、时间、地点、距离、环境及一般情况时,it 也常常可以省译。

1. It is much to be regretted that Mr. Puzo died at so young an age.
   普佐先生英年早逝,真令人惋惜。

2. The ground is still wet. It must have rained heavily last night.
   地面仍然很潮,昨晚肯定下过大雨。

3. It never occurred to me that he was illiterate.
   我从未想过他竟是个文盲。

4. Computers make it possible to run the complicated experiment automatically.
   计算机能使复杂的实验自动进行。

5. It is only the ignorant who despise education.
   只有愚蠢无知的人才会蔑视教育。

(六) 省译系动词

1. These references are valuable.
   这些参考资料很有价值。

2. We're on shaky ground. I think we're pretty close to divorcing.
   我们的婚姻摇摇欲坠,与离婚也就一步之遥了。

3. I'm now 55 yet the fear is still fresh.
   现在,我已经 55 岁了,但当时的恐惧仍记忆犹新。

4. He was in a stormy mood.
   他勃然大怒。

(七) 省译名词

1. Let's make **things** better.
   让我们做得更好。
2. A man has five items in his bathroom: a toothbrush, shaving cream, razor, a bar of soap, and a towel from the Marriott. The average number of items in the typical woman's bathroom is 337. A man would not be able to identify most of these items.
   男人浴室里有五件宝:牙刷,刮胡膏,剃须刀,一块肥皂,一条毛巾。一般女人的浴室里平均有337样东西,其中的大多数,男人不知道是干啥用的。

原文中的 a towel from the Marriott 若译作"一条万豪酒店的毛巾",节奏会显得比较缓慢。由于本句要表达的重点是男人浴室陈设之简单而非毛巾出自何处,所以省译 the Marriott,译成"一条毛巾"就行了。顺便提一句,万豪国际集团(Marriott International Inc.)是全球著名的酒店管理公司,目前集团经营及授权特许经营的近3000家酒店遍布全美及全球67个国家和地区。

二、从修辞角度

(一) 省略英语句子中重复出现的一些词、词组或意义

1. Both Judy and Robert have had **previous marriage that ended in divorce**, and they have a 3-year-old son.
   茱迪和罗伯特都曾有过离婚史。现在,夫妇俩有了一个3岁的儿子。

如果不做省略,译成"……以前都有过婚姻且婚姻都以离婚而告终……",就显得不精练。

2. Customers are anyone from wealthy Kuwaiti businessmen to celebrities, producers, directors, **guys who head software companies and Fortune 500 companies**.
   从富有的科威特商人到名人、制片商、导演、软件公司经理以及《财富》杂志500强的老板,顾客遍及各行各业。

此句若译作"……领导软件公司的经理和《财富》杂志500强企业的老板们……",就显得啰嗦而欠简略。

(二) 省略一些可有可无的词或词组

1. Taming fear is **what Blaine believes magic is all about**.
   布莱恩相信,征服恐惧就是魔术精神。

如果此句译成"征服恐惧就是魔术全部关于的精神",既累赘又不清楚,省去"全部"和"关于",无损原意,反觉自然。

2. Though Robert has never **physically abused** his wife, he admits he has a quick temper.
   罗伯特从未打过老婆,倒是经常发脾气,这一点他自己也承认。

若译成"虽然罗伯特从未对他的老婆进行身体的虐待……"就显得啰嗦。

3. Archaeologists say the find may solve some of the mysteries **surrounding** the Inca civilization.
   考古学家称此次发现也许会解开印加文明之谜。

若译作"……解开围绕印加文明的谜",语言就显得有些不自然。省去"围绕",无损原意,语言反而更明净。

4. Parents often **favor one child over another**.
   家长往往偏爱一个孩子。

这个译文比"家长往往偏爱一个孩子,不喜欢其他孩子"简洁自然。

(三) 把英语复合句译成汉语紧缩复句

把英语复合句译成紧缩复句,可使译文语言简练,更加符合汉语习惯。

1. If I see him, I'll speak to him.
   译文一:如果我见到他,我就告诉他。(假设复句)
   译文二:见到他我就告诉他。(紧缩复句)

2. Since it has been decided, let's start now.
   译文一:既然已经决定了,我们就开始吧。(推断句)
   译文二:决定了就开始吧。(紧缩复句)

3. The more he looked at that face, the more suspicious he became.

译文一:他越看这张脸就越觉得可疑。(连锁复句)

译文二:这张脸他越看越可疑。(紧缩复句)

4. I'll let you know as soon as it is arranged.

译文一:等事情安排好了我就通知你。(条件复句)

译文二:一安排好就通知你。(紧缩复句)

附一　课堂讲练材料

1. It is typical of many towns along the lake, composed of winding, cobblestone streets, waterside restaurants and cafes with the surrounding sharp hills as a backdrop, tourist hotels with predominately German and Italian vacationers, and plenty of shopping.
2. But some couples are almost constantly at each other's throats, with their marriage on the brink of divorce, as their kids witness yelling, name calling, unresolved disputes and lingering anger.
3. The videotape, captured over 10 weeks, revealed the inner workings of marriages filled with tension, mistrust, accusations and shouting.
4. The future lies in building robots capable of grasping the difference between good and evil, machines that can even harbor a sense of purpose.
5. In some arguments, one had a tendency to flee rather than resolve things, either by leaving the room or focusing on the TV.
6. After retreating into his Indiana home, Alexander, his vision fuzzy, spent his time checking his mail with a magnifier.
7. He now goes out in public, and makes regular trips to a local coffee shop with his friends.
8. The movie apparently struck a chord with audiences, becoming the biggest Easter weekend opening in history, grossing a record ＄30 million.
9. For the next 21 days, the kids wake at 7 a.m., make their own breakfast and pack their own gear.
10. My memory is terrible when it comes to names.

11. Part of the way our program is set up is that the physical tiredness helps to break down defenses that kids have.
12. Next week, magician David Blaine will outdo his previous stunts of being buried alive and turned into a human ice cube, by performing a death-defying stunt that no one else had dared even attempt.
13. When capacitors are connected in parallel, the net capacitance is the sum of the individual capacitance.
14. She was looking for skilled climbers, women who could take two months off from their jobs, women who could leave their families behind for an extended period. And women who had a certain attitude.
15. Neither approach would necessarily provide normal vision, but the primary goal is to allow people to see form and light, and thereby gain mobility and self-reliance.
16. She is currently engaged in a two-year study of childcare for the Nuffield Foundation and has found that as many as 75 per cent of parents rely on their own parents at some time or other.
17. She always picks holes in whatever I do.

附二 课外扩展训练材料

Mass Production

Long ago goods were manufactured by craftsmen, who were skilled workmen. A craftsman was proud of each article he made. He spent a long time in making it and took great care over its manufacture, and people paid a high price for it when it was finished. All the luxurious Persian carpets, the beautiful Chinese pottery and the hand-made lace of certain European countries were made in this way. But these articles were bought only by the rich. Poorer people had to be satisfied with goods that were roughly and cheaply made.

When the population of Europe increased, there was a demand for goods of better quality. These goods had to be produced in factories and workshops where hundreds of workers were employed. The invention of the steam engine helped manufacturers by giving them cheaper power to work their machines. Machines took the place of men. Production was increased. People were able to buy articles of good quality at low prices. The age of mass production had arrived. A "mass" is a large number or quantity. Mass production means the manufacture of a large number of identical articles by the use of machinery. Cars, radios and cameras are examples of the many types of article that are mass produced today.

第五节　重复法

英语力避重复。为避免重复,英语常用一个动词接几个宾语或表语;或用了一个动词,后面相同的动词便加以省略;或大量使用代词以避免重复名词。汉语则不怕重复,所以在英译汉过程中,遇到上述情况时则可以采用重复某词的手法进行翻译。重复法(repetition)实际上也是一种增益法,只不过所增补的词是前文刚刚出现过的词。尽管翻译力求省略一些可有可无的词,但为了文字清楚、突显原文精神或增加表现力,在保证译文与原文在思想内容一致的情况下,有时也可运用重复法对一些关键性的词加以重复。

一、为了文字清楚

(一) 重复名词

1. Mr. Hill is a friend of my father's rather than my brother's.
   西尔先生是我父亲的**朋友**,不是我哥哥的**朋友**。

2. We guys always hear the rules from our women. Here are ours.
   我们男人总是听女人制订的**规则**,以下是我们男人的**规则**。

3. The big company has its disadvantages.
   大**企业**有大**企业**的弊端。

4. In the 26 years since, Star Wars has changed the way movies are watched, shown, seen and made.
   在之后的26年当中,《星球大战》改变了人们制作**电影**,放**电影**,看**电影**的方式。

5. Behind every successful man, there is a woman, and behind

every unsuccessful man, there are two.

每个成功男人的背后都有一个**女人**，每个不成功男人的背后都有两个**女人**。

6. Fear not that the life shall come to an end, but rather fear that it shall never have a beginning.

不要害怕**你的生活**将要结束,应该担心**你的生活**永远不会真正开始。

7. I don't care about the London season! It is too matrimonial. People are either hunting for husbands, or hiding from them.

我才不稀罕伦敦的什么社交季节！这里的社交活动就知道围着婚姻转,不是寻觅合适的人选做**老公**,就是避开**老公**偷欢。

（二）重复动词

1. We should think more of the collective than of ourselves.

我们应该多**考虑**集体的利益,少**考虑**自己利益。

2. It grew strength from the young people who rejected the myth of their generation's apathy; who left their homes and their families for jobs that offered little pay and less sleep; from the not-so-young people who braved the bitter cold and scorching heat to knock on the doors of perfect strangers; from the millions of Americans who volunteered, and organized, and proved that more than two centuries later, a government of the people, by the people and for the people has not perished from this Earth.

竞选活动的声势越来越大则是源自那些年轻人,他们拒绝接受认为他们这代人冷漠的荒诞说法；他们**离开家**,**离开**亲人,从事报酬微薄、极其辛苦的工作；同时也源自那些已经不算年轻的人们,他们冒着严寒酷暑,敲开陌生人的家门进行竞选宣传；更源自数百万的美国民众,他们自发地组织起来,证明了两百多年以后,民有、民治、民享的政府并未从地球上消失。

3. Nabil had vanished. So had his children, and so had his wife.

纳贝尔**人间蒸发**了,他的孩子**人间蒸发**了,他的妻子也**人间蒸发**了。

4. When the bombs fell on our harbour and tyranny threatened the world, she was there to witness a generation rise to greatness and a democracy was saved.

   当炸弹袭击了我们的海港、独裁专制威胁到全世界,她见证了美国一代人的伟大崛起,见证了一个民主国家被拯救。

5. Oh, let us ask no question of it, what it is or is not.

   嘿,我们还是别**追究**了吧,别**追究**它是什么,不是什么。

(三) 重复代词

1. There is new energy to harness and new jobs to be created; new schools to build and threats to meet and alliances to repair.

   我们亟待开发新能源;**我们**亟待创造新的工作机会;**我们**需要修建新学校;**我们**需要应对众多威胁;**我们**需要修复与许多国家的关系。

2. She is my wife, my lover, my best friend.

   她是**我**妻子,**我**爱人,**我**最好的朋友。

3. That boy of his, that Howard, he doesn't appreciate.

   可是他**那个**儿子,**那个**霍华德,那小子不知好歹。

4. He had his value.

   他有**他**的可贵之处。

5. He is outspoken without being undiplomatic, straight-forward without being untactful.

   他率直,但讲究方式;**他**直言,但讲究谋略。

(四) 重复形容词

1. Everybody knows who's cool and who's not. It's obvious.

   人人都知道谁**酷**,谁不**酷**,一目了然。

2. One of the lessons of history is that nothing is often a good thing to do and always a clever thing to say.

   历史给我们的教训是:没有什么事永远是可做的**好事**,也没有什么话是永远可说的**好话**。

（五）重复副词

1. Poetry is simply the most beautiful, impressive and widely effective mode of saying things, and hence its importance.
   诗歌是**最**优美、**最**动人、**最**有效抒发感情的方式，因此很重要。

2. She never took singing lessons and she never learned to read music—she learned "by ear".
   她**从未**上过声乐课，**从未**学过识谱，她是靠"听"学会的。

3. She is never too aggressive, never too withdrawn.
   她做人**从不**咄咄逼人，**也从不**畏畏缩缩。

二、为了突显原文精神

（一）重复原文中的重复用词

1. Since that day, I have never missed a Wednesday—Patricia have received a card from me every Wednesday, every week, every month, every year.
   自那天后，我没错过一个星期三——**每**年、**每**月、**每**周的**每**个星期三，帕特丽夏都会收到一张我送的贺卡。

2. Business is business.
   公事公办。

3. Behind all this glare, behind all this storm, I see that small group of villainous men, who plan, organize, and launch this cataract of horrors.
   在刺眼的灯光**后面**，在暴风雨**后面**，我看到一小撮恶棍在策划，组织，发动一场灾难性战争。

4. That was a big, big wake-up call.
   那是一个**很大很大**的闹钟。

5. The ability to celebrate your successes, and know you deserve to celebrate them, may well be the most important skill of all.
   庆祝成功并知道成功值得**庆祝**，或许正是你最重要的潜能。

6. They are all dead, and it's your fault. Your fault.
   他们都死了。**是你害的**！**你害的**！

7. I know you didn't do this just to win an election and I know

you didn't do it for me. You did it because you understand the enormity of the task that lies ahead.

我知道你们的所作所为并不只是为了赢得大选，**我也知道**你们做这一切并不是为了我。你们这样做是因为你们明白摆在面前的任务有多艰巨。

8. Mosquito bye bye bye.

蚊子杀杀杀。

(二) 用同义词重复原文的重复用词

1. If it feels like the end of the world, that's because it is—the end of the world as we knew it.

如果感觉犹如**世界末日**来临，那是因为一个我们熟悉的**世界**结束了。

2. Blessed is the person who is too busy to worry in the daytime, and too sleepy to worry at night.

白天忙得没有时间**烦恼**，夜里困得没有精力**发愁**的人，是真正有福的人。

3. Even if I suffer with the people, even if I have all the problems that people have, I can leave. I can start again but they are stuck.

尽管我和大家一道吃苦，**虽然**别人遇到的问题我都遇到了，但我可以离开，我可以重新开始，而他们却无法脱身。

有译者发现，有时候若采用重复原文词或用同义词重复原文词的方法翻译使用了重复手段的原文，意义不仅不明反而让人读后不知所以。如 And smile, smile, smile. 只有避免使用重复手段，译成"让微笑永远充满你的心田"译文才能令人信服。可见，翻译中重复法的使用也要视情况而定。

三、为了增强表现力

(一) 运用成语

汉语中有大量的成语，这是汉语的一大特点。成语精练简洁，念起来顺口，有节奏感，并具有丰富的表现力，如运用得当，可使文字生动活泼，增强修辞效果。英译汉时可酌情考虑使用成语，使译文文字优美。如：

first success	初战告捷
old enemy	多年夙敌
calm	泰然自若
vague	模模糊糊
evasive	躲躲闪闪
ignorant	愚昧无知
fair	公平合理

1. The huge number of mummies from one period of time provides an unparalleled opportunity for new information about the Incas.

   大量同一时期的木乃伊为进一步研究了解印加文明提供了**千载难逢**的好机会。

2. *Primetime* watched them yell at each other and use bad language in front of the kids.

   在《黄金时间》节目里他们当着孩子的面相互漫骂,**出言不逊**。

3. Almost instantly I understood.

   刹那间我**茅塞顿开**,**豁然开朗**。

(二) 运用词的重叠

1. Day and night she works hard in her laboratory.

   她在实验室里**日日夜夜**、**勤勤恳恳**地工作。

2. Elinor joyfully treasured her words, as she answered...

   埃莉诺在答话时,**乐滋滋**地斟词酌句……

3. Andrea stood transfixed in front of the television, neither moving nor speaking, for more than half an hour.

   安德鲁**一动不动**、**默默无言**地在电视机前站了足足半个多小时。

(三) 运用对偶词组

汉语不怕重复,因为汉语的重复并不给人单调乏味的感觉。相反,如果使用得当,重复可以起反复强调的作用,还可增强文章的思想性和艺术性。

1. Eating and drinking, that fellow idled about and did no decent work.

   那家伙**大吃大喝**,**东游西荡**,不务正业。

2. You shouldn't have said anything against this.
对这件事你不该说三道四。
3. Despair gives courage to a coward.
人急造反,狗急跳墙。

(四) 重复原文已有的重复句子

1. Against yourself you are calling him, against the laws you are calling him, against the democratic constitution you are calling him.
你聘用他,于你自己不利;你聘用他,有悖于法律;你聘用他,违反民主宪法。
2. If he wishes to float into fairyland, he reads a book; if he wishes to dash into the thick of battle, he reads a book; if he wishes to soar into heaven, he reads a book.
如果想飘入仙境,他就读书;如果想投身激烈的战斗,他就读书;如果想一飞冲天,他就读书。
3. Let us resist the temptation to fall back on the same partisanship and pettiness and immaturity that has poisoned our politics for so long. Let us remember that it was a man from this state who first carried the banner of the Republican Party to the White House.
让我们抵制重走老路的诱惑,避免重新回到令美国政治长期深受毒害的党派纷争和由此引发的遗憾和不成熟表现。让我们牢记,正是该州(伊利诺伊州)的一名男子首次将共和党的大旗扛到了白宫。
4. And so, my fellow Americans, ask not what your country can do for you; ask what you can do for your country.
My fellow citizens of the world: ask not what American will do for you, but what together we can do for the freedom of man.
因此,美国同胞们,不要问国家能为你们做些什么,而要问你们能为国家做些什么。
全世界的公民们,不要问美国将为你们做些什么,而要问我们共同能为人类的自由做些什么。

附一 课堂讲练材料

1. The anger is very toxic to these kids, to their self-confidence, to their ability to resolve conflicts in their own lives down the road.
2. These bubbles improve the transfer of force from a player's foot to the ball, making it go faster.
3. Other Nobel laureates fly first class or start charities with their prize money. For Nash, who is doing research again.
4. Michael is clearly a male. This should not even be an issue. Anybody who watched the medical evidence, the medical testimony, in this case will clearly see that Michael, medically, is clearly a male.
5. They packed the eggs in dozens.
6. In a few minutes the women began to come in by twos and threes, pulling down the sleeves of their blouses.
7. Millions and millions of people had seen apples fall, but it was left to Newton to ask why they fall.
8. I would begin going to bed at sunset and rising with the bean of day: ten to one, it would vastly improve my health.
9. When they met again, each had already been married to another.
10. Empty vessels make the greatest sound.
11. He who has health has hope; and he who has hope, has everything.
12. It is a good horse that never stumbles.
13. Joys shared with others are more enjoyed.
14. Money is a good servant but a bad master.
15. His first stunt was in 1999, when he buried himself alive in coffin for seven days and seven nights.
16. Thompson, author of *Best Friends, Worst Enemies*, says almost every school has an "in" crowd, popular kids who decide what's "cool".
17. "So I become a bigger person," says Cross, "a more knowledgeable person and, I think, a better person for having taken the risk."
18. The salon's owners deny any responsibility.

19. There are two things to aim at in life: first, to get what you want; and, after that, to enjoy it. Only the wisest of mankind achieves the second.
20. Live all you can; it's a mistake not to. It doesn't so much matter what you do in particular, so long as you have your life. If you haven't had that, what have you had?
21. Teachers become the guide on the side, instead of the sage on the stage.
22. Britons regard their monarchy very much like the way Americans regard their flag, said Celia Sandys, a granddaughter of Winston Churchill and author of *Churchill: Wanted Dead Or Alive*.
23. Babies whose mothers drank heavily before they were born had significant problems in conducting a message through the nerves at both one month and one year of age.

附二 课外扩展训练材料

Fast Food Scraps Threaten Rat Plague?

Britain is facing a sharp rise in its rat population as growing numbers of people leave fast food scrape in the street, an environment group warned. Keep Britian Tidy said rodents were abandoning their traditional haunts undergroud and were roaming the streets, enticed by discarded remnants of burgers, pizzas and crisps. "The rat population is on the rise and soon it'll be as common to see a rodent on our street as it is to see a dog or cat," said group Director, Sue Nelson. The practice of dumping fast food litter and scraps on the street rather than in the trash—with young men the worst offenders—was behind the rise. According to the *National Rodent Survey in 2001*, Britain's rat population has grown by nearly one quarter since 1998 and is now estimated at 60 million, two million more than the human population. On average a rat can give birth every 24–28 days and just a single pair of rats can produce a colony of 2,000 a year. Around 200 Britons a year contract Weil's Disease—an infection which can lead to kidney or liver failure and eventually death and which is carried in rat's urine. To highlight the issue, Keep Britain Tidy launched a cinema ad entitled "How close do you want them to get?" The ad culminates in a shocking image of a young woman sleeping in a bed of rats—echoing the nightmare scenario from James Herbert's classic horror tale *The Rats*, in which mutant rodents begin to prey on humans.

第六节　反面着笔法

英语和汉语都有肯定概念和否定概念之分,但是由于英语和汉语的思维习惯和表达方式不同,两种语言用来表达否定概念和肯定概念的词汇、语法及语言逻辑都有很大的差别,具体到词、词组或句子,肯定和否定表达形式往往不能吻合。一味按原语形式翻译有时不符合汉语表达习惯,有时则不足以传达原文语义和修辞色彩,造成译文发生信息缺失和信息不足现象。例如,这句流行于美国高校教师中的 Publish or perish 不能译为"发表还是消失",而须用反面着笔法译为"不出书就出局"或"不出书不上岗"。同样,No bargain! 须译为"一口价!"才符合原意。因此在翻译时,原文本来是正说的,译文常常需要从反面着笔;或者,原文本来用肯定语气,译文却需用否定语气。这就是反面着笔法(mutual transformation of negative and affirmative expressions)。

一、正话反说

英语在表达否定意义时,除了使用否定词外,还有形式否定、含蓄否定等,而汉语否定意义的表达方法却几乎都含有明显的否定词,如"不""没有""无""未""毋""勿"等。

(一) 动词

1. No one **ignores** a film that resonates with the day's headlines.
   没有人会**无视**一部内容与当今新闻头条相同的电影。
2. Towering genius **disdains** a beaten path. It seeks regions hitherto unexplored.
   卓越的天才**不屑**于走别人走过的路,而是寻找迄今尚未开拓的领域。

3. Their hobby is to **keep** searching for more information about their past.
   他们的兴趣在于**不断**搜寻更多有关他们过去的信息。

4. Pictures only **puzzle**.
   图案只会使人**不解**。

5. Before our good-byes, Shelley **startled** me.
   在我们最后道别前,谢莉说了一句话让我**惊诧不已**。

6. All my cares were over, my happiness **overflowed**.
   一切忧患已告结束,我的幸福**言之不尽**。

7. If we **lose sight of** taking care of and rewarding our employees, we won't be the company we're capable of becoming, whether we achieve long-term value for the shareholders or not.
   要是**不**照顾员工,**不**回报员工,那么无论是否为股东实现了长期价值,我们都不可能成为我们有能力成为的那种公司。

(二) 副词

1. Lose weight safely and **forever**.
   安全减肥,**永不反弹**。

2. Will we **soon** all be arrested?
   我们**不久**都会被捕吗?

3. We may **safely** say so.
   我们这样说**万无一失**。

4. The subversion attempts proved **predictably** futile.
   不出所料,颠覆行径/企图最终没能得逞。

5. Take care of your brother while I am **away**.
   我**不在**的时候,你要照顾好弟弟。

6. He walked **slowly** back to his office to read the two long letters in which the whole story was made clear.
   他**不紧不慢**地走回办公室,去阅读那两封足以使真相大白的长信。

(三) 形容词

1. State inspectors say enforcement is generally **lax**, in part

because of the high cost of testing for MMA.
州检查人员说,该禁令的执行**并不严格**,部分原因是 MMA 的检测费过高。

2. We're on **shaky** ground. I think we're pretty close to divorcing.
我们的婚姻很**不稳定**,与离婚也就一步之遥了。

3. He is **the last** person to accept a bribe.
他**绝不可能**受贿。

4. The organization has produced six **murder-free** years in America's capital: a political leader's dream.
由于该机构的努力,美国首都 6 年**没发生过一起谋杀案**——这是所有政治领袖在位时都渴望实现的政绩。

5. Quite often people have bits of their past which they have never told to even their husbands or wives. It just takes someone a bit more **distanced** to coax it out.
人们难免有一些陈年旧事不愿告诉任何人,包括自己的丈夫或妻子,这就需要**不那么亲近的**人诱导他们说出来。

6. I tried county shows, old people's homes, Women's Institute meetings and genealogy magazines, but many of them proved **wrong** for this service.
我曾到郡展销会、老人院、妇女协会会场和家谱杂志社去做宣传,发现这项服务在很多地方都**推广不开**。

7. Ted Robinson has been **worried** all the week.
整整一周,特德·鲁滨逊**担心不已**。

8. Recognizing who the customer was, the manager was most **apologetic** and reprimanded the assistant severely.
经理认出了顾客,**连赔不是**,还狠狠地斥责了店员。

(四) 前置词

1. It is **beyond** his power to preside over such an important meeting.
主持这样重要的会议是他力所**不能及**的。

2. These angels would carry a new prayer to heaven, this time

one of thanksgiving for a surprise **beside** my wildest dreams.
这些天使会给天堂带去新的祈祷,这次送去的是感恩,感谢上帝赐我惊喜——一个我无论如何也梦想不到的惊喜。

3. He is **under** the weather.
    他**不舒服**,生病了。

4. Strength alone knows conflict, weakness is **below** even defeat, and is born vanquished.
    只有强者才懂得斗争,弱者甚至失败都**不够资格**,生来就是被征服的。

5. Good advice is **beyond all price**.
    忠告是**无价宝**。

(五) 连词

1. Study hard, or you will be bound to fail in the final examination.
    努力学习,**不然**期末考试肯定不及格。

2. Not every boy given an 8mm movie camera before he is ten turns into a Hollywood genius.
    并非每个**不到**10岁就得到8毫米摄像机的男孩都能成为好莱坞电影奇才。

(六) 名词

1. He is determined to prove his **innocence**.
    他决心证明自己**无辜**。

2. What makes life dreary is the **want** of motive.
    没有了目的,生活便郁闷无光。

3. The most important thing in creating **endurance** is strengthening the trust between management and the people who do the work.
    在创造**长盛不衰**企业的过程中,最重要的是加强管理层与员工之间的相互信任。

4. We can have a go at wearing masks, and role-play "**trick-or-treating**".

我们可以戴着面具玩，还可以假扮"**不请客就捣乱**"的捣蛋鬼。

在此，有必要补充一些"正词反译"的信息。所谓"正词"即词的正身。若这个正身表示相反的词义，英译汉时便需要正词反译。正确的译法是在正词的前面加"反""防""对"等具相反意义的字眼。如：

hunger march	反饥饿游行
obscenity law	反猥亵法
spy film	反特片
pornography campaign	反黄色书、画、电影的运动
terror war	反恐战争
riot police	防暴警察
fire wall	防火墙
earthquake drill	防震演习
pollution law	防污染法
China policy	对华政策

（七）短语

1. Carrying 65-pound packs on their backs, they are expected to **keep pace**. Water breaks are taken only at scheduled intervals—no exception.

   要求他们背负65磅的行装，**不许掉队**，连喝水也只能遵守安排，不得特殊。

2. I was **surprised** at his coming at all.

   没料到他竟然来了，我很惊讶。

3. Your temper is **more than** I can bear.

   我受不了你的脾气。

4. **Instead of** being an expense, these benefits actually reduce company cost of doing business.

   这些津贴不但**没有**增加公司开支，反而降低了运营成本。

5. **A great deal** of time/money/energy has been spent on the project.

   不少时间/金钱/能源都花在那个工程上了。

6. I am willing to **go through just about anything** to find it for my students.

我愿**不惜一切代价**为我的学生找到它。

7. **A clear conscience** is a **soft pillow**.
   问心无愧,高枕无忧。

8. He **got clear away**.
   他逃得无影无踪。

9. The article is **full of** pretty phrases.
   文章不乏华丽辞藻。

10. **Stay** there!
    别动!

(八) 句子

1. But that he was prevented, he would have accomplished his design.
   若不是受到了阻挠,他早就完成了设计。

2. Misfortunes tell us what fortune is.
   不经灾祸不知福。

3. The country seems to boast every kind of produce known to man except the pumpkin I want for Oct. 31.
   这个国家似乎出产人类已知的各种农产品,可唯独没有我10月31号要用的南瓜。

4. Explanations produce blank stares.
   单凭嘴说,听众不会明白。

5. I'll see you dead before that happens.
   我绝不同意你的办法。

6. I arrived late and couldn't get a bath or a meal. That's good hotels for you!
   我来晚了,澡无法洗,饭也没有,你们的宾馆客服就是这样**不周到**。

7. One man's guess is as good as another.
   一切猜测都**不准确**。

8. It is too much of a good thing that a famous scientist is always wanted for all sorts of meetings and ceremonies.
   出了名的科学家总被邀去出席各种会议或参加这样那样的典礼。这真是**过犹不及**!

二、反话正说

英汉之间的差异常常造成肯定与否定表达难以吻合的现象。如英语否定表达"Do't stop running"须译成汉语的肯定句"继续跑"才符合原意。在此,有必要补充一些"反词正译"的信息。所谓"反词"即某词加了表示否定意义的前后缀,如"mis, un, dis, non, a, less, free"等。这种反词若表示正意,英译汉时便需要反词正译。如:

misinterpret	误读
misfortune	灾祸
untie	打开领结
unemployment	失业
disarm	裁军
nonsense	胡言乱语
anhydrous	缺水的
timeless	永远的

(一) 动词

1. He is **disliked** by many.
   许多人都厌恶他。
2. I **unwrapped** the hamburger and surveyed the surrounding scenery.
   我一边打开汉堡包包装纸,一边打量四周的风景。

(二) 副词

1. I **never** lose sight of that.
   我一直把这个理想铭记在心。
2. He resigned **dishonorably**.
   他辞职了,真丢面子。
3. I **never** see her but I want to kiss her.
   我一看见她就想吻她。
4. It **never** rains but it pours.
   一下雨就下大雨。

(三) 形容词

1. A **discontented** man knows not where to sit easy.
   贪婪者坐无宁时。

2. He has bouts of **uncontrollable** coughing.
   他一阵阵地咳嗽，难以控制。

3. WBShare your knowledge to continue a **timeless** tradition.
   和别人分享你的知识吧，那才是**永恒**之道。

4. But the fear of being **penniless** again has never left him.
   然而他始终担心自己再一次**一贫如洗**。

5. The old man is **toothless**.
   这个老人**牙齿全掉光**了。

6. I just felt **incredible** relief.
   我只是感到**如释重负**。

(四) 名词

1. Spielberg is known as the master of **disquiet**.
   斯皮尔伯格被称为"**忧虑大师**"。

2. A negative relationship is one where you have to interact，but it's characterized by conflict, **disagreement**, **dislike** or **disrespect**.
   合不来的关系是你不得不进行交流的一种关系，此种关系的特点是矛盾、**争论**、**厌恶**或**藐视**。

3. Born into postwar **uncertainties** in 1946, he grew up with a sense of vocation
   他生于战后**动荡**的1946年，从小到大都有一种使命感。

(五) 短语

1. We should **lose no time** in getting everything ready for the seminar.
   我们应当**抓紧时间**把研讨会的一切准备工作做好。

2. He took **no little** pains over it.
   他在这件事上花费了**很多**功夫。

3. He is old, **none the less** he works like a young man.
   他虽然上了年纪，但干起活来还像个年轻人。

4. After her call, I could think of **nothing else**.
   接听她的电话后,我满脑子想的**都是这件事**。

(六) 句子

1. You **do not have to** spend more than five minutes either reading Howard Schultz's book, or visiting with him, to realize that values drive Starbucks.
   你只需花5分钟不到的时间读舒尔茨写的书或当面采访他,便会明白是价值观在推动星巴克公司前进。

2. He says **it is not hard to understand why**.
   他说个中原因容易理解。

3. **It's not an accident** that the attrition rate at Starbucks is four to five times lower than the national average for retailers and restaurants in America.
   星巴克公司的人员自然缩减率比全美零售商和餐饮店的平均水平低3/4至4/5,是很自然的事。

4. Live all you can; it's a mistake **not to**. It doesn't so much matter what you do in particular, so long as your have your **life**. **If you haven't had that**, what have you had?
   享受人生,否则就会枉活一世。只要拥有生命,怎样生活都无关紧要。**除了生命**,你还拥有什么?

5. They **no longer** cared whether they lived or died.
   他们已把生死置之度外。

6. Why I did this was **not** at first **apparent** even to my own perceptions.
   我为什么这样做,起初连我自己都莫名其妙。

7. Offering these benefits **did not make him wildly popular with** his shareholders.
   开始提供这些津贴的时候,股东们对他都**颇有怨言**。

8. We grumbled a little now and then, to be sure. But there's **no love lost** between us.
   有时咱们也闹点小别扭什么的,不过始终**相亲相爱**。

三、双重否定的译法

双重否定(double negation)汉译时往往译为肯定表达。如：

1. Not a day passes without shooting and bombardments between those two countries.
   两个国家每天都用枪炮对轰。
2. He is nothing if not a scoundrel.
   他简直是个十足的流氓。
3. Not for nothing does a weasel come to a chicken and give New Year greetings.
   黄鼠狼给小鸡拜年一定有目的。
4. Nothing great was ever achieved without enthusiasm.
   热情成就伟业。
5. Nothing is impossible for a willing heart.
   心之所愿,定会成真。

附一　课堂讲练材料

1. Wars have never stopped polluting the earth.
2. I can not read the long letter other than cursorily.
3. She was irritated at being denied the opportunity to get a pay rise.
4. But as she still continued to think Mr. Crawford very plain, she never mentioned him.
5. Silk is distinct from rayon in every respect.
6. The middle of the room is clear.
7. I was clear out.
8. During this period Smedley was particularly effective in bringing together people with different political concerns.
9. Few people are free from care.
10. He himself was getting old and the cares of government were becoming too much for him.
11. Sam spoke nothing in reply, but he thought within his own heart.

12. Don't worry! Everything will be all right.
13. At the most, he will experience feelings of anxiety, shame, insecurity and helplessness.
14. Her husband is now freed of anxiety.
15. And now a new anxiety seized me.
16. Nothing has changed.
17. The three months in between seemed to last forever.
18. Be cautious about revealing too much to a co-worker, superior, subordinate, or mentor, or befriending at work or in business too quickly, too soon, too high up, or too low down.
19. Casual, not so close friendships are preferable in business.
20. What we've talked about inside Starbucks is building an enduring company.
21. Storms have become more intense and weather patterns more erratic.
22. We can not estimate the value of modern science too much.
23. There is much to be desired for the government to crack down bribery and corruption.
24. Although the actual cause remains elusive, scientists know a few things

附二 课外扩展训练材料

Dishing Up a Quality Seal for Authentic Eateries

So long soggy spaghetti, tasteless tagliatelle and papery pizza at least if the Italian government's taste police get their way. Ministers said they wanted to clean up the red-white-and-green credentials of the estimated 60,000 restaurants around the world passing themselves off as Italian. So the government is creating a certificate that will be awarded to deserving establishments abroad from the 300 or so in the Middle East and 25,000 in Europe. The dual aim is to promote Italy abroad and ensure tastebuds are being tickled by authentic Mediterranean fare. "There are people out there who don't realize pizza is an Italian word and ask us what we call it," lamented Adolfo

Urso, deputy industry minister, at a news conference. And Agriculture Minister Gianni Alemanno said even if eateries did flaunt Italian roots, it was often a false claim. "Most have nothing more Italian about them than the name above the door or a tricolor flag draped outside," he said. The certificate, still without a name, would ensure restaurants offered genuine Italian menus and used authentic produce, instead of ingredients such as a German cheese marketed with the Italian-sounding name of cambonzola. Some argue that Italy's taste police will be toothless because restaurants will have the final say on whether or not they want to be tested under the voluntary scheme.

第七节 合译法

所谓合译法(combination),是指把原文中两个或两个以上的词合译为一个词,将两个或两个以上的简单句合译为一个句子,或将一个复合句在译文中用一个简单句来表达。

一、同义词的合译

把两个或两个以上的同义词合译成一个词,使译文文字清爽整洁。

1. Then, slowly, **slipping** and **sliding** down the glass, it would melt, its beauty fleeting.
   (雪花)慢慢地从玻璃上滑下来,滑着化着,美丽瞬间逝去。

此译文将 slipping 和 sliding 这两个同义词合成一个"滑",文字简洁明了。

2. He was **kindly, generous and obliging.**
   他乐善好施。

用"乐善好施"将 kindly, generous 和 obliging 三个褒义词合译,文字忠实,语义概括。又如:

3. He feels **exhausted or fatigued** most of the time.
   他大部分时间都觉得非常疲倦。

4. As goalkeeper broke down in tears at the final whistle, millions of

men, women and children wept unashamedly with him.

比赛结束的哨声响起时,守门员忍不住热泪滚滚,(英国)数百万**男女老少**也泪如雨下。

5. He was **jealous and envious** of his brother. He resented that his younger brother was so successful.

   他**嫉妒**弟弟,愤恨弟弟取得了如此巨大的成功。

6. Before we had been universally **loathed and detested**. now we marveled from afar as the Japanese took us to their hearts and England became the most popular team among neutrals.

   过去我们为世人所**厌恶**,而今我们惊讶地发现日本球迷热爱我们,英格兰球队已成为中立球迷中最受欢迎的一支球队。

7. In designing advertisements for other countries, messages need to be **short and simple**.

   为其他国家设计广告,用词须**简短**。

二、非同义词的合译

将内在意义存在一定相关性的一些非同义词合译在一起,能使译文信息圆满的同时,还可使文字更易为读者接受。

1. My idyll would have been perfect had it not been for a **persistent** bee that began **buzzing** around me.

   要不是有只蜜蜂在身边**嗡嗡个不停**,我一定会非常安闲自在。

通过原文与译文的对比,将 persistent 与 buzzing 合在一起进行翻译的处理方式是成立的。

2. The **soft green** of the trees had changed to **wiry** branches.

   树木已经**枝枯叶落**。

3. It smelled a **sweet, intense** smell of fruit.

   它发出了水果的**浓香味**。

此处的合译需要译者有一定的综合能力或概括能力,否则很难进行恰如其分的合译。由于合译法在该译文中的使用准确到位,译文因而精练顺达。看来,适当地运用合译,不失为一种好的翻译策略和技巧。

4. In real life, however, children often don't **see or hear** an argument's happy ending.

然而,在现实生活中,孩子们所见所闻的家庭纷争结局常常很不幸。

"所见所闻"是 see or hear 的等值译文,此类情况英译汉时会碰到不少。

5. He has **a repeated buzzing or other noises** in his ears.

他耳朵里常有嗡嗡的声音。

三、固定词组的合译

英语和汉语各自有一套独特的语言表达系统。在英语中,词的粘合力和搭配能力较强,一个动词往往可以同多个名词或多个介词搭配,一个介词也往往与多个名词搭配,构成不同的动词短语和介词短语。在翻译时,无需逐词译出,可考虑用汉语的固定搭配,或者四字结构、四字成语去翻译,这样译文会更流畅,更符合汉语的行文习惯。如:

1. All the ones we have seen here have **four-star abilities with five-star abilities**.

我们在此看到的人都是些**眼高手低**之辈。

2. We should **stick to** the Four Cardinal Principles and **press ahead with** reform and opening-up.

我们应该**始终坚持**四项基本原则,改革开放。

3. He **threw on** a coat and left home **in a hurry**.

他套上一件衣服,**匆匆忙忙地**离开了家。

4. Here are 10 **dynamic** verbs that belong in a **rich** vocabulary.

这里有10个**表现力强、内涵丰富**的动词。

5. I was **examined and re-examined**.

我受到**再三**诘问。

四、习语、谚语和俚语的合译

英语中还有很多在语言发展过程中出现的习语、谚语和俚语,有时也宜用成语进行合译处理。如:

| to be mindful of personal gains and losses | 患得患失 |
| to be on thin ice | 如履薄冰 |

to be wild with joy	欣喜若狂
beyond cure	不可救药
to blow one's own horn	自吹自擂
to call white black	颠倒黑白
as easy as turning over one's hand	易如反掌
to fish in troubled waters	浑水摸鱼

1. Kino hurrying towards his house, **felt a surge of exhilaration**.
   基诺加快步伐，**欣喜若狂**地朝自己的家走去。

2. It is the tears of the earth that **keep** her smiles **in bloom**.
   是大地的泪水让她的微笑**花开不谢**。

3. Some other women will make you feel **dependent** on each other. For most of the time, they have **common appearance** and they are **not ambitious** but to live **steadfastly**. They will deal with the things that their husbands don't want to handle. They will also give birth to children, support their parents and make the whole family a good state. This kind of women are the best partners for men in the second half of their life.
   还有些女人给你**相依相伴**的感觉，而这些女人大多样貌平平，欲望不高，但踏踏实实地生活，老公不愿处理的人事都由她们出面，还要生孩子、孝敬父母、稳固家庭后方的阵地，这种女人是男人后半辈子特别好的伴儿。

五、单句的合译

汉语书面语由于书写速度较慢的原因，呈两个明显的特征：一是追求简单明了；二是带有几分书卷气。而英语则为追求准确清楚，有时甚至不惜使用多个句子进行表达，若照直译成汉语，很难造出简单的汉语句子，因此难以明了。例如：

1. Sorry about the socks. I'll remember.
   我会记住袜子的事。

此句若译成:"关于袜子的事,实在抱歉,我会记住的。"读者定然不明其意,但是把原文几个句子合成一句进行翻译反而言简意赅。又如:

2. He took out a match and lit the candle. A light lit up the darkness.
   他掏出火柴,点燃蜡烛,照亮黑暗。

3. She wasn't really listening. She was thinking about something else.
   她没有认真听,脑里想着别的事情。

4. We are all alike. We all have families.
   我们同样都有家。

5. I have read your articles. I expected to meet an older man.
   看过你的文章,想不到你这么年轻。

六、复合句的合译

英语复合句可根据上下文的需要译为汉语的简单句,这也是一种合译。如:

1. I was wandering when I saw a notice outside a Sunday School.
   闲逛时看到主日学校外贴着一张通知。

2. It was my liver that was out of order.
   我的肝出了毛病。

3. The secret of being miserable is to have leisure to bother about whether you are happy or not.
   痛苦的秘密在于有闲工夫担心自己的幸福。

4. The judge said that it was difficult to comprehend why the police acted so in this matter.
   法官表示难以理解警察这么做的动机。

5. I've told you time and again not to speak when adults are speaking.
   我一再告诉你大人说话时别插嘴。

附一　课堂讲练材料

1. We scrimped and saved so we could keep up with the mortgage and our student loans.
2. He answered matter-of-factly.
3. I wanted to stop worrying about life and start enjoying it.
4. The creature didn't answer. It just looked at Jamie.
5. It made no move to eat.
6. If you want to go someplace, tell me. I'll take you.
7. That's why I go out so much.
8. Jaime hugged his mother around the waist.
9. Accomplishment is often deceptive because we don't see the pain and perseverance that produced it.
10. All through the night Sandy worked cutting the skin of the dog.
11. Uncle Tom screamed loudly, a cry of fear.
12. With every gesture, with every word, Don Corleone made it clear to Luca Brasi that he was valued.
13. These personal experiences were all valued to a degree which is difficult to parallel in earlier poets.
14. And as he had his techniques, so had she hers.
15. He quizzed me about where I had been last night.
16. Answer our argument, and your business is done.
17. When we assembled here on the 4th of March, 1987, there was great anxiety with regard to our currency and credit.
18. My parents worry if I come home late.
19. Worrying yourself to death won't help it!
20. If anybody has troubled you, I will take care of him.
21. He had recommended his daughter to her care when he was dying.
22. The boy was nimble and jumped clear of the truck.
23. It was clear that I could not hope to deceive him.
24. Our diurnal existence is divided into two phases, as distinct as day and night.

25. It was obvious that Israel had no intention of complying.

附二　课外扩展训练材料

Yaser's Complaint

Steve and Yaser first met in their chemistry class at an American university. Yaser was an international student from Jordan. He was excited to get to know an American. He wanted to learn more about American culture. Yaser hoped that he and Steve would become good friends.

At first, Steve seemed very friendly. He always greeted Yaser warmly before class. Sometimes he offered to study with Yaser. He even invited Yaser to eat lunch with him. But after the semester was over, Steve seemed more distant. The two former classmates didn't see each other very much at school. One day Yaser decided to call Steve. Steve didn't seem very interested in talking to him. Yaser was hurt by Steve's change of attitude. "Steve said we were friends," Yaser complained. "And I said friends were friends forever."

(《跨文化交际英语教程》)

第八节　分译法

所谓分译法(division),是把一个单词或短语从原文中拆分出来译成一个句子,或将原文的一个简单句拆译成两个或两个以上的句子。

一、把原文的单词译成句子

单词的分译(word division)就是将某个单词单独拿出来,翻译成一个句子。那么,什么样的单词常被挑出来,享受如此特殊的待遇呢?

(一) 副词

翻译初学者翻译时常常发现若是没有某个副词从中作梗,句子翻译易如反掌。此时,翻译老手的经验是,把这个讨厌的副词挑出来单独译成一句,不与主句搅在一起翻译。如:

1. They tried **vainly** to blame us for the breakdown in the truce talk.
   他们企图把破坏和谈的罪名强加在我们头上,**但没有得逞**。
2. **Not surprisingly**, he was constantly receiving complaints from all of them about his not giving value for money.
   他们常常议论他的不是,说他光拿钱不干活,**这一点毫不奇怪**。
3. **Characteristically** Mr. Arnold concealed his feelings and watched and learned.
   阿诺德先生不动声色,四处查看,打听信息。**这是他一贯的工作特色**。
4. The ball's best review has come from England's star midfielder David Beckham who calls the ball's accuracy "exceptional". **Incidentally**, Beckham is sponsored by Adidas and helped design the ball.
   英格兰队中场球星贝克汉姆对此球评价最高。他说,此球的准确性十分"突出"。贝克汉姆是阿迪达斯的代言人,还参与了设计此球。**当然,这是题外话**。

(二) 形容词
英译汉时,除副词外,形容词也常常享受单独译成句子的待遇。例如:

1. Women are **ambitious**, **bold**, **mischievous**, **colorful** and **imaginative**. They are **more confident**, **competitive**, **visionary** and have a stronger presence.
   女性有志向,她们大胆、淘气、有趣,富有想象力。与男性相比,她们更加自信,更喜欢竞争,更爱幻想,表现力也更强。
2. The guest was pleased by the distinction but not **overwhelmed**.
   来宾对这种破格礼遇感到十分受用,但没有**受宠若惊**。
3. **Elegant**, **passionate**, a strong career woman and a devoted mom, Michelle Obama has already become a role model with an army of fans as she prepares to become the nation's first lady.
   她**优雅大方,充满热情**,是个成功的职业女性,是位称职的母亲,在即将成为美国第一夫人之时,米歇尔·奥巴马已经有了一大批"粉丝"。

4. He feels **drowsy**, **dizzy** and **nauseated**.
   他昏昏欲睡,头晕目眩,还想吐。
5. The elements are less reserved and **distinct**.
   宇宙各种元素的活跃程度比以前高,界限却不如以前分明。

(三) 名词

不仅副词,有时某些名词的翻译也令人十分头疼,所以初学者会觉得如果没有某个名词的话,句子就好译多了。如果这样,不如把这个捣蛋的名词及其关联词从主句中挑出来单独翻译成一句,不与其他词语搅和在一起译。例如:

1. They are more comfortable with **hierarchies**, **title silos** and **processes**.
   男性更能适应社会等级,更能接受头衔差别,更能享受升迁的过程。
2. Details of the continuing **probe** are just now emerging.
   这项调查工作在继续进行,有关细节刚刚显露出来。
3. **The truth** is I have had someone in mind for some time but I've been postponing telling my parents.
   实际情况是,这段时间我已有了心上人,不过我一直拖着,没告诉父母。
4. It was our **mistake** to have kept nagging you.
   我们老是在你耳边唠叨,是我们不对。
5. I wanted to laugh at their **harmlessness**.
   它们无法作恶了,我真想放声大笑!

二、把原文的短语译成句子

英译汉时,有时如果不将某个短语单独从原句中挑出来译成单独的一句汉语的话,很难译出通顺易懂、符合汉语表达习惯的句子来。由于这类短语是英语为母语者独特的思维习惯和行文习惯的结果,与汉语为母语者的思维与行文习惯不兼容,因此有必要做短语分译(phrase division)处理。例如要想成功翻译 It was morning, and the new sun sparkled gold across the ripples of gentle sea. 须将 the ripples of gentle sea 进行分译,使汉语在结构上有别于原文。此时可考虑译成:"清晨,初升的太阳照着平静的海面,微波荡漾,闪耀着金色的光芒。"这样译文念起来意思清楚,行文漂亮。

1. Handsome young men must have something to live on, **as well as the plain.**
   美男子与凡夫俗子没有两样,也要有饭吃,有衣穿。
2. D'urberville's bad temper cleared up **at sight of** her and he laughed heartily.
   见到她,德伯维尔怒气顿消,开心地笑了。
3. Please reply **at your earliest convenience.**
   您要是方便,请尽早回信。
4. My parents stared at each other **in silence** for a while.
   一时间,父母面面相觑,沉默不语。
5. **With his failures in life** came the fears for the future.
   他生活屡屡失意,对前途忧心忡忡。

三、把简单句译成两个以上的句子

英语的葡萄句式决定了某些英语句子长而复杂的特点,而汉语句子竹子式的结构决定了汉语字句的积累性,即句子较短,句型结构较为简单。所以,英译汉时,常将英语原句拆成几个短句进行分译,这就是句子的分译(sentence division)。例如:

1. American prisoners are permitted to write censored letters.
   允许美军战俘写信,但信要经过审查。
2. And the stranger understood and appreciated.
   陌生人明白了她的意图,心里充满感激。
3. And later on he had a sketch he prized very much.
   后来他画了一幅素描,将其视为珍宝。
4. Sorrow and trouble either soften the heart or harden it.
   悲哀和烦恼不是使人心软,就是使人心狠。
5. A book is the same today as it always was and it will never change.
   一本好书过去如此,今天如此,将来也如此,永不改变。
6. Mother sounded jealous of my in-laws.
   听母亲那口气,她好像嫉妒我公公和婆婆了。

7. Interest in Obama's fashion has soared since she won particular praise for the purple sheath dress and black belt she wore in June when her husband clinched the nomination as the Democratic Party's presidential candidate.

今年6月,在奥巴马接受民主党总统候选人提名的仪式上,米歇尔凭一件紫色紧身套裙和一条黑腰带赢得盛赞,此后人们对她的时尚品味兴趣大增。

附一 课堂讲练材料

1. I left them arguing in this way and went to the train station to get a morning paper.
2. The houses around the field were all emptied and the people ordered to stay somewhere in the village.
3. This was to be the beginning of London's "Great Fear".
4. He is her half-brother by her father's first marriage.
5. We'd like to inform you that our counter sample will be sent to you by DHL by the end of this week and please confirm it ASAP so that we can start our mass production.
6. You may get a 5% discount if your order is on a regular basis.
7. He became as exhilarated as if his tender for building a mansion had been accepted.
8. Everyone talks about what goes into the body and no one talks about what comes out.
9. The group also urged new projects to alleviate a serious lack of toilets in many part of the world.
10. Underwear makers in France report soaring sales of such garments to girls as young as 10.
11. The islanders were warned that a storm was coming.
12. We thought that they had decided not to get married but their quarrel was just a storm in a teacup.
13. It stormed so hard that all the electricity went out.

14. John stormed in the meeting waving a piece of paper about.
15. Two of the victims died on Friday and the other Saturday when herds of elephants stormed two farming villages near a forest.
16. Don't take the boat out in the storming weather.
17. It is too stormy to sail today.
18. It's late and you should sleep.
19. Her mother closed the door and the room became its night self then, full of deep corners that swallowed up the dark.
20. Faces brighten with comprehension.

附二 课外扩展训练材料

Dengue Fever

Dengue fever is a mosquito-borne infection. The disease is characterized by high fever, headache, bone or joint and muscle pains, and rash. Dengue haemorrhagic fever is a potentially deadly complication that is characterized by high fever, haemorrhagic phenomena, often with enlargement of the liver, and in severe cases, circulatory failure.

The global prevalence of dengue has grown dramatically in recent decades. The disease is now endemic in more than 100 countries in Africa, the Americas, the Eastern Mediterranean, Southeast Asia and the Western Pacific. Southeast Asia and the Western Pacific are most seriously affected.

Some 2,500 million people—two fifths of the world's population—are now at risk from dengue. WHO currently estimates there may be 50 million cases of dengue infection worldwide every year.

There is no specific treatment for dengue fever. However, careful clinical management by experienced physicians and nurses frequently saves the lives of DHF patients. With appropriate intensive supportive therapy, mortality may be reduced to less than 1%.

No dengue vaccine is currently available. Prospects for reversing the recent trend of increased epidemic activity and geographic expansion of dengue are not promising. In recent years public health authorities have emphasized disease prevention by mosquito control through community efforts to reduce larval breeding sources. Although this approach will probably be effective in the long run, it is unlikely to impact disease transmission in the near future.

(*English Language Learning*)

第六章 句子的翻译(二)

第一节 被动语态的几种译法

被动语态(passive voice)在英语中的使用极为广泛,其被动含义有两种表达方式,一种有形式标志,即"系动词 be ＋过去分词(＋ by ＋ 施动者)";另一种没有形式标志,即根据句子的语义和逻辑,用主动的形式表示被动的含义。凡是不必说出主动者、不愿说出主动者、无从说出主动者或为了上下文的连贯,均可使用被动语态。汉语中也有被动句,其表现形式也有两种:一种含有"被""受""挨""遭""给""叫""为(被)……所"等字样;另一种是用主动形式表达被动含义。相比较而言,汉语中使用被动式的范围要狭窄得多,因此在翻译英语的被动语态时,常常需要做一些句式上的改变和调整。

一、译为汉语主动句

被动语态在汉语中的使用不多,因此在翻译英语中广泛使用的被动句时,很多时候要考虑用主动句翻译英语的被动句。例如:

1. Other aspects of culture must be researched and understood if marketers are to avoid blunders.
   营销商想要避免重大失误,还须研究理解有关文化的其他方面。
2. The magnitude of the financial burden generated by buying a home, financing college for one's children, and laying the groundwork for a comfortable retirement cannot be fully appreciated in the abstract, so here are some concrete figures.
   因买房、供子女上大学、防老所带来的经济负担之重,仅用抽象概念不易理解,所以在此我列出一些具体数字。
3. These acts of mass murder were intended to frighten our nation into chaos and retreat.

这些大规模屠杀行径企图恐吓我们的国民,迫使我们陷入混乱状态,迫使我们退却。

4. Around 44% of children said their dreams were affected by the books they had been reading.
   约44%的儿童认为阅读的书籍影响到了他们的梦境。

5. Foresight and common sense are all that are needed as you go from room to room and imagine what would happen in an earthquake.
   你需要做的只是巡视你的房间,设想地震时房中会发生什么,用你的常识来进行预测。

二、译为汉语无主句

汉语被动句中主语多表示受害者,如"他被盗了""她在外面受气了"。此外,汉语不习惯大量使用被动态,因此,英语被动句也常被译成无主句。例如:

1. Great strides have been taken in search of a cure, and preventative efforts have also been made.
   治疗方面已有长足进步,预防方面也投入了一些精力。

2. With a commitment from the global community, marginalization, human insecurity and inequality can be overcome and create far better results in human development.
   有了全球社会的支持,就能够消除相互排斥现象、人身不安全感和不平等因素,使人类发展更创佳绩。

3. A noted academician suggests that a publicity campaign needs to be done to reassure the public about the use of genetically modified (GM) food.
   一知名学者建议开展宣传活动,让公众放心使用转基因食品。

4. Many strange new means of transport have been developed in our century, the strangest of them being perhaps the hovercraft.
   20世纪发明了许多奇特的新式交通工具,其中最奇特的也许要数气垫船。

5. You are supposed to pay right after the books are delivered.
   书到后应立即付款。

三、译为汉语被动式

与英语被动句一样,汉语被动句除表示不如意、遭遇不测等情况外,有时还用来表达事实及态度的客观性。所以,翻译时也可考虑保留原文的英语被动语态。例如:

1. Most injuries during earthquakes occur when people are hit by falling objects while entering or leaving buildings.
   地震中的大多数伤亡,是在人们进出建筑物时被坠物击中造成的。

2. In the countryside, birth control has been accepted by more and more families.
   在农村,计划生育已为越来越多的家庭所接受。

3. People fear that the world would be in a mess if human beings are cloned some day.
   人们担心如果将来某一天人类会被"克隆",世界将会变得一团糟。

4. She was loudly applauded.
   她大受欢迎。

5. For a long period to come, most of China's elderly will continue to be provided for by their families.
   在未来相当长的一段时间里,中国大多数老年人仍旧要由家庭赡养。

四、译为汉语的"是……"结构

不少有经验的译者用"是……"结构翻译英语被动语态,效果很好,初学者不妨借来一用。例如:

1. The main reason was that the camellia (flower) used in it was traditionally used for funerals in many South American countries.
   主要原因是香水中使用的山茶(花)在南美许多国家传统上是用

在葬礼上的。

2. I won't get caught.

   我是不会被抓到的。

3. Hitler was armed to teeth when he launched the Second World War, but in a few years, he was completely defeated.

   希特勒在发动第二次世界大战时是武装到牙齿的,可不出几年,就被彻底击败了。

4. Solutions to these problems cannot be achieved by any nation or region on its own.

   这些问题仅靠一个国家或一个地区的力量是得不到解决的。

5. The left ear is controlled by the right side of the brain.

   左耳是由右脑控制的。

附一 课堂讲练材料

1. In the present war allegedly for human rights, damages are made by computers, not by the weapon in a warrior's hand.
2. This extended cooperation must be intended not to limit but to enhance mobility of ideas and freedom of the scientists within the system.
3. Most cars in the earliest days of the auto industry were what were called "assembled cars".
4. The Mode T became the first car in which the vast majority of parts were built by either a single auto manufacturer, or by a supplier that was partially owned by our company.
5. They are going to build an apartment house here next year. It is going to be built beside the Office Building.
6. There will be a Teaching Symposium at 2:00 p.m. tomorrow. All the faculty is expected to attend.
7. Poverty in industrialized countries is defined by a household disposable income less than half of the country's overall median income.
8. In the wake of a devastating conflict that inflicted enormous economic damage and cost millions of lives the United Nations was established as a world body

responsible for collective action for the resolution of conflict.

9. As for children, it was universally agreed that time in front of the TV set must be strictly rationed and supervised.

10. It is generally considered not advisable to act that way.

11. A good archer is not known by his arrows, but his aim.

12. The Labor Department say workers were not paid overtime for time spent changing clothes.

13. Under *the Fair Labor Standards Act*, employers are generally required to pay workers time-and-one-half their regular rate of pay for hours worked over 40 per week.

14. One 50-mile drive took the team six hours, with four wide rivers to be crossed and the open-top truck having to be freed from mud six times.

15. Mules and packhorses are being used to take supplies up to the main camp at Huariconca, in a 1,000-ft-deep gorge.

16. Science is often referred to as a doubled-edged sword, increasing our wealth and comfort while leaving people in fear of dangers like human cloning.

17. Do not be surprised if you are offered milk, coffee or soda with a meal.

18. On the whole such a conclusion can be drawn with a certain degree of confidence, but only if the child can be assumed to have had the same attitude towards the test as the other with whom he is being compared, and only if he was not punished by lack of relevant information which they possessed.

19. We are taught that business letters should be written in a formal style rather than personal one.

20. Illness must be correctly diagnosed before they can be treated with medicine.

附二　课外扩展训练材料

A Defense Against Cancer Can Be Cooked Up in Your Kitchen

There is evidence that diet and cancer are related. Some foods may promote cancer, while others may protect you from it.

Foods related to lowering the risk of cancer of the larynx and esophagus all have high amounts of carotene, a form of Vitamin A which is in cantaloupes, peaches, broccoli, spinach, all dark green leafy vegetables, sweet potatoes, carrots, pumpkin, winter squash, tomatoes, citrus fruits and Brussels sprouts.

Foods that may help reduce the risk of gastrointestinal and respiratory tract cancer are cabbage, broccoli, Brussels sprouts, kohlrabi and cauliflower.

Fruits, vegetables, and wholegrain cereals such as oatmeal, bran and wheat may help lower the risk of colorectal cancer.

Foods high in fats, salt, or nitrite-cured foods like ham, and fish and types of sausages smoked by traditional methods should be eaten in moderation. Be moderate in consumption of alcohol also.

A good rule of thumb is cut down on fat and don't be fat. Weight reduction may lower cancer risk. Our 12-year study of nearly a million Americans uncovered high cancer risks particularly among people 40% or more overweight.

Now, more than ever, we know you can cook up your own defense against cancer. So eat healthy and be healthy.

No one faces cancer alone.

第二节 名词从句的翻译

英语中的名词从句(nominal clause)主要包括主语从句、宾语从句、表语从句和同位语从句四种形式,其在句中的功能与名词或名词词组相同。形式上,名词从句主要由 what,whatever,whoever 等关系代词和 that,which 等关系连词以及 where,why,when 等关系副词引导。

一、译为词或词组

有经验的译者常将英语名词从句译成词或词组,效果很好,初学者不妨也尝试一下。这种方法不仅能译出文从字顺的译文,还能锻炼译者的语言概括能力和语言综合能力。例如：

1. He quizzed me about **where I had been last night**.
   他问我**昨晚去过哪儿**。
2. **Where you stumble** becomes your opportunity to make corrections, to learn and grow.
   跌倒的地方就是你改正错误、吸取教训、迅速成长的地方。
3. When someone asked him **how he was doing**, he would reply, "If I were any better, I'd be twins!" He was a natural motivator.
   如果有人问他**近况**，他会说："如果还能再好，我就成双胞胎了！"他是个天生的乐天派。
4. **Whatever is precious** in a cargo is carefully on board and carefully placed. **Whatever is delicate and fine** must be received delicately and its place in the mind thoughtfully assigned.
   贵重物品应小心搬运，谨慎摆放；而**易碎物品**则应细心收纳，妥当安置。
5. I'll try to make up **what I have missed**.
   我要把**缺掉**的补起来。

二、以代词 it 作形式主语的译法

如果代词 it 作形式主语而主语从句放在句子后面，翻译时既可将主语从句提前，也可不提前；代词 it 如果需要强调，也可以译出。

1. It's important to know where you should go for protection when your house starts to shake.
   发现房屋开始摇晃时，第一时间就知道该去哪儿躲避非常重要。
2. It doesn't matter whether we go together or separately.
   一起走或是分开去都可以。
3. It was apparent that he knew nothing about how to repair cars.
   很明显，他对汽车修理一点都不懂。
4. It was obvious that the administration didn't intend to apologize for

the prisoner abuse.

显然,该国政府不想就虐囚事件道歉。

5. It was plain to see how old and firm the girlish heart had grown under the discipline of heavy sorrow.

一望便知,在苦难的重压下,她那颗少女之心已经变得苍老而坚韧。

三、从句单译

将从句内容单独译出,同时将从句所修饰的词和主句部分合并译出。这种方法适用于同位语从句及表语从句的翻译。

1. **Why I did this** was not at first apparent even to my own perception.

为什么这么做,起初连我自己都不清楚。

2. So far, popular reaction to NASA's announcement that **its scientists have discovered evidence of life in a meteorite from Mars** has been pretty positive.

宇航局宣称科学家已在火星陨石中发现生命迹象,对此消息,公众目前反应积极。

3. We haven't yet settled the question **where we are going to spend our summer vacation**.

到什么地方过暑假,我们还没有决定好。

4. That is **why heat can melt ice, vaporize water and cause bodies to expand**.

为什么热能使冰融化,使水蒸发,使物体膨胀,就是这个原因。

5. I put it to you **whether that's the best solution of the problem**.

我请你考虑,看看这究竟是不是解决问题的最佳答案。

附一 课堂讲练材料

1. He has developed a theory that human behavior can be described as a continuum based on a willingness to undertake risk.
2. New DNA evidence taken from the exhumed body of Dr. Sam Sheppard

provides the most compelling piece of evidence that he was wrongfully convicted of murdering his wife in a trial that transfixed America more than four decades ago.

3. It is true that a modern economy is guided by the "invisible hand" of market forces, in which the demands of millions of buyers channel the production of goods and services.

4. Thus, looking at the total picture, it is dubious that anyone would seriously believe that the turning of the economic wheel could be a one-man show or linear in its cause and effect.

5. But if success is the goal, it seems clear to me that the fast track is headed the wrong way.

6. In fact I am concerned that the use of outsider in personal statements is becoming so prevalent that it biases US admission committees against Chinese applicants.

7. Foreigners with little ability to skin through piles of documents to find specific information can now use a computer search to locate what they want.

8. People come to such parties for the conversation as well as the food, so where people are seated can promote the success of a gathering.

9. What we found is that to achieve quality in a product, or by inference, in a life, you have to look enthusiastically for mistakes.

10. But what I would like to focus on is the difference, as I perceive it, between Europeans and Americans.

11. That work is mathematics, and that it should have to justify itself by its applications, as a tool for making the mundane or improving the ephemeral, is an affront not just to mathematics but to the creature that invented it.

12. Some big brain had the idea that, because in some instances the ENTER key does something that resembles the function performed by the carriage return key on an electric typewriter, people new to computers would find the keyboard friendlier if the key were labeled RETURN.

13. And there was always the possibility that a small electrical spark might accidentally bypass the most carefully planned circuit.

14. In each occasion there is an affirmation that by together advancing knowledge we can extend the frontiers of human freedom.
15. What personal knowledge the author has had, of the truth of incidents such as here are related, will appear in its time.
16. Why Earth would be such a fascinating place for UFOs to visit is left unexplained.
17. Rather we must ensure that the multilateral institutions which regulate international trade and investment, are redirected so that they better reflect the needs of developing countries.
18. This does not mean, however, that the government cannot influence the economy to develop in more socially responsible directions.
19. This popular stereotype reflects the implicit American value that everyone ought to advance in life on his own efforts, and that it is "bad" in an important sense to have had someone else's help (especially one's family's help) in becoming successful: People with inherited money and access to power have something to apologize for, not crow about.
20. Furthermore, it is obvious that the strength of a country's economy is directly bound up with the efficiency of its agriculture and industry, and that this in turn rests upon the efforts of scientists and technologists of all kinds.

附二　课外扩展训练材料

Jesus in the Garden

After leaving the upstairs room, Jesus and his apostles go out to the garden of Gethsemane. They have come here many times before. Jesus now tells them to keep awake and to pray. Then he goes a little distance away, and gets face down on the ground to pray.

Later Jesus comes back to where his apostles are. They are asleep! Three times Jesus tells them they should keep awake, but each time he returns he finds them sleeping. "How can you sleep at a time like this?" Jesus says the last time he comes back. "The hour has come for me to be handed over to my enemies."

Just at that moment the noise of a large crowd can be heard. Look! The men are coming with swords and clubs! And they are carrying torches to give them light. When they get closer, someone steps out from the crowd and comes right up to Jesus. He kisses him, as you can see here. The man is Judas!

Jesus asks: "Judas, do you betray me with a kiss?" Yes, the kiss is a sign. It lets the men with Judas know that this is Jesus, the man they want. So Jesus' enemies step forward to grab him. But Peter is not going to let them take Jesus without a fight. He pulls out the sword that he has brought along and strikes at the man near him. The sword just misses the man's head and chops off his right ear.

(My Book of Bible Stories)

第三节　定语从句的翻译

在汉语中,定语成分(包括词和词组)一般位于中心词的前面;在英语中,单个词作定语一般放在所修饰的名词之前,而定语词组或从句一般紧随所修饰的名词之后,但有时也会被其他句子成分隔开,因此在翻译时首先要加以识别。常见的定语从句(attributive clause)的翻译方法有以下几种:

一、译为汉语定语

将定语从句译成汉语定语的做法一般适用于限定性定语从句,要求译者有很好的归纳概括能力。如:

1. They have fostered several youngsters **who had no home to go to**, till they got started in the world.
   他们抚养几名**无家可归的**少年——直到他们踏足社会。

2. When someone asks you a question **you don't want to answer**, smile and say, "Why do you want to know?"
   当别人问你**不想回答的**问题时,可以笑着说:"你为什么想知道?"

3. Marry a person **who likes talking** because when you get old, you'll find that chatting to be a great advantage.

找一个**爱聊**的人结婚吧,因为年纪大了后,你会发觉喜欢聊天是一个人最大的优点。

4. In a top-heavy social structure **where an aging population outnumbers the younger generation**, the physical and financial resources needed to care for the old may prove inadequate.
   在一个**老年人多于年轻人**的失衡的社会结构中,照顾老人所需的人力和财力十分有限。

5. We must ensure that globalization benefits not only the powerful but also the men, women and children **whose lives are ravaged by poverty**.
   我们必须确信全球化既能保证强势群体受益,也能保证**贫困的弱势人群**受益。

6. Stay away from glass, windows, outside doors and walls, and anything **that could fall**, such as lighting fixtures and furniture.
   远离玻璃制品、建筑物外墙、门窗以及其他**可能坠落的**物体,例如灯具和家具。

二、译为并列结构

英译汉时,可考虑将定语从句译成汉语的并列句子结构。如:

1. My heart is full of happiness, **which I like to share with others.**
   我的心中充满欢乐,想与人分享。

2. If there is anyone out there who still doubts that America is a place where all things are possible; **who still wonders if the dream of our founders is alive in our time; who still questions the power of our democracy**, tonight is your answer.
   如果还有人对在美国是否凡事都有可能存疑,还有人怀疑美国奠基者的梦想在我们所处的时代是否依然鲜活,还有人质疑我们的民主制度的力量,那么今晚,这些问题都有了答案。

3. John is a clean-cut, great-looking guy **who likes his father and mother, who frowns on drugs, who takes his profession seriously, who likes to have a good time, who enjoys the company**

of the opposite sex, and who has his own goals and values. He's a boy with no surprise up in his sleeve.

约翰是一个干净利落,相貌伟岸的人,他热爱父母,厌恶毒品,工作认真,爱享受生活,喜欢与异性为伴,有自己的目标和价值观,是一个不会有惊人之举的孩子。

4. There were shouts of "smoke!" from the newspaper sellers, **who still sold their papers**, instead of just giving them away.

卖报人大喊"起火啦!"但没有扔掉报纸逃命,还在坚持卖报纸。

5. We also have taped information about how to apply for a visa **that people can get by telephoning the embassy for instructions.**

我们还录制了如何申请签证的信息,您可拨打使馆电话收听。

三、合译法

英译汉过程中,可将定语从句融合为句中某个部分,如谓语、补语等进行翻译。如:

1. This is a mineral **you've got to have water to make.**
   这种矿物质无水则不能形成。

2. We have seen the decency of a loving and giving people **who have made the grief of strangers their own.**
   我们更看到了有着爱与奉献精神的人民将陌生人的悲痛视为自己的悲痛。

3. I knew every spot **where a murder or robbery had been committed, or a ghost seen.**
   我知道什么地方发生过盗窃案或凶杀案,什么地方闹过鬼。

合译法指把定语从句与其他字、词、词组或句子合在一起翻译,从而将复合句译成汉语单句。

4. I stand here today humbled by the task before us, grateful for the trust you have bestowed, mindful of the sacrifices borne by our ancestors. I thank President Bush for his service to our nation, as well as the generosity and cooperation **he has shown throughout this transition.**

我今天站在这儿,为我们眼前的任务感到谦卑,为你们给我的信任感激,为我们先人的牺牲不被忘怀。我多谢乔治·布什总统对国家的服务,以及他在**整个权力过渡过程中展示的慷慨与合作**。

5. As brighter areas of the image eject more electrons than the darker or shaded portions, an electronic image is produced in **which varying degrees of positive charge duplicate light intensities seen in the scene being pictured.**

因为图像较明亮的部分比黑暗的部分或者阴影部分发射的电子多,所以产生的电子图像随正电荷的变化强度使正在描述的荧幕上的光强度成倍增强。

四、译为偏正复句

一些定语从句实际上起着相当于原因、目的、结果、条件、转折等状语从句的作用,这类句子可译为各种相应的偏正复句。如:

1. She actually works—works for the State **which did its best in those dark years to prevent her from working.**

她是一个实干家,实实在在地为政府工作,而这个政府在那黑暗年代里却竭尽全力妨碍她工作。

2. ...and, therefore, I say that if you should still be in this country when Mr. Martin marries, I wish you may not be drawn in, by your intimacy with the sisters, to be acquainted with the wife, **who will probably be some mere father's daughter, without education.**

所以我说等马丁先生结婚的时候,你若是还待在这个地方的话,我愿你不要因为同姐妹们的亲近关系而结识他太太,她可能只是一个农夫的女儿,没有受过教育。

3. A civilization **that encourages the motive of self-interested calculation to rule every sphere of social life** is on a sure path to moral bankruptcy.

如果一种文明鼓励人们一心为己,任自私行为肆虐于社会生活的各个方面,那么,这种文明注定会道德沦丧。

4. In 2014, Dr. Werner died, and Mrs. Werner's children grew concerned about leaving their mother in the old neighborhood, **where she loved to walk alone at night.**

2014年沃纳大夫去世，子女们感到把寡母留在老家不太放心，因为她常爱在晚上独自外出散步。

5. We will build the roads and bridges, the electric grids and digital lines that **feed our commerce and bind us together.**

我们将修桥筑路，铺设电缆网络和数码线路，以协助商业发展，也让大家紧密相连。

附一　课堂讲练材料

1. Since each stay was only for a single year, I always bought an inexpensive bike that constantly needed to be taken to the ubiquitous bike repairmen.
2. We think of a math whiz as someone who can do in his head what a calculator can do on silicon.
3. It is a way to produce an exact genetic replica of yourself that will walk the earth years after you're gone.
4. The advancement of knowledge and science defines one such global arena where men and women can work together to contribute to human freedom in its fullest sense of a better life for all humanity.
5. The company decided it was "impracticable" to inspect all the plasma-collection sites itself, and decided to rely instead on FDA reports which it did not, in fact, review.
6. Young graduates need to make difficult choices that will determine their future direction.
7. To have an apple a day can help you keep the doctor away.
8. Manpower is needed for the domestic market and workforce, instead of over-relying on multinationals who owe no allegiance to the country.
9. The telephone call is a breaking-and-entering that we invite by having telephones in the first place.
10. The customer's photo is taken with a digital camera and then printed

on stamp sheets, a process that takes about five minutes.
11. Weapons of mass destruction are now available to regimes who have little respect for human life.
12. Follow your bliss means to follow a course in life that is most exciting and challenging for you and to follow a direction that brings you the greatest personal and professional satisfaction.
13. Technology is only just beginning to let us search the skies for the clues another civilization might offer.
14. If it has done nothing else, however, the new coincidence of scientific and theological versions of creation seems to have opened up a conversation that has been neglected for centuries.
15. Not long ago a very interesting lecture on the psychological problems that occur among foreigners living in China was given in Beijing.
16. I have a five-year-old daughter whom I bike to and from nursery school.
17. In the second place, in the psychological arena a condition has emerged which affects both our desire and our ability to read or even to watch TV intensively.
18. This fact helps explain the deep-seated emotions that underlie America's gun control debate.
19. Nevertheless, it is also parental responsibility to instill in their children character values that would guide them toward wise decision.
20. Most astronomers now accept the theory that the universe had an instant of creation, that it came to be in a vast fireball explosion 15 or 20 billion years ago.
21. When he was refused, Oven ran out of the hospital but returned minutes later in his car, which he drove through the glass doors and down a 30-meter corridor to reception.
22. But we recognize that our officers can make mistakes or in some cases that there is more information that can be shown later that will help the applicant qualify for a visa.
23. Two Canadian otters at a sanctuary in Scotland have been placed under 24-hour protection from aggressive local otters who are confused by

their "foreign accents", a newspaper reported.
24. There is also the ethical issue of intentionally putting unborn children through genetic experiments that have potentially disastrous results.

附二 课外扩展训练材料

Environmental Art

During the 1950s artists, such as Robert Rauschenberg (b. 1925) via his Assemblages, took further the role of art as consciousness-raising, by including objects from the everyday world into their works. For instance, one of Rauschenberg's paintings, abstract expressionist in style, included a radio; others are free-standing, consisting of apparently incongruous objects assembled by the artist. These works try to make us more aware of our environment and of the narrow line which divides the rational and the irrational. They free our minds from considering our world as fixed and immutable.

One of the developments of the use of assemblage is the breaking down of barriers between sculpture and painting. In the sense that assemblages are three-dimensional, they can be called sculptures; yet none of the traditional materials or working methods of the sculptor have been used. Post-war sculptors themselves have redefined their work, in terms of their working methods and materials. David Smith (1906—1965) extended the boundaries of sculpture in the 1950s by making works from welded metal strips, so making us aware of the landscape, which we see through the gaps between the metal of the works themselves. Others, working from a similar impetus to assemblage artists, used the junk of industrial society as material for sculptures. John Chamberlain (b. 1927), for instance, makes his works from parts of wrecked cars, which he welds together and then paints. His working method of welding is close to that of modern industry, but his use of wrecked cars reminds us of the inherent dangers of the products of society, while the fact that he transmutes this wreckage via paint and the balancing of forms refutes conventional notions of beauty.

The sculptor Anthony Caro (b. 1924) has more recently pursued the implications of David Smith's work, making elegant sculptures from ready-made steel parts normally used in industry, which he welds together and sometimes paints a uniform bright colour. These parts are in themselves slender, though the size of the sculpture is often large. Usually placed in outdoor settings, they have the effect of defining the surrounding space, rather than displacing it, as traditional sculptures do. So again we have an art which makes us more aware of ourselves and our environment.

Environmental art soon took assemblage further again with artists transforming whole rooms into works of art. Edward Keinholz (b. 1927), for example, created Roxy's (1961), evoking a room in a brothel, with ordinary, rather tatty furniture complete with juke-box playing 1940s tunes, juxtaposed with such surreal objects as a clothed tailor's dummy whose head is replaced by a boar's skull. This evocation of the sordidness of a brothel derives its power from the mixing of the mundane with the incongruous, and is harder hitting because we walk around in it rather than being mere outsiders.

(The Illustrated Encyclopedia of Western Art)

第四节 状语从句的翻译

状语从句(adverbial clause)的作用是用来修饰主句中的动词、形容词或副词。从语序安排上看,汉语中状语成分的位置较为固定,而英语则比较灵活;从类别上看,英汉语状语都可以表示地点、时间、原因、目的、结果、条件、让步、行为方式、比较关系等。在这几种状语中,由 when,while,before,after 及 until 引导的状语从句比较特殊,因为它们除了表示时间关系外,还可根据具体情况理解为其他类别的状语或与主句并列的结构。下面我们只集中探讨几种比较特殊的状语从句的翻译。

一、when 或 while 引导的状语从句翻译

when 或 while 引导的状语从句除了表示时间外,还常常表达并列、对比、条件、转折、让步等关系,翻译时宜灵活机动。

1. A woman will say, "Thanks A Lot" when she is really ticking off at you. It signifies that you have offended her in some callous way, and will be followed by the "Loud Sigh".
   当女人其实在责备你时,她会说:"多谢。"这表明你已经无情地触犯了她,接下来,你会听到"大声的叹息"。(译为时间状语)

2. While demand for executives is likely to outpace supply for years, word is spreading that job-hopping, in the long run, can hurt a career.
   尽管管理人员可能在若干年内仍然供不应求,人们还是普遍认为,跳槽从长远看对事业发展不利。(译为让步状语)

3. Forty-one percent of the 12,000 people who responded to the council's survey said they were most productive in the morning, while 38 percent said they hit their stride in the evening.
   该委员会收回的 12,000 份问卷中,有 41% 的人认为自己晨间效率最高,38% 称自己的最佳状态在夜晚。(译为并列结构)

4. While I admit that the problems are difficult, I don't agree that they cannot be solved.
   我承认这些题不好解,但并不认为不可解。(译为转折状语)

5. Can any society survive when its citizens are all engaged in a furious competition to carve up the spoils?
   如果一个社会的全体公民都在争权夺利,那么这个社会能逃得过瓦解的命运吗?(译为条件状语)

二、before, after, until, till 等引导的状语从句的翻译

before, after, until, till 等引导的状语从句不仅可表达时间概念,有时还可用来表示某种逻辑关系,翻译时宜根据上下文灵活处理。例如:

1. It certainly won't be another 34 years before I see him again.
   下次见他肯定不用再等 34 年了。

2. Conditions are extremely dangerous in fog, rain and at night. It is just a matter of time before a plane crashes in Swaziland.
   雾天、雨天和夜间的情况极度危险,迟早会有飞机在斯威士兰坠毁。

3. Guess was sentenced to 18 months in prison, but spent only three months behind bars before she was paroled.

   盖斯被判入狱 18 个月,不过仅三个月后就获得了假释。

4. New British sports minister Richard Caborn has been lampooned by the media after he revealed a startling lack of knowledge about his country's top sportsmen.

   英国新任体育大臣理查德·卡本居然不知道国内顶尖运动员的情况,因而遭到媒体的冷嘲热讽。

5. We danced and danced until a lot of people joined in.

   我们跳呀,跳呀,慢慢地很多人陆续加入进来,与我们一起跳。

三、常见状语从句的翻译

一般性状语从句的翻译十分灵活,需要在准确掌握原文的基础上,适当运用前面学过的技巧进行处理。例如:

1. They should also avoid jokes, since what is considered funny in one part of the world may not be so humorous in another.

   广告用语还应避免开玩笑,因为某个地方认为逗乐发笑的事,换了另外的地方就不那么可乐了。

2. When marketers do not understand and appreciate the values, tastes, geography, climate, superstitions, religion, or economy of a culture, they fail to capture their target market.

   营销商如果不重视不了解一种文化的价值观、品味、地理、气候、迷信、宗教以及经济等,就占领不了目标市场。

3. Lead is toxic, especially for children, because it hampers brain development.

   铅毒性大,对儿童尤其有害,会阻碍大脑发育。

4. Such a study is well worth the effort, even though some aspects of English and the meaning of many words, have changed since Shakespeare's day.

   这种学习方法值得一用,虽说英语的某些习惯用法以及许多词的意义自莎士比亚以来已经发生了变化。

5. One American food company's friendly "Joly Green Giant" (for advertising vegetables) became something quite different when it was translated into Arabic as "Intimidating Green Ogre".

一家美国食品公司并无恶意的"快乐绿巨人"(蔬菜广告)译成阿拉伯语就完全变了味,成了"吓人的绿魔鬼"。

附一 课堂讲练材料

1. I missed the precise moment, sometime between my grammar and graduate schools, when TV went from tolerated vice to vital social custom, one practically necessary for membership in the community.

2. After a quarter century in which each major party has routinely accused leading figures in the other of breaking assorted laws, it may now take an egregious scandal to rock the public.

3. The human race is likely to be wiped out by a doomsday virus before this millennium is out unless it starts to colonize space, top British scientist Stephen Hawking warned.

4. Dr. Sheppard served 10 years in prison before the United States Supreme Court, ruling that his trial was tainted by excessive press attention, ordered a retrial.

5. While the Government has assembled a list of 291 species of animals, birds, insects and plants that are endangered, it has not so far passed legislation that protects them.

6. Fermat's last theorem owes its fame to its age—it was born about five years before Issac Newton—and its simplicity.

7. It won't be long, however, before these technical barriers are breached.

8. Until the late 1940s, when television began finding its way into American homes, companies relied on print and radio to promote their products and services.

9. While beauty itself may be only skin—deep studies show our perception of beauty may be hardwired in our brains.

10. Should there be urgent situation, press the red button to switch off the electricity.
11. The *New Scientist* report did not identify the candle brands or say which countries manufactured them, describing them only as having been made in "the Far East".
12. Much as he likes her, he does get irritated with her sometimes.
13. Therefore, although technical advances in food production and processing will perhaps be needed to ensure food availability, meeting food needs will depend much more on equalizing economic power among the various segments of populations within the developing countries themselves.
14. If you want to insure against all the other terrible things that might happen to you or your car, you can take out a comprehensive policy.
15. He shut the window with such force that the window broke.
16. Electricity is such a part of our everyday lives and so much taken for granted nowadays that we rarely think twice when we switch on the light or turn on the radio.
17. Because we are both prepared to proceed on the basis of equality and neutral respect, we meet at a moment when we can make peaceful cooperation a reality.
18. Since this gives individual voters and states more discretion in deciding the legality of abortion, the debates on the issue have become highly volatile.
19. The audience kept quiet till the concert came to an end, when they gave a loud applause.

附二 课外扩展训练材料

Smashing the Ulcer Myths

Movie star Tom Cruise complained that the stress of shooting his film *Eyes Wide Shut* gave him a stomach ulcer. Well, sorry, Tom, but the latest scientific evidence shows most ulcers develop not as a result of stress or diet but because of infection with a bacteria called Helicobacter Pylori.

This organism spreads when infection faeces come into contact with hands, food or water. Most people seem to be infected during childhood.

The bacteria weakens the stomach's protective lining making it more susceptible to the damaging effects of the acids and enzymes our bodies produce to digest food.

Ulcer Myths and Facts

It's a myth that stomach ulcers develop from emotional stress, despite the Hollywood insistence in many films that this is a scientific truth. Here are the facts about ulcers:

◆ You're most likely to develop a duodenalulcer if you are a man between the age of 30 and 50, or a woman over 60.

◆ The most common symptom is a gnawing or burning pain in the abdomen. This often occurs between meals and in the early hours of the morning. It may last from a few minutes to a few hours and be relieved by eating or taking antacids.

◆ Less common ulcer symptoms include nausea, vomiting, loss of appetite and loss of weight.

◆ Smoking cigarettes increases your chances of getting an ulcer and slows the healing of existing ulcers.

◆ Coffee, tea, colas and foods which contain caffeine seem to stimulate acid secretion in the stomach, aggravating the pain of an ulcer.

◆ Although emotional stress is no longer thought to cause ulcers, people often report that it increases ulcer pain. Physical stress—like undergoing major surgery or sustaining severe injures—does increase the risk of developing ulcers.

◆ Spicy, fatty, or acidic foods aren't thought to be linked with ulcers.

◆ Taking drugs like aspirin can increase the chance of developing stomach ulcers.

If you think you have an ulcer, see your doctor as soon as possible. There are a number of tests available to confirm the presence of Helicobacter Pylori and ulcers can be treated with drugs and are normally eradicated within a few weeks. These days surgery is seldom necessary.

(Nicky Pellegrino)

第五节 标点符号的灵活处理

1949年4月1日,驻宁大专院校学生举行游行示威,反饥饿,反内战,反对假和平,要求真和平。此时,国民党政府派出大批特务警察进行镇压,制造了震惊全国的"四·一"惨案。几天后,在原中央大学礼堂隆重举行追悼会。会场挂满挽联,其中有副标点符号撰写的挽联:

? ?? ???
! !! !!!

这副无字挽联不仅强烈质问和控诉了反动派,而且表示了血债血还的坚定决心。由此幅妙联想到目前大学生中普遍存在的两种现象:一是书写过程中不注重标点符号;二是在理解原文及翻译过程中忽视标点符号的表情达意功能。

总体而言,除了没有顿号和书名号外,英语标点符号(punctuation)和汉语标点符号差别不大,但使用场合有所不同,表达的意义也有所不同,尤其是破折号、冒号、分号和逗号。英译汉时这些标点符号要予以足够重视。

一、破折号

汉语破折号(dash)表示意义的转折,或表示后面是解释性内容,常用于习语的表达,如"马尾串豆腐——提不起来","外甥打灯笼——照舅(旧)","猪八戒照镜子——里外不是人"等;或表示声音的拖长,如"立正——!"而英语破折号使用频率更高,既可以表示解释、说明,也可以表示结论,还可以表示对比、原因,或提出问题,所以翻译时宜根据语境灵活处理。如:

1. This is the source of our confidence—the knowledge that God calls on us to shape an uncertain destiny.
   这是我们信心的源泉——是对主感召我们塑造不确定命运的认知。(译为解释性内容)

2. He had told all his worries now—all except the worst.
   他已经把自己所有的烦恼都抖出来了——除了那件最糟的。(译为补充性内容)

3. She doesn't care a button for me—with her confounded little dry manner.

瞧她那副冷若冰霜的小样——根本不把我当回事。（译为说明性内容）

4. But the boy has justification for the kick—she hit him first.
这男孩儿踢了人还挺有理——他说是她先动的手。（译为解释性内容）

5. Go into the library—I mean, if you please.
进图书馆——我的意思是，假如你愿意的话。（译为解释性内容）

有时，英语原文中出现的破折号可以被其他标点符号取代，如：

6. But you can argue that learning another language well is more taxing than, say, learning to play chess well—it involves sensitivity to a set of complicated rules, and also to context.
可以说，学好外语比学下棋更费力，因为学语言要求对一整套复杂的规则以及语境非常敏感。（破折号被逗号取代）

7. A south China woman said to be the oldest in the country—and possibly the world—has died of natural causes at age 119, a state-run newspaper reported.
据中国一家国营报纸报道，一名据说是中国最长寿（也可能是世界上最长寿）的南方妇女于本周二自然死亡，享年119岁。（破折号被括号取代）

8. The magazine's editors also spent time peering into the fashion choices of Republican vice presidential candidate Sarah Palin—her rimless glasses, step-toe pumps and up do hairstyle.
杂志编辑们也对共和党副总统候选人莎拉·佩林的时尚选择做了番评论。佩林戴着一副无框眼镜，爱穿露趾凉拖，而且总是梳着高高的发髻。（破折号被句号取代）

有时，虽然英语原句没出现破折号，但依据汉语需要，英译汉时可适当增加破折号或用破折号取代原来的标点符号。例如：

9. It is so easy now to see the irony of smoking: Children do it to be like adults, who smoke but wish they didn't.
如今，吸烟的讽刺意味是显而易见的——孩子们吸烟是为了模仿大人,而吸烟的大人们却后悔自己学会了吸烟。

10. Clark in "Handle with Care": A bittersweet case of double identities.
《小心翼翼》中的克拉克——一个具有双重人格、令人又喜又忧的角色。

二、冒号

冒号(colon)在汉语中用来提示下文,常见于人物讲话的内容前。在英语中,冒号除了这一功能外,还可用于解释前文或引出具体的事例,翻译时可视情况保留冒号,或删除冒号,也可取代原文的冒号,或增加原文没有的冒号。如:

1. They were now clustered round their mama in the drawing room: She lay reclined on a sofa by the fire-side, and with her darlings about her looked perfectly happy.
   他们此时都在客厅里,正簇拥在母亲周围,而母亲斜靠在炉边的沙发上,身边是心爱的儿女,看上去十分幸福。(用逗号取代冒号)

2. Remember that the man who can shoulder the most risk will gain the deepest love and the supreme accomplishment.
   记住:那些敢于承担最大风险的人才能得到最深的爱和最大的成就。(增加冒号)

3. The shorter men included: a doctor, a best-selling author, a champion skier, a venture capitalist who'd made millions by the age of 25.
   这帮矮个子男人中间有一个医生、一位畅销书作家、一名滑雪冠军、一位25岁时身家就达到数百万美元的风险投资家。(删除冒号)

4. I was excited about the idea of having a clone of myself in the beginning: I might start life all over again and redress the mistakes made in the past, and then I could live longer to see a better future.
   起初,想到"克隆"自己,我就十分兴奋。我想,要是真能那样的

话,我的生活就能重新开始,就能避免犯同样的错误,就能够长寿,能够享受到更美好的未来。(用句号取代冒号)

5. Nuclear power's danger to health, safety, and even life itself can be summed up in one word: radiation.
核能对健康、安全,甚至对生命本身构成的危险可以用一个词来概括——辐射。(用破折号取代冒号)

6. "A razzle dazzling performance from the mighty Michelle," was the London *Evening Standard*'s verdict on her arrival.
伦敦《标准晚报》这样评价米歇尔:"魅力米歇尔的一场光彩夺目的演出。"(用冒号取代逗号)

7. Remember the three "respects". Respect yourself, respect others, stand on dignity and pay attention to your behavior.
记住三个"尊重":尊重自己;尊重别人;保持尊严,对自己的行为负责。(用冒号取代句号)

8. A spokesman said: "Although they discuss very different things during their gossiping sessions, men and women agree on one thing—talking with mates, work colleagues or partners makes them feel like they belong."
发言人说:"尽管男人和女人闲聊时的话题大不相同,但他们在一点上是一致的,那就是与朋友、同事或伴侣聊天会让他们有归属感。"(保留冒号)

三、分号

分号(semicolon)在汉语中多用于一个长句中的两个并列成分之间,而在英语中,分号仅表示比逗号长一点、比句号短一点的停顿,翻译时宜灵活处理。如:

1. Her grandmother's World War Two generation had embraced motherhood and rejected careers; her mother's postwar generation rejected motherhood and embraced careers.
她祖母是二战时代的人,取为母之道而弃事业;她母亲属战后的一代人,弃为母之道而取事业。(保留分号)

2. I don't want ifs and buts; swallow your medicine at once.

别泡蘑菇了,马上吞下你的药。(用逗号取代分号)

3. Don't speak evasively; give me a definite answer.
   别遮遮掩掩的了,请给我个明确答复。(用逗号取代分号)

4. Reading makes a full man; conference a ready man and writing an exact man.
   读书使人充实,讨论使人机智,写作使人精确。(用逗号取代分号)

5. And there were people of all sorts in this crowd: injured soldiers, barely able to walk; workers, some helpful while others mean and thoughtless; old women with crying young children; kind and cruel people alike, all thrown together in this endless stream of bodies.
   这帮人真是形形色色:有几乎无法行走的伤兵;有打工者,他们有的乐于助人,有的卑鄙自私;有带着顽童的老妇;有善人,有恶人,所有人都一股脑汇入这毫无尽头的人流之中。

6. Risk makes you feel good; you relish the focus, the intensity of the moment.
   冒险使你感觉良好,使你品味全神贯注的感觉,品味那一刻的高度紧张。(用逗号取代分号)

7. Science is provisional; it progresses from one hypothesis to another, always testing, rejecting the ideas that do not work, that are contradicted by new evidence.
   科学不是永恒的,它总是从一个假设发展到另一个假设,总是在验证,总是在抛弃那些不可行的思想,抛弃那些与新数据相矛盾的观点。(用逗号取代分号)

四、逗号

逗号(comma)在英语中除表示句间的停顿外,有时还用于列举一连串的事物,相当于汉语中的顿号,翻译时宜根据汉语的构句方式采取恰如其分的方法保留逗号,删除逗号,增加逗号,或用其他标点符号取代逗号。如:

1. From Florence the river Arno runs down to Pisa, and then it reaches the sea.

阿诺河从佛罗伦萨流经比萨入海。（删除逗号）

2. Is there a difference between stupidity, foolishness, dumbness and, say, plain one-headedness?

    愚钝、愚蠢、愚笨和"一根筋"之间有没有区别？（用顿号取代逗号）

3. It happens in Hilton.

    盛世聚首,尽在希尔顿。（增添逗号）

4. All sovereign states, large or small, strong or weak, rich or poor, are equal members of the international community.

    世界上所有主权国家,不分大小、强弱、贫富,都是国际社会的平等一员。（用顿号取代逗号）

5. I can say to you, without any flattery, that your way of delivery is more inventive and fruitful than others.

    我可以对你说——我这样说毫无奉承之意——您讲课的方式比别的教授的讲课方式更有特色,更有效果。（用破折号取代逗号）

6. The people most in demand, and most likely to job hop, are in finance and accounting, sales and marketing, and include those filling general manager posts.

    市场最紧俏、跳槽最频繁的是财会、销售和营销等行业的人,还包括职业经理人。（用顿号取代逗号）

附一 课堂讲练材料

1. The barbed shaft of love had penetrated his dull hide. Six weeks—appropinquity—opportunity—had victimized him completely.

2. The judge removed the scarecrow, which had apparently been manning the watchtower for days, and took it to the court as evidence.

3. A number of head teachers in France—where school uniforms are practically unheard of—have slapped a ban on showing off thongs and tummies, the French daily *Le Parisien* said on Friday.

4. Broadly speaking, human beings may be divided into three classes:

those who are toiled to death, those who are worried to death, and those who are bored to death.

5. But if you create a headless clone of just your body, you have created a ready source of replacement parts to keep you—your consciousness—going indefinitely

6. But that's assuming higher education remains the key to upward mobility—a big "if", warn some, who foresee a time not too distant when degrees are not so prized, and skipping college might be a wiser career choice.

7. No one will ever know—certainly he never knew—how much money he owed.

8. He also noted that reindeer portrayed as pulling Santa's sleighs were all female—male reindeer lose their antlers before the winter while females keep them until the spring.

9. But some foods seem to have a timeless taste appeal and an enduring ability to leap on to clothing—red wine and coffee figured prominently on both the 1991 and 2001 lists.

10. Redheads may actually have another trait that makes them stand out—sensitivity to pain, specialists reported.

11. Nearly a quarter of the public bus drivers in India's capital—known for their appalling safety record—lack basic driving skills and hundreds of them have vision problems, a survey says.

12. They found that the risk of admission for heart attacks increased by 25 percent on June 30—the day of the England-Argentina match—and the following two days.

13. The implication is that the majority are not fully alert in the middle of the day—the traditional time for a siesta in hot countries.

14. One of Britain's most exclusive grocery stores needs a new chocolate taster—and will pay 35,000 pounds a year for the successful candidate.

15. They didn't pick this or that kind of job out of passion; the circumstances of their lives did the choosing for them.

16. The firm said in a statement it owed $250 million to the government while the government had not paid $112 million in dues—a vicious

circle increasingly common in a recession-hit economy where firms and supplies no longer have any cash.

17. Under Chinese Patent Law, a design patent may be attached to any design, shape, pattern, color, or combination thereof, of a product, which creates an aesthetic feeling and is suitable for industrial application.

18. A real life-and-death drama between two television stars has enthralled Singapore as a young actor saved his dying girlfriend by donating part of his liver.

19. Jail guards may not know, for example, how to respond to disturbed inmates who simply are not capable of standing in an orderly line for meals; a common result is that the inmates are put in solitary confinement.

20. Norway struck an unprecedented blow for sexual equality when the government said it would force companies to guarantee that at least 40 percent of board members are women.

21. Its findings come at a time when young Britons are increasingly being drinking, which has serious health risks.

附二 课外扩展训练材料

The Cutty Sark

Historically, London is one of Britain's great trading ports. So today there are many sights along the river Thames which reminds the visitor of Britain's maritime past. One of the most interesting places to visit is Greenwich in the South East of London, where you can go round the famous Cutty Sark.

The Cutty Sark is a type of sailing ship called a clipper. They launched her in 1869, and wanted her to be the fastest ship in the China tea trade. For that is what the ship carried—tea, from the Far East. In those days there was a lot of competition among the ship owners to bring home tea from China as quickly as possible. In 1954, many years later, they moored the Cutty Sark at Greenwich so that visitors can admire her.

When you look round the ship, you see lots of things which tell the story of the sailors who spent months on board the clipper. You can see the hold where the tea chests were and also the bales of wool that the ship later carried. When they built the Suez Canal, steamers took over the tea trade and the Cutty Sark started to carry wool from Australia.

The sailors' quarters were worth a visit. The sailors slept in bare wooden bunks with straw mattresses. Conditions for the officers were better, but still bad by modern standards. In the front part of the ship you can see the kitchen or galley, and the carpenter's workshop. The living and working areas were very small and very uncomfortable for the sailors on long voyage. It is hard to imagine what their life was like; they worked at least twelve hours a day, seven days a week, often in cold, wet and dangerous conditions. And the men only earned a few pounds a month.

There is an exhibition of ships' relics on the Cutty Sark, as well as a collection of figureheads from many different ships.

Up on the deck again, you can look up at the complicated rigging on the masts. There were only about 28 men to handle the ship, even in the strong gales around the Cape Horn, in South American! The steering wheel is on deck too, so the helmsman had no protection at all from the wind, rain and sea.

(Charlotte Greg)

第六节 长句的翻译(一)

英语的句法特点是关系词丰富,重视空间构建,即以主谓结构为主干,然后运用各种关系词把有关的材料组成各类枝干,依附或嵌扣在主干上;汉语则偏重运用活动词,甚至尽量省略关系词以达到活动词集中和突出的效果,汉语句法的特点是按照各动作实际上或逻辑上的时间顺序来安排各活动词在句子结构中的先后位置。

由于英汉两种语言的句法特点有上述明显差异,为了使译文易于理解、形式得当,翻译时首先必须理清原文的句法结构,抓住全句的中心内容,弄清句子各层次之间的逻辑关系,将注重空间构建的结构转化为汉语的时间动作先后顺序的结构。

一、保持原文语序

按照原句的顺序翻译,有时可避免译文产生混乱,又可维持原文结构。并列复合句、带宾语从句或表语从句的主从复合句一般可按照原文的思路和顺序来译。如:

1. His heart was not in school, but in the woods, where he often escaped alone, trying to shut out the sights, sounds and smells of his alcoholic home.

   他的心并不在学校,而在他经常独自躲藏的树林,在那里,他试图摆脱自己那酒鬼家庭的混乱、声响和气味。

2. The first elected Russian president, the man who declared what once was the world's largest nation, the Soviet Union, extinct, Boris Yeltsin resigned on December 31, 1999 after eight years in power.

   俄罗斯第一位民选总统、宣告世界最大国家苏联解体的一代巨人、叱咤俄罗斯政坛八年的叶利钦于20世纪最后一天黯然辞职。

3. Girl, bathing on Bikini, eyeing boy, finds boy eyeing Bikini on bathing girl.

   穿比基尼的女孩看着男孩,发现男孩正在打量游泳女郎身上的三点式。

4. When a manager of a State-owned enterprise is sought, for example, practical experience and achievements are taken into consideration, not just which certificates he or she once obtained from an obscure management training programme.

   比如,某国有企业在招聘经理时,会考虑实际工作经验和实际取得的成就,而不仅仅是应聘人员是否曾获得某不知名的管理培训课程的证书。

5. The two-year-old World Toilet Organization, which aims to raise global awareness of toilet and sanitation standards, marked its

annual World Toilet Day with a call for people to speak out against poorly designed or filthy latrines.

成立两周年的世界厕所组织以提高全世界厕所及卫生标准意识为己任,在一年一度的世界厕所日呼吁人们对设计蹩脚的或不洁的厕所说"不"。

二、改变原文语序

(一) 先将表达原因、条件、事实等的内容译出,再翻译表示结论、态度的部分

1. I visited the neighboring villages, and added greatly to my stock of knowledge, by noting their habit and customs, and conversing with their sages and great men...
   我去过邻近许多的乡镇,观察当地风俗习惯,与当地圣贤接谈,知识大有长进。

2. My heart sank. Some of them did not weigh more than 135 pounds. Others looked too young to be on trouble.
   我心一沉:这帮人中有的体重不到135磅,有的显得太稚嫩,根本应付不了可能出现的麻烦。

3. The accumulation of new data during the past decades has brought a refinement of some earlier views and concepts.
   几十年来,由于不断地积累资料,以前的一些观点和思想得以进一步完善。

4. Fed up with people targeted by false rumors turning up dead or wrongfully arrested, the mayor of a small Colombian town has made gossip a crime punishable by up to four years in prison.
   哥伦比亚某镇镇长不堪虚假谣言致使一些人冤死或蒙冤入狱的困扰,颁布法令规定恶意流言飞语为犯罪行为,可获刑四年。

5. Like a ship's sails the wings billow out as the insect flies, altering shape to take advantage of the wind and steer the animal through the air.
   昆虫飞行时,翅翼像船帆一样随风张起,并不断改变形状,就这样,昆虫利用风力在空中飞行。

（二）先译出作为背景信息的内容，再将主语中心词和谓语部分一起译出

1. He should have thought twice before taking such a rash action.
   采取如此轻率的行动之前，他应该三思才是。

2. Methane bubbles from the sea floor could, in theory, sink ships and may explain the odd disappearances of some vessels, Austrian researchers reported on Tuesday.
   据澳大利亚研究人员周二报告，来自海底的甲烷气泡理论上能造成沉船事故，这可以解释船只神秘的失踪现象。

3. What experts call the criminalization of the mentally ill has grown as an issue as the nation's inmate population has exploded and as corrections officials and families of the emotionally disturbed have become alarmed by the problems posed by having the mentally ill behind bars.
   全国范围内监狱犯人人数暴涨，管教人员和精神病人的家属十分担忧把精神病患者关进监狱所引发的种种问题，看来专家们所谓的精神病人犯罪已经成了一个棘手的问题。

4. Just five years later, with Microsoft choking on its own growth, Mr. Gates hired a business manager, Steve Ballmer, who had cut his teeth at Procter & Gamble, which sells soap.
   仅仅5年之后，为了应对微软飞速发展产生的瓶颈，盖茨雇佣了史蒂夫·鲍尔默作商务经理。鲍尔默只在宝洁公司初试身手，卖过肥皂。

5. Burger King is marketing the product through a Web site featuring a photo of its King character reclining fireside and naked but for an animal fur strategically placed not to offend.
   在汉堡王公司宣传该产品的网页上有一幅特写照片，汉堡王的标志卡通——国王——光着身子斜倚在火炉边，仅策略性地搭着一张兽皮，以防冒犯观众。

第六章 句子的翻译(二)

附一 课堂讲练材料

1. The timings of the games, in the early morning or at midday, have posed a dilemma to millions of soccer-mad Britons used to watching games in the evenings or at weekends and desperate to follow England and Ireland's World Cup progress live.
2. The shrinkage of the Sun to this state would transform our oceans into ice and our atmosphere into liquid air.
3. Does it matter whether we sense our place in nature so long as we have cities and technology?
4. What has changed, many experts believe, is that Americans have grown more reluctant to cast stones at friends and neighbors who fail to meet the moral standards they set for themselves.
5. These crimes, characterized by the trading of power for benefits, are believed to have an undermining effect on the nation's legal system, reform and development, if they are allowed to continue.
6. Government expenditures and aid programs were substantially restructured to invest in jobs and basic social services, including nutrition, health, and education.
7. Governments also took a strong lead in promoting more rapid progress towards gender equality by giving special emphasis to female education, improving family planning services, technologies to lessen women's workloads, and equal opportunity legislation.
8. Millions have migrated to urban slums, where poverty, overcrowding, and poor situation make life almost unbearable and where the chief form of entertainment involves sophisticated communication technologies constantly parading the images of wealth before the realities of poverty.
9. These sealed cooling systems, it is claimed, can actually provide payback within a matter of months because of the water and effluent cost savings and the removal of the need for a chemical treatment plant and the resultant chemical costs.
10. That is why in America marketing and public relations are so

pervasive—because Americans believe that language can be used to change the way people think, and that language is used to express oneself.

11. Tissue samples taken from Dr. Sheppard's body, which was exhumed under a court order last fall, show he is excluded as a donor of the blood found at the murder scene.

12. *The weekly* said that under the proposed rules, pet owners could be prosecuted if they failed to give dogs, cats and rabbits what they needed — including adequate food and water, enough space and companionship.

13. The census was brought forward by one day because of the number of weddings scheduled for the original date of July 18 would have made it impossible to complete the count, they said.

14. Father Christmas will have to rely on horses and husky dogs to pull his sleigh this year in case reindeer spread highly infectious foot-and-mouth disease which has plagued Britain this year.

15. Swaziland's international airport has no working control tower or radar system, and lighting for night time landings is so poor that pilots are forced to fly by memory, the government has been told.

16. Truancy sweeps around Britain recently revealed thousands of children missed school and turned up some ridiculous excuses, the Education Ministry said.

17. I don't think I could bear to see the good name I've earned taken away from me in the course of a political campaign.

18. I would feel very childish and ridiculous bombarding the teacher with questions I could answer for myself with a little thought.

19. The research suggests that the potential for fulfilling workplace friendships is a new weapon in the war for talent—as dual-income families become the norm, traditional social networks break down and we adopt more self-centered urban living styles.

附二 课外扩展训练材料

BUSINESS LETTERS

Letter 1: Compensation Trade

Dear Sirs,

We thank you for your letter dated September 10, in which you agreed to offer us 400 Sewing Machines, Model FK-2, under compensation trade agreements.

As to the payment for the above sewing machines to be imported by us, we propose to make payment by three equal annual instalments, namely, one third of the total value of the sewing machines to be paid each year within three yeas.

From your letter we also notice that you are going to buy back each year 5,000 dozen shirts to be manufactured with your sewing machines. As this is only a very small quantity of our output, we suggest, in the spirit of compensation trade, that you accept our counter sale products each year to a value not less than our instalment payment to you in the same year.

We shall appreciate it very much if you will consider our proposal most favorably and we trust it will lead to the beginning of a long and friendly co-operation between us.

Yours sincerely,
×××

Letter 2: About Processing According to Supplied Samples

Dear Sirs,

Thank you very much for your letter of August 2 enquiring about the possibility of manufacturing Leather Bags according to your samples.

We are pleased to inform you that we have been doing business of processing according to supplied samples and processing with supplied materials for years, in addition to our ordinary import and export transactions. Our leather products are superior in materials and excellent in workmanship, and we have won the confidence of customers abroad in our commercial integrity.

As to prices, we find it difficult to work out an exact price before receiving your samples and knowing the quantity of your order. Therefore, please inform us of the quarterly or yearly quantity we may expect from you, as the quantity of your order will be an important factor in pricing.

We assure you of our close co-operation at any time and look forward to receiving your samples at an early date.

Yours sincerely,
×××

第七节 长句的翻译(二)

一、分句

英语长句之长，主要是由于并列句、从句多，嵌入成分多，分词及动名词短语多，名词短语多，介词短语多和形容词短语多。英语的句子结构是以主谓结构为主干而搭建的空间结构，其特点是形式完整、重点突出；而汉语句子则以时间或逻辑关系为脉络、以动词为表现形式的平面结构，其特点是思路清晰、上下连贯。在英译汉过程中可以句中关系代词如 which, who, that 等，连词如 and, but, if, before 等，介词如 by, in, for 等为句界，以汉语动词为中心，将较长的、内容较复杂的从句或词组译为并列结构，或译为独立句，以保证忠实原义，译语自然流畅。这种分句方式可采用以下几种方法：

(一) 将一句分为几个短句

1. The more we can enjoy what we have, the happier we are. It's easy to overlook the pleasure we get from loving and being loved, the company of friends, the freedom of living where we please, even good health.

   我们越知足，就越幸福。施人以爱，被人所爱，朋辈相伴，自由

第六章　句子的翻译(二)

择居,乃至身体健康,这一切所带来的快乐却易为我们所忽略。

2. I'm going to keep doing what I was doing long before the cameras ever showed up and what I'll be doing long after they're gone: Working to give every American the same opportunities I had, and working to ensure that every child has the chance to grow up and achieve his or her God-given potential.

我将继续做早在这些摄影机出现以前我就已经在做的、摄影机离开后我依然会长期做下去的事情——努力让每个美国人拥有与我相同的机会,尽力保证每个孩子都有机会健康成长,都有机会发挥其天赐的潜能。

3. This is, for instance, one of the main reasons why over the last ten centuries scientific progress has been mostly associated with universities, where scholars from many different disciplines were gathering together.

比如说,在过去的一千年中,科学进步基本上与大学有很大关系,一个主要原因就在于此。毕竟,大学是许多不同专业的群英荟萃之地。

4. In most of Europe, where grocery marketing is still a part of the daily rhythm, one can buy tomatoes, lettuce, and the like picked on the day of purchase.

在欧洲大部分地区,逛菜市场仍然是人们日常生活的一部分,那里可到买西红柿、莴苣,还能买到当天采摘的其他新鲜蔬菜。

5. In the late summer of that year we lived in a house in a village that looked across the river and plains to the mountains.

那年晚夏,我们住在一个小镇里,从我们的房子,可看见隔河的平原,平原与远山相连。

(二) 将句中的某个部分单独译出

1. Sleep is influenced by the circadian timing system, a bundle of neurons, embedded deep in the brain, that regulates

production of a sleep-inducing chemical called melatonin and sets natural bedtime and rise time.

睡眠受体内生理节奏定时系统的影响,这种系统是嵌在大脑深处的一束神经元,能对诱发睡眠的一种叫做褪黑素的化学物质进行调节,并控制自然的入眠和起床时间。

2. The politicians were then to have a working dinner at Downing Street as Sarah Brown hosts what the British press is calling a "girls' night in", also at the prime minister's official residence.

之后,首脑们将在唐宁街用工作餐,布朗夫人也将在首相官邸为莅临的各位夫人举办一个被英国媒体称为"夫人之宴"的欢迎晚宴。

3. Women still have a complex and contradictory relationship with their own image according to a poll released on Tuesday that found 25 percent of those questioned would rather win the "America's Next Top Model" TV show than the Nobel Peace Prize.

一项于本周二公布的民意调查显示,女性对自身形象问题仍然持一种复杂而矛盾的心态:25%的受访者称,与获得诺贝尔和平奖相比,她们更希望在"全美超模大赛"中获胜。

4. Dr. Richard Friedman of the Cornell Weill Medical Center in New York said he is treating 25 percent more people because of the recession, with patients suffering from insomnia due to anxiety and some even being diagnosed with clinical depression.

纽约康奈尔·威尔医学中心的理查德·弗里德曼医生称,经济危机发生后,他收治的病人增加了25%,有些病人因焦虑而失眠,有些人则患上了抑郁症。

5. The ever-increasing demand for private cars could be halted by more investment in public transport.

增加公共交通投入,可以抑制不断增长的私车需求。

二、合句

(一) 如果原文中一个长句后跟着一个短句,或者短句在前长句在后,而这个短句是对长句的解释或总结,那么一般可以将两句合为一句翻译

1. The Class of 2017 will receive the most financial aid in Harvard history, with $147 million in scholarships alone. That is up 8 percent from last year.
   2017届新生将获得哈佛建校史上最高额度的助学金,仅奖学金就达1.47亿美元,比去年增加了8%。

2. HOV stands for "heavily occupied vehicle", and the road sign means that if you are driving a passenger automobile on that stretch of highway during the morning and evening rush hours, you had better have at least two other people in the car with you. Otherwise, you may be pulled over and given a $100 fine.
   HOV是英文"高承载车辆"的缩写,此路标的意思是如果在早晚高峰时段驱车通过该路段,车上至少要有两人同行,否则就可能被勒令停车交纳100美元罚款。

3. For example, the distribution of applicants is truly random. The applicants cannot select which officer they talk to, nor can the officers select which applicants they interview. This is one of the ways we try to make sure that improper influence cannot be brought to bear on the process.
   比如,签证申请者的分配是随机的,申请者不得选择签证官,签证官也不得选择申请者,这也是我们为确保工作过程不受非正常影响所采取的一项措施。

4. One weekend evening a concert was being held near the room where he was poring over a book. The noise disturbed him so much that he couldn't concentrate.
   一个周末的晚上他正在房间潜心读书,附近开起了音乐会,吵得他无法集中精力。

5. Games are valuable programming, fought over by broadcasters

around the world as networks and cable channels proliferate. And Jordan is at the center of it all.

由于联播网和有线频道的激增,球赛成了电台、电视台极为重要的一档节目,世界各地媒体为此展开了竞争,使得乔丹一下子成了炙手可热的竞争对象。

(二) 如果原文用连续的几个短句表达一个中心意义,那么翻译时可将其合为一句

1. It had been noted with concern that the stock of books in the library has been declining alarmingly. Students are asked to remind themselves of the rules for the borrowing and return of books, bearing in mind the needs of other students. Penalties for overdue book will in the future be strictly enforced.

   近来图书馆藏书剧减,在此特提醒同学们遵守借还书规定,并考虑其他同学的借阅需要,凡今后借书逾期不还者,将严格课以罚金。

2. Confucius was a believer in moral action and in what we today call human development. He advocated the establishment of harmony within the social order.

   孔子信仰道德的力量,信仰今人所谓的人类进步,提倡建立和谐的社会秩序。

3. The key to success is not information. it's people. And the kind of people I look for to fill top management spots are the eager beavers. These are the guys who try to do more than they're expected to. They're always reaching. And reaching out to the people they work with, trying to help them do their jobs better. That's the way they've built.

   成功的关键不在信息,在于人。我需要的高层管理人员须是兢兢业业的实干家,一心想着如何超额完成任务。他们一贯的工作作风是乐意向同事施以援手,帮助他们把工作做得更好。

4. These people are motivated by risk, uncertainty, novelty, variety. They thrive in ambiguous situations. They like intense experiences, they are inner-directed. They believe

they can control their fate. Whatever comes up, they believe they can handle it.

这些人追求风险性、不确定性、多样性和新奇感,即使在前景未卜的环境中也能施展才华。他们享受紧张刺激,从心底相信自己有能力掌握自己的命运,无论发生什么事,都自认为能伸缩自如。

5. We identify the species at risk, diagnose what's wrong, but then we don't treat them. it's absurd.

我们确定了濒危物种,分析了问题症结,就是不采取措施,这不荒唐吗?

三、and 的多种译法

英语句子结构严谨,关联词各司其职,以保证句子的语法正确,意义完整。前面已讨论过由各类关系代词、关系副词、关系连词等引导的定语从句、状语从句、名词从句的翻译,现在来看看连接词 and 的多种用法及其翻译。

1. The fundamental task of family planning is to control the growth of the population **and** improve the quality of people.

计划生育的基本任务就是控制人口增长,提高人口素质。(表示并列)

2. France's state administration is notorious for its use of jargon, **and** according to a report in daily newspaper *Le Monde*, a large majority of the country's population is unable to decipher official documents.

法国政府机构素有好用术语的坏名声。据《世界日报》报道,大多数法国民众无法"破译"官方文件。(表示连贯)

3. Leaders recognized that work-life programs have tremendous financial impact in terms of productivity and employee retention, **and** that a commitment to helping employees balance their personal responsibilities is a win-win.

公司领导层认识到,"工作和生活计划"能提高公司的生产力和凝聚力,给公司带来巨大收益,同时有助于员工平衡个人责权,

是一项双赢策略。(表示连贯)

4. Oil-rich Venezuela takes the beauty industry very seriously **and** has gained a reputation as a "factory" of international beauty contest winners.

   石油生产国委内瑞拉十分重视"美女制造业",因而有专门制造国际选美比赛优胜者的"工厂"之称。(表示结论)

5. He said workers should turn up in shirt sleeves **and** then they wouldn't need air-conditioners turned up so high.

   他说职员们应该穿衬衫上班,这样就无需把冷气开得太大。(表示结论)

6. Seasonal differences in what mothers ate during pregnancy, and infections occurring at different times of the year could both have an impact on the health of a new-born baby **and** could influence its life expectancy in older age.

   母亲在怀孕期间所吃的食物因季节不同而不同,一年里不同时间流行的传染病也不一样,两者都会对新生儿的健康产生影响,进而影响到他们步入老年后的寿命。(表示递进)

7. He thinks drivers should be aware of the impact music has on them **and** advised them to either choose slower tunes or to turn down the volume to reduce distraction.

   他认为司机应该意识到音乐对自己的不良影响,建议他们要么选择曲调舒缓的音乐,要么把音量调低,集中注意力开车。(表示递进)

8. She fills two converted bedrooms with clothes—one for casual and a second for glam—**and** staying organized worked for singer Fergie who on Wednesday made *People* magazine's 2008 list of best dressed women.

   女歌星菲姬的衣服占了整整两间卧室——其中一间专放休闲装,另一间放礼服,而一向会"收拾"的她于本周三获评《人物》杂志"2008年度最佳穿着女性"。(表示递进)

9. According to the law, governments at various levels have to include retiree affairs in their planning, **and** increase investment in undertakings for the elderly year by year.

根据这项法律,各级政府必须把老年人问题列入工作计划,并逐年向老年人事业追加投资。(表示递进)

10. The wise never marry, **and** when they marry they become otherwise.

    聪明人都是未婚的,结婚的人很难再聪明起来。(表示对比)

附一 课堂讲练材料

1. He would have to win a declaration of innocence for his father from a court, before he could collect damages, which could run as much as $2 million.
2. I don't know why people think that housewives are unhappy or unfulfilled. We don't sit around moaning about loss of status and lack of stimulation. I love my new status. I am having a fantastic time.
3. Even in the dark ages of television, when one actually had to get up and walk a few feet to change the channel, the shows themselves were commercial-laden and thus discontinuous.
4. In science, one makes much more progress out of a single innovative idea than the steady effort of hundreds of more conventional research scientists—which, by the way, is also necessary, although not sufficient for the fastest progress.
5. We're seeing information technology reach the point that all transformational technologies reach when they are no longer controlled by just a small group of skilled professionals, and they cross over a mass acceptance and ambiguity.
6. The new DNA testing also revealed that a recently rediscovered sample of blood, taken from a large spot on a closet door in the bedroom only a foot from where Mrs. Sheppard was killed, did not match either Dr. or Mrs. Sheppard.
7. New Zealand and Australian cities continued to show they are probably the best bet for cheap but high quality living, with scores consistently around 50 or below while at the same time ranking in the top 30 for

quality of life in another Mercer survey released in March 2002.

8. The lucky winner of the prize promoting the revamp of *New Scientist* magazine won't be able to collect the award until death when he or she will be cooled to a temperature at which decay of the body stops and then suspended in liquid nitrogen in a state known as preservation.

9. If we read at all we probably do so on the bus or subway to and from work; when we arrive home at night, exhausted by our nine-to-five, drone-like existence, we are much more likely to watch TV, an activity which, since the advent of the remote control, demands less mental and physical energy than ever.

10. There is no more difference, but there is just the same kind of difference, between the mental operations of a man of science and those of an ordinary person, as there is between the operations and methods of a baker or of a butcher weighing out his goods in common scales, and the operations of a chemist in performing a difficult and complex analysis by means of his balance and finely graded weights.

11. Friendship and mutual respect, however, do bring real rewards. They foster a human bond that cannot easily be dissolved by differences in viewpoint, or the complexity of international affairs or even the hurts and suspicious of history.

12. Pushing exports in industries where a country has a natural advantages has proven a winning strategy time and again. Nor does any other nation lose.

13. Today's world is a harsher place. Developed countries are still in the grip of recession and a developing nation may face retaliation for even the most innocuous form of "non-tariff barrier"—for example, tax incentives for certain industries.

14. Although the size of the task waiting to be carried out is daunting and there are many hurdles to be overcome, it would be wrong to end my address on a note of pessimism. Many countries have already made considerable progress in this regard.

15. The lack of doctors and medicines remains a serious problem in rural areas, and maternal and child health care is also lagging behind.

16. The birth rate has stabilized at a low level, and the natural population growth rate dropped to below 10 per thousand last year.
17. If you work long hours, you are likely to spend the rest of your waking hours socializing as it helps you to relax and that means you are unlikely to have enough sleep.
18. The article urges government workers, especially leading officials, to carry out their activities strictly in accordance with the laws and statutes, and to be models by maintaining the dignity of the Constitution and the law.
19. In Austria, adults born in autumn (October—December) lived about seven months longer than those born in spring (April—June), and in Denmark adults with birthdays in autumn outlived those born in spring by about four months.
20. As he spoke of this a light came into his eyes, and a faint smile appeared on his lips.

附二 课外扩展训练材料

A Letter of Apology

DEAR POSTAL CUSTOMER:

The enclosed was found loose in the mails or has been damaged in handling in the Postal Service (whichever is applicable to the enclosure).

We realize your mail is important to you and you have every right to expect it to be delivered intact and in good condition. The Postal Service makes every effort to properly handle the mail entrusted to it but due to the large volume, occasional damage may occur.

When a Postal Office handles large quantities of mail daily, it is imperative that mechanical methods be used to maintain production and insure prompt delivery of the mails. It is also an actuality that modern production methods do not permit personal attention to individual pieces of mail. Damage can occur if mail is insecurely enveloped or bulky contents are enclosed. When this occurs and our machinery is jammed, it often causes damage to other mail that was properly prepared.

  We are constantly striving to improve our processing methods to assure that an occurrence such as the enclosed can be eliminated. We appreciate your concern over the handling of your mail and sincerely regret the inconvenience you have experienced.

General Post Office

第七章　语篇的翻译

有道是：因字成句，因句成篇。显然，语篇(text)是高于句子的，能在一定语境支配下表达相对完整的思想，具有独立交际功能。只要具备了这些基本特征，无论是一个单词、一句话、一次交谈、一则广告、一封书信、一首诗歌，还是一次长篇演讲、一部万言小说，都可视作语篇。语篇翻译是翻译的高级阶段，是对各种翻译方法和技巧综合运用的理想翻译单位。只有通过语篇翻译练习，各种翻译技巧才能得到不断巩固和加强，最终达到融会贯通的高级境界。

第一节　语篇的理解和翻译

一、语篇翻译的基本步骤

为清楚语篇翻译的全部过程，在此以美国著名律师、演讲家罗伯特·格林·英格索尔的一段演讲词为例。

> The past rises before us. We hear the roar and shriek of the bursting shell. The broken fetters fall. The heroes died. We look. Instead of slaves we see men and women and children. The wand of progress touches the auction block, the slave pen, the whipping post, and we see homes and firesides and schoolhouses and books, and where all was want and crime and cruelty and fear, we see the faces of the free.

请将原文与以下译文进行对比：

> 过去的一切涌现在我们眼前。我们听到爆炸的炮弹在咆哮，在呼啸。断了的镣铐散开了。勇士们牺牲了。请看，眼前不再是奴隶，而是男人、女人和儿童。进步的魔杖，触及奴隶拍卖市场，触及农奴种植园，

也触及鞭刑柱,于是我们看到了田园、家舍、学校和图书。从前,这里有的只是贫困与罪恶,残酷与恐惧,现在,我们看到的是一张张自由的笑脸。

通过对比,不难发现以上由凌樟彦先生完成的翻译虽然采取句子到句子的直线式翻译,但译者并未把句子视为各自为政的个体,而是将它们视为相互关联的有机整体,引入了衔接、照应与连贯等基本的谋篇要素。由此,我们可以总结出以下有关语篇的翻译规律:

1. 翻译过程是一个上步决定下步、一步决定一步、步步相接、环环相扣的过程;
2. 翻译还是走了下步,回头看上步,一步一回首的过程;
3. 句子作为翻译的基本单位须始终接受衔接、照应、连贯等谋篇要素的调节和制约,从而使单句连成一体,构成目的语篇;
4. "目的语篇"须忠实再现"原发语篇"的内容,不得随意增删修改。

总之,在翻译的操作层面上,译者始终都应从具体的"句子"而非抽象的"语篇"入手,由句子到句子,由段落到段落,最终完成整个语篇的翻译。

二、语篇的具体类型

(一) 语篇的文体风格

按照语篇语言学(textlinguistics)的观点,不同的交际环境、交际内容、交际目的、交际方式决定着不同形式的文体。而文体风格虽有受不同文体内在规定的一面,但在很大的程度上是作者个人文化修养、地位、身份、交际动机与意图等主观因素以及交际的场合、所扮演的角色、所处的社会、文化、历史背景等客观因素决定的。据此,对语篇文体风格的分析可从以下几个方面加以把握:

1. 从体裁上分析,有小说、诗歌、散文、戏剧、公文等文体;
2. 从表述方法上分析,有叙述、描写、议论、说明、抒情5种文体;
3. 从正式程度上分析,有庄严、正式、商议、随便、亲密等文体;
4. 从语言特色上分析,有华丽、朴实、简洁、讽刺、反语、幽默等风格;
5. 从修辞特点上分析,有比喻、夸张、排比、反问、反复、对比、省略、倒装等手段。

正确把握原文文体对翻译实践的成功开展十分有益。

(二) 语篇的具体类型

风格的不同决定了语篇类型的不同,语篇类型是决定翻译策略的一个重要因素,因此应以语篇分类为切入点研究异化和归化的问题。掌握异化和归化问题可分6个层次进行:

1. 须求异化的是:条约、法典、政府公文及文献;
2. 可考虑使用异化法的是:一般学术理论、科技情报及著述;
3. 可使用异化,同时须考虑使用归化的是:新闻报道及分析、报刊特写;
4. 异化、归化兼顾的是:传记、游记、札记及文艺小说;
5. 可考虑归化的是:舞台或电影剧本、抒情散文;
6. 为达到可读性与艺术性的完美结合,须求归化的是:诗词歌赋。

三、语境通观

语篇翻译的基本单位是词句,但不同于词句翻译,其不同之处在于语篇翻译有完整或相对完整的语境,要求译者在特定的语境内对原文进行通观,否则可能只见树木,不见森林,无法有效落实译文。

(一) 语境通观的方法

为使译文完整忠实,不留疑窦,对原文进行通观的方法是:

1. 分析语篇的主题或中心思想。语篇一般都要围绕一定的主题(theme)或话题(central ideas)展开。找出语篇的主题,可以把握整个语篇的思想脉络,这对于实现原文和译文的意义对等具有重要意义。
2. 分析语篇的情景语境。情景语境是语篇赖以生存的语言环境,如事件、场合、时间、地点、人物活动及其角色关系,以及语篇所反映的人物地位、身份、态度、动机和社会、文化、时代、历史背景等。把握情景语境,有助于译文恰当地反映原文情景语境所发挥的交际功能。
3. 分析语篇的衔接手段。语言要组织成为语篇,需要借助各种衔接手段。研究语篇的衔接关系,有助于加深我们对语篇的语义联系、语篇结构和语篇功能的认识与理解。

总而言之,译者要从翻译角度出发,用译者的眼光审读原文,把握:

1. 原文讲了些什么?
2. 怎么讲的?
3. 为什么这么讲?
4. 这么讲用意何在?
5. 译文该如何再现之?
6. 什么时候该"补白",即对言外之事做必要的交代。
7. 什么时候该"表白",即对言外之意做适当的显豁。

(二) 语篇的组织结构把握

语篇的组织结构也是语境通观的重要方面。语篇的组织结构是由语篇的交际目的、环境、方式、题材、体裁、语言风格、修辞手段等多种因素决定的。语篇的结构关系大体有以下几种:

1. 顺序关系结构:即语篇按事物发展的时间顺序关系、空间顺序关系、冲突的激烈程度来组织;
2. 层次关系结构:即句子不是横向直线发展,而是分成几个意义层次纵向展开,但都从属于一个主题或主题句;
3. 递进关系结构:即句子采取环环相扣、层层推进的方式排列,语义也随之前呼后应,逐步递升,直到推出一个结论来;
4. 平衡关系结构:即句子以平衡方式排列,在层次上是平等的,没有先后之别,各自围绕主题的某个侧面展开叙述,句子结构大体相同或相似,总体上呈现一种平衡关系结构,但在表意方式上往往采取对比手段,或对比两种相反的事物,或对比同一事物两个对立方面,正反兼说,互相照应。

当然,一个语篇不可能具备以上所有特征。实践中,只需在最突出最有代表性地反映一个语篇特征的某个方面进行分析,不必面面俱到。一般情况下,注意原文的段落层次划分即可。

四、语篇的谋篇布局分析

写作离不开谋篇布局,其目的是使文章前呼后应,言之有序。体裁、题材不同,谋篇的具体方式会有所不同,动笔翻译之前可从谋篇布局的角度认真审读原文,把握原文的整体行文线索和具体构段方式,使译文避免跑题变调,散漫纠结。例如:

第七章 语篇的翻译

On Sanya's sunny stretch of coastline along the sleepy southernmost tip of Hainan Island, you are more likely to find bored buffalo than bouncy beach babes. That is unless you strolled past as one of China's hottest pot acts, Yu Quan, was shooting its new music video when the beach came alive as a swarm of shiny new cars careened around with rims and sunroofs sparkling.

译文一：沿着海南岛寂静的南端，在三亚阳光灿烂、蜿蜒伸展的海岸线旁，你更可能碰到疲惫的水牛，而非充满活力的海滩青年，除非你漫步时正好路过中国最火爆的流行动感组合之一"羽泉"在拍摄新的音乐电视片。随着一批靓丽的新车云集于此，汽车的轮胎金属盖和遮阳篷顶在炎热的阳光下熠熠闪光，这时的海滩才活了起来。

译文二：海南岛最南端——三亚的海边，阳光灿烂，寂静安详。海滩上，后生们活跃的身影难得一见，只有水牛在那儿懒散无语。漫步海滩，撞见中国最火爆的流行动感组合之一"羽泉"拍摄音乐电视片，此时这里新车大批云集，金属用具、遮阳篷在炎热的阳光下熠熠闪光——海滩活了起来。

该例描写的是海南岛的南部风光。原文以空间为线索，从寂静写到喧哗，从远写到近，行文铺排有序，条理井然。而译文一却散漫游离，杂乱无序，没能再现原文内容。

阅读是一回事，翻译则是另一回事。就翻译而言，除理解原文的精神和内容，还须把握原文的行文线索及构段方式，只有这样，才能使译文言而有序。如：

He had flown in just the day before from Georgia where he had spent his vocation basking in the Caucasian sun after the completion of the construction job he had been engaged in the south.

译文一：他刚从格鲁吉亚坐飞机回来，他在那儿度假，享受高加索的阳光，他在南方从事一项建筑工程，任务已经完成后。

译文二：他先在南方做一项建筑工程，工作结束后，去格鲁吉亚度假地享受了一番高加索的阳光，昨天才坐飞机回来。

原文句子未按照时间顺序排列，而是通过着眼于句子的修饰关系和紧凑连接方式来再现时间关系。译文一没有把握原文的构句方式，因而未按中文读者所习惯的时间顺序关系进行构句。

五、衔接、照应和连贯

一篇文章无论有多少层次、多少段落,其总体结构形式无外乎起、承、转、合几个组成部分。起是文章的开头,合是文章的结尾,承和转是文章的主体。承、转的意思就是"承接转进",即衔接、照应、连贯,而"承接转进"不仅使文章的内容充实完备,更使行文清晰明了。

(一) 衔接

内容上的"承接转进"是通过行文上的"承接转进"表现出来的,所以承转的关键在于衔接(cohesion),而衔接就是运用适当的词语及语句形式进行连接。总体而言,衔接包括文章中段落与段落之间的连接、段落中语句与语句之间的连接。语篇翻译中,衔接是否得当,直接影响译文质量。

一般而言,说明文和议论文行文的承转相对明显,段落与段落之间常有相应的词句进行衔接,翻译时比较容易。而记叙文、描写文、小说等的承转则相对含蓄,段落与段落之间不一定有相应的词句进行衔接,翻译存在一定难度。不管原文如何,译文要具体问题具体分析对待,努力使译文在行文上相衔接。例如:

> Another stereotype borne out by the lives of the *Millennial Minds* is that genius often seems to be, as Edison himself put it, one percent inspiration and 99 percent perspiration. From Leonardo da Vinci to Brunel, Mozart to Fritz Haber, an almost pathological devotion to their work characterizes many *Millennial Minds*.
>
> This devotion brought some to an early grave: Marie Curie, for instance, was killed by radiation from her years of work with radium. For many others, it meant unfulfilled personal lives, failed marriages and, in the case of Boltzmann and Turing, suicide.
>
> "千年精英"的生平证实了另外一种传统观点,即爱迪生自己所称的:天才是1%的灵感加99%的汗水。从列奥纳多•达•芬奇到布鲁内尔,从莫扎特到费里茨•哈伯,许多"千年精英"几乎对工作表现出近乎病态的献身精神。
>
> **正是这种献身精神**使一些精英英年早逝,如玛丽•居里因多年致力于镭的研究而死于辐射。**正是这种献身精神**使一些精英享受不到完美的私人生活、成功的婚姻,所以有的像玻尔茨曼和图林那样选择了自杀。

第七章 语篇的翻译

原文中的 This devotion 以及 for instance 将上下两个段落进行了有效的衔接,使文章一气呵成,没有脱节。译文在原文的基础上,考虑中文的行文习惯,将衔接进行了更为明确的突显,使上下段的衔接更为自然和明晰。

文章段落之间需要承转衔接,段落的语句之间也需承转衔接。由于体裁题材不同,构段的方式就会不同,翻译时要从实际出发,根据行文的线索和构段方式具体问题具体分析处理,努力使译文段落承接转进有条不紊。如:

The envelope wasn't sticking out of the pocket. Thinking it had slipped down inside, I reached to get it. It was gone.

译文一:信封没有露出口袋,想是滑到里面去了,我伸手去掏。不在了!

译文二:衣兜口没有露出信封,我想大概是滑进兜里去了,便伸手去摸,可是——不在!

比较以上两个译文,可以发现,译文二由于加上了"便""可是",使行文有如行云流水一样自然而晓畅,不仅充分翻译出原文的意旨,表达效果还更胜一筹。

由于英汉语的行文方式不同,符合英语的表达习惯未必符合汉语的表达习惯。换言之,某种行文方式在英语中属于正常现象,到了汉语中就不正常了。如果英语原文在核心句之间进行补叙和插叙,即使没有出现具体的衔接词语,整体行文也是流畅的,但是如果将原文照直译成汉语,译文的行文就会显得上蹿下跳,前言不搭后语。因此,在英译汉中,要再现原文内容,相关的语句衔接必不可少。例如:

Bill was a door-to-door salesman I'd delivered packages for in high school.

译文一:比尔是一个我中学时代送过包裹的挨门挨户兜售货物的推销员。

译文二:比尔是上门搞推销的,上中学时,我曾替他送过货。

译文一没有很好地处理原文补叙,文字长而晦涩。而译文二则在翻译时进行了必要的技术处理,并用"曾"这一衔接词对原文的时间关系加以显豁。

可见,衔接是语篇的重要特征。语言要组织成为语篇就需借助各种衔接手段。研究语篇的衔接关系,有助于加深我们对语篇的语义联系、语篇结构和语篇功能的认识与理解。英语语篇的衔接手段主要有以下几种:

1. 连接:指通过连词、副词、短语等连接成分来体现语篇中的各种逻辑关系。

   1) 表示顺序或列举:first, second, for one thing, for another, first of all, in the first place, to begin with, next, then, last, finally 等。
   2) 表示递进或增补:and, also, and...too, furthermore, besides, in addition, moreover, what's more 等。
   3) 表示转折或对比:but, though, yet, still, however, nevertheless, instead, on the contrary, on the other hand, by contrast, in contrast with 等。
   4) 表示例证或解释:for example, for instance, namely, that is to say, in other words 等。
   5) 表示因果:for, therefore, thus, hence, so, consequently, as a result, for that reason 等。
   6) 表示推论:in conclusion, in sum, in short, in a word, in brief, on the whole, to sum up, to summarize 等。

2. 词汇衔接(lexical cohesion):指通过某些关键词汇的复现或同现来体现语篇的语义联系。

   1) 原词复现:如 **The two girls** on the campus read English. From the other end of the campus Sandy watched **them**.
   2) 同义词复现:如 She got a lot of presents from her future husband. **All the gifts** were wrapped in red paper.
   3) 近义词复现:如 Birds did not **chirp**. The leaves did not **rustle**. The insects did not **sing**.
   4) 上下义词复现:如 You can get a **book**, a **writing pad** and a **pen** from her.
   5) 反义词复现:如 I **hate** you and you don't **like** me.
   6) 互补词同现:如 According to comedian George Carling, football is a ruthless, **warlike** game, but baseball is a warm and **pastoral** one. Football takes place on the gridiron while baseball is played on a

field. A defensive football player tackles the opponent, but a baseball player only tags one. A violation in football draws a **penalty**, but a mistake in baseball is merely an **error**.

7) 词汇链同现：如 A great number of high school graduates continue their education in one of the many colleges or universities in this country. After four years, they receive a **bachelor's degree or perhaps a doctor's degree.**

词汇衔接是语境的重要组成部分。英语的句群内,甚至相隔较远的语篇内,有时会产生重复关系、同义关系、反义关系、上下义关系、部分和整体关系等,构成词语之间的衔接机制。因此,翻译初学者要仔细研读原文,善于捕捉这些起衔接作用的词语,对原文做出正确的解读,避免误解、误译。

3. 结构衔接（structural cohesion）：是语篇中某一结构与上文另一预设结构相比较而存在的承启关系,也是语境的重要表现形式。结构衔接一般可分为替代（substitution）和省略（ellipsis）两种。替代又分人称替代、名词替代、动词替代和句子替代。省略可分名词省略、动词省略和句子省略。若忽视了结构衔接,也会导致误解和误译。以代词为例,英语中代词的使用频率大大高于汉语,使用代词可避免单词的重复和句子的臃肿,但有时也会出现指代不明的现象,翻译时如照搬照译,势必给译语读者造成理解障碍。因此,遇到这种情况,可通过语境来明确指代关系。如：

Because everyone uses language to talk, everyone thinks **he** can talk about language. But talking about **it** is one thing, and using **it** correctly is another.

译文一：因为人人都用语言讲话,人人都认为他能谈语言。但是谈论它是一回事,正确使用它又是另一回事。

译文二：人人用语言交流,因此人人都以为自己有资格谈论语言。殊不知,谈论语言是一码事,正确使用语言则是另一码事。

译文一因照搬原文表达方式而指代不明,引起歧义;译文二则用同义词的复现克服了这一问题,行文明了而清楚。

(二) 照应

为使语篇精神前后一致,要求行文上需表现承接转进的同时,遣词造句也要前后照应。所谓照应(reference)是指用语篇中的一个成分作为另一成分的参照点,从而形成照应关系。换言之,译文前后的遣词造句要团结互助,彼此配合,不能各自为政,否则译文会散乱难读。例如:

We see them all as they march proudly away under the flaunting flags, keeping time to the grand, wild music of war—marching down the streets of the great cities— through the town and across the prairies— down to the fields of glory, to do and to die for the eternal right.

我们全都看见了,看见他们在迎风招展的旌旗下**雄赳赳**地向远方行进,伴随着**庄严**、**激越**的战斗乐曲,**步伐整齐**地走过大都市的长街,**穿过乡村集镇**,**越过**茫茫草原,一直走向光荣的战场,为永恒的正义去流血牺牲。

为再现原文,译文在选词方面前后照应,选择了同类的与战争相关的褒义词来译文中的关键词语,取得了较好的翻译效果。又如:

Its advertisement showed a picture of a pile of dirty clothes on the left, a box of the company's detergent in the middle, and clean clothes in the right. Unfortunately, **the message** was incorrectly interpreted because most people looked at **it** from right to left, the way Arabic is read.

这家公司的广告画面上,左侧是一堆脏衣服,中间是该公司生产的一盒洗衣粉,右侧则是洗干净了的衣服,倒霉的是**该信息给曲解了**,因为当地人大多习惯从右向左看,阿拉伯语就是这么读的。

Message 有"口信、消息、信息"等意,根据前面的选词,用"信息"照应并翻译是不为过的。

一般而言,照应可分五类:

1. 人称照应:指用人称代词作为另一成分的参照点。如:Tom married the girl he had long kept his eyes on. They visited **her parents but not his.**

2. 指示照应:指用名词性指示词(this, that, these, those)、定冠词和指示性词(here, there, now, then)作参照点。如: **Here is the news**. An explosion took place in Spain.

3. 比较照应：指用形容词和副词的比较级及其他具有比较意义的词语（but, same, similar, such, equal, different, otherwise, likewise）作参照点。如：I know I can't, **but** I just cannot help.

4. 前后照应：
1) 承前关照，如：Listen to **this**! We are going to have a new teacher.
2) 承后关照，如：Mary didn't appear. **It** puzzled all of us.

5. 意合连接，也叫零形式连接，是指不借助连接成分而通过句际间的逻辑关系来体现语篇的语义连贯。如：I'll tell you, Governor, if you'll only let me get a word in. I'm willing to tell you. I'm wanting to tell you. I'm waiting to tell you.（句子通过首语 I'm 和尾语 to tell you 多次反复，突出了逻辑联系，深化了"咱很想告诉您"这一主题，从而实现了前后照应）

此外，一些表示逻辑关联的关系，如时间关系、因果关系、转折关系、解释说明等，也可视为照应。总之，翻译语篇须有大局观念，应选择适合篇章行文整体性的词句。

(三) 语篇的连贯

语篇的连贯(continuity)指语言片段以语篇意向为主线，所形成的语义、逻辑上的连贯性。这种连贯性可通过连接词语来衔接，也可按一定的时空、逻辑关系来贯通。译者在翻译过程中，须把每个词、每句话放在语境中去认识，从中领会原文作者的写作意图，进而做出适当翻译。例如：

We owe protection to those men first, and we owe the security for their families if they die. I say it! I voice it! I proclaim it! And I care not who in heaven or hell opposes it!

译文一：我们首先幸亏有了这些人的保护，如果他们不幸牺牲，我们要保护他们家人的安全。我提出它！我表达它！我呼吁它！不管谁反对！

译文二：我们感谢这些人的保护，如果他们光荣牺牲，我们就要肩负起保护他们家人安全的职责。我提出来！我表达己见！我呼吁！不管谁反对！

译文二恰如其分地运用原文作者使用的重复法,成功实现了语篇的连贯,还表达出了强烈的感情色彩:我们要肩负起保护他们家人安全的职责。

六、段落的分合

一般而言,语篇翻译只需按原文的段落层次进行既可。但是,英汉语行文习惯不同,按原文的段落层次翻译有时不合汉语的行文习惯。在这种情况下,翻译时可对原文的段落层次划分做适当的技术处理,予以拆分或合并。例如:

He was a little man, barely five feet tall, with a narrow chest and one shoulder higher than the other and he was thin almost to emaciation. He had a crooked nose, but a fine brow and his colour was fresh. His eyes, though small, were blue, lively and penetrating. He was natty in his dress. He wore a small blond wig, a black tie, and a shirt with ruffles round the throat and wrists; a coat, breeches and waistcoat of fine cloth, gray silk stockings and shoes with silver buckles. He carried his three-cornered hat under his arm and in his hand a gold-headed cane. He walked every day, rain or fine, for exactly one hour, but if the weather was threatening, his servant walked behind him with a big umbrella.

仔细阅读原文,不难发现翻译时若不重新进行分段处理,译文条理可能有欠清晰。试比较一下原文与下面的译文:

他个头矮小,高不过五尺,瘦骨伶仃,身板细窄,且一肩高一肩低。他长着一副鹰钩鼻子,眉目还算清秀,气色也还好,一双蓝眼睛不大,却炯炯有神。他头戴金色发套,衣着非常整洁:褶边的白衬衣配一条黑色领带,质地讲究的马甲外配笔挺的套装,脚着深色丝袜和带白扣的皮鞋。他腋下夹顶三角帽,手上挂根金头拐杖,天天散步一小时,风雨无阻。当然落雨下雪时自有仆人亦步亦趋,为他撑伞。

译文对原文进行了适当的技术处理,将"他"的外貌描写挑出来作为一段进行翻译,将"他"的行为描写作为另一段进行处理,显得层次分明、条理清楚。

翻译语篇时,不仅可视具体情况对原文的段落进行切分,还可对原文的段落进行合并。有时若依原文的段落来译,行文会因为缺乏有机联系而显得松散拖沓。此时,若将原文段落进行合并,使之在译文中成为一个整体,便可使译文行文符合汉语的阅读心理。例如:

> A spirited discussion springs up between a young girl who insists that women have outgrown the jump-on-the-chair-at-the-sight-of-a-mouse era and a colonel who says that they haven't.
>
> "A woman's unfailing reaction in any crisis," the colonel says, "is to scream. And while a man may feel like it, he has that ounce more of nerve control than a woman has. And that last ounce is what counts."
>
> 这时,一位年轻的女士同一位上校展开了热烈的辩论。她坚定地认为当代女性已有很大进步,不再像过去那样一见到老鼠就吓得跳起来。上校则认为女性过去现在都一样。他说:"女人一遇危险必然高声尖叫。男人虽然也想叫,但和女人相比他的胆量就大了那么一丁点,能够管住自己的嘴,而这一丁点胆量却很能说明问题。"

比较一下原文和译文,会发现合译后的段落更为紧凑、合理。

另外,要注意独句段、独词段的翻译。如果独句段、独词段在文章的中间,并且与上下段落关系密切,翻译时可合并;如在文章的结尾,翻译时也要视具体情况具体处理。如:

> Our travel arrangements were also carefully planned so that no routine could be detected.
>
> Sometimes we traveled singly, sometimes in groups of two, three, or four, sometimes with an agency representative along, sometimes not. Usually, when accompanied, it was by Collins, who was becoming as omnipresent as the radio in each of our hotel rooms.
>
> 我们的旅行安排也经过周密计划,让人找不出规律。有时我们单人独行,有时两人、三人或四人同往,有时有专家陪同,有时又没有。一旦有专家陪同,此人往往是柯林斯。柯林斯可说是无所不在,就像无线电一样,每个旅馆房间都看得到。

译文视原文具体情况进行了合段处理,营造了联结紧密、贯通一致的效果。

从一般意义而言,原文层次与层次之间关系的密切程度是段落分合的重要依据,而译文的行文习惯则是对原文段落拆分或合并的参考因素。当然,翻译不宜妄改原文的结构形式,对原文的段落进行拆分、合并只能偶尔为之,且须有理有据,适度有序。

七、语境

所谓语篇的连贯,还要注意译文应与原文的情景语境(context)相吻合,比如译笔下的人不可脱离其原有身份,所叙述的事、所描写的物不可违背其原有场合,切忌出现"语不适境"的译文。例如:

The lady at the desk in the hotel was quite friendly, full of stories of girls waiting for a divorce.

译文一:那家旅馆写字台后的那位夫人很友好,她知道许多关于等待离婚的姑娘们的故事。

译文二:那家旅馆的前台女接待挺友善,会讲很多有关女人闹离婚的故事。

在该句中,由于介词短语 in the hotel 的限制关系,将 lady 和 desk 分别译成"夫人"和"写字台"是不妥的,而 girls 因其修饰语 waiting for a divorce 的作用,显然不能译成"姑娘们"。

译者在翻译过程中,有时需要将情景语境与文化语境结合起来理解,并针对原文的文化背景做出必要的信息补充和诠释,使译文能为读者所接受。例如:

Hygeia herself would have fallen sick under such regimen; and how much more this poor old nervous victim?

译文一:即使哈吉娅本人吃了这种东西也会生病,何况这个神经过敏的老可怜虫呢?

译文二:即使健康女神哈吉娅本人吃了这种东西也会生病,何况这个神经过敏的老可怜虫呢?

不留疑窦是成功翻译的一大要素,译文二根据语境增加了"健康女神"一词,如此处理是成功的。又如:

The next day he awoke with the sun.

译文一：第二天,他和太阳一起起床。

译文二：第二天,他和太阳公公一起起床。

译文一易给读者造成太阳也睡觉的印象,而译文二增补上"公公"之后,使译文充满童趣,符合儿童的认知心理,也能为成年读者所接受。

在具体情境的翻译中,语境也会被赋予一定的定向性,要求我们的理解活动在一定的范围内进行,例如《永别了,武器》是以战争为背景的,这就是一种定向性。

There was much traffic at night and many mules on the road with boxes of ammunition on each side of their pack-saddles and gray motor trucks that carried men, and other trucks with loads covered with canvas that moved slower in the traffic.

译一：晚上交通甚繁,有许多骡子走过,鞍子驮着军火箱子,灰色的摩托货车装着人,此外,还有一些装货的货车,上面帆布盖着,走起来较慢。

译二：夜间,这里运输繁忙,路上有许多骡子,鞍的两侧驮着弹药箱,灰色的卡车上装满了士兵,还有一些辎重车辆,用帆布盖着,在路上缓慢地行驶着。

显然,译文一中 traffic, men, loads 等词的翻译没有考虑到原文对情景的定向作用,即战争的背景。根据上下文,这里白天都极少有行人,为什么到了晚上反而"交通"繁忙呢?显然,这是军队向前方输送"辎重"的"运输"车队,车上也不是一般的"人",而是"士兵",这样才有战争的氛围。正所谓"上什么山唱什么歌",一切应以不同的语境因素为转移。

总之,翻译初学者在翻译中宜加强语篇意识,从语篇分析的角度审视语篇整体及其诸层次上的转换,使译文连贯流畅,文通理达。

附一 课堂讲练材料

A Man in My Eyes

We found him in a small, businesslike office hardly large enough to hold the big old-fashioned roll-up desk and a chair or two. Perhaps there was a safe; I can't remember. The office was protected by some iron bars, and there was a uniformed attendant at the door who admitted us after Mr.

Whitney had given the word he would see us.

I found him a man square of jaw, cold of eye, his face rather unexpressive—much what I had expected. He runs his gambling place as a business—and it is a matter of pride with him that it is conducted in an efficient, businesslike way. It is said that his profits are two million dollars a season, and I doubt this just as one doubts the salaries of motion picture stars.

However, the man had a strong personality. He interested me. I liked him. I wanted to talk to him, but it was difficult. He was not a very communicative person. Soon I asked him how much he lost a season in the way of bad checks and bad debts. He said approximately two hundred thousand dollars, which he didn't seem to consider heavy. As he spoke of this a light came into his eyes, and a faint smile appeared on his lips.

附二 课外扩展训练材料

Pines

The pine, placed nearly always among scenes disordered and desolate, brings into them all possible elements of order and precision. Lowland trees may lean to this side and that, though it is but a meadow breeze that bends them, or a bank of cowslips from which their trunks lean aslope. But let storm and avalanche do their worst, and let the pine find only a ledge of vertical precipice to cling to, it will nevertheless grow straight. Thrust a rod from its last shoot down the stem; it shall point to the center of the earth as long as the tree lives. It may be well also for lowland branches to reach hither and thither for what they need, and to take all kinds of irregular shape and extension. But the pine is trained to need nothing and endure everything. It is resolvedly whole, self-contained, desiring nothing but rightness, content with restricted completion. Tall or short, it will be straight.

(John Ruskin)

第二节 描写文、记叙文和小说的翻译

记叙文(narration)、描写文(description)、小说(fiction)本属不同体裁,但鉴于三者均具备词汇丰富、语言现象丰富、情态丰富、风格多样等文体特征,且均不流于表层意义的传达,强调感染力,故在此一并进行探讨。

记叙文、描写文、小说的共性要求译者在翻译过程中须在深层理解上下工夫,在把握作品的写作背景、创作意图、原文的发展层次、各种语法现象、词的内涵意义和文章的总体风格的同时,重点放在叙述角度、叙述线索的处理和描写的布局上,避免白开水似的翻译,注重神似,力争达到形神兼备的再创作佳境。

一、叙述角度和叙述线索的处理

翻译描写文、记叙文和小说首先要注意叙述的角度。一般说来,叙述或采用第一人叙述方式,或采用第三人称叙述方式,基本从一而终,少有变换,即便有所变换,也会有相应的词句或段落作为过渡,又称语言标记。同样,翻译的时候叙述角度通常不要随意变换,特别是英汉叙述习惯不同,为避免译文行文脱节,可对原文的叙述习惯进行变通处理。如:

> The door shut with a click. She was outside on the step, gazing at the winter afternoon ... There was a cold bitter taste in the air, and the newly-lighted lamps looked sad. Sad were the lights in the houses opposite. Dimly they burned as if regretting something. And people hurried by hidden under their hateful umbrellas, Rosemary felt a strange pang.

> 店门"咔嗒"一声关上了。罗斯玛丽站在店外的台阶上,久久地凝视着冬日的残阳……空气中飘浮着苦寒的滋味,华灯初上,散发出悲哀的光芒,对面屋子里的灯光也悲哀无言,隐隐约约,闪烁着遗憾。街上行人步履匆匆,头顶撑着讨厌的伞。一阵从未有过的痛楚涌上罗斯玛丽的心头。

原文通过"她"即罗斯玛丽为着眼点,通过"她"的眼睛一贯而下进行叙述,行文有条不紊。由于英汉在行文上的差异,译者没有照搬原文的行文方式,而采取了灵活的处理,叙述角度清晰明了。又如:

On the bus ride home, I stand, protecting my pumpkin from the tight press of passengers. As usual, people are staring at me, one of the few foreigners in a city of 4 million. Their eyes alight on the thing I clutched to my chest. They are curious, wanting to know what the foreigner has bought that she guards so carefully.

站在回家的公交车上,我护着我的南瓜以免被乘客挤破了。像往常一样,人们盯着我瞧,在这座400万人口的城市中,外国人很少很少。他们一直盯着我怀中紧抱着的玩意儿,很好奇,想知道这个老外到底买的是什么,居然如此小心地护着。

原文以"我"为着眼点,通过"我"来展开叙述,掌握了这一点,译文行文会比较干净整齐。

翻译时不仅要注意原文叙述的角度,还要注意原文叙述的线索。一般情况下,作者往往以时间的推移、地点的变换为线索,或以事件的发展、人物的活动为线索,或以事物的象征意义为线索展开叙述,使一条主线无形之中贯串始终。有时为达到行文张弛有致的目的,作者或用顺叙,或用倒叙,甚至以插叙的形式进行追叙、补叙或分叙。了解叙述的线索,就能较好地把握叙述的脉络,对理解原文并有效落实译文无疑有一定帮助。例如:

He carried her downstairs, counting the creaks on the way. Together, they settled in the kitchen table, and the adult in him slipped away. Two children now, they pressed their noses against the glass.

他抱着女儿,一步一步默数着楼梯的台阶数悄悄走下楼来,坐到厨房靠窗的餐桌边。此刻的他,童心盎然,与女儿一道,把脸紧贴在窗户上往外看。

原文用了插叙、叙述角度的变换等手段进行描写,译者可在充分把握原文叙述线索的同时,用坚持叙述角度不变的方式,以最大程度地传达出原文张弛有度的叙述风格。

二、描写的翻译

记叙文、描写文和小说的成功创作离不开成功的描写。描写分景物描写和人物描写。翻译时宜把握原文描写的性质和方法,清楚原文是客观描写(objective description)还是主观描写(subjective description),是白描

(general description)还是细描(specific description),从而设法再现之。

(一) 景物描写

景物描写主要针对场面、环境、情景等要素,视文章的目的进行客观或主观描写。客观描写中名词、动词多,形容词、副词少,遣词造句不带感情色彩,翻译时应避免使用感情色彩浓重、主观判断强烈的词语;主观描写通常富于感情色彩,多运用修辞手法和带有主观判断性质的词语,翻译时应尽量再现之。例如:

> Springs are not always the same. In some years, April bursts upon our Virginia hills in one prodigious leap and all the stage is filled at once, whole choruses of tulips, arabesques of forsythia, cadenzas of flowering plum. The trees grow leaves overnight.
>
> In other years, Spring tiptoes in. It pauses, overcome by shyness, like my grandchild at the door, peeping in, ducking out of sight, giggling in the hallway. "I know you're out there," I cry. "Come in!" and April slips into my arm.

> 年年岁岁花相似,岁岁年年春不同——4月有时不知怎的一跃,就落在弗吉尼亚的山坡上,大自然转眼生机勃勃。郁金香展开歌喉,连翘献上优美的舞姿,洋李奏起华彩乐段。一夜之间,林木着装,绿叶瑟瑟。
>
> 4月有时又悄然而至,像我的小孙女一样,羞羞答答地倚在门外,向里探头,一闪又不见了,咯咯的笑声在门厅回荡。"我知道你在那里藏着呢,"我喊道,"进来!"春天这才溜入了我的怀抱。

又如:

> The air that sweeps the South Sea Islands is fragrant with flowers and spice. Bright warm days follow clear cool nights, and the rolling swells break in a never-ending roar on the shores. Overhead the slender coconut palms whisper their drowsy song.

> 散发着鲜花和香料芬芳的微风,轻轻吹拂着南太平洋诸岛。明媚温暖的白天与清澈凉爽的夜晚交相更替。奔腾咆哮的巨浪拍打着海岸,树影婆娑的椰林低声吟唱着催眠曲。

两段原文皆用了许多富于主观判断性质的词语和修辞手法,赋予描写对象以强烈的感情色彩。翻译时应准确把握原文描写的性质,注意不要将主观描写译成了客观描写,不要将客观描写译成主观描写,从而背离原文风格,同时须将原文着意使用的拟人的修辞手段所表现的感情色彩翻译出来。

在手法上,描写如前所叙还可分为白描和细描。白描是捕捉描写对象的典型特征并进行勾勒,以展示描写对象的概貌;细描则是对描写对象的细节进行具体细致的临摹,使描写对象纤毫毕现。翻译时宜把握原文描写的手法,以充分再现原文。例如:

> For a time, the sun suddenly fell back into the unsteady sea, though not completely. Yet it struggled with might and main and, in the long run, it broke through the mist and darted out of the boiling sea. Up, up it rose, adding to itself strength and glory at every step. It dazzled with vigour, driving away darkness, cold, and misery from earth, and bestowing men with light, warmth, and happiness.

> 转眼间,太阳忽然又重坠到起伏不定的海上,好在没有整个儿沉没。接着,它用尽力量挣扎,结果又冲破浓雾,从沸腾的海洋奔进而出。它升得越来越高,每一升级,都增加了它的力量和光彩。它闪射着活力,驱走了地上的黑暗、寒冷与愁惨,赠给人类以光明、温暖与喜悦。

原文采用了大量的摹状词对描写对象的细节进行具体入微的描写,从而生动再现了太阳升起刹那间的情状。对这种描写,翻译时不能做简括处理,须尽力使译文描摹的对象如原文一样生动起来。

(二) 人物描写

一般而言,人物描写包括肖像描写、心理描写、行为描写、语言描写等等,以便从不同侧面表现人物的精神面貌和思想感情。一般性质的语篇对人物的描写多集中于肖像和语言描写两个方面,翻译时宜把握英汉两门语言在表达习惯上的差异,具体问题具体分析处理,以再现原文描写对象的形象。例如:

> The fellow stood in the street, on the other side of a green Volkswagen, his chest resting on the car's roof. "Yes, you." He was about nineteen, long black hair brushing his shoulders, a curling mustache, like a limp black snake draped on his upper lip, the ends dangling near his chin. "You been staring at us, man, like every day. Standing here and staring."

> 那个嬉皮士就站在路边,隔着一辆绿色大众汽车对杰里说话。他

的胸口就贴在车顶上。"没错,就是你。"他大约有十九岁,长长的黑发盖到了肩膀,卷曲的胡子就像一条软塌塌的黑蛇蜷缩在他的上嘴唇上,头尾正好垂挂在两边脸颊上。"喂,老兄,你好像每天都在看我们。就站在这里,盯着我们看。"

肖像描写主要描写人物的外表,包括人物的音容笑貌、神情姿态和服饰打扮,让读者对描写对象有一个清晰的印象。该例描写的主要是一个嬉皮士的容貌和行为特征。从原文看,该人容貌及行为特征都很特别,译文就要译出其特别之处。

言为心声。人物的性格及思想感情是通过具体语言表现出来的,语言描写得当往往能使人物形象栩栩如生。因此,翻译中涉及语言描写的时候宜充分考虑原文特定的人物性格和环境气氛,分清译者自己的语言和原文人物的语言。例如:

"I'm trying to get Mom to let me bring you home," Jamie told the creature. "I know you're not really a pet. You're a friend ... sort of. But I can't let you stay out here in the cold. Winter's coming soon. It gets really cold here then. And sometimes Mom doesn't let me go outside when it snows."

译文一:"我会设法说服妈妈让我把你带回家,"杰米对这只动物说,"我知道你其实不是一只宠物。从某些方面看……你是一位朋友。而我不会让你待在这冰冷的地方。冬天马上就要来了。到那时,这里真的很冷。而且,下雪的时候,妈妈总不让我出来。"

译文二:杰米对小动物说:"我在想办法,要妈妈让我把你领回家。因为,你不是宠物,你是我的朋友。可不能让你住在冰冰凉凉的地方。冬天要来了,这里会很冷很冷的。下雪后,妈妈就不会让我随便出来了。"

这是一个九岁男孩对小狗说的一番话,译文一书卷气十足,显然将译者自己的语言与文章中人物的语言混同了起来,致使译文中人物的语言因为不符合特定的环境气氛及年龄特点而缺乏个性化特征。又如:

In his work, he preferred to use "common objects from anywhere: a pitcher, a mug of beer, a pipe," to tell the story. "They're what I wrap up my thoughts in. They're parables."

在作品中,他喜欢用"信手拈来的普通物品,比如一个有柄水罐,一杯啤酒,一只烟斗"进行表述。他说:"我用它们包裹我的思想。它们其实就是寓言。"

从原文不难看出,著名艺术大师马蒂斯的谈吐不俗,意味深长,因而翻译他的言谈话语,行文须再现其语言风采,否则遣词造句就不像是马蒂斯嘴里说出的话了,从而使人物形象失去了原有的光彩。

涉及语言描写翻译的时候,须从宏观上把握原文特定的环境气氛和人物语言风格。涉及人物对话翻译时,可遵循口语表达习惯,注意译文的行文不要拗口。如:

Little John was shouting his prayers:"Please God send me a new football for my birthday."

His mother, overhearing this, said, "Don't shout dear, God isn't deaf."

"No, but Grandad is, and He's in the next room," John replied.

小约翰大声祈祷:"上帝啊,请您在我生日那天送我一只新足球吧。"

他妈妈无意中听到后,说:"亲爱的,别喊,上帝不聋。"

"上帝不聋,可爷爷聋呀,他在隔壁房间呐,"约翰回答道。

总之,翻译口语表达时不要有悖于口语的表达习惯,使对话显得有失和谐。同时,还要做到将原文的一般性语言与个性化语言区别开来,努力再现原文人物的个性化特征。又如:

"You know who's sub-human, man? You. You are. Going to school every day. And back home on the bus. And do your homework." The guy's voice was contemptuous. "Square boy. Middle-aged at fourteen, fifteen. Already caught in a routine. Wow."

"你知道什么是下等人吗,先生?是你,你就是。每天上学,然后乘公交车回家,之后做家庭作业。"那家伙的语气很轻蔑,"哇噻,多规矩的孩子!才十四五岁就像个中年人了,天天都在循规蹈矩了。"

嬉皮士提倡非传统的宗教文化,批评西方国家中层阶级的价值观,他们着不寻常的衣饰,过着不寻常的反主流的生活。作为嬉皮士,这个家伙为突出自己反抗习俗、反时政的特征,说出的话故意离经叛道。

三、避免白水翻译

许多描写文、记叙文和小说原作十分优美感人,犹如一杯新茶清新芬芳,略带苦涩,健脑提神,可有时不幸给译成了一杯淡而无味的白开水,有翻译理论家称之为"白水翻译"。如:

We are at home when the news comes that they are dead. We see the maiden in the shadow of her first sorrow. We see the silvered head of the old man bowed with the last grief!

译文一:当他们的死讯传来时我们正好待在家中。我们看见那个处女陷入第一次悲哀之中。我们看见那个老人长满银发的头最后一次悲哀地低垂着。

译文二:他们死去的噩耗传来,我们正在家中。我们看见那位少女浸没在有生以来第一次悲伤的阴影之中。我们看见那位老人为人生最后一次哀恸,垂下了白发苍苍的头!

原文将悲伤写得很美很动人,好似一盘美味佳肴,色、香、味俱全,但译文一却寡淡无味,原作神韵尽失。在充分欣赏原文之美的基础上,为再现原文的美,译者须有较好的语言修养,方能拿出较为令人满意的作品。
试比较下面的原文与译文:

The Goober was beautiful when he ran. His long arms and legs moved flowingly and flawlessly, his body floating as if his feet weren't touching the ground. When he ran, he forgot about his acne and his awkwardness and the shyness that paralyzed him when a girl looked his way. Even his thoughts became sharper, and things were simple and uncomplicated—he could solve math problems when he ran or memorize football play patterns. Often he rose early in the morning, before anyone else, and poured himself liquid through the sunrise streets and everything seemed beautiful, everything in its proper orbit, nothing impossible, the entire world attainable.

落花生跑起来很带劲。他四肢修长,跑起步来上下协调,如行云流水,完美无瑕,仿佛脚不着地,身在飘移。跑步时,他就会忘记脸上的青春痘,忘记面对女孩子目光时的窘迫、羞涩和笨拙。甚至,在他跑步或默记橄榄球阵式时,思维也变得敏锐了,一切都化繁为简了——复杂的数学题都迎刃而解了。

他经常一大早起床,比谁都起得早,然后迎着曙光,跑过大街小巷。这时候一切看起来分外美丽,一切都显得井然有序。世上没有办不到的事,整个世界仿佛都在他的掌控之中。

上面这段译文选自南京青年译家刘雪城的翻译力作《巧克力战争》。该译作中多有创造性的文字表达,例如此段的表达让人觉得非这样说不可,否则就达不到原文所达到的效果。

附一 课堂讲练材料

On Beauty

A young man sees a sunset and, unable to understand or to express the emotion that it rouses in him, concludes that it must be the gateway to a world that lies beyond. It is difficult for any of us in moments of intense aesthetic experience to resist the suggestion that we are catching a glimpse of a light that shines down to us from a different realm of existence, different and, because the experience is intensely moving, in some way higher. And, though the gleams blind and dazzle, yet do they convey a hint of beauty and serenity greater than we have known or imagined. Greater too than we can describe; for language, which was invented to convey the meanings of this world, cannot readily be fitted to the uses of another.

That all great art has this power of suggesting a world beyond is undeniable. In some moods Nature shares it. There is no sky in June that it does not waken the vision of a greater beauty, a vision which passes before it is fully glimpsed, and in passing leaves an indefinable longing and regret. But, if this world is not merely a bad joke, life a vulgar flare amid the cool radiance of the stars, and existence an empty laugh braying across the mysteries; if these intimations of a something behind and beyond are not evil humour born of indigestion, or whimsies sent by the devil to mock and madden us; if, in a word, beauty means something, yet we must not seek to interpret the meaning. If we glimpse the unutterable, it is unwise to try to utter it, nor should we seek to invest with significance that which we cannot grasp. Beauty in terms of our human meanings if meaningless.

(Pieces of Mind)

附二　课外扩展训练材料

Black Dog

One January morning, the captain got up early and walked down to the beach. It was a cold winter's day with the sun still low in the sky. My mother was upstairs with my father, who was now very ill. That year the winter was long and hard, and we knew my father would not see another spring.

I was getting the table ready for the captain's breakfast. Suddenly, the door of the inn opened and a man stepped inside. I had never seen him before. He wore a sailor's short sword by his side, and I noticed he had only three fingers on his left hand.

I asked him what he wanted and he said, "I'll take a glass of rum." But before I could fetch it, he told me to come near him. "Is this table for my old friend Bill?" the stranger asked, with a terrible smile.

I told him I did not know his friend Bill and the breakfast was for a man who was staying at the inn. "We call him the captain," I said.

"Does he have a sword cut on his face?" he asked.

"Yes," I said.

"That's Bill," said the stranger. "Is he here?"

I told him the captain was out walking, and the man waited, like a cat waiting for a mouse. I did not like the look on his face and was sure the captain would not be pleased to see him.

When the captain came back, the man pulled me behind the door. The captain opened the door and walked across the room.

"Bill," said the stranger.

The captain turned quickly and saw us. The colour went from his face and he looked old and sick. "Black Dog!" he said. He stared at the stranger. "And what do you want?"

"I'll have a glass of rum," said Black Dog, "then you and I'll sit and talk like old friends."

I fetched the rum and they told me to go away. I went out of the room, but the voices became louder.

"No, no, and That's the end of it!" I heard the captain shout. "If one is caught, we'll all be caught!"

There were more shouts, and then the sound of the table crashing over. Next, I heard the sound of swords, then out ran Black Dog with blood running down his shoulder. He ran out of the inn and along the road. In a few seconds, he had disappeared from sight.

The captain watched him go, then said, "Jim, quick! Bring me rum."

He turned and went back into the inn, but he could only just stand on his feet. I realized he was feeling ill and ran to fetch the rum. Then I heard him falling and hurried back to find him on the floor.

My mother heard the noise and came downstairs. We lifted the captain's head. His eyes were closed and his face was a terrible colour.

At that moment Dr. Livesey arrived to see my father. He looked at the captain and said to my mother: "His heart can't take much more of this. I told him drinking rum would kill him, and it nearly has."

The captain opened his eyes and tried to sit up. "Where's Black Dog?"

"There's no Black Dog here," said the doctor, "Get on your feet and I'll help you to your bed."

(*Treasure Island*)

第三节 论说文的翻译

论说文(argumentation)是应用最为广泛的一种文体,其功能在于说明、阐释、陈述和论证。论说文一般包括社会科学论著、研究报告、文献资料和报刊社论等,其特点是遣词严肃、庄重、典雅;句法结构繁复,谋篇布局缜密。翻译论说文可从这两个基本特点着手。

一、注重遣词的严肃、庄重、典雅

论说文用词正式,概括词、抽象词很多,翻译时要反复斟酌以求准确把握词义。此外,论说文基调端庄凝重,因此译文不能太俚俗,也不得文白夹杂,还要注意用词,而且在风格和程式上要与原文保持一致。如:

Every man who rises above the common level has received two educations: the first from his teachers; the second, more personal and important, from himself...

每一个人尖儿大凡接受两种教育,一是拜师学艺,二是自学成才,后者尤为重要。

原文语言正式,用语标准,但是译文中"人尖儿"虽是一个正确的译文,但作为俚语,与原文的风格相悖;另外,"大凡"作为一文言表达,使译文文白相杂。建议译作:"每一个拔尖人才都接受过两种教育:第一种是从师;第二种更直接也更为重要——自学。"

二、注意句法结构的繁复及谋篇布局的缜密

翻译论说文时,须宏观上把握全文中心思想,理解总体结构和谋篇布局的脉络,如若不然,译文会流于形式,疏漏百出。例如:

The normal Western approach to a problem is to fight it. The saying, "When the going gets tough, the tough get going," epitomizes this aggressive, combat-ready attitude toward the problem-solving. No matter what the problem is, or the techniques available for solving it, the framework produced by our Western way of thinking is fight. Dr. De Bono calls this vertical thinking: the traditional, sequential, Aristotelian thinking of logic, moving firmly from one step to the next, like toy blocks being built one on top of the other.

译文一:西方解决问题的正常途径是战斗。"艰难之路,惟勇者行"的谚语说明这种解决问题的态度是挑衅性的、剑拔弩张的。无论问题是什么,或有什么解决的诀窍,西方的思维方式是拉开架势干一场。德博诺医生称这为纵向思维,即传统、连续、亚里士多德式的逻辑思维,固执地一步步走下去,就像是玩具积木一块块搭上去一样。

译文二:西方解决问题的方法通常是同它斗。谚语"艰难之路,唯

勇者行"体现了这种进攻性的、好斗的解决问题的态度。无论什么样的问题,无论解决问题的技巧怎样,我们西方思维方式所创造的解决问题的模式就是同它斗。德博诺博士认为西方思维方式属于纵向思维,即传统的、连续的、亚里士多德式的逻辑思维,固定地从一步迈向下一步,好像玩具积木一样一块搭在另一块上面。

逻辑关联是联系论据与论点的纽带,是作者实现缜密布局的有效手段,但逻辑关联是通过具体的语句表达出来的,要再现原文的内在逻辑关联,译文行文就要把握语意上的贯串,注意语句间的扣接。译文一行文松散,句与句间缺乏逻辑关联,甚至歪曲了原文的基本意思,可见译者并没把握好原文的布局格式,译文因而出现了误译及流于形式的现象。

论说文旨在摆事实讲道理,通过运用概念、判断进行推理和论证,提出观点或主张。议论文一般由论点、论据、论证三部分组成。论点是作者提出的主张和观点;论据是作者用来证明论点的理由和事实;论证是作者用论据证明论点的过程和方法。翻译论说文首先要关注论据与论点之间的内在联系,把握行文上的逻辑关联。例如:

> Just as Darwin discovered the law of development of organic nature so Marx discovered the law of development of human history, the simple fact, hitherto concealed by an overgrowth of ideology, that mankind must first of all eat, drink, have shelter and clothing before it can pursue politics, science, art, religion, etc.; that, therefore the production of the immediate material means of subsistence and consequently the degree of economic development attained by a given people during a given epoch form the foundation upon which the state institutions, the legal conceptions, art, and even the ideas on religion, of the people concerned have been evolved, and in the light of which they must, therefore, be explained, instead of vice versa, as had hitherto been the case.

正如达尔文发现有机自然界的发展规律一样,马克思发现了人类历史的发展规律,即繁茂芜杂的意识形态所掩盖的一个简单事实:人们首先要吃、要喝、要穿、要住,然后才能从事政治、科学、艺术、宗教等活动,所以与生存息息相关的物质资料的生产,会为某个民族在某个时代带来一定程度的经济发展,而这又构成了国家制度、法律观念、艺术以及宗教思想的基础。在解释人类历史发展中的诸多问题时,必须运用马克思所发现的这一规律。

附一 课堂讲练材料

Why People Work

Jobs and work do much more than most of us realize to provide happiness and contentment. We're all used to thinking that work provides the material things of life—the goods and services that make possible our modern civilization. But we are much less conscious of the extent to which work provides the more intangible, but more crucial, psychological well-being that make the difference between a full and an empty life.

Historically, work has been associated with slavery and sin and punishment. And in our own day we are used to hearing the traditional complaints: "I can't wait for my vocation", "I wish I could stay at home today", "My boss treats me poorly", "I've got too much work to do and not enough time to do it." Against this background, it may well come as a surprise to learn that not only psychologists but other behavioral scientists have come to accept the positive contribution of work to the individual's happiness and sense of personal achievement. Work is more than a necessity for most human beings; it is the focus of their lives, the source of their identity and creativity.

Rather than a punishment or a burden, work is the opportunity to realize one's potential. Many psychiatrists heading mental health clinics have observed its healing effect. A good many patients who feel depressed in clinics gain renewed self-confidence when gainfully employed and lose some, if not all, of their most acute symptoms. Increasingly, institutions dealing with mental health problems are establishing workshops wherein those too sick to get a job in "outside" industry can work, while every effort is exerted to arrange "real" jobs for those well enough to work outside.

And the reverse is true, too. For large numbers of people, the absence of work is harmful to their health. Retirement often brings many problems surrounding the "What do I do with myself?" question, even though there may be no financial cares. Large numbers of people regularly get headaches and other illness on weekends when they don't have their jobs to go to, and must fend for themselves. It has been observed that unemployment, quite aside from exerting financial pressures, brings enormous psychological troubles and that many individuals deteriorate rapidly when jobless.

But why? Why should work be such a significant source of human satisfaction? A good share of the answer rests in the kind of pride that is stimulated by the job and by the activity of accomplishing.

(Leonard R. Sayles)

附二　课外扩展训练材料

Health and Wealth, Which to Prefer?

"Health is wealth!" This is an old saying which the majority applaud. As a rule, the wealthier you are, the weaker your health is, but this cannot be applied to all.

A person that has health can afford to challenge all hardship. For example, coolies, who are usually stout and strong, though having only two stable meals a day or even one, are very energetic. With their energy, they earn their living. Although such occupation brings little reward as compared with the energy they have exerted, they enjoy life whatever things may be.

Business is based on health. Surely, in good health a student can absorb knowledge more readily. And, being in good health, a scientist can achieve more success whereas, the weak learner loses his ability to tackle the complex technical problems.

Frequently we find millionaires clinging close to their doctors for they seldom have enough exercise to bring forth better health. Their lack of exercise slackens the readiness of growth of the antibodies to resist the attack of diseases.

We can take the famous wealthy film star, Elizabeth Taylor as an example. Does she find real happiness, having to frequent the hospital and at the edge of death? So, what can we benefit from wealth if we do not have health?

(《英语模范作文》)

第四节　说明文的翻译

说明文(exposition)通常采用分类、比较、举例等方法对事物进行介绍说明,给读者提供有关知识。因此,翻译说明文,首先要使译文清楚明确,避免含糊其辞。例如:

For the battery first three times using, please make sure the battery is completely used up and charged for over 12 hours, this can keep the battery capacity in good condition. This product is specially designed for PSP, and can be connected to PSP console, and an USB PLUG is enclosed which provide power supply for other USB products.

电池前3次使用时,请确保电池中的电量被彻底耗空,并且充电12小时以上。这样可以使电池的容量保持一种良好状态。本产品专为PSP设计,可以连接PSP主机,并附USB插头,所述USB插头用于为其他USB产品提供电源。

这一段取自PSP的外部充电器"产品说明书"。原文条理清楚、行文通顺。既然说明文的目的是为了通过介绍产品来提供知识,那么说明文的翻译就力求准确,同时还应明确,否则"越说越不明"。

说明文注重知识性、科学性,其语言不同于记叙文、描写文或论说文,遣词造句通常较为平实,行文较为简洁,无太多的修饰语,文章精神无需从深层次进行挖掘。因此,翻译说明文,行文也要平实简洁,不拖泥带水,用语准确、科学。例如:

Aside from herbs' healing substances include cinnabar and other minerals, insects, and such strange materials as deer horn, tiger bones, cicada shells, frogs and toads. Liquid concoctions are usually thick, brownish or black, and often more or less bitter. This has led to the saying: "Efficacious remedies are bitter in the mouth but beneficial to the body."

除了花花草草之外,用来治病的"药"还包括朱砂等矿物质和昆虫,以及一些奇奇怪怪的东西如鹿角、虎骨、蝉蜕、青蛙与蟾蜍。煎成的汤药通常汁浓,带棕色或呈黑色,且多少有些苦涩,所以成语说:"良药苦口利于病"。

原文介绍了草药之外的其他可以用来治病的东西,语言客观平实。译文也不拖泥带水,简洁明了,毫无夸大之辞。

附一 课堂讲练材料

The Female Mosquito

No matter who you are or where you come from, one thing is certain: you are acquainted with the mosquito—although you probably wish you weren't. Mosquitoes are everywhere. They can be found all over the world, and they come in more than 2,500 species. Somewhere, at some time, you have surely met at least one.

No one loves mosquito. But unfortunately the mosquito may decide that she loves you. She? Yes, she. Did you know that only the female mosquito bites? Well, it's true. And it's not because she's friendly; she needs blood to reproduce.

Do you know how the female mosquito decides whom to bite? She's quite selective, and she chooses her victims carefully. First, she uses sensors to find her victim. These sensors are located on her two antennae and her three pairs of legs. With these sensors, she tests your body moisture, body warmth, and chemical substances in your sweat. If she likes what she finds, she bites. But if you don't appeal to her, she'll reject you for someone more appetizing. The next time a mosquito bites you, just remember that you were chosen. You're special.

If the mosquito likes you, she settles onto your flesh very gently, and she breaks your skin with her proboscis tip. Proboscis tip? What's that? It's a kind of mouth and it sticks out just below the mosquito's eyes. It contains six sharp instruments called stylets. She stabs all six stylets into your skin at once, and if she hits a blood vessel, she'll get a full dinner in about a minute. All this usually takes place so quickly and quietly that you may not have suspected anything was happening.

Why does a mosquito bite itch? The itch is not really from the bite. It's from the saliva the mosquito mixes with your blood to keep it from clotting as she sucks it up her proboscis tip. By the time the itching begins, she has gone.

And then what happens? Well, after her delicious dinner, the mosquito is tired. She just wants to find a place to rest. Heavy with your blood she picks a spot—on a leaf or a wall or a stone—to quietly lay her eggs. Just one drop of blood will produce hundreds of eggs.

Where is her mate? Well, their relationship is over, and he's no longer around. Their mating took place before she bit you. She will live one to two months and lay eggs four or five times during this time.

All mosquitoes, male and female, pass through their early stages of development in or near water. In fact, mosquito eggs will not hatch without water—although the eggs can survive up to five years on dry land waiting for water. It is not surprising that heavy rains produce large numbers of mosquitoes.

But why? Why did nature bother to create mosquitoes? Just to annoy us? Probably that wasn't the main reason. Male mosquitoes live on the nectar of flowers, and some scientists believe that they pollinate the flowers as they fly from one to the other. Of course, mosquitoes have to reproduce, and unfortunately that's where you and I come in. Like it or not, mosquitoes are here to stay. Ouch! (Slap!) One just bit me!

(《提高阅读技能》)

附二　课外扩展训练材料

How to Learn a Foreign Language Through Translation

Every man who rises above the common level has received two

educations: the first from his teachers; the second, more personal and important, from himself.... In my French and Latin translations I adopted an excellent method, which, from my own success, I would recommended to the imitation of students. I chose some classic writers, such as Cicero and Vertot, the most approved for purity and elegance of style. I translated, for instance, an epistle of Cicero into French; and, after throwing it aside till the word and phrases were obliterated from my memory, I re-translated my French into such Latin as I could find; and then compared each sentence of my imperfect version with the ease, the grace, the propriety of the Roman orator. A similar experiment was made on several pages of the Revolutions of Vertot; I turned them into Latin, returned them after a sufficient interval into my own French, and again scrutinised the resemblance or dissimilitude of the copy and the original. By degrees I was less ashamed, by degrees I was more satisfied with myself; and I persevered in the practice of these double translations, which filled several books, till I had acquired the knowledge of both idioms, and the command at least of a correct style. This useful exercise of writing was accompanied and succeeded by the more pleasing occupation of reading the best authors. The perusal of the Roman classics was at once my exercise and reward.

(Edward Gibbon)

第五节 新闻报道的翻译

传媒语篇主要指报刊、电台、互联网等大众传播媒介的新闻报道和评论。由于传媒(mass communication)报道题材不同,传播工具的层次各异,其分类界限也是相对的。为了清楚表述,此处的传媒语篇主要指新闻报道文体,即严肃的报刊、电台、网站等传播媒介在报道或评论政治、时事性事件时所使用的文体。

由于新闻报道时间性强,需用最小的篇幅传播尽可能多的信息,这就规定了其语篇在结构和语言上的特殊性。新闻报道的结构特点是,把报道的中心成分放在文章的开头,然后再交代有关过程和细节,总体而言其模式呈倒金字塔形状(inverted pyramid format),内容主要回答五个 W 和一个 H,即 what-where-when-who-why-how? 其基本程式与汉语报刊文体一致,所以汉译时一般不调整其段落结构和语篇整体框架,宜将重点集中于报刊文体语言特色的准确把握上。

一、再现原文的词汇特点

(一) 用词追求新奇的效果是传媒语篇的突出特征之一

传媒用语的特点之一就是追求新颖、时尚,惯常使用派生、附加、合成、拼缀及缩略等手段,创造新词,因此新词、临时词毫不鲜见,如 working poor(穷忙族)、playing cute(扮萌),Bollywood 由 Hollywood 演变而成,指的是印度电影业,有人译作"宝莱坞"。译者在翻译新闻文字时,一定要仔细揣摩上下文,勤于查询工具书,以求准确把握词义,切忌想当然或望文生义。确属首次使用的新词可依情况,采用试译加注的方法。

(二) 传媒语篇的另一突出特征是赋予某些习语特殊的含义,追求意外效果

用词追求意想不到的效果常促使作者采取一些特别手段,如将习语进行转义,例如 pants 现在的意思为"垃圾、废话",bad hair day 指"糟糕的一天",New Man 指"不遵循男人传统思维方式的新新男人"。汉译时要注意辨别新闻职业语言与日常词汇的区别。

(三) 要避免使用主观感情色彩较浓的词汇以保证新闻的真实、客观

译文的句法结构要以原文为依据,一般不宜太复杂,要保证较强的可读性、真实性、客观性。试比较:

> A police postmortem has yet to determine the official cause of death, but friends and relatives of the 52-year-old super chef were in no doubt that he had shot himself. "He tried to do too much," said his wife, Dominique. "He was worn out; He's just had enough."

> 警方尸检还没有确定这位 52 岁超级厨师的真正死因,但其亲朋好友却断定他是开枪自杀的。"他想要做太多的事情,"其妻多米尼克说,"他精疲力竭,他只是受够了。"

(四) 要重视语言正式程度

总体而言,新闻报道语言属于标准英语,汉译时可使用与其对应的现代汉语,行文尽量避免极端化:过俗则有失严肃,过于正式则会降低可读性,不能满足大众化阅读要求。如：

> A Romanian man plans to complain to consumer authorities about the poor quality of a rope he used in a failed attempt to hang himself, Romanian papers reported. "You can't even die in this country," 45-year-old Victor Dodoi was quoted as saying in the daily *Adevarul*. The newspaper said Dodoi's relatives found him hanging from a tree in his garden and managed to cut the rope with a knife. He was taken by horse-drawn cart and then by ambulance to a hospital in the northern town of Botosani. Dodoi said he would file a complaint with the Consumer Protection Authority about the quality of the rope, which was easily cut, as soon as he is released.

> 据罗马尼亚报纸报道，一罗马尼亚男子打算向消费者保护机构投诉他上吊所用的绳子存在质量问题。《真理》日报援引45岁的维克多·多铎伊的话说，"在这个国家，你连死都困难。"报纸说，多铎伊的亲戚发现他在自家花园的树上上吊，立刻用刀割断绳子，先用马车，后用救护车把多铎伊送到北部城镇波托萨尼的一家医院抢救。出院后，多铎伊宣布他将就绳子的质量问题向消费者保护机构投诉——它太易割断了。

原文中的 complain to consumer authorities about the poor quality 若依字面意义译成"向消费者保护机构抱怨绳子质量不好"，译文就会有失正式。

二、再现原文的句法特点

从句法上看，媒体语篇具有以下特征：一是出于简洁的需要，常省略冠词、介词、动词、代词、助动词等；二是出于真实和客观的需要广泛使用直接引语和被动语态；三是不强调时态，往往主句用动词过去时，从句用一般现在时；四是为提供背景之需多用简单句，同时增加补加定语、状语、同位语、插入语等。译者在翻译传媒语篇时，宜针对以上特点，包括前面提及的词法特点，做出相应的处理。请看下面一篇报道：

> Anz $200,000 ($112,000) dispute between two New Zealand companies has been resolved in an unusual out-of-court settlement—a best-of-three 1 arm-wrestling match. The chief executives of the small telecommunications companies—Teamtalk Ltd. and MCS Digital

Ltd.—squared off after their firms were unable to reach an agreement on access to a mobile radio network. The dispute had already been the subject of a complaint with competition regulators and was heading for the courts. "Sure, losing hurts but not nearly as much as paying lawyers bills," defeated Team Talk Chief Executive David Ware told reporters.

两家新西兰公司以一种非同寻常的庭外和解方式——三局两胜扳腕子比赛解决了一场涉及金额20万新西兰元(11.2万美元)的争议。情况是这样的:蒂托公司和MCS数字因无法就一个移动无线网络的使用权达成协议,于是这两家小型电信公司的总裁拉开架势单挑。此前,他们已经就这一争议向行业竞争调解机构提出过申诉,并准备对簿公堂。结果,蒂托公司总裁输掉了扳腕子比赛。他对记者说:"失败固然令人痛心,但跟高昂的律师费相比,这种失败要好受一点点。"

这是一篇典型的媒体语篇,简明,短小精悍,结构紧凑,笔锋犀利。只有三句,却把一场争端的解决描绘得淋漓尽致。作者采用了夸张、生造词、俚语等手段,以加强新闻的真实性、娱乐性,比如作者用了新闻界惯用的造词术,创造了 a best-of-three 1 arm-wrestling match,汉译时译作"三局两胜扳腕子比赛"较为恰当。对于原文的引语,译者予以保留,以求报道的客观性,减少主观性。另外,译者在传达原文的语调上没掺杂个人情感,实事求是地译出了原文的意义。

三、新闻报道标题的翻译

今天是阅读爆炸的时代,放眼浩如烟海的因特网、微信、图书报刊,如何从中获取重要信息及自己想要的信息?前辈们总结的经验值得借鉴:"看书看皮,看报看题"。"看报看题"的阅读建议向翻译初学者翻译传媒语篇提出了一个翻译重点,即标题的翻译,因为好的标题必定是抓人眼球的,如果标题没有吸引力,很少有读者会耐心地阅读正文。可以说,标题的翻译关系到新闻报道的死活与成败。那么,如何翻译英语新闻报道的标题呢?现以本书第七章第五节附二的题目翻译为例加以说明:

A Family Adventure
译文一:一个家庭的历险(直译)
译文二:不走平常路(意译)

译文三:全家总动员,骑车游美国(意译加注释)
译文四:多德一家的逍遥游(意译)

译文一中用了"历险"一词,但通观全文,读者会发现报道中的多德一家只是中止工作和学业全家一起去周游全美国,途中并没有任何历险经历,看来原文的"Adventure"与汉语的"历险"在意义上是不等值的,因而译文虽是直译的结果,但不忠实。不忠实的译文,题目再有吸引力也是不足取的。

译文二用了一语双关,表面指多德一家骑自行车周游全美国这件事,实际上暗指这家人中断正常的工作及学习不惜冒卖掉房子的风险借钱全家一起去游玩这件不寻常的举动。撇开原文题目,根据报道内容意译题目是一个不错的选择。

译文三脱离原标题,直接点明报道的内容,言简意赅。与此同时,还借用目前较火的"总动员"一词,这种题目对那些热爱"玩具总动员"和"汽车总动员"的读者不能不说存在一定的阅读诱感。

译文四与前面两个译文一样,采用了意译的方式,不仅告诉读者这篇报道的内容,还恰当借用了庄子的"逍遥游"来点明这一家人对此次游玩的享受与无悔。与上例一样,很多标题的翻译可能有多个版本,那么,如何确定众多译文中哪个是最好选择?翻译初学者不妨自问:这些标题中哪一个最能让自己产生阅读渴望?如果答案是译文四,那就毫不犹豫地选择译文四吧。

附一 课堂讲练材料

Hostile Takeover Brews at Harbin Beer

The world's two largest brewers, the US based Anheuser-Busch Ltd. and South Africa based SABMiller, are locked in a struggle over a potential takeover of Harbin Brewery Group. Harbin Brewery Group ranks forth in the Chinese beer market in terms of sales. The current market value of the Hong Kong listed company (HK0249) is estimated at HK＄3 billion (US＄384 million).

SAB purchased 29.6% of the shares of Harbin Beer in June last year to become the largest shareholder of the company. It also signed an "exclusive strategic investment agreement" with Harbin Beer. Harbin

Beer, however, unilaterally announced the termination of this agreement on May 1, stating that SAB did not fulfil all of its commitments made in the agreement.

Anheuser-Busch Ltd. responded immediately. On May 2, it announced it would take over a company called Global Conduit holdings Limited (GCH), which had just signed an agreement 40 days earlier to purchase 29.07% shares for HK＄1.08 billion from a window company of the Harbin government. The purchase gave Anheuser-Busch the second largest stake in Harbin Beer.

SAB reacted on the same day with the announcement of a plan to make a general offer of HK＄4.3 per share for all Harbin Beer shares. The market value of Harbin Beer was HK＄3.22 per share on April 30.

(《财经》)

附二　课外扩展训练材料

A Family Adventure

What is amazing about the Dodd family is not who they are, but the extraordinary adventure they chose to go on together.

Up until last summer, Gary Dodd was working as a minister and Faith Dodd was employed at a doctor's office. They lived with their twin teenagers, Rebekah and Andrew, both 15, at a house in Nashville, Tenn.

But last summer, the Dodds did something unusual. They quit their jobs, pulled their children out of school and took a loan against their house. Together, the family set out to see America from the seats of their bicycles.

The plan is to criss-cross the country. The trip began in Seattle. But it really started with a casual family conversation.

"Andrew and Rebekah and I were driving home from church one evening and I was telling the kids that I needed to get in better shape, and before they graduated, and since they were twins, that I wanted to spend more time with them," Gary Dodd said. "I just said that and Rebekah just quipped, 'well, let's bike across America.'"

Instead of treating it as an offhand remark, the rest of the family seized on the idea. "My thought was extremely random and for me just to say that I have no idea what hit me for me to say such a thing," Rebehah Dodd said. "But I'm glad I did."

The Dodd parents knew that time is a bandit when you have children. Before you know it, time with friends replaces time with family. Gary and Faith said they wanted one last grab at their children's childhoods, as their kids approached the end of high school.

Teenagers seem to have the energy to try anything, but Faith—who is in her 40s—took a deep breath when she heard the plan. "Could this body do it?" Faith Dodd asked herself.

In the meantime, their plan was drawing some mixed reactions from their friends. "We had many people very supportive of the trip. They would hear it and say 'oh, that seems like it would be a lot of fun'" Faith Dodd said. "But then, we would have some people who would look at us as though we had lost our mind, and would call us crazy."

The Dodds are making their own video diary of the experience and taking hundreds of photographs. Andrew Dodd, meanwhile, is maintaining the family Webb page.

"The Internet has been great. We've been able to post journals and type e-mails to people, and people have been able to stay in contact with us."

"I haven't had to answer the phone. I haven't been on call," he said. "It's really been liberating just to be out and to do your own thing and to go your own way and just to have an adventure every day."

Rebehah Dodd has been similarly enjoying the thrills of the unknown. "I look forward each day to getting up and thinking, 'What's the ride going to hold today?'" she said.

"We realize we're making some sacrifices," she said. "We might have to sell our home when we get back to help for the trip, but it's worth it and I would do it again in a heartbeat."

(《扬子晚报》)

第六节 演讲语篇的翻译

演讲(lecture 或 speech)是一种极受欢迎的交流形式,其功能在于"传道""授业""解惑"、宣传、煽动等。演讲内容涉及政治、经济、军事、外交、社会、文化、文学、教育等各个领域,演讲者来自各行各业,可能是总统的就职或告别演讲,可能是政治家深谋远虑的外交演说,或是社会活动家的慷慨激昂之辞,或是教师针对性强的讲座,也可能是某工人在一次请愿中一时冲动登上讲台的即席发言……演讲由于不同于其他文体或语篇的特点,对演讲者有极高的要求,例如要求断句须准确,否则就会引起误会。如:

1. 麻子无头发黑脸大脚不大好看。
2. 麻子无,头发黑,脸大,脚不大,好看。
3. 麻子,无头发,黑脸,大脚,不大好看。

上面三句话由于断句的不同,意义迥异,所以演讲者十分重视断句。此外,节奏感的把握也很重要,可增加演讲的表现力。当然还有其他许多方面须注意,特别是演讲稿的文字准备工作及翻译。

一、演讲语篇的特点

概括起来,演讲语篇一般有以下两大特点:

(一) 遣词严肃但不乏意趣,庄重不失灵动,典雅不失亲和力

Four million bodies in chains—four million souls in fetters! All the sacred relations of wife, mother, father, and child trampled beneath the brutal feet of might. And all this was done under our own beautiful banner of the free.

400万人系着锁链,四百万人戴着镣铐!谁无妻子,谁无父母,谁无子女,这一切神圣的关系都遭到强权野蛮的践踏。然而,这一切,又都是在我们这美丽的自由旗帜下干出来的。

原文带有强烈的感情色彩,文字严肃,铿锵有力,掷地有声,译文较好地传达出了原文的神韵和特点。

(二) 演讲多使用煽动性的文字

You ask, what is our aim? I can answer in one word. It is victory. Victory at all costs—victory in spite of all terrors—victory, however long and hard the road may be, for without victory there is no survival.

　　要问我们的目的是什么？我可以用两个字回答，那就是胜利。不惜一切去夺取胜利，不惧一切去夺取胜利！胜利！胜利！无论道路多么漫长，多么崎岖，要夺取胜利！没有胜利就不能生存。

原文的文字选择极尽煽动之能事，译文同样也在译词选择上下了一番工夫，基本上起到了与原文相似的表达效果。

（三）演讲强调缜密的谋篇布局

由于演讲旨在解析思想、阐明观点、辩明事理、展开宣传攻势，因此内容虽然复杂，但表现形式清楚易懂，用语准、精，长句不多，有浓厚的主观色彩，而且为突出其表现力常常使用修辞，如排比、重复等。试比较：

　　I see a world at peace, adorned with every form of art, with music's myriad voices thrilled, while lips are rich with words of love and truth—a world in which no exile sighs, no prisoner mourns; a world on which the gibbet's shadow does not fall; a world where labor reaps its full reward; where work and worth go hand in hand; where the poor girl trying to win bread with the needle—the needle, that has been called "the asp for the breast of the poor"—is not driven to the desperate choice of crime and death, of suicide or shame.

　　我看见的是一个太平的世界，有各种形式的工艺美术为它增色生辉，有千变万化的乐曲在激荡回响，而人们的谈吐尽是爱与真的言语。在这个世界，没有流放者的叹息，没有囚徒的哀伤；在这个世界，没有绞架投下可怕的阴影；在这个世界，劳动会得到充足的报偿；在这个世界，工作与价值并驾齐驱；在这个世界，试图靠针头线脑来换取面包的穷姑娘不会被逼进犯罪、死亡、自尽和耻辱的绝境，而缝衣针曾经被人称为"睡在穷人胸膛上的毒蛇"。

原文内容复杂，但由于排比句恰如其分的使用，原文精神清楚易懂。为突出原文的表现力，译文采取了同样的修辞，如排比、重复等进行翻译，起到了与原文相似的表现效果。

二、演讲语篇的翻译要点

(一) 把握原文的正式度

Ladies and Gentlemen, Dear Colleagues:

  Because I am the Vice-Chancellor of the oldest of the foreign universities represented here today, I have been chosen to speak on their behalf. I am pleased to be their voice in presenting our heartfelt congratulations to the professors, teachers, researchers and students of Peking University on the 100th anniversary of its foundation.

女士们、先生们、尊敬的同道们：

  由于我是今天在此派有代表的各外国大学中最古老的大学的副校长，所以被推选代表他们讲话。我很高兴作为大家的代言人，表示我们衷心的祝贺，向北京大学的教授们、教师们、研究人员们和学生们祝贺北大成立一百周年。

在此若将 Dear Colleagues 译成"尊敬的同事们"，听众肯定会惊讶：牛津大学副校长怎么会和北大的师生是同事呢？译成"尊敬的同道们"则较得体。their voice 意为"代言人"。voice 是一个普通的英语词，通常解释为"噪音、说话声"，但在词典里也有"发言人、代言人"这一释义。本篇是公共演讲文体，句子结构较正式，但在规范的完整句中，用词大多是普通词。译者要像演讲者那样激发听众的感情，吸引听众的注意力，获得听众的理解与共鸣，特别是掌握好语言的正式程度。

(二) 照顾原文的句法结构

译文要照顾原文的句法结构，不宜使用过多的长句，也不宜使用过多的短句以免行文松散零乱。试比较：

  I see a race without disease of flesh or brain—shapely and fair, the married harmony of form and function—and, as I look, life lengthens, joy deepens, love canopies the earth; and above all, in the great dome, shines the eternal star of human hope.

  我看到一个在肉体和精神方面都没有疾病的种族，他们的体态匀称而优美，形态美和心灵美非常和谐地结合在一起。正如我所看到的：人的寿命延长了，生活的乐趣更浓了。爱的气氛弥漫大地，最重要的是，在浩瀚的天顶，闪耀着一颗永恒的人类希望的星星。

原文只有一句,但译文视情况对这一长句做了适当的拆分处理,但译文行文不显松散零乱,反而紧凑集中。

附一 课堂讲练材料

Hillary Clinton's Exit Speech
7 Jun 2008

Thank you so much. Thank you all.

Well, this isn't exactly the party I'd planned, but I sure like the company.

I want to start today by saying how grateful I am to all of you, to everyone who poured your hearts and your hopes into this campaign, who drove for miles and lined the streets waving homemade signs, who scrimped and saved to raise money, who knocked on doors and made calls, who talked and sometimes argued with your friends and neighbors, who emailed and contributed online, who invested so much in our common enterprise, to the moms and dads who came to our events, who lifted their little girls and little boys on their shoulders and whispered in their ears, "See, you can be anything you want to be."

To the young people like 13 year-old Ann Riddle from Mayfield, Ohio who had been saving for two years to go to Disney World, and decided to use her savings instead to travel to Pennsylvania with her Mom and volunteer there as well. To the veterans and the childhood friends, to New Yorkers and Arkansans who traveled across the country and telling anyone who would listen why you supported me.

To all those women in their 80s and their 90s born before women could vote who cast their votes for our campaign. I've told you before about Florence Steen of South Dakota, who was 88 years old, and insisted that her daughter bring an absentee ballot to her hospital bedside. Her daughter and a friend put an American flag behind her bed and helped her fill out the ballot. She passed away soon after, and under state law, her ballot didn't count. But her daughter later told a reporter, "My dad's an ordinary old cowboy, and he didn't like it when he heard mom's vote wouldn't be counted. I don't think he had voted in 20 years. But he voted in place of my mom."

To all those who voted for me, and to whom I pledged my utmost, my commitment to you and to the progress we seek is unyielding. You have inspired and touched me with the stories of the joys and sorrows that make up the fabric of our lives and you have humbled me with your commitment to our country.

18 million of you from all walks of life, women and men, young and old, Latino and Asian, African-American and Caucasian, rich, poor and middle class, gay and straight, you have stood strong with me. And I will continue to stand strong with you, every time, every place, and every way that I can. The dreams we share are worth fighting for.

Remember we fought for the single mom with a young daughter, juggling work and school, who told me, "I'm doing it all to better myself for her." We fought for the woman who grabbed my hand, and asked me, "What are you going to do to make sure I have health care?" and began to cry because even though she works three jobs, she can't afford insurance. We fought for the young man in the Marine Corps T-shirt who waited months for medical care and said, "Take care of my buddies over there and then, will you please help take care of me?" We fought for all those who've lost jobs and health care, who can't afford gas or groceries or college, who have felt invisible to their president these last seven years.

I entered this race because I have an old-fashioned conviction: that public service is about helping people solve their problems and live their dreams. I've had every opportunity and blessing in my own life, and I want the same for all Americans. Until that day comes, you will always find me on the front lines of democracy, fighting for the future.

The way to continue our fight now, to accomplish the goals for which we stand, is to take our energy, our passion, our strength and do all we can to help elect Barack Obama the next President of the United States.

Today, as I suspend my campaign, I congratulate him on the victory he has won and the extraordinary race he has run. I endorse him, and throw my full support behind him. And I ask all of you to join me in working as hard for Barack Obama as you have for me.

I have served in the Senate with him for four years. I have been in this campaign with him for 16 months. I have stood on the stage and gone toe-to-toe with him in 22 debates. I have had a front row seat to his candidacy, and I have seen his strength and determination, his grace and his grit.

In his own life, Barack Obama has lived the American Dream. As a community organizer, in the state senate, as a United States Senator, he has dedicated himself to ensuring the dream is realized. And in this campaign, he has inspired so many to become involved in the democratic process and invested in our common future.

Now when I started this race, I intended to win back the White House, and make sure we have a president who puts our country back on the path to peace, prosperity, and progress. And That's exactly what we're going to do by ensuring that Barack Obama walks through the doors of the Oval Office on January 20, 2009.

...

You know, I've been involved in politics and public life in one way or another for four decades. During those forty years, our country has voted ten times for President. Democrats won only three of those times. And the man who won two of those elections is with us today.

We made tremendous progress during the 90s under a Democratic President, with a flourishing economy, and our leadership for peace and security respected around the world. Just think how much more progress we could have made over the past 40 years if we had a Democratic President. Think about the lost opportunities of these past seven years on the environment and the economy, on health care and civil rights, on education, foreign policy and the Supreme Court. Imagine how far we could've come, how much we could've achieved if we had just had a Democrat in the White House.

We cannot let this moment slip away. We have come too far and accomplished too much.

Now the journey ahead will not be easy. Some will say we can't do it.

That it's too hard. That we're just not up to the task. But for as long as America has existed, it has been the American way to reject "can't do" claims, and to choose instead to stretch the boundaries of the possible through hard work, determination, and a pioneering spirit.

It is this belief, this optimism, that Senator Obama and I share, and that has inspired so many millions of our supporters to make their voices heard.

(to be continued)

附二 课外扩展训练材料

Hillary Clinton's Exit Speech
7 Jun 2008

So today, I am standing with Senator Obama to say: Yes we can. Together we will work. We'll have to work hard to get universal health care. But on the day we live in an America where no child, no man, and no woman is without health insurance, we will live in a stronger America. That's why we need to help elect Barack Obama our President.

...

We'll have to work hard to bring our troops home from Iraq, and get them the support they've earned by their service. But on the day we live in an America that's as loyal to our troops as they have been to us, we will live in a stronger America and that is why we must help elect Barack Obama our President.

This election is a turning point election and it is critical that we all understand what our choice really is. Will we go forward together or will we stall and slip backwards? Think how much progress we have already made. When we first started, people everywhere asked the same questions: Could a woman really serve as Commander-in-Chief? Well, I think we answered that one.

And could an African American really be our President? Senator Obama has answered that one.

Together Senator Obama and I achieved milestones essential to our progress as a nation, part of our perpetual duty to form a more perfect union.

Now, on a personal note, when I was asked what it means to be a woman running for President, I always gave the same answer: that I was proud to be running as a woman but I was running because I thought I'd be the best President. But I am a woman, and like millions of women, I know there are still barriers and biases out there, often unconscious.

I want to build an America that respects and embraces the potential of every last one of us.

I ran as a daughter who benefited from opportunities my mother never dreamed of. I ran as a mother who worries about my daughter's future and a mother who wants to lead all children to brighter tomorrows. To build that future I see, we must make sure that women and men alike understand the struggles of their grandmothers and mothers, and that women enjoy equal opportunities, equal pay, and equal respect. Let us resolve and work toward achieving some very simple propositions: There are no acceptable limits and there are no acceptable prejudices in the twenty-first century.

You can be so proud that, from now on, it will be unremarkable for a woman to win primary state victories, unremarkable to have a woman in a close race to be our nominee, unremarkable to think that a woman can be the President of the United States. And that is truly remarkable.

To those who are disappointed that we couldn't go all the way, especially the young people who put so much into this campaign, it would break my heart if, in falling short of my goal, I in any way discouraged any of you from pursuing yours. Always aim high, work hard, and care deeply about what you believe in. When you stumble, keep faith. When you're knocked down, get right back up. And never listen to anyone who says you can't or shouldn't go on.

As we gather here today in this historic magnificent building, the 50th woman to leave this Earth is orbiting overhead. If we can blast 50 women into space, we will someday launch a woman into the White House.

...

That is what we will do now as we join forces with Senator Obama and his campaign. We will make history together as we write the next chapter in America's story. We will stand united for the values we hold dear, for the vision of progress we share, and for the country we love. There is nothing more American than that.

And looking out at you today, I have never felt so blessed. The challenges that I have faced in this campaign are nothing compared to those that millions of Americans face every day in their own lives. So today, I'm going to count my blessings and keep on going. I'm going to keep doing what I was doing long before the cameras ever showed up and what I'll be doing long after they're gone: Working to give every American the same opportunities I had, and working to ensure that every child has the chance to grow up and achieve his or her God-given potential.

I will do it with a heart filled with gratitude, with a deep and abiding love for our country, and with nothing but optimism and confidence for the days ahead. This is now our time to do all that we can to make sure that in this election we add another Democratic President to that very small list of the last 40 years and that we take back our country and once again move with progress and commitment to the future.

Thank you all and God bless you and God bless America.

第七节　科技语篇的翻译

科技语篇(science variety)与文学、媒体、演讲等语篇迥然不同,具有自身鲜明的特点：

在行文方面,为更清楚地说明某种产品、某个现象或某种实验,科技语篇常借助公式、表格、图形等,这是其他文体中十分少见的；

在语法方面,科技语篇中被动语态使用频率高,一般现在时使用很多,句子结构完整,很少使用不完整句或省略句；

从词汇方面看,实验指示中多用短词、小词,一般科技文章中多用长词、大词,复合名词也较多；

在篇章结构方面,科技语篇组织谨严,观点清楚,逻辑严密,结构紧凑,合乎逻辑顺序,没有插叙、倒叙等。

总之,科技语篇清晰、准确、精练、严密、正式,唯有如此,才利于科技信息的交流。因此,翻译时应注意:

一、遣词准确无误

由于科技语篇术语较多,同一词语在不同行业中的意义不尽相同,有时甚至相差很大,因此,翻译时不能望文生义。

试比较:

> The queen has wings for a time, and one day she flies away with a winged male. The male dies soon afterwards, but the queen, without her wings, finds a good place for her new nest and begins to lay eggs there. Worker ants will feed her and protect the eggs, and they will build as big and as safe a home as they can.
>
> 雌蚁在一段时间内是有翅膀的,会在某一天与一只长翅膀的雄蚁飞走。很快,这只雄蚁会死去,而褪去翅膀的雌蚁则会找一个合适的地方作她的新窝,并在那里产卵。工蚁会去喂养她,并保护那些蚁卵,尽其所能来建设一个又大又安全的家。

原文中 The queen 不是指"女王",而指"蚁后"或"雌蚁",同样 male 不能译成"男性",须依照上下文译为"雄蚁",to lay eggs 不译成"生蛋",而得译作"产卵"。可见科技翻译中不能见字就译,须在理解原文的基础上,根据语篇的行业特点,进行准确的翻译。

二、注意行业特点,遣词要前后一致,不生造词汇

老话"隔行如隔山"有时也不无道理。科技翻译中,要留心行业特点和术语,对看似熟悉的词汇认真对待,否则可能错译,或无意识中就触犯生造词汇之大忌。试比较:

> In the ant society each worker has a special job. Some workers take care of the young, some carry out building work, and some are soldiers and do the fighting.
>
> 在蚂蚁社会中,每一个工蚁都有专门负责的工作。有些工蚁照管幼蚁,有些则从事建筑,还有一些是兵蚁,专司打仗。

原文的焦点是蚂蚁,所以 worker 的翻译得照应前文,译成"工蚁",the young 就得考虑译成"幼蚁",而 soldier 译作"兵蚁"也是顺理成章的事。其实,有关蚂蚁社会的各个译名已为生物界所确定,译者的任务不是再造出新的译名,而要在原文的基础上,将其意义忠实准确地传达给读者。

三、忠实原文格式

科技文章格式固定,结构严谨,层次分明,环环相扣,翻译时一般不要随意改变其固定程式。试比较:

> Each cylinder therefore is encased in a water jacket, which forms part of a circuit through which water is pumped continuously, and cooled by means of air drawn in from the outside atmosphere by large rotary fans, worked off the main crankshaft, or in the larger diesel-electric locomotives, by auxiliary motors.
>
> 因而,每个气缸都围着一个水套,水套形成循环水路的一部分,由水泵驱动水在回路中不断地流动,并由大型旋转风扇从外部鼓入空气使水冷却。所谓的大型旋转风扇是由主曲轴带动的,而在大型电力传动内燃机车上则由辅助电动机带动。

原文仅为一句,它通过英语特有的定语从句结构,一句套一句,层层推进。汉译时肯定不能套用原文的句式,只可根据其特点,因句制宜,充分运用前面学过的有关翻译手段,或分译,或合译,或重复,准确传达出原文的内容。

四、重视逻辑性与科学性

科技语篇讲究文章的逻辑性与科学性,要求翻译时不能偏废任何一面。例如:

> The children's upper and lower limbs were examined with a machine that stimulated the nerves using a machine that passed a mild, painless electric current through the skin and recorded the electrical activity of the nerves to determine if they were damaged.
>
> 研究者用一台能刺激神经的机器检测孩子们的四肢,机器发出的微弱、无痛电流穿过孩子们的皮肤,记录下神经的电流活动,这样便可以确定神经是否受到损害。

科技语篇科学性强，逻辑性强，翻译时不能用非科学、无逻辑的形式来进行，因而译文无论从遣词造句还是行文习惯上都得将两者很好地结合起来。原文是一个典型的科技语篇——科学、严谨，译文也尽量做到了科学和严谨。

五、汉译时要注意层次结构，避免罗列堆砌现象

有伟人说过，科学是掺不得半点虚假的，那么将国外科学引入国内时也来不得半点虚假，这便要求译者有严肃认真的工作作风及一丝不苟的精神，否则可能失之毫厘，差之千里。请比较下例：

The range of a voltmeter may be extended by means of a series resistor called a multiplier as show in Fig. 2. The full scale reading of the meter alone may be 15 volts. With the multiplier 250 volts may be required to move the pointer to full-scale，135 volts across the multiplier and 15 volts across the meter.

如图2所示，采用一种称为倍增电阻的串联电阻器即可扩大伏特表的量程。量表单独使用时的满刻度读数可以为15伏。倘有倍增电阻，指针偏转到满刻度的读数可达150伏，其中倍增电阻两端之间的读数为135伏，表头内的读数为15伏。

原文为典型的科技读物，有数字，有专业术语，有专业知识，对于仅对科技了解一点皮毛的译者而言，在动手翻译前应积极了解相关知识，翻译时注意原文的层次结构，认真译出原文内容，不罗列堆砌信息，这样，翻译工作才能为读者所接受。

六、掌握必要的专业知识

一些资深译者称，真正好的翻译都是"万金油"，此言不无道理。对科技语篇的掌握，译者虽不能达到专家的程度，起码的了解还是需要的，否则即使译语没有什么问题，也难符合专业要求。因此，着手翻译科技语篇前，最好找到相关领域的汉语资料，花一定时间阅读，以便熟悉专业用语、基本概念及表述，更重要的是了解必要的专业知识，实现成功翻译。试比较：

HDL cholestero is "high density" because it has a high amount of protein and not very much fat. The HDL molecules find excess cholestero in the blood stream and carry it back to the liver for disposal. This is why it is good. If HDL levels are too low, it means there aren't enough around to carry away excess cholesterol and you will be at a risk for CHD

高密度脂蛋白的高密度在于它含有大量蛋白质和少量脂肪。高密度脂蛋白分子能发现血流中的多余胆固醇,并将其输送回肝脏进行处理,因此它对人体有益。如果体内高密度脂蛋白含量较低,那意味着没有充足的高密度脂蛋白来运送多余的胆固醇,人就可能得冠心病。

附一 课堂讲练材料

Go to the Ant

There are more ants than any other kind of land animal in the world. A million ants can live in a few trees, and the ant is a social insect. That means that ants live in societies in which they depend on one another. The societies are not all exactly the same. There are differences because there are ants of very many kinds—more than 15,000 kinds, in fact. But in general each kind has ants of three main types: queens, males, workers.

The queen has wings for a time, and one day she flies away with a winged male. The male dies soon afterwards, but the queen, without her wings, finds a good place for her new nest and begins to lay eggs there. Worker ants will feed her and protect the eggs, and they will build as big and as safe a home as they can.

In the ant society each worker has a special job. Some workers take care of the young, some carry out building work, and some are soldier ants and do the fighting.

Some ants remind us of farmers. Their workers gather seeds and store them underground. If the seeds begin to grow, the ants throw them away round the edge of the nest. There the growing seeds become fields of "ant rice".

The ants have a good many enemies. They include birds, bears, and "ant-eaters" of various kinds. In some cases other ants are their worst enemies, just as man's worst enemy is man. In some parts of the world red ants march in large armies to attack the homes of black ants. Meanwhile, the black ants are blocking the entrances to their tunnels with all the stones and mud that their engineers and workers can find.

Some ants make life very uncomfortable for anyone who goes near their colony. But other ants find us very useful. They like the food we eat, and so they come into our houses and gardens to get it. They visit us in thousands when we have a picnic.

Studies of ant life tell us that these creatures live in colonies, keep farms, go to war, carry off slaves, and have a society rather like our own. But do they think? Are they intelligent? Probably the worker ants who get the food do not know what they are doing. They are controlled entirely by instinct.

附二 课外扩展训练材料

What Makes a Millennial Mind?

Since 1000 AD, around 30 billion people have been born on our planet. The vast majority have come and gone unknown to all but their friends and family. A few have left some trace on history: a discovery made, perhaps, or a record broken. Of those, fewer still are remembered long after their death. Yet of all the people who have lived their lives during the last 1,000 years, just 38 have achieved the status of Millennial Minds—That's barely one in a billion. Those whose lives *Focus* has chronicled have thus become members of possibly the most exclusive list of all time. And choosing who should be included was not easy.

From the beginning, the single most important criterion was that the Millennial Minds are those who did more than merely achieve greatness in their own time, or in one field. Thus mere winners of Nobel Prizes had no automatic right to inclusion, nor artists who gained fame in their own era, but whose reputation has faded with changing fashion. The achievements of the genuine Millennial Minds affect our lives even now, often in ways so fundamental it is hard to imagine what the world was like before.

Not even transcendent genius was enough to guarantee a place in the *Focus* list. To rate as a Millennial Mind, the life and achievements also had to cast light on the complex nature of creativity: its origins, nature—and its personal cost.

Nature or nurture?

So, with the list now complete, what do the lives and achievements of the *Focus* Millennial Minds tell us about this most precious of human commodities?

Firstly, it shows that genius can emerge from any background: poor or wealthy; academic or barely literate. Faraday's father was a blacksmith, Pasteur's family worked as tanners, the mathematical genius Gauss was the son of a labourer. In contrast, the philosopher Friedrich Nietzsche came from a long line of intellectuals, John Von Neumann was born into a family of wealthy Hungarian bankers, and rocket pioneer Wernher Von Braun was the son of an aristocrat.

In the making of a Millennial Mind, parental influence emerges as vastly important, although its impact is not as simple as it may seem. Some clearly inherited the abilities of their intellectual forebears: economist John Maynard Keynes, for example; Charles Darwin; and the founder of quantum theory, Max Planck. Others, such as Isambard Kingdom Brunel, Marie Stopes and Rachel Carson, clearly benefited from inheriting their parents' feisty personalities.

But for some, the parental influence was less positive. Mozart was robbed of his childhood by his ambitious and overbearing father, while Newton was abandoned by his mother at an early age, leaving him so bitter that he dreamed of killing her. Childhood unhappiness is a strikingly common feature of the lives of Millennial Minds. Loneliness, parental absence and traumatic events that threaten the security of the family appear time and again. Charles Dickens, Sigmund Freud, Marie Curie and Linus Pauling had childhoods blighted by financial disasters ranging from debt to the collapse of family businesses. Perhaps the need to take refuge from such traumas in an inner world sowed the seeds of these Millennial Minds.

Child prodigies

Some Millennial Minds conform to the stereotype of being precocious children: the mathematician Gauss correcting his father's accounts at the age of two, for example, or the teenage Edison's high-tech entrepreneurship. Yet some took much longer to reveal their genius. Darwin, Pasteur and Faraday showed no interest in science until their 20s, while young Einstein's teachers famously suspected he was mentally retarded.

Intellectual health

Another stereotype borne out by the lives of the Millennial Minds is that genius often seems to be, as Edison himself put it, one percent inspiration and 99 percent perspiration. From Leonardo da Vinci to Brunel, Mozart to Fritz Haber, an almost pathological devotion to their work characterizes many Millennial Minds.

This devotion brought some to an early grave: Marie Curie, for instance, was killed by radiation from her years of work with radium. For many others, it meant unfulfilled personal lives, failed marriages and, in the case of Boltzmann and Turing, suicide.

While one might envy their lasting status, few Millennial Minds enjoyed lives of unalloyed success, happiness and recognition. Fewer still made fortunes out of their genius; for our final Millennial Mind, web inventor Tim Berners-Lee, eschewing personal wealth was crucial to his Millennial Mind status.

One thing is certain. Had these 38 remarkable people not lived, our lives today would all be the poorer.

参考译文

第一章 课堂讲练材料

广 告

广告已经成为一项非常专业化的活动。今日商界,供通常大于求,为说服客户购买自己的品牌,同行之间竞争激烈,他们无时无刻不在提醒消费者自己品牌的存在,宣传自己产品的种种优势,所采用的方法就是——广告。

制造商们利用报纸、宣传画做广告,有时在商业电台节目里用花钱买广告歌的形式促销自己的产品,还雇迷人年轻女子做销售四处分发产品样本,更组织各种比赛活动并给优胜者颁奖。很多时候,制造商还在当地影院的电影银幕上投放广告,不过最重要的一个广告手段则是在电视普及率较高的国家把广告植入节目之中。总之,在广告上,制造商们常常投入大量资金。

作为消费者,我们购买自认为最好的产品。之所以认为某个产品最好,是因为广告就是这么说的——某些消费者从来不驻足自问:广告说的都是真的吗?

(杰克·富兰克林)

第二章 课堂讲练材料

年 轻

年轻,并非人生旅途中的一段时光,而是一种心灵状态;并非粉腮朱唇和矫健的身姿,而是头脑中的一个意念,思维中的一种潜能,情感世界中的一股灼灼生气,人生大好春光中蓬勃着的一抹新绿。

年轻,意味着乐于舍弃舒适的生活,四海闯荡;意味着具备超越羞怯和欲望的勇气。或许60岁的男人比20岁的小伙子更多地拥有这种勇气。人是不会仅仅因为时光的流逝而衰老的,放弃理想没有理想的人才是老人。

　　岁月可以在肌肤上留下道道皱纹,但丧失热情却会给灵魂刻下深深的印迹。忧虑、恐惧、缺乏自信只会让人胸无大志,沦为尘土。

　　无论60岁还是16岁,人人都会受到好奇心的驱使,都会对未来对人生际遇中的欢乐怀着孩童般无尽的渴望。在你我心灵的深处都有一部无线电台,只要它从人群中、从无限的时空中永不间断地接受美好、希望、喝彩、勇气和力量的信息,你我就会青春永葆。

　　一旦这部电台坍塌,心灵就会被玩世不恭、悲观绝望的寒冰覆盖,即便只有20岁,但你已垂垂老矣!如果这部电台始终矗立于心中,去捕捉每一束乐观向上的电波,你便可望在80岁高龄甚至在撒手人寰的那一刻依然拥有一颗年轻的心。

(塞缪尔·乌尔曼)

第三章　课堂讲练材料

我的人生目的

　　我的人生一直受着三种质朴而又十分强烈的激情支配,即对爱之渴望、对知之求索、对人之苦难的万分悲悯。这三种激情,犹如狂飙挟我四处漂泊,穿越苦海的深渊,飞临绝望的边缘,游移不定。

　　我寻求爱,因为爱能带来狂喜——它是如此令人心醉神往,我愿舍弃余生来换取这片刻的欢娱;我寻求爱,因为爱能消除孤独——颤抖的灵魂在世界边缘望着冰冷、荒凉的无底深渊时所感到的那种孤独;我寻求爱,因为在爱的交融中,我看见了圣者和诗人所预知的天堂景象的神秘缩影,这正合我心之所求,虽然人生似难臻此境,我最终会不负所求。

　　我怀着同样的激情为知识而上下求索。我曾希望理解芸芸众生,我曾渴望了解星星缘何闪烁,我也曾努力领会毕达哥拉斯赋予数的力量——主宰万物流变之力。仅此而已,虽无斐然之绩,却也算小有成就。

　　爱和知识引领我超凡入圣,但悲悯又把我拉回凡尘。声声悲号在我心中回响不绝:饥饿的孩子、惨遭压迫者折磨的苦难者、因依附儿孙而被视为可憎负担的老年人以及整个孤独、贫困和痛苦的世界是对理想人生的嘲讽。我渴望减轻罪恶,却无能为力,我也同样遭受到痛苦的煎熬。

　　这就是我的人生。我觉得此生并未虚度。若有可能,我将欣然再一次度过如此人生。

(伯特兰·罗素)

第四章 第一节 课堂讲练材料

1. 产量减少到了25%。
2. 到2018年,世界石油年产量预计将下降到50%。
3. 这一设备的误差率降低了3/5。
4. 今年我厂这种机器的产量预计是1980年的3倍。(或:今年我厂这种机器的产量预计比1980年增长了2倍。)
5. 约翰逊跑完200米正好用了22秒。
6. 史密斯医生那天正好给30位病人看了病。
7. 爆炸在千分之几秒内便可以完成。
8. 今年南京市区建造了数以百计的高楼大厦。
9. 在建造这座装有现代化电子设备的礼堂时花费了几千万人民币。
10. 这种改进型车床比原先未改进的车床快了20%。
11. 2013年这座钢铁厂的钢产量比2012年增加了近100%。
12. 与旧式冰箱相比,它的主要优点是重量和噪音都减少了3/4。
13. 由于高压突然增加2倍,这台精密仪器里的阀门一下子全都烧坏了。
14. 在较为老式的同轴电缆系统中要每隔8英里安装一个放大器。在较新式的同轴电缆系统中,传输信号的频率高出很多,所以要每隔4英里安装一个放大器。
15. 合同附件中规定的提成率适用期为5年,时间从接受技术之日起算,此后,每年将减少1%。
16. 除前一条款提到的酬劳外,聘方将以毛销售额的2.50%支付给受聘方作为佣金。这笔佣金每月支付一次,在次月的最后一天支付。

第四章 第一节 课外扩展训练材料

我眼中的朱镕基

接到大年初一与厦门市政界、商界领袖一道参加春节团拜会的邀请,儿子们兴奋不已,但一听说届时将有领导发表讲话就抗议了——"不去!"于是，苏珊只得和孩子们待在家里。事后她后悔至极，因为上台发言的不是别人，是朱镕基！

同许多美国人一样，我对政客对演说都不厌其烦，然而出现在我们面前的朱先生不是一个政客而像一位长辈——甚至可说是朋友，坦诚地向我们道出他内心对中国的忧虑和期盼。而且，他风趣诙谐，基本让听众从头笑到尾。

朱先生谈及的话题十分严肃，诸如国有企业的改革、日益臃肿的政府机构、中国对亚洲邻国承担的义务、不使人民币贬值的决心、环境保护的必要性、铲除腐败的重要性。自始至终，听众们都兴奋地坐在椅子边沿，时而点头同意，时而捧腹大笑，而这位机敏的政治家和长辈始终面容严肃，不露声色，这令我想起了深得美国人喜爱的脱口秀节目主持人乔尼·卡森。

朱先生毫不隐讳自己的好恶。当他眼珠一转说他恨VCD的电视广告太多时，在座的人都笑了。随即他又向我们吐露，他最爱看的节目是脱口秀，他希望更多的人能够畅所欲言。朱总理这样谈话并不令人惊奇，因为他谈话从不兜圈子。

朱镕基出生于湖南的一户贫苦人家，我想他一定生来就抱负远大，因为他总是着眼于未来，而不是崇拜过去或故步自封。他不怕直面挑战，不闪烁其词。他直截了当的作风得罪了不少安于现状的人，却赢得了另一些人的敬佩，这些人不欢迎政客的口头支票，而是希望拥有真正的领导者和实际的结果。

这就是朱先生给我的最终印象：他不是政客而是胸怀理想的领导者。为媚俗，政客们必须花言巧语、玩弄手腕、朝令夕改，而胸襟远大的领导者却从不乏忠实的追随者。

中国是幸运的，曾有过许多伟大的领导者，他们个个似乎都顺时应势而生！由于出了个毛主席，中国结束了一个世纪的外来压迫，中国人民团结起来参加革命。由于出了个社会主义市场经济的设计师邓小平，中国正逐渐走向成熟。今天，在李鹏总理领导下的十年稳定和坚实的发展以后，中国进入了一个可能是最有成效同时也是最困难的时期，正如中国古话所说："创业维艰，守成不易。"

厦门人民（包括我们这些被中国人民接纳的外籍人士）都以新年伊始朱镕基来访为荣。令大家欣慰的是，有了朱镕基掌舵，中国最好的日子还在后头呢。

（威廉·N.布朗）

第四章 第二节 课堂讲练材料

1. 虽然他很有钱,但生活俭朴。
2. 约翰在考试时乱猜答案,结果全答错了。
3. 不要为他提心吊胆,他想怎么做就怎么做吧!
4. 自他做了那桩生意以后,就发了大财啦。
5. 小孩子很喜欢模仿别人。
6. 你的提议正在考虑之中。
7. 一般人做了坏事惯于支吾其词。
8. 我怀疑他讲的话,因为他曾对我撒过谎。
9. 他经常发脾气,但是她还是尽心侍奉他。
10. 跟心爱的人闲聊到深夜是非常快乐的事。
11. 他真是个怪人,我们同他开玩笑,他竟然勃然大怒。
12. 约翰偷了主教的银器,可是主教以德报怨把银器送给了他,令他羞愧万分。
13. 老师对学生谆谆教诲。
14. 这是颠扑不破的真理。
15. 那件小事不需要小题大做。
16. 政府坚持施行较前更严的宗教迫害,实在是种下了祸根,注定要招致阴谋活动与暴动。
17. 他有改变局势的能力,但却总是深藏不露。
18. 这乞丐无家可归。
19. 他散播毫无根据的谣言,目的在于败坏你的名誉。
20. 扫人兴致是不礼貌的行为。
21. 他千方百计想弄个一官半职,但都没起到作用。
22. 他的演讲一结束,就博得全场喝彩。
23. 凡是熟知内幕的人,取得成功的机会就大。
24. 他从未发觉那个笑话讲的就是他。
25. 他负债累累,但你从来不予同情。
26. 虽然你很爱你的女仆,但你的父母一定反对这桩门不当户不对的婚事。
27. 他是一个伪君子,只是在假装帮助你罢了。
28. 在篮球队中,弗兰克的球艺远在队友之上。

29. 一个人如果墨守成规,便无法体验丰富多彩的人生。
30. 除了说她必会自食其果之外,我再想不出更强烈的谴责言辞了。
31. 这首诗的最后一句最为精彩。
32. 别这样丧气,振作起来,面对现实吧!
33. 他最讨厌不劳而获的人。
34. 看完了这篇故事后,他感动得流下了热泪。
35. 总统向人民发表广播讲话。
36. 他说他今晚不能去听歌剧,因为有别的事要做。
37. 假若你这样做,我就跟你一刀两断。
38. 有些人好像运气一直都很不错。
39. 为了养活一家人,他拼命工作。
40. 假若你们信口雌黄,将来必定会后悔的。
41. 有人说做广告只消夸大其词就行。
42. 鲍勃对玛丽真是唯命是从。
43. 他偶尔会放浪形骸连续纵饮三日。
44. 你的金玉良言对他只不过是一阵耳旁风。
45. 他们坐在那儿含情脉脉地瞧着对方。
46. 我要找管家理论去,我想知道他昨天为何要说那些无礼的话把信差打发走。
47. 威尔逊先生怕老婆,他太太才是一家之主。
48. 威利叔叔给我家丢人现眼。因为他酗酒,所以没有人提起他。
49. 你意气消沉,喝杯(波尔多红)葡萄酒会使你觉得精神好些。
50. 她泄露了秘密,因此失去了惊叹奇妙的效果。
51. 他是在银行做事,但是看他太太那副阔绰的样子,你还以为银行是他家开的呢。

第四章 第二节 课外扩展训练材料

身体语言

我们彼此交流时不只用言语,还用非言语方式。对此,我们大多数时候都毫无意识,例如我们扬眉、摆手、碰到对方的目光后扭头望向别处,坐在椅子上不时调整坐姿,还以为这些只是些随意的偶然动作,殊不知研究者们近年发现交流中已然存在着一整套如言语系统一样稳定而全面的非言语交流系统。

每个文化都有自己的身体语言,每个人孩提时代都是一边习得口头表达一边掌握其间细微差异。法国人讲法语,使用法式身体语言。英国男人与美国男人一样跷二郎腿,但方式不一样。交谈过程中,美国人结束一段话时往往会垂一下头或手,或者低一下眉眼,结束一个提问时会扬扬手,翘翘下巴,或瞪瞪眼睛,使用将来时态时,往往做出一个前倾的动作。

第四章 第三节 课堂讲练材料

1. 我最讨厌迈克呼啦呼啦喝汤的样子。我看了真气得要发疯。
2. 珍妮,别跟我捣鬼,我对你的诡计和手段一清二楚。
3. 我们饿极了,10分钟就把妈妈做的苹果馅饼吃得精光。
4. 他想骗我们,但在他阴谋得逞以前我们就看穿了他。
5. 他利用关系替我们弄到了音乐会前排的位子。
6. 我没法讲这个笑话,我忘了当中最好笑的部分。
7. 酒后开车简直是拿命开玩笑。
8. 比尔一定是哪根筋不对,他的举动真奇怪。
9. 他没听到你说的话,他魂不守舍似的。
10. 别给我卖关子,告诉我现在确切地讲到什么地方了。
11. 他们怎么可以随便取消音乐会呢?真可恶!
12. 史密斯靠拍马屁得了势。
13. 你们两个一道去好啦,我不想当电灯泡。
14. 别这么脚踩两只船了。你必须做出选择。
15. 这次我们真的是错失良机!那笔交易原可让我们猛赚几百万的。
16. 我们大吃特吃薯条和小甜饼,一直吃到肚子撑得发痛。
17. 住在纽约市,你就要学会对周围的噪音听而不闻。
18. 我不想来,他却好说歹说地要我来。
19. 哪怕你稍微动一下脑筋,事情就不会这么一团糟了。
20. 你不能丢下我不管,我真的需要你的帮助。
21. 这道菜做的真难吃!谁烧的?
22. 老板威胁要炒保罗鱿鱼,后者才停止说上司们的坏话。
23. 哈罗德总是拍老板的马屁。

24. 玛丽的确是个电视迷。她整天都窝在电视前吃零食。
25. 我们坐彼得买的小型快艇去兜风。
26. 假如我妻子发现这件事,她必定会兴风作浪的。
27. 在这次难得令人无法置信的考试里,我看来只能得个大鸭蛋。
28. 那家伙看样子像个大人物。
29. 我只是个小萝卜头,说话起不了什么作用。
30. 算了吧,她从来就没这想法。
31. 喂,老兄,出口在哪儿呀?
32. 萨姆的太太离开他时,他消沉了好几个星期。
33. A:他知道自己已经才竭智穷了吗?
    B:我想他已经意识到了,但还在故作镇定。
    A:估计他会碰壁的。你最好敬而远之。
    B:一看到他无助的样子,我就禁不住想拉他一把。

第四章 第三节 课外扩展训练材料

为什么研究文化

　　文化的掩蔽性远远大于其暴露性。奇怪的是,文化掩蔽的内容最能瞒过的竟然是泡于该文化里的人。多年的研究结果表明,我们真正首先需要理解的不是外国文化,而是我们自己的文化。不仅如此,我们对外国文化的研究成果只是理解问题的中介,最终目的是要深入了解本国文化,而了解外国文化就是为了给本国文化带来活力和觉醒,即一种生命动力,这种生命动力只有当我们经历了强烈反差的冲击之后才能获得。

　　对于我们门外汉而言,花点时间研究文化,既能学到对己有用的知识,又能加深自我了解。整个过程,虽说时有挫折,但总体而言引人入胜,且终会有所收获。了解自己的最佳途径就是认真对待别国文化,这样才能注意到自己与他人之间具体存在哪些差异。

(《跨文化交流》)

第四章 第四节 课堂讲练材料

1. 我们对这一观点要去其棱,磨其凸,光其面。

2. 这个人就像一只骄傲自负的公鸡,以为太阳升起是为了听它打鸣。
3. 这种观点推销不出去。
4. 如何包装一个人的思想非常重要。
5. 这一观点很粗糙,尚需打磨。
6. 劝导对他好像水过鸭背似的不起作用。
7. 甚至最有教养和最有文化的人,在谈话中也有打绊儿、说错话儿的时候(比喻会出错)。
8. 他对此想法不买账(他对这种观点不认可或不屑一顾)。
9. 好想法总是能找到市场的。
10. 这种观点一文不值。
11. 玛丽和她妈妈长相酷似。(不宜直译:玛丽和其母像两个豌豆。)
12. 史密斯要求见面,我当时就估摸着他是醉翁之意不在酒。(不宜译为:史密斯有斧头要磨。)
13. 我们确实在提出(快速批量制造、机械化生产)新观念。(本句用"制造""生产"都不太符合汉语表达习惯,只能意译。)
14. 我们这一周想出了许多新主意。
15. 他以令人惊叹的速度提出了许多新观点。
16. 俗话说,衣柜里面藏骷髅,见不得人的事家家有。(用形象比喻加解释说明,再加上喜闻乐见的顺口溜,容易为读者理解。)
17. 请别把我的高保真收音机给鼓捣坏了!(原文中有个 monkey 猴子形象,有顽皮、捣蛋的含义,译文用"鼓捣",基本传达了喻义。)
18. 那些调皮的男孩子用拇指顶着自己的鼻子,摇动手指,相互嘲弄着对方。(原文中有 thumbed one's nose,译文中也用同类喻体,同时增加了说明,使喻义更加突出。)
19. 他一点自己的思想都没有,只会鹦鹉学舌。(原文中有 parrot,译文中有鹦鹉学舌,言简意赅。)
20. 那个年轻姑娘真是异想天开!
21. 他离开了伙伴,就像老鼠离弃了沉船。(喻体加解释,使喻义突出明了。)
22. 没有你,巴黎成了一座陈尸所。认识你之前,巴黎就是巴黎,我把它看成天堂,然而它现在成了一片荒凉而寂寞的沙漠,像一个没有时针、分针和秒针的钟面。
23. 作为一个作家,我所能贡献的只有这么几篇故事和散文,它们像我心头温和夏日里绽放的花朵。

24. 一些书需要浅尝,另一些书却要生吞,只有少数的书值得细细咀嚼慢慢消化……
25. 不义之财宛如建筑在沙堆上的宫殿。
26. 阳光透过棋盘格子般的中隙,掠过他睿智的肩头,撒下亮晶晶的圆片,宛如跳动的金币。

第四章 第四节 课外扩展训练材料

如此提高知名度

某位诗人新近创作的诗集出版了。面对成功,自豪之情自不待言,但令人懊恼的是,新书几乎无人问津,于是诗人便找老友诉苦。"问题出在名气上。"朋友说,"当务之急是提高名气,这样才能赢得读者。知名度一高,大作自然就不愁销了。""这个我懂,"诗人道,"可——我该怎么办才好呢?"

"书呆子!干吗不在报上登个广告呢?"朋友微笑回答。

"但我总不能在广告上说我是个多么多么出色的诗人,我的诗如何如何值得一读吧?"

"当然不行。不过,别急,我可以助你一臂之力。"

有了朋友这句话,诗人的心情顿时轻松不少。打那以后,他天天坚持看报,对报上的广告栏目格外留意,但令他失望的是,报上一直没出现有关他诗集的广告。时间一久,就差不多把广告的事给忘了。

一天清晨,诗人正在用餐,门铃响了。他离开餐桌去开门。门一开,一个大汉牵着一只大狗站在诗人面前。

"我来拿钱。"大汉恶声恶气道。

"什么钱?"诗人莫名其妙,"也许您认错门了吧?"

"扯淡!"大汉嚷道。"你说过一条狗两英镑。"

"可我并不需要狗呀,"诗人说道。

"哈!你不要狗!"大汉不耐烦了,"你让我大老远赶到这里,居然一毛不拔!"大汉边嚷,边拉开了架势。

"我这么瘦弱,对手那么强壮,"诗人暗自掂量,"若交起手来,我哪是他的对手……"只好付给大汉两英镑将狗买了下来。

诗人拿些肉把狗喂饱后将它锁进厨房,回头又开始工作。可是没过多久,门铃又响了。

他透过窗户朝外一望,只见至少有六个人,各牵一只狗站在自家门前。"怎么回事?"他自言自语道。

蓦地,他想起了登广告的事。他抓过一摞报纸,一张一张翻看。翻着翻着,一则《寻狗启事》赫然映入眼帘。《寻狗启事》上写着:柯克先生愿出两英镑酬金以寻回那条首次唤起他诗歌创作灵感的爱犬。

(D. H. 巴柏)

第四章 第五节 课堂讲练材料

罢 也!

肖恩·列侬携其蜚声世界的母亲大野洋子及一帮朋友,来到纽约一家人气很旺的餐馆。列侬的女友找到工作人员,要一张可供7人就餐的餐桌。

"要等45分钟",工作人员说,"留个名,好吗?"

"大野,"姑娘答道。

"嗯!罢也?"工作人员一愣,嘴上却问,"这么说,您不想等?"

"大野,"姑娘重复道。

"罢也?!"此时工作人员彻底糊涂了,问,"您倒是要不要餐桌呀?"

姑娘指了指大野洋子。不出几分钟,肖恩一干人就落座了。

(《读者文摘》)

文 字

字典里有大量阳光、健康、快乐的词条,多为动听的辞藻。的确,美好的辞藻有很多,你我生命中确有许多快乐的理由,这并非意味着我们应该对事物的阴暗面保持缄默,该出手时还是得出手的。不过,在树立健康积极的态度方面,应该多使用哪类词条呢?心理学验证了这样一个简单事实,即只要稍加留意我们使用的言辞,就能受益良多,能避免自我毒害。真的,字眼,可以构建一个美梦成真的生活。通过文字,我们创造力量,这种力量或许是阴暗的,或许是微笑的,它们陪伴我们并可能统领我们。

第四章 第五节　课外扩展训练材料

不　累

　　不久前,某位知名国会议员认识了一位报童,这孩子每天送报。虽然个头非常矮小,背的报纸却又多又沉,可敬的议员先生动了恻隐之心。
　　"孩子,"他问,"这么多报纸,你累不累?"
　　对此仁慈的关怀,孩子愉快作答:"不累,先生,我不识字。"

(《读者文摘》)

第四章 第六节　课堂讲练材料

1. 新版的巴特利语录秉承其铁面无私的民主宗旨,为那些无名氏的作品大大增加了篇幅。
2. 我自己也是个福尔赛,本来轮不到我来说,可是我是一个纯(种的)混血儿。
3. 他对那硕大无比的笨拙的红海龟抱一种友好而轻视的态度。那些海龟怯生生地缩在甲胄里,以奇怪的方式做爱,会闭上眼睛兴致勃勃地吃水母。
4. 那一次,吉姆·霍尔本来没有错,但无罪而被判了罪。吉姆认为法官心里完全明白却与警察狼狈为奸制造了这起重大冤案,所以当司各特法官宣布判处他五十年活着的死亡以后,他怀着对这个虐待他的整个社会的仇恨,站起身来在法庭上大声咆哮,直到他被半打穿蓝上衣的仇敌拖出去。
5. 他知道他挨得起饿,这种本领是自小就练成了的。当时看到母亲把自己一份吃的省下来让孩子们多分几口,作为长子的他说出这样一个伟大的谎言:"我不饿,我再也吃不下了。"他照着母亲这个勇敢的榜样,去止住几个小弟弟令人心酸的啼哭。
6. "你是怎么打死山羊吓死老虎的?"梅宾小姐说着,嘴里发出一串令人不快的笑声。
7. 我的意思不是说我们在联合国中突然遭遇失和的威胁。

第四章 第六节　课外扩展训练材料

结果好,就是好

　　一个晴好温暖的下午,威尔决定骑自行车去乡下逛逛。

阳光中的乡间小路,宁静祥和,威尔边骑边欣赏,当骑上一座陡峭的小山包时,他任自行车飞奔而下,没留意山脚是道急转弯,等注意到时,不料一只狗冲出农家小院,狂吠着向他扑将过来。

威尔猛踩刹车,绕开了狗,可速度太快自行车没法正常驶入弯道,冲过马路,一头撞上对面的河堤。幸好,无车辆经过,有惊无险。

威尔从地上爬起来。此时,狗主人出现了。见威尔毫发无损,狗主人把他领回自己家,递上一杯鲜奶。

呆了不多时,威尔再次蹬上自行车。道别时,他对狗主人道:"结果好,就是好。"

第四章 第七节　课堂讲练材料

1. 海关官员:您有什么需要(说)报关的吗?
   男人:唔——有的。我想(说)申报我爱我妻子。
2. 儿子:妈妈,我值多少钱?
   妈妈:儿子,你对于我来说值 100 万。
   儿子:好,那你能给我其中的 5 元吗?
3. 病人:医生,我打鼾很响,让自己无法入睡。我该怎么办?
   医生:到另一间屋子去睡。

第四章 第七节　课外扩展训练材料

黑　豹

她立于丛林之中,安静、独立、沉着,散发着动物的魅力,这种笼罩着她周身的气氛,向四面八方辐射。她不求吸人眼球而自然引人注目,没有扭捏,毫不作态。月光下,她溜滑的毛皮黑亮发光,肌肉纤维在皮肤底下扭动,像火石上击出的火花,在暗示体内将释放出具有摄人魂魄速度的电能。她凶猛,但不残忍;高贵,但不傲气;迷人,但不卖弄风情。

突然,一股看不见的力量使她昂扬起来!从她专注的目光、热烈的表情,透过她翡翠玛瑙般眼睛徐徐燃烧的灵魂之火,使人联想到那股看不见的力量。她在阴影中看到了什么?莫不是可以与她的辉煌媲美的伴侣?他的雄风能够释放她温柔的心灵?或者被利爪熟练的一击而无力地倒在她脚下成为美食的对象?她凭直觉懂得适时发出一击,期盼着美妙时刻的到来。

她高视阔步时,水一般的动感像火山熔岩一样流过她的躯体,动作的波浪从她的胸骨开始,再经过腔丛、胯部,继而是强健有力的双腿,连绵起伏。她的动作遒劲而不紧绷,有力而不吃紧。她壮实的脚爪轻轻着地,踏着切分节奏,好像抚摩大地;她弯弯的脊柱曲线犹如猎人的弯刀蓄势待发。她像蛇一样盘踞着,正要准备一击,然后腾空而起,爆发出闪电般的愤怒。

她将有什么样的命运?她是勇猛的猎手,还是媚人的妖女?

(L. B. 科利特)

第四章 第八节 课堂讲练材料

1. 在古旧的大梁因不胜重荷吱吱呀呀的抗议声中,主人拉紧了绳子,随后,点点滴滴的亚麻子油就沿着石槽流入一个旧油桶里。不久,大梁下沉,吱呀声更大;磨轮隆隆,骆驼喘息。伴随着这阵阵嘈杂声,闪光的亚麻子油如洪水般喷涌而出。

2. 我们已经没有退路,要退只有含垢忍辱,沦为奴隶了。囚禁我们的锁链已经铸就,波士顿平原上已可听到锁链郎当的响声。

3. 那里有一大间屋顶很低的房间,装着稀里哗啦响的机器,机器旁边,一些穿着白衬衫、罩着蓝布围裙的男子在工作。她跟着他,怯怯地走过那些响动的机器,眼睛直看着前面,脸上微微发红。

4. 接着车站一阵震动,渐渐地震动得使人心惊肉跳,表示列车快要到了。火光和热气,煤烟和红灯。一片咝咝声,一阵乒乒乓乓的响,铃声当当,汽笛呜呜。路易莎走进了一个车厢,斯巴塞太太走进另一个车厢。在暴风雨中,小小的车站如同沧海中的一座孤岛。

5. 幼儿发现嗓音那天起就在设法利用它,一般说来,最初像是感到痛苦似的尖叫。一个月后开始咿呀咿哑,后来叽里咕噜,稍后就自个儿轻轻地哼哼唧唧,不久就长出牙齿,能够说话了。

6. 有着各种沙龙的济尼斯离墨哈利斯和温尼麦克大学15英里,乘大型隆隆作响的钢制市际电车需要半个小时,医科学生常到济尼斯去搞"劫掠"。

7. 那辆马车哗啦哗啦地冲过街道拖过拐角,吓得女人们在车前尖声喊叫,男人们互相扯拉,并把孩子们拉到路旁。

8. 我不接受人类末日的说法。因为人能传宗接代而说人是不朽的,这很容易。因为即使最后一次钟声已经敲响并消失在海上最后一块无用的礁石之旁时,还会有一个声音,那就是人类微弱的、不断的说话声,这样说也容易,但是我不能接受这种说法。我相信人类不仅能传宗接代,而且能战胜一切。

9. 寒来暑往,冬去春来,一年四季仿佛围绕着乔舒亚旋转。他成了詹尼弗生活的中心。在她的眼皮底下,他一天天长大起来:看着他蹒跚学步、咿呀学语,逐渐懂事,她天天都感到惊喜不已。他呢,情绪变化无常,时而凶野、咄咄逼人,时而羞赧、逗人喜爱。
10. 随着电话交谈日渐产生疗效,我们的心情渐渐轻松起来,突然,在离帕特和我正在使用的电话机只有几英寸的窗户外面,轰轰隆隆一声炸响。

第四章 第八节 课外扩展训练材料

时间危机感

今天,想花很短时间做很多事的人不在少数,持此类时间观念的人可能有一种"时间危机感"。"时间危机感"是一种行为综合征,症状为坚持不懈地尝试实现超人的发挥。不久前,人们还认为"时间危机感"是美国人,特别是生于经济大萧条至第二次世界大战结束这一时期美国男性的典型文化特征,如今它已不再为这一代美国男性公民所专有,亚洲的"工薪阶层"也产生了这种"时间危机感",整个世界由于经济全球化而迅速感染上这种"时间危机感"。

这种时间观念产生的最重要的一个结果便是,在交际活动中,较快的话语交际参与者基本上对较慢的参与者评价不佳。而这些具有"时间危机感"的人往往倾向于认为谨言慢行之人观念保守、有欠合作、故步自封、不求进取。由此,可看出"时间危机感"的真正含义牢牢地建立在追求进步的信念基础之上,即未来永远好于过去。

(《跨文化交际英语教程》)

第四章 第九节 课堂讲练材料

1. 你骗不了我。(注:此语源自美国的密苏里州。据说,该州的商人十分精明,做生意时极少上当。久而久之,该词便有了"非常精明"这一约定俗成的概念。人们使用它时暗示对方,别把说话人当成傻子,本人是不会上当的。翻译该词时要透过现象看本质,译出深层含义。)
2. 三个骑马的人已经由幕后破墙而出,第四匹马刚刚露出一点侧面。这是一匹浅白色的骏马,代表的是死亡。这就是《圣经》"启示录"中的四骑士。(注:《圣经》启示录中的四骑士代表的是人类四大灾害,即战争、饥荒、瘟疫和死亡。)

3. 这一则报道将被束之高阁,锁进保险箱里,不过他知道,潘多拉的灾难盒终究是关不住的。(注:潘多拉是希腊神话中的人物。普罗米修斯窃取火种来到人间。主神宙斯为了惩罚他,派潘多拉带了一只盒子来到人间。那只盒子里面装着各种各样的灾祸,一旦打开就会祸害人间。)

4. 你以为自己可以打败曾经与上帝作过战的人?你以为自己可以打败曾经把米迦勒打得逃到地球上来的人?(注:米迦勒系《圣经》里的人物,天使长之一,曾率领众天使与魔鬼撒旦战斗。)

5. 跟我说说看,在各各他你那超凡的力量是怎么遭劫的!(注:各各他是耶稣蒙难的地方。)

6. "听我说,巴恩,在发掘报道题材方面,她还真有点"羯摩",这显然不需要火箭科学家的头脑也能想得到。有点猜疑是正常的嘛。(注:羯摩是佛教用语,又称"业",泛称一切身心活动,一般分为身业"行动"、语业"言语"和意业"思想活动"。)

7. 华盛顿"老卫士"中名望很高的罗伯特·奥兹·查尔斯夫人站在迎宾行列中,热情地抓住琼莉的手说:"看到你真高兴,感谢上帝,你是最后一位了。"(注:"老卫士"系指共和党保守派。)

8. "那是拉里·沃尔德特。"
"他是什么人?"
"是纽约专门报道上流社会活动的摄影记者。他收藏的小约翰·F. 肯尼迪的照片是世界上最多的。"

9. 他睡得并不怎么沉,仿佛在做梦。有些东西他忘了。他似乎是在某个学校里。是在他自己的学院里。显然他正要去参加考试,他竭力要在脑海中回想起课程的全部内容,而有一些却想不起来了。他看见一个房间,里面放着一排排桌椅,他却又好像忘了什么东西。他记不起来那是什么。维恩公式、瑞利—琼斯定律、普朗克定律、斯忒藩定律、玻尔兹曼常数⋯⋯对于某一特定波长 λ 来说,辐射磁通量 W_m 等于第一个常数乘以 λ 倒数的 5 次方,再乘以⋯⋯姓名、公式、方程式——所有这些一股脑儿闪过他的脑际。他想把它们一下子回忆起来,但做不到,有些事已踪迹杳然。他思绪奔涌,苦苦追忆,一心想找到它们。最后他猛然间醒了过来,或者说恢复了意识。他朝暗中仰望,突然喃喃低语,就像在做祷告,或像回答口试中的一部分:"5.6697 乘以 10 的负 8 次方 W_m 的负 2 次方 K 的负 4 次方。"接着,他心不在焉地重复了两遍,一时间也不知自己说的是什么意思。过后他明白了,这是斯忒藩常数 Σ 的实际数值,有了它,就能计算出在一定温度下,一个黑体单位面积上的电磁辐射通量。

第四章 第九节 课外扩展训练材料

背包大使

中国国家媒体星期一提醒说,不要把美国驻中国大使受到的热情接待错误理解为两国问题得到了解决。骆家辉是第一位担任美国驻华大使的华裔美国人。星期五,他自己带着行李抵达,然后乘坐一辆低调的汽车离开机场,媒体一片哗然。

但是,封他为"背包大使"的新华社提到骆家辉必须应对的一系列问题,如贸易摩擦、军事关系和美国债务问题。新华社说,骆家辉的任务比他中国之行的行李还要重。《环球时报》也提到骆家辉的低调到任,说他"有可能是历史上最知名的美国驻华大使",但同时指出,他的华裔血统并不意味他在维护美国利益时会采取比较柔软的立场。

第四章 第十节 课外扩展训练材料

达美尔品质链猪肉

达美尔与合作伙伴保证:每一头猪都拥有自己的身份证明,身份证明上详细记录其产地、品种、年龄、种猪、饲养周期和饲养方法。

科学配方而成的饲料、无污染的饲养环境、对兽药使用的严格控制使得猪肉拥有更好的口感和安全性。

作为品质链的合作伙伴,农场养殖人员承诺:尊重动物的福利,严格遵守养殖、屠宰和运输的各项相关规定。

为保证猪肉的口感和质量,种猪均来自达美尔所认可的育种群,并在达美尔指定的农场饲养。

为保证肉质鲜嫩,自屠宰后到运至门店的整个过程,我们始终将温度维持在摄氏0—4度之间。

("达美尔猪肉"广告)

第五章 第一节　课堂讲练材料

1. 符拉迪沃斯托克（注：中国传统称海参崴）正在结束其与世隔绝的状态，接待外国游客的人数逐年增多。来访者都是受到特别邀请的。但就是这么一小部分外国人的到来，也已经使得该市不发达的旅游基础设施不胜负担了。

2. 一大批骗子与走私分子正从东部进入德国，这将使德国守卫和控制其新拥有的东部边界显得非常吃力。

3. 为寻找高收入工作，为子女谋求更好的受教育机会，农民大批涌往首尔。以过去的 8 年为例，该国农民占总人口的比例已从 27％下跌至 18％。农民的大量涌入，使首尔不堪负担。市区出现的种种问题，归根结底，大多是城市人口激增造成的。

4. 他们有自己的欢乐与悲哀。

5. 一些分析家猜测，成批购买飞机以及过多新航线的开辟，使该航空公司的财力几近枯竭。

6. 这种形势使党内具有改革思想的领导人为之绞尽脑汁。

7. 这位男子被（一女子）引诱到伦敦北部的一所房子里。他与这个女子在一起有卿卿我我之嫌的情景被人偷偷地录了下来。

8. 巡查官会在半夜两点突然冲进她的房间，试图当场抓住她做风流事的把柄。

9. 美国负责东亚和太平洋事务的前助理国务卿理查德·霍尔布鲁克在《外交事务》杂志上撰文，纪念珍珠港事件 50 周年。文章说："日本人动辄就要提醒别人，说他们的资源如何贫乏，又是如何容易受制于人。"

10. 我倒不是有先见之明，而只是碰巧来到图们参加了一年之中最盛大的节庆活动——庆祝农历正月十五元宵节。

11. 大马尼拉市刮起了一股兴建宾馆之风，这种情况自 1976 年以来第一次出现。1976 年，马尼拉有 7 家宾馆落成开张，并举办了国际货币基金会和世界银行年会。

12. 深圳的官员正全力以赴使深圳经济特区成为一个自由贸易区，为此，他们正在改造港口设施，因为进出口货物有望激增。

13. 有望在今后几个月签订的这项合同是这支部队向外购买军火最大的一笔生意,此举将有助于其防空和火力投射能力的提升。
14. 上海想通过开发浦东经济区实现其振兴经济的雄图大略,但这要看它是否有能力筹集到数十亿美元的资金,改进该市陈旧不堪的交通系统。
15. 去年马来西亚政府拨出大笔资金用于改善该国的基础设施。
16. 亚美尼亚和阿塞拜疆之间的冲突已经延续了6个月。自2月份以来,冲突引发了多起群众集会、罢工及种族暴力事件,使整个高加索地区处于一种极大的动荡之中。
17. 裁员会提高行业效率,但也可能引发害怕被解雇的工人闹事。
18. 这场运动触发了工业富国与第三世界穷国之间的对立。前者刚刚成为环境保护主义者,而后者则把外来的干涉看成是对自己主权的侵犯。
19. 美国农场出租者们担心,去年的农业复苏(靠的是联邦政府的大量拨款)会因这场干旱而前功尽弃。
20. 昨天,在此地一家烧伤整形外科专科医院,医生们全力抢救拉姆斯坦飞行表演惨祸的十名烧伤者,他们是被飞机坠毁时雨点般溅落的火油团烧伤的。
21. 现在轮到记者提问了。
22. 我的小叔子有了一个儿子后,她(婆婆)便对这个孙子呵护备至。
23. 这一年叶利钦从一个无足轻重的我行我素者一跃成为现代史上的一个显赫人物,而独联体的诞生则给这一年画上一个圆满的句号。
24. 从11月下旬开始,布什很可能要出访日本、韩国、澳大利亚和印度尼西亚。此行结束的重头戏在火奴鲁鲁:12月7日布什要在那里作短暂停留,出席日本偷袭珍珠港50周年纪念仪式。
25. 当时谁也没有注意到他有脱离联邦的野心。
26. 许多名人都十分谦虚。
27. 得到军队支持的右翼派系策划了这场政变。
28. 我绝不犹豫。
29. 这位老人说他一辈子都是享乐主义者。
30. 他的经济收入来源于一些非法活动——赛马登记赌注、赌博、放高利贷和一些可疑的工会活动。

第五章 第一节　课外扩展训练材料

秋之湖

　　我仍清晰地记得故事发生的季节。秋叶飘零，洒落一地。你我曾经孩童般戏水畅游过的小湖盖满落叶，在太阳下闪着光。那时我们幸福过。哦，我认为我们幸福过。其实你早就想离开我，只是不忍告诉我罢了。在那美丽的夜晚，眼望湖水，恍然中听见你说：我们的故事已到尽头。

　　秋雨扼杀着所剩无几的暑气，而很久以来你也一直在扼杀我奄奄一息的爱。我现在仍然觉得自己不会再去经历另一段爱情故事。你把一切都带走了。我只有默然伫立，早已明白自己会是那个遭遗弃的人。我凝望着湖水，恍惚中，生命正离我而去。

（《疯狂英语》）

第五章 第二节　课堂讲练材料

1. 在废物回收利用方面,德国人在世界上是领先的。
2. 就是在英国政府实施"国家育儿策略"4年以后,也只有1/7的8岁以下儿童能享受此项服务。
3. 结不结婚,这是一个值得考虑的问题。
4. 经济丑闻被新闻媒体曝光加剧了民主党内部各派系之间的争斗。
5. 看看为学生所设置的课程门类之繁多,我们不难发现,学生要选一门符合自己兴趣和能力的课程是多么困难。
6. 例如,美国烟草业就力图在中东和北非大力推销香烟,在这些地区,美国烟草的出口量增加了27%。
7. 选择这个工作会惹人笑话的。
8. 同时也有人反对,说文化的进步始终是以城市为中心向外辐射的。
9. 20多年前,美国海洋学家约翰·艾萨克就曾提出过把冰山从南极牵到世界上比较干燥的中心区的主张。
10. 当"药房连锁"主动给出建议时,他们比从前多留了几分戒心。
11. 为了保持观赏性,每一次绝技的危险度都在加大。
12. 该公司设计的新式足球也提高了精确性,而且摸起来更"柔软"。
13. 观众的需要各不相同。
14. 这种被称为"飞火流星"的足球是专门为2002年世界杯设计制作的,与

1998年世界杯足球赛所用的阿迪达斯三色球相比,"飞火流星"的精确度增加了25%,速度提高了10%。
15. 哈代还认为家长应该记住每个孩子都有优缺点。
16. 不是每一个接触到MMA的人都有不良反应,制造商说,该化学用品的危险性并不比其他美甲产品要高。
17. 几乎所有夫妻都或多或少地会吵架,内容小到脏碟子和扔在地上的臭袜子,大到彼此缺乏信任和沟通。夫妻之间的"战斗"内容真是五花八门。
18. 依靠5台摄像机和300个小时连续拍摄,《黄金时间》节目前所未有地窥视到两个现实美国家庭的内部世界。
19. 心理学家一直认为,父母的不和会伤害孩子的情感健康,而这项新研究又进了一步,它提示这种伤害会影响到孩子的身心健康。
20. 化石骨骼证明它们共同的祖先"比我们以前想象的还要古老"。
21. 列斯和香侬在高中时就热恋了,还未毕业,他们就怀上了大儿子。
22. 她正在找一个单身妈妈合住。
23. 一旦获得下载和压缩的内容,就很容易被分享,那将更难控制了。
24. 8岁的汤姆出生时就缺一只耳朵。
25. 随着数字化娱乐方式的增多,业内专家注意到用户需要用新的办法寻找更多的娱乐方式。
26. 在繁忙的美国机场,这种错误将意味着每天有1,000名乘客被保安扣压,会造成许多航班误点,引起乘客的愤怒。
27. 为防止数字化节目被盗版商复制发行,好莱坞电影公司希望数字化保护措施到位。
28. 他认为自己是"一个肩负重大神秘使命的救世主"。他发疯般逐字逐句地阅读《纽约时报》,说是要寻找来自外星人的密信,天天乱拨收音机,说是要收听来自太空的信号。
29. 他们吃简单的饭菜,住寒冷的窑洞,靠微弱的灯光长时间工作。

第五章 第二节 课外扩展训练材料

动物的运动趣闻

骆驼属慢行动物,动作虽缓,却不乏耐力。作为名副其实的负重动物,骆驼承载重量可达半吨,负重行走每日可达30英里。

大袋鼠长着一双长而有力的后腿,身材健壮。袋鼠虽重约200磅,其沉重的身体却能腾空跨越9英尺高的栅栏。做空中腾越动作时,这种跳跃型有袋动物用其粗大的尾巴保持平衡,控制方向。

昆虫的力量不容低估:小小蚂蚁能搬动相当于其体重50倍的东西,善飞的蜜蜂如果被拴在一个小小的带轮的负荷上,便可拉动相当于其重量300倍重的东西。

大象可谓肌肉的标志,单就象鼻子而言,就有40,000个肌肉组织——约为人体肌肉数的70倍!象鼻子无所不能,不仅能将大树连根拔起,还能把细小的针头从地上捡起来。

跳蚤是世界上最擅长跳远的动物,能跳13英寸,相当于其自身长度的350倍!按此比例推算,一个身高6英尺的人就应该跳大约2,000英尺,即相当于7个足球场那么远的距离。事实是,至今无人能跳过30英尺。

远东地区的耗子跳蚤当属精力最旺盛的跳跃型动物,能以每小时600次的速度连续跳三天。

据记录,有着骄人成绩的蠓虫是肌肉运动最快的动物。这种行动敏捷的小昆虫每分钟可振翼133,000次,比人眨一下眼皮的速度还要快100倍——而人眨一下眼皮所需的时间是1/25秒。

无论是掠过陆地,飞越天空,还是穿越海洋,鸟都应算是佼佼者。鸵鸟虽重达300磅,但两条腿比任何动物都跑得快,每小时可达30英里。印度的雨燕每小时飞行速度达100英里以上,仙企鹅据说每小时可游22英里,按这种速度比较,它与海洋中游得最快的哺乳动物——海豚相比,毫不逊色。

(《英语世界》)

第五章 第三节 课堂讲练材料

1. 汤姆逊家收到一封邀请函,还附带一张赠券。信尾是一则说明,表明该邀请由"阿兹德公司提供"。
2. 他自信,这批成本仅"几十美元"的芯片不出两三年便会遍布各地。
3. 卡萝尔的指甲修长、坚挺、美丽,曾经是她的骄傲和幸福。
4. 导演乔治·卢卡斯称他在讲述一段故事。
5. 他说:"好的,开始打。"你就打啊打,一直打到他说"停"。
6. 另一个提示是他们所使用的材料有刺鼻难闻的化学气味,这种强烈的气味能使人流泪。
7. 为把重点放在拉斯维加斯与赌博无关的方方面面,我们一起真正努力过。

8. 旅游局发起了一轮针对家庭的猛烈广告宣传攻势。
9. 人们早先对印加文化的了解来自零散的墓地,仅靠这些墓地保存的几具木乃伊,难以对印加人的生活方式做出明确结论。
10. 夫妻双方都认为自己结婚太早,且在信任、沟通、为人父母及花多少时间在一起等事情上有矛盾。
11. 沙利文想到类似处境的妇女可能更多,于是创建了 Co-Abode.com 网站。去年该网站发展成了全国性的资源网站。
12. 它的攀爬能力使它比周围其他哺乳动物更有优势,不过这只是推测而已。
13. 想更快、更便宜且更具动感吗?
14. 在其中一座墓里,发现了约 300 磅重的生棉、一个印加贵族和一个婴儿的躯体,还有食品、陶器、动物皮以及酿造奇卡酒用的谷物等 70 种物品。
15. 比赛的意义远远超过娱乐和游戏。
16. 人类的步行流畅优美。
17. 随便用什么方式自杀都行,凭什么我还要遭这份罪?生活已经没有什么可留恋的了。
18. 从录像带可以看出,校霸在对受害者拳打脚踢时其他孩子只是漠然地观看。
19. 假如你输入"Will Smith",这个数字化中心将从它所链接的许多装置和网站中进行搜索。
20. 在我的学生中,大约有五个作法自毙者。
21. 对此球褒贬不一的部分理由可能是,该足球的结构如此之新,可能许多人对它不熟悉。
22. 如果一场足球赛已趋完美,改进后的足球是否能使其更精彩?
23. 迄今为止,球员对此球的评价褒贬不一。比利时守门员教练抱怨此球"太轻"。据说巴西队中场里瓦尔多也认为此球"太大、太轻"。
24. "厄尔尼诺"现象——这个引发世界范围内久旱及特大洪水的罪魁祸首,正从四年的沉睡中苏醒过来,但它的来势还无法预测。
25. 在大家津津有味地听他调侃完票房收入情况后,拉什风趣地说他希望环球公司的账能比自然公司好。
26. 三胞胎中的一个宝宝已会走路了,另一个会爬了,第三个也会坐了,三人都在学叫"爸爸"。
27. 布雷洛克这家新公司——"生发联合公司"设在旧金山的分公司,专门提供保存头发的服务,直到科学发现治秃头的良法。
28. 运输和能源方面的支出是必须慎重权衡的重要因素。
29. 读史使人明智,读诗使人灵秀,数学使人周密,科学使人深刻,伦理学使人庄重,逻辑修辞之学使人善辩。

第五章 第三节 课外扩展训练材料

有限的土地

曾几何时,似乎美国有足够的土地供人周游,足够的河流修建大坝,足够的谷地搁置不用,足够的空间修公园建城市,足够的森林供砍伐,足够的草地供耕耘。俱往矣!未被开发的土地时代已经结束!现在,土地被认领,被圈用,被瓜分成一座座城市、一块块农场、一片片工业园。

与此同时,人口在持续增长,需要工作场所、娱乐场所,需要更多的土地建工厂,更多的海滩供人日光浴,更多干净的河流养殖更多的鱼。除增长的人口外,我们的现代技术也有各种需要必须满足,例如需要更多的煤能、电厂,汽车必须有高速公路和停车场,飞机必须有空港。

林林总总,哪一样不在鲸吞宝贵的空间!仅高速公路和快车道每年就占用200,000公顷土地。由于城市的无序扩张(即城市向边缘地区发展),2008年前有望吃掉大片土地。不过,美国土地也只有这么点家底供人们周游了。

第五章 第四节 课堂讲练材料

1. 这座小镇和沿湖的很多小镇一样,有曲曲折折的鹅卵石街道,也有背靠峭壁的水边餐馆和咖啡馆,旅馆里的游客以德国人和意大利人居多,各家商店也很热闹。
2. 某些夫妻几乎总在大吵大闹,婚姻处于离异边缘,而他们的孩子则亲眼目睹了父母无休无止地叫嚷和谩骂,以及无法解决的争执和绵延不绝的怒火。
3. 在长达10多个星期的偷拍录像带上,人们看到自己的婚姻内容充满着紧张、不信任、指责和叫骂。
4. 将来的机器人能够理解好与坏之别,甚至还拥有一定的目的感。
5. 发生争吵时,其中一方有时不是积极解决问题,而是选择逃避,或弃家出走，或闷声看电视。
6. 在印第安纳州深居简出的亚历山大视力模糊，成天拿个放大镜阅读邮件。
7. 现在他能出门了，可以经常与朋友一起上当地的咖啡馆了。
8. 这部电影显然打动了观众，创造了历史上复活节电影放映的票房纪录，共赚得 3,000 万元。
9. 在以后的 21 天中，孩子们每天早晨 7 时起床，自己做早餐，自己整理行装。
10. 我记名字的能力糟透了。
11. 我们计划的部分内容就是用身体疲倦击破这些孩子的防线。
12. 下星期，魔术师大卫·布莱恩将超越他以前被活埋的绝技，通过完成一项没有人曾经尝试的死亡挑战——把自己变成一个人体冰块。
13. 并联电容器的总电容是单个电容之和。
14. 当时她正四处寻找既有登山经验，又能脱离工作两个月，可以长时间无需照管家庭的妇女，而且这些妇女要有积极姿态。
15. 这两种装置均不一定能使患者恢复正常视力，但起码能让患者看到轮廓和光，可以让患者自己行动，从而获得自信。
16. 她正为挪菲德基金会进行一项为期两年的育儿研究，研究中发现有 75% 的年轻父母或多或少地依靠自己的老父老母帮忙照看孩子。
17. 我干什么事她都要挑毛病。

第五章 第四节 课外扩展训练材料

大规模生产

很多年前，商品制造者是些手艺人，即技术工人。手艺人对亲手制成的每一件作品都感到自豪，因为件件都投入了大量时间，精工细作，一旦成形，就有人出高价购买。奢华的波斯地毯，精美的中国瓷器，欧洲的手工蕾丝，无一不是这样制成的，但只有富人买得起，穷人只得选购做工粗糙、价格低廉的。

随着欧洲人口的增加，对所需产品的质量有了更高要求。高质量产品开始在工厂、车间，由数以百计的工人生产。而蒸汽机的发明为制造商提供了更为廉价的动力，机器取代人工，生产规模得以提高，人们得以用低价买到高质量产品。大规模生产的时代到来啦！"大规模"是大量或大批的意思。大规模生产意味着用机器生产出大量相同产品。汽车、收音机、照相机就是今天大规模生产的例证。

第五章 第五节　课堂讲练材料

1. 愤怒是对这些孩子的伤害,伤害他们的自信心,伤害他们在生活道路上自己解决纠纷的能力。
2. 这些泡沫改进了球员力量的传递,使球速加快。
3. 当其他诺贝尔奖得主用奖金坐着头等舱飞来飞去或热衷于慈善事业时,拉什却又开始了自己的研究。
4. 迈克显然是男人,这本来就不该受到质疑,任何人看到这个案例中的医学证据,都会清楚地看出麦克在医学上是个不折不扣的男人。
5. 他们把鸡蛋成打地成打地装箱。
6. 几分钟后,女士们放下衣袖,三三两两地走进来。
7. 无数人看过苹果落地,但苹果为何落地这个问题却由牛顿提了出来。
8. 我要开始早睡早起,这十有八九能大大改善我的健康状况。
9. 他们再次见面时,一个已是有妇之夫,一个已是有夫之妇了。
10. 满瓶不响,半瓶叮当。
11. 拥有健康者就拥有希望;拥有希望者,就会拥有一切。
12. 人有失错,马有失蹄。
13. 与众同乐,其乐更乐。
14. 须作金钱主人,勿为金钱奴隶。
15. 他第一次的绝技表演是在1999年,那次他把自己活埋在一个棺材里达七天七夜。
16. 汤姆逊是《最好的朋友,最坏的敌人》一书的作者。他说,几乎每一个学校都有一个团伙,由风头十足的孩子决定什么是"酷"。
17. 克罗斯说:"这样我就能成一个了不起的人,一个更有见识的人。我认为,吃遍苦中苦,方为完美人。"
18. 该美容院的老板却把责任推得干干净净。
19. 人的一生有两大目标;第一,得到你想要的东西;第二,享受你得到的东西。只有最聪明的人才能实现第二目标。
20. 享受人生,否则就是一种谬误。只要拥有生命,怎样生活无关紧要。除了生命,你还拥有什么?
21. 现在,老师成了学生身边的向导,而非高高在上的圣人。

22. 温斯顿·丘吉尔的孙女,《丘吉尔:消亡或生存》一书的作者塞丽娅·桑迪斯说,英国人对待君主制的方式很像美国人对待美国国旗的方式。
23. 酗酒孕妇所产的婴儿,无论是一个月大,还是一岁以上,在神经传导信息方面都存在严重问题。

第五章 第五节　课外扩展训练材料

快餐残渣养鼠为患

一环保组织发出警告:由于越来越多的人把吃剩的快餐扔在大街上,英国的老鼠数量正在急剧上升。"保持英国清洁"组织说,人们抛弃的汉堡包、比萨饼和土豆条残渣正在诱使习惯于地下活动的鼠类转到大街上游荡。"老鼠数量正在增长,不久,在街上看到老鼠就会和看到猫狗一样平常。"该组织负责人苏·尼尔森说。老鼠增多的背后是往大街上而非垃圾箱里乱扔快餐垃圾和残渣的行为——年轻人是罪魁祸首。根据《2001年度全国鼠类调查》,英国的老鼠数量自1998年来已增长了近1/4,目前估计为6,000万只,比英国人口还多200万。老鼠平均每24至28天可生产一次。仅仅一对老鼠一年就能繁殖出一个2,000只的鼠群。每年约有200个英国人感染威尔氏症,即一种能导致肾或肝功能衰竭直至死亡的传染病,病源就在老鼠的尿液中。为引起人们对这一问题的关注,"保持英国清洁"组织推出了名为"你希望它们靠得多近?"的公益广告。公益广告的高潮是一幅令人惊骇的画面:一个年轻姑娘睡在一张满是老鼠的床上——这是对詹姆斯·赫伯特的经典恐怖故事《老鼠》中梦魔般景象的模拟。在那个故事中,变异老鼠在捕食人类。

第五章 第六节　课堂讲练材料

1. 战争一直在威胁着地球。
2. 我只能草草地看一看。
3. 她没有得到涨工资的机会,非常生气。
4. 她依然认为克劳福德先生其貌不扬,因此从不提他。
5. 真丝在各方面都与人造丝截然不同。
6. 屋子中间没有放东西。
7. 我是一文不名了。

8. 这一时期,史沫特莱特别善于把具有不同政治倾向的人聚拢在一起。
9. 没有人是无忧无虑的。
10. 他年事已高,力不从心,胜任不了国事的操劳。
11. 萨姆没有作答,但心里不免嘀咕。
12. 别发愁,一切都会好起来的。
13. 他能体验到的不外是忧虑、耻辱、不安和无助感。
14. 她丈夫如今不必提心吊胆了。
15. 现在我不由得提心吊胆了。
16. 一切还是老样子。
17. 等待中的三个月冗长难熬,遥遥无期。
18. 要谨慎,别对同事、上司、下属、师长透露太多;在工作中或生意上不要交友过快、过早、过于高攀或过于低就。
19. 随意而疏远的友谊在生意场上是可取的。
20. 我们在星巴克内部讨论的是如何建立长盛不衰的公司。
21. 风暴更加猛烈而天气更加变幻无常了。
22. 现代科学的价值,无论如何重视也不过分。
23. 政府打击贪污腐败的力度很不尽如人意。
24. 虽然真实的病因仍令人捉摸不透,但科学家已掌握了一些资料。

第五章 第六节 课外扩展训练材料

意式餐馆合格证

可以跟味道平平的意式细面、没滋没味的意式干面、味同嚼蜡的比萨饼说再见了——至少在意大利政府的"风味警察"开展行动之后。

意大利政府表示,他们打算对世界各地打着意大利招牌的 6 万家左右餐馆进行彻底清理。为此,他们正在制作一种证书,用以颁给合格的海外意式餐馆,甄选范围包括中东约 300 家以及欧洲 25,000 家意式餐馆。此举目的有二:一是在海外宣传意大利国家形象,二是保证人们的味蕾能体验到正宗地中海食物的美妙滋味。工业部副部长阿道弗·乌尔索在记者招待会上哀叹道:"外面有些人连'比萨'是个意大利文单词都不知道,还问我们管比萨饼叫什么。"农业部长吉亚尼·阿莱曼诺说,即使有些餐馆吹嘘自己源自意大利,那也值得推敲,"大多数意式餐馆只有门上的名字和挂在门外的三色旗是真正的意大利货。"这种尚无正式名称的证书,可以确保餐馆供应正宗的意大利菜肴,食材也是地道意大利产品,而不像"卡朋佐拉"干酪那样,出售时冠以意大利名号,实际上却是德国货。不过,有人认为意大利的"风味警察"起不了什么作用,毕竟这一计划以自愿为基础,是否接受,最终由餐馆自行决定。

第五章 第七节　课堂讲练材料

1. 我们省吃俭用,以便能按时还上房贷和我俩的学生贷款。
2. 他就事论事地回答。
3. 我要开始无忧无虑地享受生活。
4. 动物没有回答,只是望着杰米。
5. 它不吃。
6. 你要是想去什么地方,我就带你去。
7. 所以,我才经常出去。
8. 杰米抱住妈妈的腰。
9. 成就常使人产生错觉,使人只看到"功成名就",看不到成就背后的痛苦和执著。
10. 整个晚上桑迪都在剥狗皮。
11. 汤姆大叔恐惧地大叫着了一声。
12. 唐·科莱奥内的每一个手势和每一个用词都表明卢卡·布拉西很受器重。
13. 他们极端推崇这些个人体验,连早期诗人都难以与之相提并论。
14. 他和她各有各的诀窍。
15. 他问我昨晚在哪儿。
16. 你们要达到目的只有驳倒我们的论点。
17. 1987年3月4日我们汇集于此为我国的货币和信誉忧心如焚。
18. 回家迟了父母要担心的。
19. 愁死不顶事。
20. 谁找你麻烦我就收拾谁。
21. 他临终时把女儿托付给她抚养。
22. 男孩儿灵巧地纵身一跳避开了卡车。
23. 明摆着不可能骗他。

24. 我们的日常生活分得就像白天和夜晚那样清楚。
25. 以色列不打算执行决议之心已昭然若揭。

第五章 第七节　课外扩展训练材料

亚沙尔的困惑

　　史蒂夫和亚沙尔是在美国一所大学的化学课上首次相识的。亚沙尔是个留学生，来自约旦。他很高兴能结交到一个美国人，可以了解更多的美国文化，因而希望与史蒂夫成为好朋友。

　　起初，史蒂夫似乎非常友好，常在课前向亚沙尔热情地打招呼，有时主动与亚沙尔一道学习，甚至还邀亚沙尔与自己一同吃午饭。可是，学期结束之后，史蒂夫与以前相比对亚沙尔好像疏远了一些，两个曾经的同班同学在学校很少见面。一天，亚沙尔决定给史蒂夫打个电话，但是史蒂夫好像并不乐意与他交谈。史蒂夫态度的巨大变化，令亚沙尔十分不快。"史蒂夫曾说过与我是朋友，"亚沙尔不满地说道，"我也向他保证一旦为友终身为友。"

（《跨文化交际英语教程》）

第五章 第八节　课堂讲练材料

1. 我任他们争来吵去，独自去火车站买了一张晨报。
2. 战场附近的房子都撤空了，人们接到命令在镇子的某处集中。
3. 伦敦陷入了"大恐惧"，现在，仅是一个开始。
4. 他是她同父异母的哥哥，是她父亲第一任妻子所生。
5. 很高兴通知您，我们的回样将于本周末用敦豪速递给您，请尽快确认，以便我们开始大规模生产。
6. 如果你方定期给我方下订单，你方便可得获 5% 的折扣。
7. 他欣喜若狂，好像他承办大厦建筑的项目中标了。
8. 人人都在谈饮食，却讳言排泄问题。
9. 该组织强烈要求新的方案上马，以缓解世界许多地方厕所严重不足的情况。
10. 法国内衣制造商报告说，这种衣服的销售量激增，购买者最年轻的仅 10 岁。
11. 岛民们已经得知警报，暴风雨即将来临。

12. 我们想他们已不打算结婚了,他们的争吵不过是小题大做而已。
13. 风雨大作,全都停电了。
14. 约翰在会上边咆哮,边挥动着一张报纸。
15. 其中一名受害者周五去世,另一个第二周周六死亡,死亡当天发生了大象成群袭击村子的事件。遭袭的两个村子以农业为生,距森林不远。
16. 有暴风雨时,不要把船驶出去。
17. 风浪太大,无法下锚。
18. 天晚了,你该睡了。
19. 她妈妈关上门,随即屋子变成了真正的夜晚,到处是盛满了黑暗的角落。
20. 明白我的意思后,他们笑了。

第五章 第八节　课外扩展训练材料

登革热

登革热是一种由蚊子传播的传染病,其临床症状为高烧、骨头或关节痛、肌肉痛以及皮疹。登革出血热则是一种可能伤及性命的并发症,临床表现为高烧、出血,常伴有肝肿大,严重时病人还会并发循环系统衰竭。

近几十年,登革热在全球范围内大规模流行起来,如今已经成为分布于100多个国家的地方流行病,非洲、美洲、地中海东部、东南亚和西太平洋地区,其中东南亚和西太平洋地区疫情最为严重。

现在,大约有25亿人,即全世界人口的2/5,受到登革热的威胁。世界卫生组织估计,全球每年可能有5,000万登革热感染病例发生。

目前对登革热没有特效治疗方案。不过在经验丰富的医护人员精心护理下,登革出血热病人一般能够脱离生命危险。采用大剂量高疗效药物并进行适当的辅助治疗,可以将登革热死亡率控制在1%以下。

登革热疫苗目前尚未开发出来。要扭转登革热不断上升的流行趋势和地区性扩散趋势,前景不容乐观。近年来,公共卫生当局重点通过灭蚊、减少幼虫繁育场所等办法预防疾病。这些办法从长远看十分有效,但对控制近期内疾病的传播收效可能不大。

(《英语学习》)

第六章 第一节　课堂讲练材料

1. 在这场声称为人权而战的战争中,破坏是由计算机造成的,而不是战士手中的武器造成的。
2. 这种广泛的合作形式旨在提高思想交流及科研人员在本系统内的自由流动。
3. 在汽车工业初期,大多数小汽车属于有"组装车"之称的那类车。
4. "T"型车成为有史以来第一种这样类型的汽车:其零件绝大多数由制造商独家制造,或由与我们公司合资的供应商提供。
5. 他们明年要在这里修建一座住宅楼,就修在办公楼旁边。
6. 明天下午两点开教研会,全体教师务必参加。
7. 工业发达国家对贫困的定义是,家庭可任意支配的收入低于全国中等收入的一半。
8. 在造成了巨大经济损失并夺去了千百万生命的毁灭性冲突之后,二战催生了联合国——通过集体行动解决冲突的世界性组织。
9. 至于儿童,人们普遍赞同对他们坐在电视机前的时间实行严格安排和监控。
10. 大家认为这样做不妥。
11. 好弓手的美名并不来自弓箭,而来自他的瞄准工夫。
12. 劳工部说,那些场主没有为工人更衣时间支付加班工资。
13. 根据《公平劳动标准法》,雇主对工人每周工作超过 40 小时的部分一般应按正常报酬的一倍半给付加班费。
14. 50 英里的车程探险队花了 6 个小时,其间,他们跨过 4 条宽阔的河流,6 次踏着泥泞的道路一路推着敞篷卡车前行。
15. 骡子和驮马被用来为他们在瓦里康卡 1000 英尺深谷里的主营地运送物资。
16. 人们常说科学是把双刃剑,在增加财富、安逸度的同时,也使人们担忧诸如克隆人类的潜在危险。
17. 用餐时,如果人家给你牛奶、咖啡或者苏打水,用不着诧异。
18. 总的来说,得出这种结论是有一定把握的,但必须具备两个条件:能假定这个孩子对测试的态度和与他比较的另一个孩子的态度相同;他没有因缺乏别的孩子已掌握的有关知识而被扣分。
19. 我们学过,写商务信件要使用规范格式,不得像私人信件那样随意。

20. 疾病必须先确诊,再用药。

第六章 第一节　课外扩展训练材料

烹制防癌食品

　　有证据显示饮食与癌症有联系。有些食物可能致癌,有些食物则可能防癌。

　　例如,可防喉癌、食道癌的食物都含有大量的胡萝卜素。胡萝卜素是维生素 A 的一种形式,存在于甜瓜、桃、硬花甘蓝、菠菜、深绿叶蔬菜、红薯、胡萝卜、南瓜、冬瓜、番茄、柑橘类水果及芽甘蓝之中。

　　有助于减少患胃、肠、呼吸道癌症危险的食物有卷心菜、硬花甘蓝、芽甘蓝、球甘蓝和菜花。

　　水果、蔬菜及纯谷物食品,如燕麦片和小麦等,可帮助降低患直肠癌的可能。

　　经高脂肪食物、盐或亚硝酸盐处理过的食物,如火腿、咸鱼、用传统方法熏制的各类香肠,食用应适量。饮酒也要有节制。

　　少吃脂肪,避免发胖是实践得出的一条有益经验。减轻体重可降低患癌危险。对近 100 万美国人进行的为期 12 年研究发现,超重 40% 以上的人属于癌症高发人群。

　　现在,人们比以往更清楚地了解如何能够在厨房做出防癌食品。吃益于健康的食品并保持健康吧。

　　让我们行动起来,共同对付癌症。

第六章 第二节　课堂讲练材料

1. 他提出了一种理论,认为可根据冒险程度把人类行为描述成一个具有一致特征的统一体。
2. 从挖掘出的塞姆·谢泼德大夫尸体中提取的新的 DNA 证据提供了最令人信服的证明,说明四十多年前令全美震惊的杀妻案中塞姆被误判了。
3. 的确,现代经济被市场这只"无形的手"左右着,千百万人的购买需求引导着商品的生产和服务。
4. 因此,要使人们真正相信经济之轮的运转是个独角戏或直线的因果关系,实在是匪夷所思。
5. 如果成功是目标,在我看来这种快节奏的方式显然选错了方向。

6. 其实让局外人帮助写简历的做法十分盛行,这使得美国大学招生委员会成员对中国学生产生了一定的偏见,对此我十分担忧。

7. 对查找中文资料有困难的老外来说,计算机搜索功能可方便其寻找所需内容。

8. 参加这样的聚会不仅为共餐,也是为了交流,因此,合理的座位安排有助于聚会的成功。

9. 我们发现,在产品上追求质量,与在生活中追求质量一样,你须认真挑出各种失误。

10. 我想讲的重点内容,也是我个人的亲身体验,那就是欧洲人与美国人有差异。

11. 这件作品就是数学。如果数学一定要靠实际应用来证明其存在价值,一定要成为一种工具来服务于平庸而短暂的人生,那就不仅仅是冒犯了数学,也冒犯了创造它的人类。

12. 脑瓜灵活的人觉得"输入"键的功能此时有点像电传打字机上的托架回返键,如果把这个键标上"回车"的话,那些刚刚使用电脑的人会觉得电脑键盘更亲切些。

13. 即便是设计最为周密的电路偶尔也会发出小小的火花,这种可能性在过去一直都得不到排除。

14. 每一次双方都达成一种共识,即我们可以通过共同推动知识的发展来拓展人类自由的疆界。

15. 对于本书所言事实的真相,作者到底有多少切身体验,将在某个时间公之于众。

16. 没有人能解释为什么地球会吸引不明飞行物的频频造访。

17. 要保证制定国际贸易和投资规则的多边国家组织,须重新进行定位,使其更好地适应发展中国家的需要。

18. 但是,这并不意味着政府不能影响经济使其朝着更有益于社会的方向发展。

19. 这一广为流行的模式反映出美国人的内在价值观,即每个人应靠自己的努力来寻求发展,依靠他人(特别是家人)的提携取得成功是很"不光彩"的。那些继承了家产与仕途的人会多少有些歉疚,不敢四处炫耀。

20. 显而易见,一个国家的经济实力与其工农业生产效率密切相关,而效率的提高则有赖于科技人员的共同努力。

第六章 第二节 课外扩展训练材料

耶稣被抓

离开楼上的房间,耶稣和门徒来到客西马尼园。他们以前曾多次来过这里。耶稣吩咐门徒专心做祷告,不要睡觉。说罢,他离开门徒,走不多远便俯伏在地,祈祷。

过了一会儿,耶稣回来,发现门徒们都睡着了!耶稣再次叮嘱他们不要睡觉,可是每次回来都发现他们睡着了。"这种时刻你们怎么能睡觉呢?"耶稣最后一次回来时说:"时辰已到,我要落入敌手了。"

话音刚落,园外人声嘈杂。看,那些家伙到了,手里拿着刀剑和棍棒!还举着火把!只见一个人走出人群,直奔耶稣。他吻了吻耶稣(在画中你可看到)。这人就是犹大。

耶稣问:"犹大,你在用亲吻作暗号出卖我吗?"是的,亲吻是个暗号,告诉与犹大同来的人,这就是耶稣,他们要抓的人。耶稣的敌人上前抓住耶稣,彼得怎会让他们轻易得手,他拔出随身携带的刀,向靠得最近的敌人砍去。刀削掉了那人的耳朵,差一点就砍在头上。

(《我的圣经故事》)

第六章 第三节 课堂讲练材料

1. 因为每次只住一年时间,所以我买的自行车都不贵,车一出毛病就去找那些遍布大街小巷的修车匠。
2. 我们认为数学高手就是能用脑子做计算器在硅芯片上所做之事的人。
3. 这种方法能够制造出一个跟你一模一样的人,可以在你离开人间多年后还活在这个世上。
4. 知识和科学的发展已提供了这样一个国际舞台,在这个舞台上男人们和女人们为所有人的美满生活通力合作,为人类自由做贡献。
5. 该公司知道他们自己去检查所有的血浆采集点"不可行",所以决定依靠食品和药物管理局的检测报告,实际上他们对这些报告从不复查。
6. 年轻的大学毕业生面临困难的抉择,这一抉择将决定他们的未来走向。
7. 一天一苹果,医生不找我。

8. 国内市场及劳资需要人力资源,而不是过分依赖那些并不忠于本国的跨国公司。

9. 电话来访是一种破门而入,我们买来电话便是对破门而入提出了邀请。

10. 用数码相机给顾客拍照,然后印到邮票纸版上,这一过程需要大约5分钟。

11. 那些对人的生命缺乏应有尊重的政府如今能搞到大规模杀伤性武器。

12. 追随天赐之福,就是追寻生命河流中最激动人心最富有挑战性的事业,并沿着一个能让你充分显示个性又能得到充分满足的方向前进。

13. 能为我们在天空中搜寻另一文明提供线索的技术刚刚起步。

14. 且不论其他,科学和宗教在创世说上这一新发现的巧合看来打开了被忽略了几个世纪的对话。

15. 不久前,北京举行了一场很有意义的讲座,内容主要涉及侨居中国的老外们的心理问题。

16. 我每天骑自行车接送五岁的女儿上幼儿园。

17. 其次是引起了心理问题,影响到我们集中精力阅读甚至是看电视的欲望和能力。

18. 这一现实有助于解释那种深藏于心的情感,而这一情感构成了美国在枪支控制问题上争论的基础。

19. 父母还有责任向子女灌输人格价值,引导他们做出明智的选择。

20. 现在,大多数天文学家接受了宇宙是瞬间创造的理论,即宇宙起源于150或200亿年前一个巨大火球的爆炸。

21. 遭到拒绝之后,欧文跑出了医院。不过,几分钟之后他又开着车转了回来,冲破医院的玻璃门,沿30米长的走廊开到了前台。

22. 我们知道,我们的官员有时也会出错,有时需要申请人下次来时带来更齐全的资料,才可帮助申请人获得签证资格。

23. 据报载,来到苏格兰一处保护区的两只加拿大水獭受到24小时的严密保护,因为它们的"外国口音"引起了当地水獭的困惑和敌意。

24. 而且,用未出生的孩子做基因实验也涉及道德问题,而这种实验有可能导致灾难的后果。

参考译文

第六章 第三节　课外扩展训练材料

新的环境艺术

20世纪50年代类似罗伯特·劳申伯格(生于1925年)的艺术家,将现实生活中的实物带进作品,从而进一步发挥了艺术唤醒人类意识的作用。例如,劳申伯格的一件表现抽象艺术风格的作品,其内容就是一台收音机;还有一些作品自成一体,内容为多位艺术家集合起来的显然互不相干的物品。此类作品试图让人们更清醒地认识到自己的生活环境,看到理性和非理性之间界限的狭窄,改变所谓世界永恒不变的观点。

集成艺术的成就之一就是打破了雕塑与绘画间的界限。从某种意义上而言,集成艺术品是立体的,可称之为雕塑品,但并未使用传统雕塑材料和雕塑方法。战后的雕塑家已就自己作品中所用的方法和材料对雕塑艺术重新进行了界定。大卫·史密斯(1906—1965)20世纪50年代扩大了雕塑的概念范围。他用焊接好的金属条进行创作,让人们通过金属之间的空隙看到自然风景。有些艺术家和集成艺术家充满着类似的激情,他们用工业社会的"废物"做雕塑材料。如约翰·张伯伦(生于1927年)创作时将小汽车的残骸焊接起来,然后上色。他的焊接方法和现代工业技术差不多,但对残骸的利用却提醒人们注意现代社会产品带来的潜在危险。与此同时,他用颜料改变了废物的本来面目,使其变成和谐的形体,以此颠覆传统的美的概念。

最近,雕塑家安东尼·卡罗(生于1924年)发展了大卫·史密斯作品的内在意义。他把通常用于工业的现成钢部件焊接起来,涂上明快的颜色,做成优美的雕塑品。整个作品的造型虽大,但各部分都很纤秀。此类作品通常置于户外,它们不像传统雕塑那样取代环境空间而是赋予空间更明确的意义。这样,又有了一种可让人们更能清楚地意识到自我及人类生活环境的艺术。

很快,环境艺术又将集成作品做了进一步推动,艺术家们将整个房间变成了艺术作品,如爱德华·肯荷兹(生于1927年)创作的《地质学教授的家》(1961年作)。这是在一妓院里创作出的一个房间,里面摆上了相当普通甚至低劣的家具,并且配着正在播放40年代乐曲的自动电唱机,唱机旁立着一个形象逼真的着衣木偶裁缝,但其头部却换上了一只公猪的脑壳。肯荷兹塑造的妓院里的种种污秽之所以逼真,是因为他把事物的平淡庸俗与彼此之间的不协调混合成一种气氛,置身其间使人更觉难堪。

(《西方艺术插图百科全书》)

第六章 第四节　课堂讲练材料

1. 我记不清确切的时间了,大概是在我读高中和研究生之间的某个时候吧,电视从可容忍的恶习变成了重要的社会习俗,成为社区居民必需的活动项目。

2. 25年来,各大党派一如既往地遣责其对立党领导人违法,不同的是,他们现在仍可以利用耸人听闻的丑闻使公众失去对对立党的信任。

3. 英国顶尖科学家斯蒂芬·霍金警告我们,除非开始向宇宙空间殖民,否则不出这个千年,人类就会被某种"世界末日"病毒灭种。

4. 谢泼德大夫在监狱服刑10年后,联邦最高法院决定重审此案,认为该案由于新闻界的过度炒作,判决有失公正。

5. 虽然政府已列出291种哺乳动物、鸟、昆虫和植物为濒危物种,但是至今还没有通过保护它们的法律。

6. 费马大定理是世界上最著名的悬而未决的数学难题。之所以出名,是因为它历时已久(它的诞生比艾萨克·牛顿还要早5年),也由于它的简洁。

7. 然而过不了多久,这些技术障碍都将被一一攻破。

8. 20世纪40年代,在电视进入美国千家万户以前,企业主要通过报纸、杂志与广播对其产品及服务进行宣传。

9. 虽然美貌本身也许只是表面一层皮,但种种研究表明,我们的审美观可能和我们的大脑密切相关。

10. 万一出现紧急情况,请按红色按钮,切断电源。

11. 《新科学家》的报道既没点明这些含铅蜡烛的品牌,也没有点明是哪些国家生产的,只是说它们由"远东地区"制造。

12. 尽管他很喜欢她,有时仍对她发脾气。

13. 尽管需要粮食生产和加工方面的技术进步来确保食物的来源,满足粮食需求更多取决于发展中国家内部各阶层同等的经济实力。

14. 如果你想保险,想防止可怕事故对你或你的车造成影响,那就投综合保险吧。

15. 他关窗户用力很猛,窗户坏了。

16. 电在我们日常生活中所占的地位非常重要,现在有人还认为电是完全理所当然的事,所以在开灯或开收音机时,很少再去想电是怎么来的。

17. 由于我们双方都愿本着平等和相互尊重的原则,这次会晤能够使和平成为现实。

18. 由于这一裁决给予每个选民及各州在堕胎合法性问题上更多的发言权，有关问题的争论变得异常激烈。
19. 观众席鸦雀无声，直到音乐会结束才响起热烈的掌声。

第六章 第四节 课外扩展训练材料

揭开溃疡的病因

电影明星汤姆·克鲁斯称他在拍电影《大开眼界》时由于精神紧张而患了胃溃疡。不过，很抱歉，汤姆，最新科学证据显示，大多数溃疡并不是精神紧张或饮食不当的结果，而是由于感染了被称为幽门螺杆菌的细菌。当带菌的粪便同手、食物或水接触的时候，细菌得以传播。大多数人似乎在儿童时期就受到了感染。

细菌削弱胃的保护性内膜，使胃更易受到我们身体产生的用于消化食物的酸和酶的损害。

溃疡神话和事实

胃溃疡由情感压力而发是无稽之谈，尽管好莱坞在许多电影里都坚称其科学性。以下是有关溃疡的常识：

- ◆ 如果你是年龄在30至50岁之间的男性，或超过60岁的女性，你最有可能得十二指肠溃疡。
- ◆ 最常见的症状是腹部因饥饿等引起的阵痛或烧灼感。这种情况大多发生在两餐之间和清晨，持续时间可能达到几分钟到数个小时，缓解方法是进食或服用制酸药。
- ◆ 较少见的溃疡症状是：恶心、呕吐、胃口差和体重减轻。
- ◆ 吸烟会增加你患溃疡的可能性，减缓已有的溃疡愈合时间。
- ◆ 咖啡、茶、可乐类饮料和含咖啡因的食物，似可增加胃酸的分泌，从而加重溃疡引起的疼痛。
- ◆ 尽管情感压力不再被看成是引起溃疡的原因，但人们经常说它加重了溃疡的疼痛。身体的压力，如外科大手术或重伤，确实会增加得溃疡病的危险。
- ◆ 辛辣、脂肪性或酸性食物与溃疡无关。
- ◆ 服药（如阿司匹林）可能增加患胃溃疡的机会。

如果你认为自己得了溃疡,那就尽快去看医生。有些检查方法可确诊幽门螺杆菌属细菌的存在。采用药物治疗溃疡,通常可在几周内治愈,目前已很少需要手术治疗。

(尼基·佩乐古里诺)

第六章 第五节　课堂讲练材料

1. 爱神的倒钩箭头把他身上的厚皮射穿了。一个半月的朝夕相处,亲近的机会很多,已令他到了神魂颠倒的地步。

2. 法官拿走稻草人(显然它已经在这个岗位上呆了不少日子)将它呈上法庭作为证物。

3. 法国的一家日报《巴黎人》周五称,法国许多中学校长(校服在法国实际上闻所未闻)对于显露丁字裤和腹部的服饰下了禁令。

4. 广义地说,人可以分为三类:辛劳而死的、忧愁而死的、郁闷而死的。

5. 如果你克隆的仅仅是自己的身体,弄出一个无头的克隆人,你就拥有了能随时替换你身体各个部件的备用品,这样一来,你,或者说你的意识,便会永无终止地延续下去。

6. 不过,这是假设高等教育对升迁仍然起关键作用(是否如此,还有很大疑问)。一些人士提出警告,预计过不了多长时间,当学位不那么受重视时,不上大学而去工作,可能是较明智的选择。

7. 没人清楚,他肯定也不清楚,自己到底欠了多少钱。

8. 他还提到图画中为圣诞老人拉雪橇的驯鹿都是雌性,因为雄鹿的角会在冬季来临之前脱落,只有雌鹿的角能保留到春天。

9. 不过有些食品似乎拥有永久的魅力以及经久不衰的力量,能够跻身品牌食品的行列,比如红酒和咖啡在 1991 年和 2001 年排行榜上都占据显著位置。

10. 专家说,红头发的人也许还有一个非同寻常的特征,即敏锐的痛感。

11. 一项调查显示,素以骇人听闻的交通安全记录出名的印度首都新德里有将近 1/4 的公共汽车司机缺乏基本的驾驶技能,其中更有数百人视力存在问题。

12. 他们发现,在 6 月 30 日英阿之战当天及此后两天内,因心脏病入院的几率提高了 25%。

13. 这暗示着大部分人在午间都不够清醒,所以气候炎热的国家传统上都有午睡时间。

14. 英国最高档的食品杂货店之一需要新聘一名巧克力试吃员,被聘用者年薪将达 35,000 英镑。
15. 他们选择工作并不是出于激情,而是出于生活环境的考虑。
16. 该公司在声明中说欠政府 2.5 亿美元,而政府也有 12 亿应付款没有给它。在经济不景气及公司和厂方都不再持有现金的状况下,这样的恶性循环越来越多。
17. 根据中国专利法,一项设计专利可以包括产品的图案、形状、式样、颜色或者其组合,它可产生一种美感并且适用于工业。
18. 两个电视明星出演的一幕生死攸关的真实故事牵动了新加坡人的心;年轻的演员捐出自己的部分肝脏挽救了垂死的女友。
19. 例如,看守们不知道如何对付那些连排队吃饭都不会的精神有问题的囚犯,结果往往是把这些囚犯单独关押起来。
20. 挪威在两性平等方面跨出了史无前例的一步:政府宣布所有公司须保证妇女在董事会成员中所占比例不得低于 40%。
21. 此项研究结果让人们看到越来越多的英国年轻人沉醉于酒精之中,这对他们的健康极其有害。

第六章 第五节 课外扩展训练材料

"女巫号"帆船

历史上,伦敦一直是英国最大贸易港口之一。现在,泰晤士河沿岸仍有许多古迹能使人回忆起英国航海贸易事业曾经的盛况。其中,最值得参观的就是位于伦敦东南的格林尼治镇,在那儿你能看到著名的"女巫号"帆船。

"女巫号"是一种"快速帆船"型的航海帆船,于 1869 年下水。船主的想法是把它打造成中国茶叶贸易中速度最快的运输船,因为它本来就是用来从远东运茶叶的。当时,为尽快从中国运回茶叶,船主之间的竞争十分激烈。多年之后,他们把"女巫号"帆船停泊在格林尼治,使今天的人们得以一睹其风采。

参观"女巫号"时,你会看到许多东西,上面记载着成年累月呆在这只快船上的水手的故事。你可以看到从前装载茶叶的箱子以及后来载运成捆羊毛的货舱。苏伊士运河建成以后,轮船接手了茶叶贸易运输任务,"女巫号"

便开始从澳大利亚运输羊毛。

　　水手们的住处值得参观。水手们睡觉的地方是光秃秃的木板铺位,上面只铺着草垫子。当官的条件要好一些,但用现在的标准衡量仍然很差。在船头,你可以看到厨房或称作船上厨房以及木工车间的地方。水手们生活和工作的空间十分狭小,极不适宜漫长的航行生活。很难想象他们当时的生活情景。他们在寒冷、潮湿、危险的条件下每天工作至少十二个小时,一周工作七天,而每月只挣几个英镑。

　　"女巫号"上还陈列着当时船舶的一些遗物以及从各种船只上收集来的许多船头雕饰。

　　拾级登上甲板,抬头可以看到错综纠缠的帆缆工具。当初仅有二十八人驾驶这条帆船,就连抗击南美合恩角的八级风暴时人员也没增加!舵轮设在甲板上,可见舵手是在毫无遮蔽风雨和海浪防护设备的情况下工作的。

(夏洛特·格雷格)

第六章 第六节　课堂讲练材料

1. 数百万狂热的英国球迷习惯在晚间或周末观看球赛,他们渴望及时了解英格兰队和爱尔兰队在世界杯上的赛况,但由于比赛时间在清晨或中午,他们面临着左右为难的窘境。
2. 如果太阳收缩到这种状态,就会把海洋变成冰,把大气变成液化气。
3. 既然我们拥有了城市和技术,那么,能否感受到我们在自然界所处的位置又有什么关系呢?
4. 许多专家认为,与以前有所不同的是,美国人虽然为自己规定了道德准则,但是对于言行不符合这些准则的朋友或邻居,他们往往不愿进行谴责。
5. 人们相信,这些以权谋私的犯罪行为,如果听之任之,对国家的法律系统、改革和发展将产生破坏性的影响。
6. 政府对支出及援助项目结构进行了重大调整,以便提供就业机会,改善包括营养、卫生和教育在内的基础社会服务。
7. 政府还发挥了强有力的领导作用以加速促进男女平等进程,特别是强调妇女的教育、计划生育服务、减轻妇女工作量和机会均等的立法等。
8. 成千上万的人迁移到都市边缘的贫民窟。那里由于贫困、过分拥挤和极差的卫生环境,生活几乎让人无法忍受;那里主要的娱乐形式是通过复杂的传播技术,不断地向生活在贫困之中的人们展示富有的梦想。

9. 据说,使用这些封闭式冷却系统在几个月时间之内就能收回投资,因为用水及排水费用节省了,而且可以省去一个化学物品处理车间以及必需的化学物品处理费用。
10. 为什么美国市场营销与公关如此盛行?因为美国人相信语言可以用来改变人们的思维方式,可以用来表现自己。
11. 去年秋天,法庭命令开棺验尸。从谢泼德大夫的尸体上取出的组织样本表明在谋杀现场发现的血不是他的。
12. 这家周报说,按照他们提出的原则,如果狗、猫、兔子等宠物的需要未得到满足,如没有充足的食物和水、足够的空间和友谊,那么宠物的主人将遭到起诉。
13. 据说,许多人准备在7月18号那天举行婚礼,原定在同日进行的人口普查看来无法完成,因此普查提前一天进行。
14. 由于英国的驯鹿能传播传染性极强的口蹄疫,圣诞老人今年只得用马和爱斯基摩狗来拉雪橇了。
15. 斯威士兰政府获悉,国际机场的指挥塔和雷达系统都已失灵,夜间降落的照明条件也很差,飞行员只能凭记忆飞行。
16. 英国教育部称,日前进行的全国性逃课清查行动查出了数千名逃学学童,他们的一些逃课理由十分荒谬。
17. 让我眼看着已经赢得的声誉在政治斗争中被破坏,我想我是忍受不了的。
18. 如果让我去问老师一连串略微动脑就能得到答案的问题,我会觉得很幼稚,很荒唐。
19. 该研究表明,由于双职工家庭已成为一种定势,传统的社会关系网在瓦解,我们采取了一种更加自我的城市生活方式,所以建立工作场所友谊关系在人才争夺战中是一件新式武器。

第六章 第六节 课外扩展训练材料

贸易往来函件

信一:关于补偿贸易

致启者:

谢谢你方9月10日的来信。信中你方同意按补偿贸易方式向我方提供

400台FK-2型号缝纫机。

  关于由我方进口的上述缝纫机的付款方式,我们建议采用三年分期付款办法,即在三年内每年支付总价的三分之一。

  从你方来信中我们也注意到:对使用你方提供的缝纫机生产的衬衫,你们每年回购5,000打。由于这仅占总产量的很小一部分,本着补偿贸易的精神,建议你方接受我方每年返销的金额不低于我方同年内分期偿付你方设备的金额。

  你方如能最有利地考虑我方建议,将不胜感激,并相信这将是我们双方长期友好合作的开始。

  此致

×××

信二:关于来样生产

致启者:

  谢谢你方8月2日来信询问按来样生产皮包的可能性。

  我们很高兴告知你们:除了正常的进出口贸易外,多年来我们还经营来样加工和来料加工业务。我们的皮革制品选料上乘,做工精细,已赢得海外客户对我们商业信誉的充分信任。

  至于价格,我们在尚未收到你方样品和知道你方订购数量之前,很难算出确切价格。因此,请把你方每季或每年想订购的数量通知我们,因为你方订购的数量是我们核算价格的一个重要因素。

  我们保证和你方在任何时候都密切合作,并盼早日收到你方样品。

  此致

×××

第六章 第七节 课堂讲练材料

1. 他须在为父亲做无罪辩诉中获胜方能获得赔偿,赔偿金可能累计高达200万美元。

2. 我不知道人们凭什么认为家庭主妇不愉快,没有成就感。我们并没有闲待着抱怨丧失了地位或感到无聊,我喜欢现在的身份,日子过得有滋有味。

3. 在电视技术还不发达的年代,人们要起身走上几英尺去转换频道。可即使在那时,也由于广告过多,播放总是断断续续的。

参考译文

4. 在科学上，一个具有独特创新思想的科学家取得的进步，比数以百计的做常规研究的科学家取得的进步作用更大。当然，后者的研究还是需要的，虽然这些研究对于迅速发展的科学是不够的。

5. 我们看到信息技术正在进入所有使事物发生变化的技术都会经历的一个重要阶段，技术不再只为少数专业人员所掌握，而为大众所接受，并且无处不在。

6. 新的 DNA 测试使用的是最近发现的血液样本，取自卧室壁橱门上的一个大血点，这个血点离谢泼德太太被杀的地方仅一英尺之隔。结果表明，新的血样与谢泼德大夫及谢泼德太太的血样均不一样。

7. 新西兰和澳大利亚各城市仍在声称它们是追求高质量低成本生活的人们的最佳选择，尽管它们的得分仍居 50 分左右或更低。不过，在默瑟 2002 年 3 月公布的另一项调查中，它们居于生活质量最高的 30 个城市之列。

8. 《新科学家》杂志设立的这一奖项旨在为杂志的改版做宣传，幸运的获奖者要到死时才能领奖。届时获奖者的身体将被冷却到足以阻止身体腐烂的低温，然后悬浮在液氮中，进入冷冻保存状态。

9. 如果我们读点什么的话，很可能是在上下班的公共汽车上或地铁里。晚上回到家里，朝九晚五、蜜蜂般的上班生活已使我们疲劳不堪，此时我们更可能做的是看电视，因为自从遥控器的问世，此项活动要求消耗的脑力和体力比以往任何时候都少了。

10. 科学家的思维活动和一般人的思维活动之间并没有多大区别，无非是面包师或屠夫的操作方法与化学家的操作方法之类的区别罢了，前者是用普通的秤来称货物，而后者是用天平和等级分得很精细的砝码来进行困难而又复杂的分析。

11. 友谊与相互尊重，会带来实实在在的回报，会建立人与人之间的纽带，这种纽带不会轻易被观点的不同或国际事务的复杂性、乃至历史上的伤害与猜忌所消融。

12. 一个国家哪些行业有天然优势，哪些行业的出口便应大力扩展，这已被反复证明是一个获胜的法宝，而其他国家也不会因此受到什么损失。

13. 当今世界形势不容乐观，发达国家仍没有摆脱经济衰退，发展中国家则可能因为实行某些无关大碍的"非关税壁垒"（如对某些行业给予赋税激励）而遭到报复。

14. 尽管我们要完成的任务规模之大令人畏惧，尽管有许多障碍有待克服，但是以悲观的调子来结束我的发言是错误的，因为许多国家在此方面已经取得了长足的进步。
15. 农村地区的缺医少药仍是一个严重问题,母婴保健也相对落后。
16. 出生率稳定在低水平上。去年,自然人口增长率降至千分之十以下。
17. 如果你长时间工作,就极可能把业余时间用于社交活动以求放松,而这意味着你可能睡眠不足,最后导致免疫力下降。
18. 文章敦促政府工作人员,特别是领导,要严格按照法律、法规办事,力争做维护宪法和法律尊严的典范。
19. 在奥地利,秋天(10 至 11 月)出生的成人大约要比春天(4 至 6 月)出生的人多活 7 个月,而在丹麦这一差异约为 4 个月。
20. 他谈及此事时,眼睛亮了起来,一丝淡淡的笑意浮上嘴边。

第六章 第七节 课外扩展训练材料

一封道歉函

尊敬的邮政用户:

您的邮件可能属于以下两种情况之一:袋内装的邮件可能原来并未封好,也可能是在邮局处理过程中遭到损坏。

我们知道您的信件对您十分重要,您完全有权力希望完好无损地收到。邮政部门尽了最大努力妥善处理委托给他们的邮件,但由于邮件量大,偶尔的损坏是难免的。

由于邮局每天要处理大量邮件,为确保工作的顺利进行和邮件的快速投递,必须使用机械设备。事实上,现代化的生产方式不允许特别关注每一份邮件。如果信件未封好,或者邮件内装的东西太多,都可能破损。出现这种情况时,机器就会发生堵塞,常会对其他封好的邮件造成损坏。

我们正在努力改进工作方法,以保证类似的损坏事故不再发生。我们十分感谢您的关心,并对给您带来的不便深表歉意。

邮政总局

第七章 第一节 课堂讲练材料

我眼中的一个人

惠特尼先生在一间井然有序的办公室里。办公室很小,只能容纳一张老式拉桌及一两把椅子,也许有一个保险柜,记不起来了。办公室四周是铁栅栏,门前有一个着制服的保安,惠特尼先生不发话不放我们进去。

惠特尼先生方下巴,冷峻的眼睛,脸上表情全无——一如我想象的那样。他将自己的赌场作为一家企业来经营,并为自己高效有序的管理方式而自豪。据说,他每季利润为200万美元,对此数据我有些怀疑,就像人们怀疑影星的工资一样。

但不容置疑的是,此君个性很强,十分有趣,我喜欢他,想与他交谈,不过有点难度,因为他不是个很有沟通能力的人。很快,我问到他每季因不能兑现的支票及坏账所造成的亏损情况,得到的回答是约20万美元,似乎对他而言不是个大数目。说到此点时,他的双眼放光,嘴唇浮现出一丝淡淡的微笑。

第七章 第一节 课外扩展训练材料

松 树

松树几乎千篇一律地生长于杂乱而荒芜的野地之中,却给四周景物带来高度的整齐与精确之感。低地的树木会旁逸斜出,就算草地上的一阵微风也会使它们弯曲,一排黄花九轮草也会使它们的树干偏向。然而,哪怕风暴和雪崩恣意肆虐,只要松树在徒直的悬崖上有一块凸出的岩石可以紧紧依附,它还是长得笔直挺拔。从它新发的嫩枝旁沿树干将一根竿子伸下去,只要这树活着,竿子必定指向地的中心。低地的树枝为了各自的需要会朝四处伸展开去,形成各种各样不规则的形态向外扩张。但是松树却锻炼得什么也不需要,一切都能忍受。松树,是坚定的整体,独立自持,但求正直,别无希冀,以有限的满足为完满。无论高矮,松树将永远把身板挺得笔直。

(约翰·拉斯金)

第七章 第二节 课堂讲练材料

论 美

某个年轻人看到落日,无从理解也无法表达心中所涌起的激情,就断定说,这是一扇通往天外另一个世界的大门。在强烈地感受到美的那一瞬间,几乎无人会怀疑这辉煌不是出自另一个世界,这个世界不但与我们的世界相异,而且由于强烈动人,在某些方面还高于现实世界。虽然这辉煌使人迷惘目眩,但它确实向我们传达出一丝美和宁静的信息,这种美与宁静远非我们所知,远非我们所能想象,也远非语言所能描绘。语言,人类创造出来用作世间表情达意的工具——是很难适用于另一个世界的。

毋庸置疑,伟大的艺术能启发人们对天外的另一个世界展开联想。有时大自然也具有同样的力量。没有一个6月的蓝天会蓝得使你不联想到你心中更蓝的蓝天——这是一个还没被完全看清便已消逝的幻景,而它在消逝时又给人留下了难以言叙的向往和惆怅。

但是,即使现实世界不是一个拙劣的玩笑,生命不是冷冷星光中一点平庸的闪亮,人生也不是穿过迷宫的一阵无聊哂笑;即使存在于现实世界之外的这个神秘实体的种种启示不是由于内心不适而产生的奇想,也不是魔鬼用来欺骗和愚弄我们的怪念,换句话说,即使美确实有其意义,最好不要试图做出解释。当我们目睹了无法用语言表达的东西时,若强行把它表达出来,这是不明智的;当遇到无法领会的东西时,若把意义强加于它们,也是无所裨益的。就人类所能理解的意义而言,美是无以名状的。

(《心灵小语》)

第七章 第二节 课外扩展训练材料

黑 狗

1月的一个清晨,船长早早起床去了海边。这是一个寒冷的日子,太阳还没升高,母亲正在楼上陪伴病重在床的父亲。那一年冬季特别漫长、寒冷,大家都清楚父亲恐怕挨不到来年春天了。

当时我正在准备船长的早餐,忽然客店的门开了,一个陌生人闯了进来。来人腰间佩着把水手专用短剑,左手只剩3根指头。

我问他要点什么,他回答:"来一杯朗姆酒。"我正要去取酒,他却把我叫过去,笑着问:"桌上的早餐是不是为我的老朋友比尔准备的?"笑容十分恐怖。

我回答说不认识他的朋友比尔,早餐是为一个住在店里的客人准备的。"我们管他叫船长,"我说。

"他脸上是不是有一道剑疤?"他问。

"是的,"我答。

"他就是比尔。他在吗?"

我告诉他船长出去散步了,于是他就耐心地等,像猫等老鼠一样。我不喜欢此人脸上的这种表情,相信船长也不愿见到他。

见船长回来,陌生人一把将我拉到门后。船长推门,走进屋子,穿过房间——

"比尔,"陌生人叫道。

船长猛地转过身,看见我们,脸色霎时变得惨白,整个人一下子显得衰老、虚弱。"黑狗!"船长叫道。他盯着陌生人,问:"你想要怎么样?"

"我想要一杯朗姆酒,"黑狗说。"然后你、我二人坐下来,像老朋友那样聊聊天。"

我取来朗姆酒,他们把我支开。我走出房间后,他们说话的嗓门越扯越高。

"不,不,不,事情到此为止!"我听见船长吼道。"如果有人被抓,谁都逃不了。"

又是几声吼叫,夹杂着桌子被掀翻的声音,然后是一阵刀剑的撞击声,旋即黑狗肩上淌着鲜血一头冲了出来。我看着他跑出客店,上了条小路,不一会儿就没了踪影。

船长见他跑了,就对我说:"吉姆,快!拿朗姆酒来!"

他转身想回客店,但无法挪动步子。我看出他生病了,赶紧跑去拿酒,猛然间听到他倒地的声音,急忙跑回——

船长已经躺倒在地。

母亲听到动静,跑下楼来。我们抬起船长的头,见他双目紧闭,面如死灰。

正巧,里佛塞大夫来看我父亲,他瞧了瞧船长,对母亲说:"他的心脏受不了这玩意儿。我早就警告他不能喝这么多酒,现在差点要了他的命。"

船长睁开眼,挣扎着要坐起来。"黑狗在哪儿?"他问。

"哪有什么黑狗!"大夫说,"站起来吧,我扶你上床。"

(《金银岛》)

第七章 第三节 课堂讲练材料

劳动有益健康

劳动给人带来的不仅仅是幸福与满足,其益处远比大多数人想象得还要多。我们都习惯于认为劳动为生活提供物质利益,如体现现代文明的商品和服务,但是对劳动在人心理满足方面所起的作用知之甚少。有关后者的作用虽说无形,但更为重要,因为它决定着一个人的一生过得充实还是空虚。

　　历史上，劳动一直与奴役、罪恶和惩罚联系在一起。即使今天，那些老一套的怨言还常常不绝于耳，如"应早点放假"、"我真想今天待在家里"、"老板待我不好"、"活儿太多，来不及做"，等等。如果真是如此，一旦获悉如下情况，你一定十分惊讶：心理学家、行为科学家已对劳动在个人幸福和成就感方面的积极作用进行了肯定。对多数人而言，劳动不仅仅是一种必须，还是生活的焦点，是身份和创造的来源。

　　劳动不是惩罚，不是负担，而是人类发挥潜能的契机。精神病诊所的很多主治医生都注意到劳动的治疗效果。许多在诊所里精神抑郁的病人，一旦从事有偿劳动，便恢复了自信，那些最严重的症状也会随之部分消失。越来越多的精神病研究或治疗机构开始建厂，病情过重、在"外面的"工厂找不到活干的病人可以在那里劳动；同时，这些机构还竭尽全力替那些身体条件允许在外从事劳动的人安排"真正的"活儿干。

　　反过来也是一样。对许多人而言，不劳动对健康有害。退休就算没有引起经济之忧，也常常会带来诸如"今后我该怎样生活才好？"之类的问题。又如许多人在周末不用上班而需自行安排生活的时候，常有头痛及其他不适感。人们还注意到失业除了造成经济压力外，还给许多人的心理上造成病痛，因此某些人一朝失业，健康状况便急转直下。

　　这是为什么呢？为什么说劳动是人获得满足的重要源泉呢？答案的关键就是：劳动及劳动所带来的成就能激起人的自豪感。

（伦纳德·R.塞尔斯）

第七章 第三节　课外扩展训练材料

健康与财富，孰轻孰重？

　　"健康就是财富！"这是老生常谈，多数人会表示赞同。通常说来，一个人愈是有钱，体质也愈是柔弱。不过，也不能一概而论。

　　体魄健康的人，有资本向任何艰难困苦挑战。例如，苦力们虽然每天仅得两餐甚至一餐粗茶淡饭，不过依旧身壮力健，能够用自己的劳动维持生活。虽然他们付出大量的劳动而仅获微薄的工钱，但是无论在什么情形下，他们都能享受生命的乐趣。

　　健康是事业的基础。一个学生，如果他的身体健康，就有精力吸收大量的知识;一个科学家,如果身强力壮,往往能取得更大的成就,而体质柔弱的学者却没有足够的精力应付复杂的学术问题。

许多富翁把看病视为家常便饭,因为他们没有好好地锻炼体格以增进健康。身体缺乏锻炼,肌肉细胞就会松弛退化,体内的抗生素也就不能成长壮大,所以就无抵抗疾病的能力。

以富有而出名的美国女星伊丽莎白·泰勒为例,她一天到晚都要寻医问诊,仿佛身处死亡的边缘,你认为她幸福吗?所以,一个人如果没有健康,财富对他又有什么意义?

(《英语模范作文》)

第七章 第四节 课堂讲练材料

雌蚊子

不管你是谁,也不管你来自何方,有一点是肯定的:你认识蚊子——尽管你可能并不想认识。蚊子到处都有。全世界都可以找到蚊子,其种类多达 2,500 余种。你肯定在某个时间、某个地方至少碰到过其中一种。

没人喜爱蚊子。可是,不幸得很,蚊子,她可能喜爱你。"她"?是的,"她"。知道吗?只有雌蚊才叮咬人。这可是事实,倒并不是因为她对人不友好,而是因为她需要血进行繁殖。

知道雌蚊是如何确定叮咬对象的吗?雌蚊相当挑剔,对叮咬对象的选择十分精心。她首先用感觉器寻找叮咬对象,这些感觉器在她的两根触角和三对腿上。借助感觉器,她可以测定你身体的湿度、体温和汗液的化学成分。如果她喜欢你,就会叮咬你。要是你对她没有吸引力,她就会转而寻找更合她品味的人。下次再有蚊子叮咬你,记住喽,你是经过挑选而成为叮咬对象的,你可是个不一般的人物。

如果蚊子喜欢你,她就会轻轻地落在你的皮肤上,然后用喙端刺破你的皮肤。喙端?喙端是什么呀?那是一种口器,就是蚊子眼睛下方向外伸出来的部分,其中有六根叫作口针的尖杀器。她把六根口针同时刺入你的皮肤。如果刺中血管,一分钟左右,雌蚊就能够饱餐一顿。所有这些活动都很快,而且是悄悄进行的,你也许毫无知觉。

蚊子叮咬处为什么痒?其实痒并非由蚊子的叮咬引起。为了防止血液凝结,蚊子在用喙端吸血时混进了唾液。是这种唾液引人发痒。等你开始痒时,蚊子早就逃之夭夭了。

然后怎样呢？喔，蚊子美餐后累了，只想找个地方休息一下。由于吸了血后身子很重，蚊子就在叶片上、墙边或石头上选一个地方静静地产卵。一滴血能够产数百颗卵。

　　她的配偶在何处？这个么，它们的关系早已结束了。他已不在附近。他们的交配发生在雌蚊叮咬你之前。这之后，雌蚊还能活一、两个月，产四、五次卵。

　　所有蚊子，包括雄、雌，都要经过早期的水中或在水附近的生活阶段，虽然蚊卵在干地缺水情况下可以存活五年之久，但事实上没有水，蚊卵无法孵化。难怪大雨过后会出现大量的蚊子。

　　但这一切是为了什么？大自然为什么要烦神造出蚊子来？就是为了滋扰人类？这可能不是其主要原因。雄蚊靠花蜜生活。有些科学家认为雄蚊从一朵花飞到另一朵花时使花受粉。当然，蚊子需要繁殖，倒霉的是，这就涉及你和我了。不管你是否喜欢，蚊子终会在人世间呆下来。哎唷！（啪！）一只蚊子刚叮了我一口！

（《提高阅读技能》）

第七章 第四节　课外扩展训练材料

用翻译学外语经验谈

　　大凡水平较高的人都接受过两种教育，一种是从师，另一种更为直接、更为重要——自学。……在做法语和拉丁语翻译时，我采用了一个极好的方法。在此，我愿从个人成功的经验出发，把它介绍给学生们效仿。我选择了一些经典作家，如西塞罗和维脱，因为他们的文体纯正优雅，最受好评。譬如，我把西塞罗的书信译成法语，然后把译文搁置一旁，等其中的词句和短语全都忘光之后，再把法语译文回译成我力所能及的拉丁语。最后，拿我那蹩脚的译文与那位罗马演说家平易、优美、用词精当的原文，逐句逐句进行对照。同样，我也拿维脱的《革命文献》做过好些页的翻译练习。我把它们先译成拉丁语，搁置一段时间以后，再把它们回译成法语，然后，就我的习作和原文之间的异同，做详细的比较。渐渐地，我对自己感到比较满意了。我坚持这种对译的练习，竟用了好几个笔记本。最后，我终于熟悉了两种语言的习惯用法，至少掌握了一种正确的文体。这种有益的书面翻译练习还要与欣赏名著这种更为愉快的活动同时或交叉进行。认真阅读罗马经典著作，对我来说既是一种练习也是一种犒赏。

参考译文

(爱德华·吉朋)

第七章 第五节　课堂讲练材料

哈啤争夺战

世界啤酒业排名前两位的大公司——美国的 AB 和南非的 SAB 在哈啤争夺战中交手。哈尔滨啤酒集团有限公司(香港交易所代码为 0249)在中国啤酒销售市场上排名第四,此前市值为 30 亿港元。

去年 6 月 SAB 曾购入哈啤 29.6% 股权进而成为第一大股东,并与后者签订了"独家策略投资者协议"。今年 5 月 1 日,哈啤宣布单方面终止此项协议,理由是 SAB 未能达到协议所规定的目标。

AB 立即出手。5 月 2 日,该公司宣布,将以 10.8 亿港元的价格收购 Global Conduit Holdings Limited (GCH),而这家公司(GCH)刚在 40 天前签约,从哈尔滨市政府在港的窗口公司手中买下了该上市公司 29.07% 的股权,从而使 AB 一举成为哈啤的第二大股东。

同一天 SAB 做出反应,通知哈啤公司董事会,发出对哈啤以每股 4.3 港元的价格进行全面收购的要约,而哈啤 4 月 30 日的市值为每股 3.22 港元。

(《财经》)

第七章 第五节　课外扩展训练材料

多德一家的逍遥游

多德一家个个令人刮目相看。这么说,不是因为他们身份显赫,而是因为他们的超凡之举——抛业弃学游美国。

去年,加里·多德还是一位牧师,妻子菲丝也只是在一家诊所打工,夫妇俩与一双 15 岁的龙凤胎儿女安德鲁和丽贝卡生活在田纳西州纳什维尔的一栋普通民宅里。

可就在夏天,平凡的多德一家做出非凡之举:夫妻俩辞去工作,领着孩子走出校园,拿房子作抵押贷款,全家骑上自行车,从西雅图出发——周游美国去啦。其实,这一举动背后并无玄机,不过因一次家人间的闲聊而起。

对此,一家之主加里是这样解释的:"有天晚上,在离开教堂回家的路上,我一边开车一边与车上坐着的安德鲁和丽贝卡闲聊,聊着聊着,就聊到自己有点超重需要健身,聊起想在他们离家上大学之前多与他们相处,随便说说而已,丽贝卡也只是随声附和,'好呀,那咱就骑自行车周游全美国吧。'"

说者无意,听者有心,最后他们真的决定一试。

对于自己当初的提议,丽贝卡是这样讲的:"我也就那么一说,搁现在我还闹不明白自己为什么会有那样一说。不过,我很高兴那样说了。"

其实,多德夫妇早已意识到,自从为人父母,时间过得飞快,加之不经意间交友之趣取代了天伦之乐,所以现在眼瞅着孩子们即将中学毕业,他们很想揪住孩子们童年的尾巴,与他们共度时光。

但是乍听这一计划,菲丝不禁深吸了一口气,想:"十多岁的孩子正是精力旺盛的时候,而我已经40多岁了,这把骨头经得起此番折腾吗?"

朋友们在得知这一消息后,反应不一。菲丝说:"赞成的很多,他们说'哇噻,肯定好玩!'有的则上下打量我们,好像我们不正常似的,有的干脆说我们疯了。"

现在人在路上,多德一家把每天的经历录下来,还拍了几百张照片放到由安德鲁负责维护的家庭网站上。安德鲁说:"网络真是个好东东,可以上传日志,也可以收发邮件,能让大家始终保持联系,但不必接电话,也不用随时待命,自由极了,说走拔脚就可以走,可以做自己想做的事,走自己想走的路,每一天都是新的。"

丽贝卡也对这种未知的生活十分享受。她说:"我每天都期待着新的一天来临,猜想新的一天又会碰到什么新鲜事儿。当然,快乐是要付出代价的,比如为了还贷,我们回去时得卖掉房子,可是值! 如果有下一次,我还会义无反顾的。"

(《扬子晚报》)

第七章 第六节 课堂讲练材料

希拉里退选演讲(续)

(2008年6月7日)

非常感谢大家,谢谢大家。准确地说,这并不是我计划中的聚会,但可以肯定地说,我喜欢大家的陪伴。

首先我想感谢你们所有人——所有倾注了心血和希望的人、不远万里

参考译文

驱车前来街道两旁挥舞自制标语的人、靠精打细算节俭克己筹集资金的人、挨家挨户敲门拜访选民打助选电话的人、因谈论我而与朋友或邻居争论的人、给我发过电子邮件并在网上投稿的人、给我们的大众企业投资巨款的人、来到选举现场把女儿或儿子举在肩头并对他们轻声耳语"瞧,只要你想,你可以做成任何事"的妈妈爸爸们、年轻人们,比如来自俄亥俄州梅菲尔德的13岁的安妮·雷德尔,她为了去迪斯尼乐园攒了两年的钱,可后来还是决定用这笔积蓄和妈妈一起来宾州做志愿者;还有老兵们、儿时的朋友们、纽约以及阿肯色州的朋友们,你们千里迢迢赶来,告诉所有愿意听的人你为什么支持我;还有出生在妇女不能参加选举年代的八九十岁的妇女们,她们曾在选举中投票。我曾经提到过一位88岁的南达科他州人弗兰西丝·斯坦恩,她在医院的病床上坚持让女儿拿来一张给缺席者的选票,她女儿和一个朋友在她床后挂上了一面美国国旗并帮她填写了选票。不久后,她去世了。可惜的是,按州法律她的选票不能生效。她的女儿后来告诉记者:"我爸爸是一个粗人,一个老牛仔,听说妈妈的选票无效时他很难过,我记忆中他在近20年内从未投过票,可这次他替妈妈投了一票。"

对所有投票给我的人、对我发誓尽我所能为你们奉献的人,为了我们共同追求的进步,我承诺我将努力不懈。

你们用编织成我们生命的有悲有喜的故事鼓励我,感动我。与你们为国家所做的贡献相比,我无比卑微。1800万人民,来自生活的不同层面,女人和男人,年轻人和老人,拉丁裔人和亚裔人、黑人和白人、富有的、贫穷的、中产阶级、同性恋者或异性恋者,你们曾站在我这一边。我也将一如既往地坚定地站在你们一边,无论何时何地,尽我所能。我们共同的梦想是值得你我为之奋斗的!

请记住,我们曾奋斗,为了那个带着年幼的女儿拼命工作学习的单身母亲,她曾对我说:"我做的一切都是为了能使我因女儿做得更好。"

我们曾奋斗,为了那个握住我的手问"你会怎样做来确保我能得到健康治疗?"并不住哭泣的女人,因为她尽管打三份工作仍付不起医保。

我们曾奋斗,为了那位身穿海军T恤为入院治疗苦等数月的小伙子,他说:"照顾照顾那边我的朋友吧!然后能不能也照顾我一下?"

我们曾奋斗,为了所有失去工作、支付不起医药费、加不起油、买不起日用品、上不起大学却在过去7年里不曾见到总统做过些什么的人。

我参加此次竞选,因为我始终怀着一个旧式的信念,那就是公共服务专门解决人们的困难、实现人们梦想。我已经尽可能地抓住了我生命中的一切机会和赐福,我同时希望所有美国人都能如此。你将永远看见我至死站在民主的最前线,为了未来而奋斗!

现在,能够继续我们的奋斗、实现我们的目标的方法,就是竭尽我们的能量、激情、力气以及其他所能帮助选举贝拉克·奥巴马,我们的下一任美国总统。

今天,我想借这一活动祝贺奥巴马所取得的胜利以及他奋斗至今所赢得的不凡竞选成绩,我将在他身后全力支持他。我请你们所有人与我一起,像支持我一样支持奥巴马。

我在参议院与奥巴马共事了4年,我和他一起参加了16个月的竞选活动,我站在台上和他面对面进行了22场辩论。我曾坐在他候选演讲的最前排,我看到了他的力量和决断、他的优雅和果敢。

身为社区组织者、州议员和联邦参议员,贝拉克·奥巴马自己的生活就是美国梦的写照。为确保这个梦想的实现他全力以赴。在竞选中,他鼓舞了无数人加入推进民主的进程,鼓舞我们为共同的未来而努力。

我开始这次赛跑时目的是赢得白宫并确定我们能够有这样一位总统,他使我们的国家和平、富足、进步。现在,具体地说,我们应该做的就是确保奥巴马参议员在2009年1月20日能够进入白宫椭圆形办公室的大门。

……

大家知道,我参与这样或那样的政治活动和公众生活已经40年了。在这40年里,我们的国家举行了10次总统选举,民主党只赢了3次,那位赢得了其中两次的人今天也在这里。

上世纪90年代,我们在这位民主党总统的带领下取得了巨大的进步——经济繁荣,我们的和平与安全政策获得了世界的尊重。

让我们想想,如果有民主党总统领导,我们可以在过去的40年里取得多么了不起的进步。想想过去7年,我们在环境、经济、人权、教育、对外政策、最高法庭上失去了多少机会。想想如果有民主党总统领导,我们可能已经走了多远,取得了多么不凡的成就。

我们不能让这一刻溜走,我们还有太多的路要走。

现在,我们面前的道路并不平坦。有人会说我们走不下去,太难了,我们无法胜任,但是只要美国依然存在,就会用我们美国的方法来对抗那些说我们不行的宣传,就会选择苦干、坚毅和开拓精神去拓展一切可能。

(未完待续)

第七章 第六节　课外扩展训练材料

希拉里退选演讲（续）

（2008年6月7日）

　　于是今天，我站在奥巴马参议员这一边，说："是的，我们能行！"我们将共同努力——我们必须共同努力使医疗普及。当我们有朝一日居住在一个让每个孩子、每个男人、每个女人都享有医疗保障的美国时，我们便拥有了一个更强大的美国。这就是为什么我们要帮助奥巴马竞选总统。

　　……

　　我们将努力让我们在伊拉克的战士回家，给予他们服役所应得的供养，而当我们有朝一日居住在一个对军队忠诚得就向他们对我们一样的美国时，我们便拥有了一个更强大的美国。这就是为什么我们要帮助奥巴马竞选总统。

　　这场选举是一个转折点，而我们必须了解我们的选择究竟意味着什么，这是当前要回答的关键问题——我们将共同前进，还是停滞不前，或者一起倒退？

　　现在，想想我们已经取得了多大的进步吧。当我们刚刚起步时，到处有人问我一个同样的问题："女人真的可以成为美国总统吗？"那么现在，我想我已经回答了这个问题。

　　"黑人可以成为美国总统吗？"奥巴马参议员已经回答了这个问题。奥巴马和我一起竖起了一块对我们国家至关重要的里程碑，这是我们永远的责任——造就一个更完美的国家。

　　说心里话，做竞选美国总统的女人意味着什么，我始终给出同样的答案，我以我是一个竞选总统的女人而自豪，但我参加竞选是因为我想成为最棒的总统。可是作为一个女人，像无数的女人一样，我知道仍然有许多往往无意的障碍横亘在面前，我想建立的是一个能够尊重和包容我们每个人的美国。

　　作为一个女儿，我得益于许多我母亲从未梦想过的机会。作为一个母亲，我担心着我女儿的未来，我想让所有的孩子都有一个更加光明的未来。

　　要创造我所想象的那种未来，我们要确保女人和男人同样理解他们的祖母和母亲所做出的努力——女人拥有平等的机会、平等的报酬、平等的尊重。

　　让我们下定决心争取实现一个十分简单的主张：在21世纪的美国，没有可以接受的限制，也没有可以接受的偏见。

　　你可以骄傲地说，某个女人在某州脱颖而出不值一提，某个女人在选举中被提名不值一提，某个女人成为美利坚合众国总统不值一提。可是，我的朋友，这绝对是值得一提的。

　　因我们没能走完全程而失望的人，特别是为这次竞选倾注了大量心血的年轻人，我虽然在目标未实现之际出局，但假如我的行为使你们放弃追求，那才是真正令我心碎的。

　　永远坚持远大的目标，努力工作，坚定地关注你所深信的。遇到障碍时，不要放弃信念；跌倒时，立刻爬起来，不要听信任何人所谓的你不行、不要继续下去。

　　正当我们聚集在这座历史悠久、富丽堂皇的建筑物之际，世界上第50位飞向太空的女性正在我们头上沿轨道运行。如果我们能将50位女性送入太空，我们为何不能将一位女性送入白宫？

　　……

　　这就是我们当前所应该做的——为奥巴马参议员和他的竞选注入我们的力量。当我们在美国的故事中书写下一章时，我们将一同创造历史。为了我们所共同持有的珍贵的价值观、幸福的前景及对国家的爱，我们将团结一致。

　　没有什么人比我们更像我们美国人的了。

　　现在，面对着你们，我从没感到过如此深受上帝福佑。我在竞选中所遇到的变化与千百万美国人日常生活中所遇到的相比，根本算不了什么。所以今天，我将带着上帝对我的赐福继续前进，我将继续做早在这些摄影机出现以前我就已经在做的、摄影机离开后我依然会长期做下去的事情——努力让每个美国人拥有相同的机会，尽力保证每个孩子都有机会健康成长，都有机会发挥其天赐的潜能。

　　我将怀着一颗感恩的心，怀着对我们这个国家深深的爱来做这些，用对明天的乐观和自信来做这些。

　　现在是我们尽已所能来确保这一切的时候了。在这场选举中，我们在这张写有今后40年总统名字的小小的名单中，加入又一位民主党人的名字，我们重新掌握我们的国家，并再次为未来的进步而奉献。

　　谢谢大家。上帝保佑你们，上帝保佑美国。

参考译文

第七章　第七节　课堂讲练材料

走近蚂蚁

与世界其他陆地动物相比,蚂蚁数量最多,几棵树上就可以生活100万只蚂蚁,蚂蚁是一种社会性昆虫。这就是说,蚂蚁是生活在社会之中的,在这些社会中,它们相互依赖。这些社会并不都完全一样。它们之所以有差别是因为蚂蚁种类繁多——事实上有15,000种以上。但是总体说来,每一种蚂蚁都有三种主要类型:雌蚁、雄蚁和工蚁。

雌蚁在一段时间内是有翅膀的,并且会在某一天与一只长有翅膀的雄蚁飞走。这只雄蚁不久以后死去,而这只已失去翅膀的雌蚁则找一个理想的地方作为新窝安顿下来,然后产卵。工蚁会去喂养她,并对她产下的卵加以保护,还尽其所能建造一个既宽敞又安全的家。

在蚂蚁社会里,工蚁都有专门的工作,如有些工蚁照管幼蚁,有些则从事建筑,还有一些是兵蚁,专司打仗。

有些种类的蚂蚁使人联想到农民,它们的工蚁负责收集种子贮藏于地下。如果种子发芽生长,这些蚂蚁就把它们撒在窝的四周,于是这些地方就成了"蚂蚁稻田"。

蚂蚁有相当多的敌人,如鸟、熊和各种"食蚁兽",而它们最大的敌人有时却是别的种类的蚂蚁,就如同人的最大敌人是人一样。世界上有些地方,红蚁用大规模的兵力攻打黑蚁的家园。与此同时,黑蚁则用工程蚁和工蚁所能提供的石头和泥浆封锁地道的进口。

有些蚂蚁使得走近蚁群的人日子很难舒畅,不过也有些蚂蚁觉得我们很受用,因为它们喜欢我们吃的食物,常爬进我们的住房和花园谋食。在我们野餐时,它们会成千上万地光临。

从对蚂蚁生活的研究中我们得知,这些生物是群居的,它们种田,进行战争,抢夺奴隶,有一个和我们人类颇为相似的社会。但是,它们有思维吗?它们有智力吗?很可能搜罗食物的工蚁并不知道它们在干什么,它们之所以那么做完全受本能的驱使。

(《成人读物》)

第七章 第七节　课外扩展训练材料

"千年精英"是怎样诞生的？

　　1000年以来，我们这个星球的出生人口已达300亿左右，其中绝大多数人终生默默无闻，仅仅只有家人和朋友知道他们，少数人或因有所发现，或因打破某项记录，而留迹史册，而死后长久被人们记忆者更是寥寥无几。在过去1000年的芸芸众生中，仅38人获得"千年精英"的地位——即每10亿人中只能挑出一位。这些生平记载于《焦点》上的人物因此可能永远名登精英录，但是确定该把谁选入这个名单绝非易事。

　　挑选工作唯一的也是最重要的标准是："千年精英"是那些不仅仅只在其所处的时代或某个领域取得伟大成就的人。因此，单凭是诺贝尔奖得主还无权顺理成章地入围，名噪一时但随时尚变迁而被淡忘的艺术家也无权入围。一位真正的"千年精英"所取得的成就时至今日应当还在影响着人类的生活，其影响之巨大，我们难以想象没有这些成就世界会是什么样子。

　　然而，即使是卓越的天才也不足以稳入《焦点》名单。要被评为"千年精英"，其生平和成就还须阐明创造力的复杂性：来源、本质及个人的付出。

先天造就还是后天培养？

　　现在这个名单已经敲定，那么通过《焦点》千年精英"的生平和成就，我们可以了解人类这个最宝贵群体的哪些方面呢？

　　首先，名单表明天才家庭背景各异：有的出身贫寒，有的降生在富贵家庭，有的出自书香门第，有的家人目不识丁。法拉第的父亲是铁匠，巴斯德全家以制革为业，而数学天才高斯是苦力的儿子。与他们相反，哲学家弗里德里克·尼采来自书香世家，约翰·冯·诺伊曼出生于富贵的匈牙利银行家家庭，而火箭先驱恩赫尔·冯·布劳恩的父亲则是贵族。

　　在"千年精英"的成长过程中，父母的影响非常重要，只是这种影响作用可能并非如表面所见的那么简单。有些人显然继承了祖先的聪明才智，例如经济学家约翰·梅那德·凯恩斯、查尔斯·达尔文及量子理论的奠基人马克斯·普郎克。也有些人分明延续了父母精力旺盛的个性，例如伊桑巴德·金德母·布鲁内尔、玛丽·斯托普斯和雷切尔·卡森。但是对另外一些人而言，父母并没给予他们积极的影响。野心勃勃、专横傲慢的父亲剥夺了莫扎特的童年，而早年遭母亲遗弃的经历使牛顿如此痛苦，他甚至幻想过杀死母亲。令人震惊的是，童年不幸成了"千年精英"生平的共同特征。他们感到孤独,缺少父母陪伴,常为威胁家庭安全的令人痛苦的事件所侵扰。查尔斯·狄更斯、西格蒙德·弗洛伊德、玛丽·居里和莱纳斯·鲍林在童年都饱受家庭经济困顿的打击,他们有的家庭负债累累,有的家庭走向破产,他们需要在内心世界寻求精神创伤的避难所。或许正是这种需要,为这些"千年精英"播下了成就事业的种子。

少年神童

正如人们所想的那样,有些"千年精英"从小就智力过人。例如,数学家高斯在两岁时就能纠正父亲账目中的错误,爱迪生十几岁就创办了自己的高科技企业。但是也有些人经过很长时间才展露天资。达尔文、巴斯德和法拉第直到20—30岁才表现出对科学的兴趣,而爱因斯坦小时候曾让老师们怀疑智力迟钝。

智力健康

"千年精英"的生平证实了另外一种传统观点,正如爱迪生自己所称,天才通常似乎是1%的灵感加上99%的汗水。从列奥纳多·达·芬奇到布鲁内尔,从莫扎特到费里茨·哈伯,许多"千年精英"几乎对工作表现出近乎病态的献身精神。

正是这种献身精神使一些人英年早逝。例如,玛丽·居里因多年致力于镭的研究而死于辐射。就其他"千年精英"而言,对工作的献身精神意味着不完美的私人生活、破碎的婚姻,以及像玻尔茨曼和图林那样以自杀结束自己的一生。

虽然人们可能嫉妒"千年精英"经久不衰的地位,但是很少有"千年精英"生前享受到真正的成功、幸福和尊敬,利用天分发了财的人就更少了。我们最后一位"千年精英"是网络的发明者蒂姆·伯纳斯·李,他不走个人致富的道路,这一点对他获得"千年精英"的地位至关重要。

有件事情我们是可以肯定的,那就是,如果没有这38位杰出人物,我们今天的生活会贫乏许多。